Research Methods for Social Work

Becoming Consumers and Producers of Research

James R. Dudley

The University of North Carolina at Charlotte

PEARSON

Boston   New York   San Francisco
Mexico City   Montreal   Toronto   London   Madrid   Munich   Paris
Hong Kong   Singapore   Tokyo   Cape Town   Sydney

To my wife, Joanna, for her support, patience, and inspiration

Series Editor: Patricia Quinlin
Development Editor: Janice E. Wiggins
Series Editorial Assistant: Annemarie Kennedy
Marketing Manager: Kris Ellis-Levy
Senior Production Editor: Annette Pagliaro
Editorial Production Service: Trinity Publishers Services
Composition Buyer: Linda Cox
Manufacturing Buyer: JoAnne Sweeney
Cover Administrator: Rebecca Krzyzaniak
Text Design: Denise Hoffman
Electronic Composition: Omegatype Typography, Inc.

For related titles and support materials, visit our online catalog at www.ablongman.com.

Between the time Website information is gathered and then published, it is not unusual for some sites to have closed. Also, the transcription of URLs can result in unintended typographical errors. The publisher would appreciate notification where these errors occur so that they may be corrected in subsequent editions.

Library of Congress Cataloging-in-Publication Data

Dudley, James R.
    Research methods for social work : becoming consumers and producers of research / James R. Dudley.
        p.   cm.
    Includes bibliographical references and index.
    ISBN 0-205-36529-9 (pbk.)
    1. Social service—Research. 2. Social service—Research—Methodology.   I. Title.
HV11.D83 2005
361.3'072—dc22

2004044769

Printed in the United States of America

10   9   8   7   6   5   4   3   2   1   RRD-VA   08   07   06   05   04

CONTENTS

chapter 3

Research Ethics and Social Work's Mandates   37

chapter 4

Understanding the Research Topic   64

chapter 5

Defining and Measuring Concepts   82

chapter 6

Focusing a Research Study   115

c h a p t e r **7**

Designing the Study   132

c h a p t e r **8**

Considering Sampling Techniques   147

chapter **9**

Constructing Surveys   162

chapter **10**

Constructing Observational Studies   183

chapter 11

Exploring Causal Relationships   197

chapter 12

Collecting the Data   225

chapter 13

Analyzing Data   237

chapter 14

Quantitative Data Analysis   245

chapter 15

Qualitative Data Analysis   271

chapter **16**

Preparing the Report   291

Research Methods for Social Work is designed to help social work students overcome many of the obstacles that interfere with their understanding of research. These obstacles include students questioning the relevance of research to their practice, wondering what statistics have to do with client well-being, and feeling intimidated by the technical nature of research methods. This text confronts these and other obstacles by introducing the research process in a clear, understandable manner and by persuading the reader to consider the important connections between research and social work.

The text has several special features. It is primarily written for Baccalaureate of Social Work (BSW) students. It can also be used in foundation research courses offered to beginning Master's of Social Work (MSW) students. Most important, the text continually points out the numerous ways in which research can facilitate good social work practice. For example, the text introduces applied research skills that equip graduates for social work employment. This book also introduces undergraduate students to the foundation material required in MSW programs.

The text is organized around the research roles of *consumer* and *producer*. Social work graduates are expected to be able to be effective consumers of research. The consumer role involves critically reading relevant research reports found in professional journals, on Websites, and in agency libraries. These consumer skills also involve learning how to apply the findings from these sources to interventions with clients. Social work graduates are also expected to be producers of research. The text introduces a wide array of applied research skills that can be used in helping clients, including constructing surveys for numerous purposes, leading focus groups, and analyzing practice interventions. Research skills and strategies are also offered for empowering clients and meeting various self-care needs.

The text addresses all of the current accreditation standards of the Council on Social Work Education (CSWE) by clearly describing a conceptualization of required research content for beginning social work students. The accreditation agency, CSWE, also requires additional foundation areas that are relevant to research methods. These additional foundation areas, which include social work values and ethics, diversity, social and economic justice, and populations at risk, are infused throughout the text in illustrations, exercises, discussion questions, and summaries at the end of chapters.

Another text feature is an emphasis on research strategies that are collaborative with clients and agency providers. This collaborative approach encourages the input and participation of the research participants in most, if not all, of the steps of the research process. In this case, research participants could be clients, family members, community residents, agency staff members, or administrators.

Participant action research, in particular, is highlighted in various sections of the text to describe how research can be utilized in bringing social change.

The text also infuses knowledge and skills of technology. Social work practitioners learn how to use various electronic tools such as a listserv, the World Wide Web, and data analysis programs. The text does this by frequently including exercises to be completed on the Internet and other assignments using electronic tools. In addition, students are encouraged to access the latest information on client populations and practice interventions from listservs and Websites of professional organizations. The text also helps students to discern the credibility of the information found on a Website. Allyn and Bacon, the publisher, also provides access to Research Navigator. This is an online search engine that helps students with their research assignments and research papers. Research Navigator requires an access code, which can be value packed free with this text. To access or to learn more about Research Navigator, go to www.researchnavigator.com. Finally, the text is user friendly to new instructors of a research methods course. Undergraduate and some graduate research courses are often taught by social work educators who do not have the time to conduct their own research. These faculty often feel underqualified to teach this course. In this regard, an *Instructor's Manual and Test Bank* accompanies the text. This manual summarizes learning objectives, important terms in each chapter, discussion topics, class exercises, and exam questions. Discussion questions are also included at the end of each chapter to provide a focus for class discussions, homework assignments, quizzes, and exams.

The chapters of the text are largely organized around the basic steps involved in conducting research. The primary attention given to these steps helps the reader put them together into an integrated, understandable whole that they can readily understand and use. A brief summary of the topics covered in each chapter follows.

Chapter 1 explains why social workers need research, defines the scientific approach and other kinds of research, explores many of the topics that social work researchers study, and outlines the similarities between research and social work practice. The roles of consumer and producer of research are introduced. Chapter 2 describes different philosophies used in conducting research and the differences between quantitative and qualitative research methodologies. Specialized perspectives on research are also introduced, including the feminist, Afrocentric, and participant action approaches. Chapter 3 introduces the mandates of social work education and their relevance for research. Social work values and ethics, diversity, social and economic justice, and populations at risk are introduced and discussed as they impact and are impacted by research. These mandates are infused throughout the remaining chapters.

Chapter 4 describes the first step in the research process—*understanding the research topic*. Tips on completing literature searches are offered, including critiquing someone else's literature review, gathering literature, and writing your own literature review. Chapter 5 introduces measurement. The chapter helps the reader to understand what measurement is and how it can be used to both generate new knowledge and confirm existing explanations helpful to social work.

Measurement instruments are highlighted that are useful in evaluating social work practice. Chapter 6 describes the second research step—*focusing a research study*. Exploratory and explanatory studies are described and distinguished. Illustrations of both types of studies are provided, and the reader is taught how to craft research questions and hypotheses.

Chapters 7 to 11 describe several dimensions of *designing a study*. These chapters describe various purposes and approaches to selecting samples, constructing data collection instruments, and exploring causal relationships. Two of these chapters focus on survey and observational studies because of their importance to social work research and practice. Single system designs are also highlighted as a tool in evaluating the effectiveness of one's practice. Chapter 12 describes the next step in the research process—*collecting data*. Several issues are considered in this chapter, including how to prepare and train data collectors. The chapter also highlights how to collect data using focus groups because of their increasing popularity in social work research.

Chapters 13 to 15 focus on the topic of *data analysis*. An introductory chapter on data analysis is followed by specific coverage of several quantitative and qualitative data analysis strategies. Chapter 16, the final chapter, describes *preparing a research report*. This chapter offers numerous techniques for implementing this final step and disseminating it to clients, staff members, funding agencies, and other stakeholders.

Rounding out the text are two helpful appendixes: the first offers a list of questions to ask when critiquing a research report; the second presents the ethical standards of the National Association of Social Workers (NASW). A glossary is also included.

Acknowledgments

Numerous people have graciously assisted in the preparation of this text. Joe Whitmeyer and Lynn Ahlgrim-Delzell, colleagues at the University of North Carolina at Charlotte, gave generous time in reviewing the manuscript. The thoroughness of their reviews resulted in many improvements. Others at UNC Charlotte offered other kinds of valuable assistance. Kayce Owens, Elizabeth Combs, Jacqueline Briscoe, Phyllis Mills, Ann Davis, and Adrienne Davis all helped retrieve a large number of articles, books, and other resources and always in supportive ways.

My social work students, mostly from one class during the fall 2003 semester, were a wonderful group to read an earlier version of the manuscript as their required text for the research methods course. They were thoughtful, patient, and generous in informing me of what was helpful and relevant to them, as well as what was unclear and made little sense. I deeply appreciate the honesty evident in their feedback and the encouragement that they gave me to proceed in completing the text. Three of these students deserve special credit: Norm Stovall, Amber Boyce, and Kathy K. Wright. Finally, my colleagues in the Department of Social Work at

UNC Charlotte helped by their encouragement and support, and my college and university provided me with a sabbatical leave to help in completing the book.

Janice Wiggins, my editor, was invaluable in helping me put the text together in a more readable fashion. Her suggestions, encouragement, and inspiration were always deeply appreciated. Pat Quinlin and Annemarie Kennedy at Allyn and Bacon provided guidance and support at various critical points from beginning to end. John and Evelyn Ward did a superb job in editing and producing the manuscript. Eight social work colleagues, selected by the publisher, deserve enormous plaudits for meticulously critiquing three versions of the manuscript. Their specific feedback was invaluable in making the text more relevant and useful for a social work research methods class. My thanks to Kathy Byers, Indiana University; John D. Clapp, San Diego State University; Adele Crudden, Mississippi State University; D. Randall Haley, Northwestern State University; Grafton Hull, University of Utah; Joe M. Schriver, University of Arkansas; Jack Sellers, University of Alabama; and Beverly A. Stadum, Saint Cloud State University.

Other social work colleagues from the Baccalaureate Program Directors' Association helped me during the early stages of conceptualizing the text and in discovering its importance to social work education. These include Grafton Hull and other members of the BPD Research Task Force (of which I was a member) that prepared a professional report for the National Institute of Mental Health in 1994 on the state of research in undergraduate social work education. This report made a convincing case for social work educators to give greater attention to research. Thanks also are due Joe Schriver and Heather Quinney for helping me obtain access to many of the journal articles published in the *Journal of Baccalaureate Social Work*.

chapter 1

Why Social Workers Need Research

Social work practice and research have more in common than you may think.

An important question to ponder as you take a course in research methods is "Why does a social worker need to know about research?" Imagine for a moment that you are a social worker and that your supervisor assigns you to complete one or more of the following tasks:

- documenting how your interventions are helping your clients
- finding out the most pressing needs of the local community
- leading focus groups on an important topic and analyzing the responses
- reading a complicated research report related to your client population
- using the findings of a research report to improve your practice
- comparing the needs of clients from different ethnic backgrounds
- convincing a funding agency that your job should be continued

All of these tasks have one thing in common: they involve the use of research skills. Also, they are among the most important tasks that professional social workers are expected to address. Take another look at the above list of tasks. How many of them do you think you could complete with some degree of confidence? If your answer is only a few or none, then you may see the importance of learning about research methods for social workers. Even if you think you can complete many of these tasks, you may still want to learn more about research methods to enhance your knowledge and skills.

This book begins where it will eventually take us—to the practical research skills needed to do social work. These skills, being evident in the tasks mentioned above, are central to social work practice at all levels—micro, mezzo, and macro. These skills are applicable if you decide to work with older people, teenagers, parents, community organizations, or small children. They have relevance in virtually every field setting in which social workers are employed, including public welfare,

1

foster care, the courts, prisons, mental health, health care, family preservation, schools, older adult centers, or neighborhood centers.

Research offers numerous tools for *describing, defining, measuring,* and *evaluating* what we are doing. First of all, research tools help us in *describing* the complex phenomena that impact on the lives of our clients. Such phenomena might be, for example, the strengths of our clients or the persistent emotional problems that interfere with their social functioning. Phenomena in the clients' social environment provide additional examples—such as what makes for a decent house, a satisfactory job, or successful family functioning.

Once these phenomena are identified and described, *defining* them comes next. Unfortunately, many of the phenomena of interest in social work are prone to being misdefined and misunderstood. An example of something that can be misdefined is the term *forced-response question,* a concept to be discussed in Chapter 2. This term is defined as a question in surveys that restricts the respondent's answer to a predetermined list of response categories. The term was clearly explained to BSW students using this definition. However, when they were asked to define *forced-response questions* on an exam, some gave the following inaccurate explanations:

- "Asking questions in such a way as to get the answers that you want."
- "A question that makes participants obligated to answer."
- "A question that leads to single-word responses."
- "A question that is offensive and intrusive."

Note that each of the above explanations reveals some inaccuracy in defining a forced-response question. Research tools help us to define the concepts we use in social work in an accurate and consistent way, whether in our informal conversations with each other or in various work activities.

Measuring a phenomenon comes next. Research tools help us create ways to measure what our clients need and how we can help them. Measurement is also important in determining whether a client has made progress on a problem and whether such progress is sufficient or satisfactory. Chapter 5 is devoted entirely to the important topic of measurement.

Measurement can lead to *evaluating* something. With measurement tools, we can evaluate our clients' progress over time as well as document a lack of progress. In addition, we can determine how much our interventions are responsible for the progress our clients are making. Because social workers are expected to have a range of skills in evaluating how they are helping people, several chapters are devoted to evaluation tools.

Research as a Source of Knowledge

Social workers also depend on research because it is a major source of our knowledge. Overall, the knowledge we obtain from researchers is essential to have if we are to be successful in helping people. The knowledge that researchers generate answers many important questions for us, such as:

- What motivates people to change?
- What makes people happy?
- How do we encourage successful family life?
- What do people need to be fulfilled, from birth to death?
- What resources are needed to maintain healthy communities?
- How can services be effectively delivered to people?
- How does a culture nurture its members?
- How can we help teenage mothers and fathers be more successful parents?
- Why are social supports so important in helping people cope?

While social workers use a wide variety of sources of information, a critical source must be the knowledge that comes from the scientific approach and its research methods. An example of how one research study provides useful knowledge is evident in a study by O'Farrell and colleagues on the connection between domestic violence and alcoholism. This study found that men who suffer from alcoholism are more likely than nonalcoholics to abuse their spouses (O'Farrell, Hutton, & Murphy, 1999). Behavioral marital therapy was introduced to a sample of couples to address their problem with alcoholism. The results revealed that as the therapy was effective in reducing the alcoholism, the violence in these families significantly diminished as well. Social workers who know about this research finding will likely consider alcoholism as one possible factor associated with family violence. The study also offers the insight that violence may at least partially be overcome by treating alcoholism.

Social workers are professionals who help people solve their problems. The help that we provide needs to be based on accurate sources of knowing. Social workers are both scientists and uniquely creative individuals. As scientists, we rely on scientific findings to inform us about how we can effectively help our clients. As uniquely creative individuals, we rely on the personal qualities we have, such as our warmth and capacity to communicate and the positive and spontaneous dynamics that we promote in our relationships with each client. Obviously, we need to be both scientific and uniquely creative in our work. Both domains reflect characteristics of who we are as helping people.

While scientific research studies are a central source of knowledge for a social worker, other sources are also important. Social workers use a wide range of sources of knowledge, including our intuition or inner voice; what seems logical; experiences of our past; our parents and others in authoritative roles; the expertise of supervisors, teachers, and others; and the policies of respected professional organizations (Marlow, 2001).

You may be able to identify some of your primary sources of knowing by considering an exercise that a group of students completed. For a period of a day, a group of students recorded every decision they made, large and small. Decisions included the route they chose to get to school, who they asked to join them for lunch, when they decided to study, with whom they talked on the phone, what they ate,

Caution In Using Intuition

While interviewing a young Cambodian mother for the first time, Anne, a social work student, senses that this mother may not be telling the truth about how she disciplines her children. The social worker suspects that this mother is abusing her children. Intuitively, Anne senses this because of the mother's hesitation and discomfort in answering a question about her method of discipline. While Anne's intuition is important to consider in this case, it will also be important to corroborate it with other sources. What are some possible reasons for suggesting that her intuition may be incorrect? What other sources of information could this social work student rely on to corroborate her suspicion about abuse?

when they went to sleep at night, what TV programs they watched, and so on. After identifying and recording each decision, they attempted to identify a source(s) of knowledge or information they relied on to make that decision. For example, the route they took to school may have been based on a road map, someone's suggestion, or trial and error. The food they ate may have been selected because it filled an immediate hunger pang, was easily accessible, or seemed nutritious.

These different sources of knowledge have varying degrees of reliability. For example, using intuition as a source may need to be corroborated by another source, such as a consultation with a supervisor or a question that can be posed to a client. The box above provides an example of the need for corroborating sources.

Some might say that our *personal beliefs* could also be added to the list of sources of knowing. Our beliefs are definitely important to us and have an enormous influence over what we do. Beliefs, however, are based more on our values than the knowledge available to us. Knowledge is distinguished from values in some distinct ways. Knowledge is "what is" in the real world, whereas values are what we believe "should be." As social workers, we have strong beliefs about what is needed by our clients, but these beliefs cannot be considered necessarily "what is," since others can disagree with us about what we believe. Beliefs will be covered more extensively in Chapter 3 in the discussion of social work values and ethics pertinent to research.

Returning to the point of social workers as scientists and creative individuals, the profession has given greater emphasis to one or the other at different times in history. Currently, we are in an era in which our scientific side needs to be strengthened. Our society demands greater *accountability* for what social workers do. Science and its research methods can help us become more accountable to our clients, the social work profession, the funding and regulatory agencies, and our society.

What Is Research?

Research, in general terms, can be defined as a critical and exhaustive investigation of something. From time to time, everyone does research to make both the big and small life decisions. For example, how did you decide to choose social work as your career goal? You may have talked to professionals or teachers in social work or other fields about what they do. You may have read material on these careers as well. Your decision likely was based on a "reseach" investigation that helped you weigh the advantages and disadvantages of going into social work.

Types of research include the following:

- *Library research* is intended to be a critical and exhaustive investigation of the literature available on a topic of interest. Library research is greatly enhanced by using computer software to facilitate the investigation.

- *Marketing research* is done by company representatives who survey people by phone or in person about their knowledge of and interest in the company's products, with the goal of promoting and selling these products.

- *Political research* is sponsored by political parties, which conduct mail and phone surveys to inquire about people's political views and election preferences, with the goal of persuading people to vote for their candidates and make financial contributions. These studies are clearly biased based on politics.

- *Media research* is conducted by representatives of newspapers, TV, radio, and magazines to gather information about people who are in the news or a special topic of interest to the public. Media research is not monitored by an independent review board that can determine if methods used are valid and ethically sound.

Distinctiveness of Scientific Research

Scientific research is also involved in information gathering and investigations. Its purpose is to produce its own form of knowledge, which is sometimes referred to as "science." Scientific research has long-standing values and principles that distinguish it from other types of information gathering. These values and principles include

- seeking to discover something that exists or is a truth
- following a special code of ethical behavior, including integrity and neutrality in conducting research, and a concern for protecting the people it studies
- being universal in its interests and representing the concerns of all of society, even though the focus may be on one subgroup of people or a narrow topic
- being intended for the public's use
- using a methodology that minimizes bias
- expecting a commitment to report findings accurately
- having a methodology that involves a systematic set of procedures that can be flexibly employed

These principles of scientific research and science are ideals that should be fulfilled to the greatest extent possible in all scientific studies. Science that rigorously fulfills the ideals mentioned above is considered "good" science. In this book, "research" will refer to scientific research. Although complex, *scientific research* has several major characteristics, including development of theory, systematic and rigorous methods, empiricism, commitment to neutrality, and obligation to an ethical code.

Development of Theory

One goal of scientific research is to determine support for existing theories; another goal is to generate new theories. A **theory** consists of several interrelated explanatory statements or propositions about a phenomenon. The propositions in theories are often referred to as **hypotheses.** Hypotheses are crafted by researchers as the focus of their studies, and data are collected to find support for these hypotheses in the real world. The concept of hypothesizing is discussed in various places in the book as a tool to help social workers develop their own theories about what works in their practice.

The best theories are those that have been substantiated or validated in the real world by research studies. An example of such a theory is the explanation that domestic violence is related to gender. Studies conducted throughout the world have documented that men are usually the perpetrators of violence against women and that violence can be explained by such things as power and control issues in domestic conflicts, the greater physical strength of men, forced sex, the presence of substance abuse, and so on (e.g., Krantz, 2002). Other studies have found support for different theories on domestic violence and its causes. One such theory is that violence is learned within families when parents behave in violent ways toward each other and their children. Children in these families can easily learn that such violence is "normal" human behavior even though it is painful and disturbing. As these children grow older, they too can easily become perpetrators or victims of violence. Still other studies have found support for theories explaining violence as a derivative of severe economic conditions and other physical hardships experienced by families.

The human behavior and social environment (HBSE) courses in social work programs give special emphasis to theories of particular relevance to social work. HBSE courses are expected to provide content on theories of "biological, sociological, cultural, psychological, and spiritual development across the life span; the range of social systems in which people live (individual, family, group, organizational, and community); and the ways social systems promote or deter people in maintaining or achieving health and well-being" (Council on Social Work Education, 2001, p. 5). Hutchison (1999) identifies several criteria for identifying well-developed theories in her course text on human behavior and the social environment, as follows:

- *Coherence and clarity.* Are the propositions and concepts of the theory clearly defined? Are they coherent? Do they make sense?
- *Comprehensiveness.* Does the theory include multiple dimensions of persons and their environments, and does it cover things that have been overlooked by other theories?

- *Testability.* Are the propositions and concepts observable, and can they be verified by research methods?
- *Compatibility with existing theory.* Is the theory compatible with other theories, particularly those that have been validated by research?
- *Significance for social work practice.* Does the theory assist in the understanding of person and environment transactions? Can it accommodate diversity issues and contribute to social justice issues? Does it suggest principles of action?

Everyone has hunches about why things happen the way that they do, such as why some clients use an agency's services and others do not, or how to succeed in college, or how do I manage the stress in my life. We sometimes call these hunches "hypotheses" or even "theories." However, we need to be cautious about referring to these speculations as theories until we know that they meet most of the criteria described above. In addition to being substantiated in the real world, we should consider how widely applicable a theory may be for different types of people.

Importance of Diversity in Theories

Many theories that are espoused or used in social work are not well grounded in scientific theory. Sigmund Freud, for example, developed the foundations of psychoanalytic theory from patients who were largely middle- and upper-class Germans with psychoneurotic problems. Similarly, Levinson's (1978) fascinating theory about the stages of a man's life is flawed because it is based on a small sample of forty young men at Yale University.

New theories are frequently being developed by researchers, particularly by those who are social workers, as, for example, in the work of Miller and colleagues (2002), as can be seen in the following example:

The Urban Hassles Scale

David Miller and colleagues found that existing studies of stress of adolescents only focused on factors primarily faced by white middle-class adolescents, not disadvantaged African American adolescents living in the inner city. These social work researchers pointed out that life in the inner city is characterized by factors such as street violence, poor housing, and drug use that are not usually evident in the suburbs; further, these factors can adversely affect adolescent development. These researchers developed an "Urban Hassles Scale" that measures some of the stressors that inner-city disadvantaged youth may face. Their nine-item measurement instrument considers hassles such as pressure to join a gang; ridicule because of good grades; working to pay family expenses; nervousness about gunshots and sirens at night; worry that someone will steal clothes, shoes, or money; and keeping fears about dangers secret from friends.

Systematic and Rigorous Methods

Scientific research is also characterized by the systematic and rigorous methods and procedures that it uses. These methods are most evident in a research process that comprises several basic sequential steps. Most of this book is organized around these six basic research steps:

1. Understanding the research topic
2. Focusing the study
3. Designing the study
4. Collecting the data
5. Analyzing the data
6. Preparing a report

Chapters 4 through 16 will list these steps at the chapter opening. The step that is the focus of that chapter will be highlighted. This will help show the relation of each particular step to the overall research process. Many of these steps also have substeps, which will also be introduced.

This presentation of these steps is intended to help you become both a consumer of research studies and a producer of research at the agency where you will be employed. These chapters describe the steps you would follow in evaluating published studies as well as conducting studies that you could carry out. The information in these chapters will help the reader to become a critical consumer of these research reports. Summaries of studies published in professional journals are cited throughout the chapters to illustrate the issues to consider in each of the research steps.

Another purpose of each of these chapters is to enable you to be a producer of research, primarily in the agencies in which you are employed or volunteer. Each step is described so that it can be easily understood and applied to a research task that could be assigned to you in a social work agency. Illustrations are included in these chapters of the works of students and social work researchers to illustrate how a producer can implement these steps.

> **Steps in the Research Process**
>
> 1. Understanding the research topic
> 2. Focusing the study
> 3. Designing the study
> 4. Collecting the data
> 5. Analyzing the data
> 6. Preparing a report

Empirical Evidence

Scientific research is also characterized by it emphasis on obtaining empirical evidence. Empiricism is defined as the collection and analysis of information concerning actually occurring phenomena in the real world. Scientific research usually involves investigating some aspect of the real world by observing it first-hand. Some or all of the senses (eyes, ears, nose, touch, smell) are used in collecting information. At times, scientific research also analyzes second-hand sources not directly observed by the researcher. Examples of secondhand sources include existing documents, such as agency case records or the results of questionnaire studies filled out by respondents who were not directly observed. Empiricism is also a familiar aspect of the work of a social worker, as illustrated by the following example on housing conditions:

A Firsthand Investigation of Housing Conditions

Assume you are conducting an empirical investigation of the housing conditions of a neighborhood served by your agency. You would likely go out into the neighborhood and observe these conditions firsthand. You could drive around the neighborhood to get an overall view and then walk from block to block to obtain a closer look. You might examine both the external and internal conditions of the housing, and you could also interview some of the residents about how they perceive their housing conditions. As the investigator, you would take special steps to avoid introducing bias in your observations. An example of a bias would be deciding to observe the size of the houses (e.g., number of bedrooms, size of the kitchen) but ignoring the physical conditions (e.g., whether the kitchen appliances work or not). Another example of a bias would be to observe housing only on the safer streets.

Commitment to Neutrality

Another distinguishing characteristic of scientific research is that the researcher is committed to being neutral and to avoiding introducing bias. *Neutrality* is an extremely important principle to follow in conducting research. Neutrality is threatened whenever the researcher consciously or unconsciously introduces a bias that can interfere with the results of a study. How can the researcher prevent a research investigation from being overly biased? The answer is that the researcher must agree to abide by a set of ethical principles. Other groups also play a role in enforcing neutrality in research. These groups include the agencies that fund a study, sponsoring agencies such as academic institutions and governmental units, and professional peer review groups.

Neutrality is built into each step in the research process. Let's take as an example how research step 1 addresses bias. A research investigation begins with "defining and understanding the research topic." As researchers complete this step, they are expected to explore the research topic in a comprehensive manner. For example, they are expected to conduct an extensive literature search about the topic to find out as much as they can about what is known. Identifying past research studies and existing theoretical explanations helps researchers define the central issue accurately. Also, if controversy exists in defining the research issue, researchers are expected to examine all important viewpoints. This is a tall order to follow just in completing step 1, but that's what is expected.

Obligation to an Ethical Code

Those who participate in scientific research are also obligated to follow an ethical code similar to the Code of Ethics promulgated by the National Association of Social Workers (NASW), which can be found in Appendix B. An ethical code obligates researchers to become well informed about ethical issues and to implement numerous measures to prevent ethical problems from occurring in their studies. Ethical problems include such things as physically and psychologically harming research participants, invading their privacy, or misrepresenting the findings of a study when it is published. Researchers are ethically obligated to prevent these ethical problems by implementing a variety of ethical safeguards, including instituting an informed consent protocol, ensuring confidentiality, and selecting researchers with the appropriate credentials. In today's world, ethical safeguards are required by most organizations that support scientific research, including all organizations with government-sponsored studies, academic institutions, and most health and human services agencies.

Chapter 3 offers an extensive introduction to many of the ethical concerns that are evident in scientific research and how these problems can be addressed. The NASW Code of Ethics is also examined in Chapter 3, particularly as it pertains to social workers' ethical obligations when either conducting or supporting scientific research.

Similarities between Social Work Practice and the Scientific Research Process

It is important to point out that social work practice and social work research have more in common than you may think. This chapter has already described how research provides social workers with knowledge for their jobs and with useful research tools. Research is also conducted in ways that are similar to social work practice, as can be seen in Table 1.1.

Consumer and Producer Roles

What do social workers need to know about research? Based on social work accreditation standards, social workers are expected to be both effective consumers and producers of research activities (Council on Social Work Education, 2001). Thus, the roles of a research consumer and research producer are explored throughout this book. Let's look more closely at these roles.

Consumer Role

As consumers of research, social workers need to be effective in "consuming" research studies that are pertinent to their professional work. The **consumer role** in-

TABLE 1.1 Social Work Practice and Scientific Research

Steps in Social Work Problem-Solving Process	Steps in Scientific Research Process
1. Develop an assessment of the client's problem.	1. Define the research problem or issue.
2. Set up goals to address or solve the problem.	2. Set up research questions and/or hypotheses to learn more about an aspect of the problem or issue.
3. Work out a plan of action to meet the goals.	3. Set up a research design to answer the research questions or test the hypotheses.
4. Carry out the action plan, which involves both worker and client taking on tasks to reach the goal.	4. Carry out the research design, which usually involves collecting data from a group of people.
5. Evaluate the progress or lack of it.	5. Analyze the data.
6. Decide whether to terminate or continue the relationship based on success in reaching the goals.	6. Present the results, including the findings and recommendations, to the stakeholders.

volves (1) understanding a study, (2) evaluating how well it was conducted and presented, and (3) applying the findings to social work practice.

First, social workers should be able to understand the research studies they read. After reading a study a couple of times, a skillful consumer will be able to understand the purpose of the study, the characteristics of people being studied, the data collection approach used, and the findings presented. These are some of the most important aspects to understand.

Second, social workers need to use critical thinking skills to evaluate how well the study was conducted. Evaluation involves being prepared to be skeptical about a study rather than assuming it was conducted and presented perfectly. Often, social workers do not think they know enough about research to assess the merits of a researcher's report. Nevertheless, all research studies have their imperfections or limitations. At times, authors of studies may leave important information out of their report or may fail to report important limitations inherent in their studies. These unseen limitations or errors are not easily found unless a critical consumer evaluates the study closely.

You may think that if a study is reported in a professional journal like *Social Work*, then it must be free of errors. This is not necessarily so, even though reports of studies in professional journals have been carefully reviewed and examined by an editorial board. Also, you may read research reports that have not been published in professional journals. These may be accessible on a Website or published by a social agency or research firm. In such cases, these reports may not have had careful reviews by an independent review group. Below are some practical guidelines for assessing the accuracy and relevance of a research report and other material presented on a Website (e.g., Lynch, Vernon, & Smith, 2001).

Critically Using Websites: Some Questions to Ask

1. What are the last three letters (domain) of the Website's address or URL (uniform resource locator)? For example,
   - .gov = federal government
   - .edu = educational
   - .com = commercial
   - .org = a nonprofit organization
   - .net = network
   - .mil = military

   These three letters convey something about the quality and likely biases of the Website.
2. Who is the sponsor of the Website? (Are the group's name, mission, leaders identified?)
3. Are dates included of the initial posting and latest revision? Are they recent?
4. What is the scope of the information? What areas of information are covered?
5. What links are provided to other Websites? Do these Websites have legitimacy and a positive reputation?
6. Is this Website reporting information authored by the sponsor or someone else?
7. How well is the Website written (its organization, clarity, ease for reading, etc.)?
8. Based on your answers to the above questions,
   A. Assess how accurate and up to date the information is.
   B. Does the Website mostly seem to present facts, opinions (interpretations of facts), or propaganda (highly opinionated or one-sided facts and interpretations)?
   C. How could you use this Website? What reservations, if any, do you have about using it?

Consumers or readers of studies develop an ability to make judgments about the quality and correctness of a reported study. You must learn to critically examine how the researcher addressed each step in the research process. You must determine, for example, such things as whether enough descriptive information was provided on how the study was conducted, if the sample was diverse enough, whether tables were presented correctly, and if the recommendations of the study were supported by the findings. The example below points out how biases can be evident in such things as the sampling approach or the composition of a sample in a study.

The Importance of Being a Critical Consumer

Numerous studies have been conducted about divorced and unmarried families. Many of these studies have focused on the extent to which the noncustodial parent, usually the father, is involved in raising the children. Most studies over the last several decades have only sought the custodial mothers' views on the fathers' involvement. The results, which have been widely published, generally suggest that these fathers have been inactive or not doing enough with their children. In recent years, a new set of studies has emerged that seeks the views of the noncustodial parent about their involvement in raising their children, and the results have tended to be more positive. Interestingly, noncustodial fathers in these studies have been claiming that they are more involved with their children than earlier suspected. Because of these findings, a tentative conclusion has been reached among many researchers that there are biases in the reporting of both the custodial mothers and noncustodial fathers (Braver & O'Connell, 1998). The latest research on this topic has tended to address these biases by consulting both parents about the fathers' involvement and then comparing their responses. The "truth" about the noncustodial fathers' involvement may be found somewhere in between these two sources.

Third, you as a consumer need to know how to apply the findings of a study to the your own practice or use. You might ask several questions, such as "What is the relevance of the study for me and my clients?" "Can the findings be generalized to the clients I serve?" "What recommendations are offered that can help my practice?"

The findings about a foster care population in Los Angeles, for example, do not automatically apply to children in foster care in Atlanta, Georgia. Neither are they likely unrelated to foster children in Atlanta. You need to think about how the characteristics of children studied in Los Angeles are similar to and different from the clients in your own city and how the city of Los Angeles is similar to and different from your city. Once you have considered these questions, you can begin to consider the extent to which you can apply the findings of the study to your practice. Ultimately, you should apply the findings with considerable caution and skepticism.

Appendix A provides guidelines for critiquing research from a consumer role perspective.

Producer Role

Social workers are also expected to become producers of research. In the **producer role,** social workers either conduct their own studies or assist others in conducting research. This book helps you develop basic competencies in conducting research and learn some applied research skills that will be useful to you in your agency.

There are numerous ways that social workers employed in social work agencies can be producers of research. You may be asked to construct a needs assessment survey, for example, to find out more about the needs of Latinos who have migrated to your community. Or you may develop a client satisfaction survey to help the agency determine if clients are satisfied with the services they are receiving. You will also need to have the skills to evaluate the impact your interventions have on the clients in your caseload. You may be asked to develop a set of questions for interviewing former clients to find out whether they are still progressing on their goals after leaving the agency.

If you are asked to conduct any of the above research studies, you may also be called on to complete other steps in the research process. For example, you are likely to be asked to analyze the data you collect. In addition, you may be asked to

TEST YOUR KNOWLEDGE

Responding to 9/11

Amanda, who works at a mental health agency, was asked by her supervisor to find out how much impact the terrorist attacks of September 11, 2001, have had on her clients' well-being. When she asked how to carry out this task, she was told to do it in the easiest and least-expensive way possible. Identify two different options Amanda can consider in completing this task. What are the advantages and disadvantages of each of these options?

either present your study findings at a staff meeting or submit them in a written report. There are many possibilities for how you produce applied research.

Several basic competencies are required to prepare you to be a research producer. Following are some of the things that you will be expected to know or understand:

- the steps in the scientific research process
- the kinds of research that are occurring in social work
- the ethics of good research
- the importance of incorporating diversity into research
- how research can support and promote social justice
- the value and importance of evaluating your practice as a social worker
- the impact of the research design in shaping the findings

Producers of research also need to have basic competencies or skills. The things that you will be expected to be able to do as a producer of research include the ability to

- construct surveys for various social work research purposes
- evaluate the effectiveness of your interventions in helping clients
- collect data as a researcher
- analyze the data you collect
- write a research report describing your findings
- give an oral presentation of your findings to other professionals

Using Critical Thinking Skills as a Consumer and a Producer

Critical thinking skills are needed in research just as they are in social work practice. These skills are especially evident in the consumer and producer roles described above. As a consumer of research, you are expected to be "critical" in your review of how researchers describe their research topic as well as how they use research methods to gather data and select research participants. Critical thinking skills are also needed in evaluating how well researchers present findings and formulate recommendations. For example, did they offer recommendations that were substantiated by their findings, or were the recommendations mostly unsubstantiated personal preferences?

You are also encouraged to be critical thinkers when carrying out your producer role. You are using critical thinking skills, for example, when you are involved in defining your focus for a study. Does your focus build on what has been learned from previous studies, for example, or does it largely overlook what others have learned? You are also using critical thinking skills when you design your study, analyze your data, present your findings, and offer recommendations. Critical thinking skills will be highlighted in Chapter 2.

Why Do Social Work Researchers Conduct Studies?

We have just explored the importance of conducting various types of applied research. Let's look at other types of research. Some social workers are employed in universities or research institutes where knowledge building is emphasized. The research they conduct is often published in professional journals and books. This type of research is often referred to as *social and behavioral science research* or *social work research*. The purposes of this research include theory building, developing and testing practice approaches, and creating descriptive accounts of phenomena previously not well understood. These researchers focus on topics related to social work practice, social problems facing their clients, social policy issues, administrative practices in social agencies, and numerous other topics.

An immense amount of knowledge has been developed by social work researchers over the past fifty years. Such knowledge has been extremely valuable because it is applied in nature and directly relevant to what social workers need. Often, social work researchers either are or once were practicing social workers.

TEST YOUR KNOWLEDGE

Discovering Outstanding Social Work Researchers

Some professional social work organizations periodically give awards to social workers for outstanding research. Examples of such organizations include the Council on Social Work Education (www.cswe.org), the National Association of Social Workers (www.naswdc.org), the Institute for the Advancement of Social Work Research (www.iaswresearch.org), and the Association of Baccalaureate Social Work Program Directors (www.bpdonline.org). Visit the Website of one of these organizations and find out if any research awards or honors have been recently bestowed on a social work researcher. Also find out who the researcher is and why their research is being recognized.

They have the same general values and ethics and agency experiences as all social workers, and because of these similarities, their studies are usually easier to understand and more relevant to social workers than studies conducted in other disciplines.

The research findings of social work researchers can be easily found in professional journals that either focus on social work or a field of practice in which social workers are employed. Examples of social work journals are *Social Work, Health and Social Work, Families in Society, Journal of Baccalaureate Social Work, Journal of Social Work Education, Children and Schools, Child Welfare, Social Work Research*.

All of these journals are published by professional social work organizations such as the National Association of Social Workers, the Association of Baccalaureate Social Work Program Directors (BPD), Family Services of America, and the Child Welfare League. The BPD is particularly important to note because it has focused on baccalaureate social work issues, as seen below:

The Journal of Baccalaureate Social Work

In October 1995, a new journal was launched to nurture scholarship and contribute to the knowledge base of social work (Schriver, 1995). This journal was to be different from other journals in several important ways. It was to focus on baccalaureate social work education issues, solicit BSW faculty contributions, and encourage BSW students to submit their manuscripts as well. The new editor, Joe Schriver, called for the journal contributors to collaborate with their clients in a mutual search for meaning and to listen to clients' voices, narratives, and constructions of reality. Diverse research methods were encouraged. Several studies have been published in this journal over the past ten years. You will find many of these studies highlighted in this book as illustrations of good research.

The *Journal of Baccalaureate Social Work (JBSW)* is a journal that BSW students may want to consider as an outlet for publishing their own research. The editors of this journal provide authors with helpful comments for improving the manuscripts they submit. Sometimes the editors will even assign someone from the editorial board to work directly with an author who needs extensive help with a manuscript. The Website for *JBSW* is www.sowo.tcu.edu/jbsw.htm. Student social work journals have also sprung up as outlets for publishing students' manuscripts. One of these journals is the *New Social Worker*. Its Website is www.socialworker.com. Another student journal is *Social Work Perspectives*, published by San Francisco State University.

Other professional journals are multidisciplined and focus on a particular field of practice, such as mental health, family services, substance abuse, or gerontology. These journals are also good sources for research conducted by social work researchers as well as research from those in other disciplines working in these fields. A few examples of multidisciplined journals are listed, with the pertinent field settings listed in parentheses. *The Gerontologist* (older adult settings), *Family Relations* (marriage and family), *Community Mental Health Journal* (mental health), *Journal of Community Practice* (community organizing), *Mental Retardation* (mental retardation), *Public Welfare* (income maintenance; child, youth, and family; and disabled and older adults), *Journal of Social Work in Disability and Rehabilitation* (disabilities), *Journal of Child Sexual Abuse* (child welfare), *Psychiatric Services* (mental health), *Journal of Studies on Alcoholism* (substance abuse). There are numerous professional journals of potential interest to social workers. Some are published by professional organizations and others by private publishing firms.

Because social work is primarily a helping profession, we must also rely on the research from other disciplines. Sociology, psychology, anthropology, and political science are among the most important disciplines we depend on for knowledge. Each of these disciplines focuses on the person-in-environment. *Sociology* provides understanding about social forces and groups that influence and socialize people. *Psychology* provides understanding of the interior life of people, including their feelings and emotions, motivations, beliefs, and thoughts. *Anthropology* emphasizes understanding of the cultures of people, what these cultures value, and how they influence and are influenced by people. *Political science* helps us understand the political arenas in which social work finds itself. Some of these disciplines also provide knowledge on how to improve the environments of disadvantaged and oppressed people. Other disciplines also provide social workers with pertinent knowledge, including social psychology, education, counseling, religion and spirituality, biology, medicine, pharmacology, history, art, and others.

Research Topics of Interest to Social Workers

Social workers are employed in a variety of field settings and encounter a diverse set of problems. Because of these realities, social workers are interested in a varied array of research topics. If a research topic is in any way relevant to the person-in-environment focus of social work, it is probably of interest to some social workers. A small sample of research topics taken from the titles of recent professional journals illustrates the varied collection of research consumed and produced by social workers:

- The voices of African American families about transracial adoptions
- Opportunities for empowering people with severe mental illness for treatment planning
- Access barriers to using prenatal care among low-income urban women
- Family caregiving among lesbians and gay men
- Designing a psycho-educational group for children from drug-involved families
- A case study in partnering with a community
- An analysis of the career paths of social work students
- Kin and nonkin social supports among Vietnamese immigrants
- Living with HIV/AIDS in the Latino culture

Equally varied are the research topics BSW and MSW students select when conducting their own studies, particularly in a research methods course. A small sampling of the topics in one social work program follows:

- Attending to the well-being of students in a BSW program
- Students' attitudes on the death penalty
- How the school social worker is understood (or misunderstood) by other school personnel
- The cultural sensitivity of social work students
- Effects of a 12-step program on a client's spirituality
- Perceptions of school violence by students in a public school
- Why some people eat meat

Once a research topic is selected, the challenges and fun of conducting research begin. Decisions need to be made about the specific focus of the study, the most important variables to be measured, who will be in the sample, what data collection approach will be used, who will collect the data, how the data will be analyzed, and what the implications of the study for social work will be. The chapters that follow describe what is involved in conducting research.

Chapter Reflections

The Book's Perspective about the People Who Are Studied

One final note about the basics of research has to do with the people being studied. Historically, the people who are studied have been referred to as "subjects" or "research subjects." The focus of social work studies are usually on clients, community leaders, and staff members. Because social workers are committed to giving people more control over their lives, it is important to remember that social work research can also give the people being studied more control as well. In a sense, they can often be viewed as our "consultants" because they have much to teach us. Therefore, the book refers to the people being studied in social work research as **research participants** or participants, not research subjects. These terms suggest that people participate and often collaborate with researchers in the important enterprise of science.

Discussion Questions

1. What are some of the ways that you use research in your everyday life?
2. Follow the exercise conducted by a group of students on pages 3–4 to find out some of your sources of knowing.
3. What are some of the ways you envision using research as a social work practitioner?

4. Check with your university library to find out what periodicals (professional journals) they have that are devoted to the specific fields of practice involving social workers.

5. Identify two or three research topics of interest to you. Explain why you have selected these topics.

6. Consider a recent news report that you saw on TV. How do you think the information shared in the report was obtained? What research skills might have been used? What biases in reporting might have existed?

7. Identify a research article on a topic of interest in a recent professional journal and bring it to your class. The purpose of a research article is to report the findings of a research study. Identify the research methods that were used in the study and report the findings, recommendations, and conclusions. In addition, identify an article that is not a research report and bring it to class. Identify the focus and purpose of this article. For example, does it describe something, such as a practice approach? Is it a literature review of a topic? A debate that presents opposing views about a controversial issue?

8. Many social problems (e.g., homelessness, divorce, and teenage pregnancy) have been studied numerous times to find out more about their causes. Look for a research report that attempts to identify the causes of a social problem and concludes by offering a description of a theory that explains the causes of this problem. Describe this theory. Then determine the extent to which you think the findings of this study provide adequate support for the theory.

References

Braver, S., & O'Connel, D. (1998). *Divorced dads: Shattering the myths.* New York: Tarchner/Putnam.

Council on Social Work Education. (2001). *Educational policy and accreditation standards.* (Corrected in 2002.) Alexandria, VA: author.

Hutchison, E. (1999). *Dimensions of human behavior: Person and environment.* Thousand Oaks, CA: Pine Forge Press.

Krantz, G. (2002). Violence against women: A global public health issue! Violence against women has an effect on public health. *Journal of Epidemiology and Community Health, 56*(14), 242.

Levinson, D. J. (1978). *The seasons of a man's life.* New York: Ballantine Books.

Lynch, D., Vernon, R., & Smith, M. (2001). Critical thinking and the web. *Journal of Social Work Education, 37*(2), 381–386.

Marlow, Christine. (2001). *Research methods for generalist social work* (3rd ed.). Stamford, CT: Thomson Learning.

Miller, D., Webster, S., & MacIntosh, R. (2002). What's there and what's not: Measuring daily hassles in urban African American adolescents. *Research on Social Work Practice, 12*(3), 375–388.

O'Farrell, T., Hutton, V., & Murphy, C. (1999). Domestic violence before and after alcoholism treatment: A two-year longitudinal study. *Journal of Studies on Alcoholism, 60*(3), 317–321.

Schriver, J. (1995). As we begin: Collaboration, listening and diverse research methods. *Journal of Baccalaureate Social Work, 1*(1), 9–12.

chapter 2

Philosophies and Perspectives about Research

What is "real"? What is "true"? In our society, it is safe to say that the dominant forms of thought are scientific, technological, empirical, and objective, as contrasted with poetic, symbolic, personal, and existential.

(Sanks, 2001, p. 6)

Chapter 1 pointed out that scientific research is supposed to be conducted in a neutral manner. While this is true, values are always evident and must be considered in research. Whenever human beings are studying other humans, values are presumed to exist. Values have a major influence on how a study is conducted. These values can usually be detected in the description of the study in a research report, whether they are explicitly stated or not. It is important for researchers to openly identify their perspectives when they begin a study and to build in ways to consider alternative perspectives as the study progresses. Welfare reform is an example of a research topic that could be examined from numerous perspectives.

Researchers can approach a topic from a wide variety of perspectives. For example, two researchers may want to study the barriers to clients using social work

TEST YOUR KNOWLEDGE

What's Welfare Reform All About?

An example of a controversial research topic is welfare reform, the federally funded program that replaced Aid to Families with Dependent Children (AFDC). Numerous perspectives exist about welfare reform that can determine how a study on welfare reform would be conducted. One perspective may point out that welfare reform programs do not provide enough child care and other employment-related support; neither do they provide much stability in a recipient's life because of the time limits on eligibility. Another view could be that welfare reform is beside the point. Instead, welfare should be replaced by an employment program that guarantees jobs for everyone. Another view might be that it is important to keep financial payments to recipients as low and short term as possible to ensure that people do not get too dependent. Still another perspective might suggest that welfare reform be eliminated and replaced by a negative income tax that provides minimal tax refunds when people's income drops below a certain level. Can you come up with other perspectives on welfare reform?

services. One researcher explores how the specific area of spirituality influences the views of one Islamic family and their service utilization. The second researcher takes a general approach to the same general topic by surveying 100 families about their views on several factors related to service utilization. In the first study, the source of the barrier has been identified by the researcher; in the second study, the researcher lets the research participants identify the barriers from a list of possibilities.

Variations in study approach are evident, on any topic, whether the topic is housing, family supports, welfare reform, or adoptions. On welfare reform, for example, one investigator may document the supports mothers need to become successfully employed. Another researcher may want to determine how a welfare family member addicted to crack cocaine disrupts the family system. A third researcher may evaluate how a particular welfare reform program increases the involvement of absent fathers. A fourth study may measure how welfare reform can save the government money.

Why is there so much variation in how studies are conducted? Are some types of research "better" or more "scientific" than others? And what about the neutrality expected in scientific research? Is research supposed to be conducted in one particular way in all cases? After all, if it is "scientific," shouldn't it follow one standard set of procedures or rules?

These and other questions are addressed in this chapter as we consider the factors that give research its underlying meaning. Specific topics covered in this chapter are:

- two distinct philosophies—deductive and inductive
- quantitative and qualitative methodologies
- some specialized areas in social work research
- critical thinking and its relevance to social work research

Inductive and Deductive Philosophies

Research is driven by two general philosophies—the inductive and deductive approaches. A **philosophy** refers to the underlying intentions or reasons for conducting the research process including the basic values and beliefs about research. These two philosophies (inductive and deductive) have very different purposes and approaches. Yet, they complement each other. Studies can usually be identified as being based on either one or the other.

Inductive Research

Research is called **inductive** when data are gathered about a phenomenon before an explanation is hypothesized or suggested. In inductive research, researchers often start with a theoretical perspective or orientation but do not have a specific explanation for the phenomenon. They may not even know much about the phenomenon they are about to observe. Inductive researchers take the position that they are prepared to learn as much as they can from the people they study. The data they collect are intended to generate new theoretical explanations about a research problem or topic.

Example of an Inductive Study

Sharon Owens (2003) conducted an inductive study that focused on how African American women coped with AIDS/HIV. She conducted unstructured interviews with 18 women who were living with this problem to obtain their perceptions of how their families both supported and hindered them in their efforts to cope with this disease. The questions that she asked were open ended and included "What would you say have been your major concerns or problems?" "What did you find most helpful in dealing with these problems?" "What did you find to be least helpful?" One set of findings focused on the women's families being a source of stress. Themes frequently mentioned emerged from several of these interviews including wanting to communicate their sickness to their families, fear that their families would not be able to help when they needed them, denial among family members that AIDS was a terminal disease, and blocked communication because of other pressing problems in these families.

Those who conduct inductive research are driven by an interest to discover new explanations and insights for how and why people and their environment function. This approach is useful when little or nothing is known about the situation. In the 1950s and 1960s, for example, little was known about the gangs that were emerging in many low-income neighborhoods, particularly in larger cities. Inductive research, using the participant observation method, was helpful in providing answers to the question of why gangs were gaining membership. One overall finding in many of these studies was that the gangs met many of the personal needs of their members, including a feeling of belonging, leadership opportunities, protection from other gangs, and socialization. *Talley's Corner* is a good example of a participant observation study of a group of unemployed men who routinely spent their time hanging together on a street corner. Little if anything was known about the lives of such men and their peer groups before this study was published.

Talley's Corner

E. Liebow (1967), a sociologist, explored the lives of a couple dozen African American men in the 1960s living in a low-income neighborhood in Washington, D.C. Liebow spent a year with these unemployed men, hanging out on the street with them. He developed enough rapport to become accepted as an "insider," and he learned about their lives through his associations with the group. In research terms, he became a "participant" in their lives. His book portrays what life was like for these men, based on what they said and what Liebow observed. A captivating, informal system of interlocking roles, friendships, and support was described in *Talley's Corner;* Talley was the leader of the group. Liebow later explained, "I went in so deep that I was completely submerged and my plan to do three or four separate studies, each with its own neat, clean boundaries, dropped forever out of my sight. My initial excursions into the street—to poke around, get the feel of things, and lay out the lines of my field work—seldom carried me more than a block or two from the corner where I started."

(McCarthy, 1994, p. 2)

Gang problems may again be important to investigate in many U.S. cities in the 21st century, since gangs are reemerging as a serious problem in many cities and are appearing for the first time in other cities.

Similarly, in the 1970s and 1980s, homelessness became a burgeoning social problem that victimized many struggling groups, not just addicted men. Former patients of mental hospitals, mothers and children, and people struggling to live on minimum wages were among the homeless population. While there was some speculation about the various causes of homelessness, little was initially known about the widely varied reasons for homelessness. Inductive studies, including case studies of homeless people, analyses of case records of homeless shelters, and participant observation studies became valuable sources of information for helping them.

Deductive Research

Research is called **deductive** when it begins by crafting a theoretical statement that explains why something is happening in the real world. This step is completed prior to data collection and should be deduced from already established theories, perhaps by adding a few assumptions. Like inductive research, deductive research is supposed to take into account what is already known from the professional literature and other relevant sources. After a theoretical explanation is crafted, the researcher attempts to find out whether it is supported or not by gathering data. Theoretical explanations are usually constructed as hypotheses. Hypotheses, which are statements that describe a specific relationship between two variables, are described in Chapter 6.

Example of a Deductive Study

Siebert and colleagues (1999) used role theory to help explain the importance of the friendship role to aging adults. Role theory in this case was defined as a perception of how people see themselves being and acting in a particular role. These researchers wanted to find out if the adults who identified with qualities that foster friendship (e.g., more social than solitary, more happy than sad, more warm than cold, more interested in others than interested in self, etc.) were more satisfied with their lives. They also examined whether the adults who were more committed to their friendship roles were more satisfied. A sample of 800 preretirement adults were surveyed to determine which of several factors influenced their satisfaction in life. They found that the more these adults identified with friendship qualities and were committed to their friendships, the higher their life satisfaction scores were. Both quantitative methods and measures were emphasized in this study.

Deductive studies are valuable in supporting or casting doubt on theoretical explanations about people and their environment. These studies can provide some of the evidence for an explanatory statement. Deductive studies can also be valuable in exploring the extent to which theoretical explanations may be evident in a wide variety of people and social groups. However, we must always be careful to consider the limitations inherent in generalizing findings from one group to another.

Deductive studies are usually concerned with generalizing their findings from a subgroup of people to a larger population. **Generalizing** means inferring that the findings from a study of a sample of participants apply to a larger population. For example, we could ask if the results of a study of a sample of 100 homeless people in Chicago can be generalized to all homeless people in this city. Also, we may want to ask if these findings are applicable to homeless people in other cities as well.

Let's look closer at some of the limitations in generalizing. It is not possible to fully generalize the findings of a study from one group of people to another simply because no two people or groups are exactly alike. We also know that the social conditions (population characteristics, condition of the economy, employment opportunities, etc.) of different cities are not identical. For example, homeless people in Chicago are not faced with the same opportunities and problems as those in Phoenix, Cincinnati, or Los Angeles.

Deductive studies are interested in investigating whether similar patterns exist in the social circumstances of different groups of people. For instance, even though the larger cities in the United States are not identical, they are similar in demographic characteristics, types of industries, housing patterns, and socioeconomic conditions. Therefore, it seems logical that their social problems would be similar as well. It is quite possible that the experiences of a social group in one city could be somewhat like those of the same type of group in another city.

The findings of deductive studies are usually generalized from a subgroup studied to the larger population from which it is drawn. When social workers want to improve services to their clients, they often end up generalizing, or applying, the findings from studies of other groups to their own client groups. Otherwise, why would someone living in Jacksonville read a research study conducted in St. Paul?

How we generalize or apply findings of studies about one group to another group needs to be done with care, caution, and an awareness that there will be some degree of error involved. The cautions to be heeded in making generalizations are discussed further in Chapter 8.

Assessment of Your Philosophical Tendencies

After being introduced to these two ways of thinking about research, it may be interesting to explore your preference for a particular research philosophy. Your preference may be for an inductive or a deductive approach. The inductive and deductive approaches are apparent in many aspects of students' work, such as writing papers, interviewing, taking exams, and conducting other personal investigations. The questionnaire in Table 2.1 will help you explore your inductive and deductive tendencies.

Quantitative and Qualitative Methodologies

Both quantitative and qualitative methods are general types of research methods. **Quantitative methods** involve analysis of numbers; **qualitative methods** involve

TABLE 2.1 **What Are Your Inductive and Deductive Tendencies?**

Please answer the following questions by circling the number that best fits your inclination. Circle one of the three numbers for each question. There are no right or wrong answers.

1. When I write papers, I usually . . .

outline my papers before writing them	am in-between	let the organization of the paper evolve as I write the paper
1	2	3

2. When I investigate something, I usually prefer . . .

to confirm ideas that I already have	am in-between	discover new ideas from other people
1	2	3

3. When I investigate something, I am most comfortable with . . .

completing what I have started even if I am not satisfied with it	am in-between	leaving it incomplete until I am satisfied with it
1	2	3

4. When I investigate something, I prefer working with . . .

numbers	am in-between	words
1	2	3

5. When I investigate something, I like to . . .

find out what's known	am in-between	delve into the unknown
1	2	3

6. When I interview someone, I usually like to . . .

be active in asking questions	am in-between	mostly listen
1	2	3

Count your total score. A score of 6–10 is a deductive tendency. A score of 11–13 is a balance between deductive and inductive tendencies. A score of 14–18 is an inductive tendency.

words. Typically, quantitative methods use structured surveys, structured observations, and examination of existing quantitative reports. Qualitative methods usually use open-ended questions in interviews, unstructured surveys, focus groups, participant observation, and examination of existing qualitative documents. However, the distinction between the methods used in deductive and inductive research is not exact. Exceptions should be noted. For example, you can conduct and analyze a structured survey as part of inductive research, and you can use unstructured methods to support or refute a hypothesis.

Quantitative and qualitative methodologies are closely linked to inductive and deductive reasoning. The deductive approach uses quantitative methodologies, whereas the inductive approach uses qualitative methodologies. Quantitative and qualitative methods are also different in other ways, as noted in Table 2.2.

Quantitative Methods

Quantitative methods are an approach to data collection that measures the quantity of something. These methods are used in deductive studies to find support in the real world for something, such as a theoretical explanation, that has been developed by the researcher. These inquiries are also focused on what the researcher has as a goal. The steps in the research process are followed in a linear pattern, with each step completed sequentially. Once a step is completed and a new step taken, it is unlikely that the previous step will be revisited and changed. This is particularly true for the research design, which is not likely to change once data collection begins.

Quantitative methods are more structured in approach than qualitative methods. Quantitative inquiries are more definite and specific about what they want to find out. Questions are asked or observations made in such a way that responses

TABLE 2.2   Characteristics of Quantitative and Qualitative Methods

Quantitative Methods	Qualitative Methods
• quantify something	• qualify something
• deductive reasoning	• inductive reasoning
• support an existing explanation	• discover a new explanation
• focused	• holistic
• linear research process	• circular research process
• structured search	• semi- or unstructured search
• forced-response questions	• open-ended questions
• data in number form	• data in word form
• statistical analysis	• word analysis

can be quantified. These quantified measures are more standardized than qualitative measures. Quantitative searches usually provide all of the potential answers to a question in the form of a set of response categories. The respondent is expected to choose the most appropriate response. These questions are referred to as "forced-response" questions.

A question, for example, may be "What is your primary source of income?" The answer to this question could be any of a number of sources, including employment earnings, savings, welfare, disability insurance, a social security pension, or your partner, friends, or family. While these responses are all in word form, they could be easily quantified. Each of the categories in this example are distinct and do not overlap, and thus each category could be assigned a number that could be entered as data into a computer. In analyzing the results of quantitative investigations, statistical methods can be used because the results are quantified in number form.

Quantitative methods have several advantages over qualitative ones. They can provide standardized measures of a concept and more accurate measures generally. Exact comparisons can be made in the participants' responses, unlike qualitative methods. Quantitative studies also often have the option of generalizing the findings from a sample to a larger population and can be used to test hypotheses. Statistical analysis, which offers many options for data analysis, can also be used.

Qualitative Methods

Qualitative methods are an approach to data collection that attempts to discover the quality of something—its peculiar and essential character. These methods are inductive in nature and attempt to discover new explanations. New explanations could be, for example, cultural barriers perceived by a Korean group to using a mental health center or the views of inner-city African American teenage males about preventing pregnancy. Qualitative inquiries are not nearly as focused as quantitative methods. They have a flexibility that allows the researcher to gather data on topics not initially identified. These holistic explorations can also provide data for understanding an issue in a larger social context.

The steps in the research process for qualitative studies are similar to those for quantitative methods, except that the process can go back and forth between steps in a circular fashion rather than being linear and sequential. A research step that has already been implemented can be revisited and modified if it benefits the study. For example, even though a data collection instrument has been constructed and data partially collected, researchers might discover some new questions they want to ask. An illustration of this can be seen in the following example. The researcher could choose to either ask these new questions of all participants or decide only to ask them of participants who have not yet been interviewed. Standardized data collection is not as important in qualitative studies, because the results are primarily used to more fully understand the participants in the study, not to generalize the findings to others.

> ### Example of a Research Design Changing over Time
>
> A participant observation study of a group of 27 people with a mental retardation label focused on the topic of stigma associated with being labeled "mentally retarded." Unstructured interviews were used to explore this topic. Early in these interviews, it was discovered that this extremely sensitive topic was difficult to explore by directly asking participants how they felt about being labeled mentally retarded. Some, for example, did not perceive themselves as having this condition or they abhorred the label. The researchers changed their interviewing approach as they discovered that some participants could discuss the topic more easily by talking about how they perceived others with this label, particularly those who functioned at lower levels than they did. These discussions often involved projecting negative attributes onto others who were labeled, followed by a more positive portrayal of their own attributes (e.g., "He is really the retarded one; he doesn't even have a job like I do."). This early discovery in interviewing led to another major finding—that these participants tended to stratify their peer group by level of functioning. These participants inevitably ranked themselves high in the "pecking order." The study goals were adjusted along the way as these findings developed.
>
> (Dudley, 1983)

Although the findings of qualitative studies are not typically intended to be generalized to other groups of people, they can have transferability potential. The findings of a qualitative study may be relevant and useful to someone else concerned about a group of people with similar characteristics and circumstances. To optimize the opportunities for transferability of findings from the study group to another group, it is important for researchers to sufficiently describe the research participants and their circumstances in their report (Tutty, Rothery, & Grinnell, 1996). Then consumers of the study will be able to judge the extent to which the findings are based on case material similar to their group.

Qualitative methods involve more semi- or unstructured searches. They ask questions or observe behaviors that are more likely to be open ended and thus less likely to be quantified. Open-ended questions do not have a defined set of response categories from which respondents choose their answers. Instead, respondents write responses in their own words in a blank space on a questionnaire or share their responses in their own words in an interview. For example, a qualitative question may be "What do you like about social work?" The responses, if they are in the respondent's own words, can be anything from "helping people" to "getting a stable job" to "reaching addicted adolescents" to "feeling that I am doing something meaningful." The types of responses to such a question can be unlimited.

Unless these naturalistic responses were forced into a smaller set of general categories by the researcher, they would not be measured in quantified form. Instead they would remain in word form. Qualitative methods usually elicit data from conversations and behaviors that are natural to what people say and do in their daily lives. The analysis of the data would honor the meaning of each response rather than dispossessing it of some of its meaning by forcing it into a quantitative measure. This latter problem is referred to as **reductionism.**

Qualitative methods also have advantages over quantitative methods. These methods are more useful when little is understood about a phenomenon and flexibility is needed in the methods used. In addition, these methods are valuable when naturalistic data are needed. Also, many concepts can only be understood in word form and cannot be reduced to variables with quantitative measures. Finally, these methods are more amenable to research participants who have difficulty reading and comprehending written material or do not have a full understanding of the English language.

While quantitative and qualitative methods are distinctly different, they can both be used in the same studies to complement each other. For example, many survey studies that are composed mostly of forced-response questions (quantitative methods) also may include one or two open-ended questions (qualitative methods). These open-ended questions are usually located at the end of the survey. Various ways to combine quantitative and qualitative methods in studies are discussed in later chapters.

Some Specialized Areas in Social Work Research

In addition to the two broad philosophies of social research (inductive and deductive) and the differences evident between quantitative and qualitative methods, there are other variations in how research is conducted. Many researchers use a specialized theoretical perspective to guide their research. These perspectives accentuate particular theories mixed with the viewpoints or values of the researcher. Some of these specialized areas are relatively new, and some are especially used by social work researchers. Three of these specialized areas are (1) participatory action research, (2) feminist research, and (3) Afrocentric research. While there is not always a consensus on how each of these specialized areas are defined and described, general descriptions are provided here based on some recent pertinent writings.

Participatory Action Research

Participatory action research (PAR), also sometimes referred to as participant action research or critical action research, is one of these specialized areas. PAR takes an interest in actively involving research participants in all or most of the steps of the process. PAR also favors studying topics that are beneficial to the research participants. Following are some of the key PAR principles (DePoy, Hartman, & Haslert, 1999):

1. Collaborate with those affected by the problem to clearly articulate the problem, its scope, and all stakeholders.
2. Articulate the purpose of the change that the research is designed to accomplish.
3. Have both professional and lay researchers on the team.

4. Train the lay researchers how to design, conduct, and use appropriate research methods.
5. Report findings in accessible formats for all stakeholder groups.

PAR is a specialized research approach that can be implemented in each of the steps of the general research process. Suggestions for how the PAR can be implemented in each step are described in Table 2.3.

Some of the principles of participatory action research (PAR) have been used in the preparation of this book. Undergraduate students have reviewed, utilized, and critiqued chapters as they were being developed, and one class of BSW students used a later draft of the text as their research methods text. PAR principles have also been used in several studies described in various chapters. In addition, an example of a PAR study that was conducted by a group of people with developmental disabilities is highlighted in Chapter 14 on pages 266–269.

The principles of PAR are an innovative way of increasing the protection of research participants in studies. Encouraging participants' input in some or all of the steps of a study gives them more understanding and interest in the study's purpose and more control over the impact it may have on them. The participatory action approach can also be used as a means of promoting social and economic justice in research studies; these points are elaborated on in Chapter 3.

The example presented in Table 2.4 illustrates how the principles of PAR can be used in conducting a needs assessment of an at-risk group in a city or county.

TABLE 2.3 How to Implement Participant Action Research in the Steps of the Research Process

Steps in Research Process	Implementing Participant Action Research
1. Understand the research topic	Involve all stakeholder groups in offering their views about the research problem (or topic) and its causes. Ask those affected by the problem to clearly articulate the problem, its scope, and all of the stakeholders.
2. Focus on research questions or hypotheses	Involve all stakeholder groups, including those affected by the problem in deciding on the research questions and the purpose of change that the research is designed to accomplish.
3. Design the study	Select a collaborative research team of professional and lay researchers to create the research design. Train lay researchers to participate in these research design decisions.
4. Collect the data	Train lay researchers to assist in data collection.
5. Analyze the data	Train lay researchers to assist in data analysis.
6. Prepare a report	Report findings in accessible formats to all stakeholder groups, including the research participants. Share specific types of formats with these groups to help in getting feedback.

TABLE 2.4　A Needs Assessment of Nonresidential Fathers Using PAR Principles

1. **Build a communitywide organization to sponsor your fatherhood initiative.** Include representatives of all relevant agencies and organizations that have an interest in fathers and families in this organization. Make sure that you have included people with varying views about how to help non-residential fathers.

2. **Based on extensive discussion within the organization, articulate a focus for your group,** including identifying target groups of fathers that you wish to help, general goals for helping them and their families, and some initial assumptions about the causes of their problems and possible solutions.

3. **Develop small committees** to gather different types of information about these fathers in the goal areas that you have articulated above. Committees can have several foci such as:

   - collecting available statistics from the U.S. Census, special U.S. Census reports, health statistics, state studies, local studies, etc.

   - reviewing the Websites of several national fatherhood organizations to find out what they offer and then calling the organizations that are most relevant to your project's goals . . .

   - talking to the staff and clients of local agencies about these topics

   - finding out more about existing programs that serve fathers

4. **Organize and report on the material collected in the prior step.** As you do this, try to make sure that it is in an format that is easy to read by all stakeholder groups.

5. **Explore funding support for your project** and involve the ideas of these funding agencies in your continued articulation of the problem and goals of your project. Also, begin articulating a program proposal for funding support. Possible funding supports could be identified earlier in the process in a general way.

6. **Decide on the methods that you will use** to conduct your own needs assessment of fathers. This will likely be an in-depth, firsthand study of the community. Possible methods to consider are focus groups, informant interviews, surveys of existing agency resources and services, other surveys of public attitudes, etc. Be sure to include ample participation of fathers' groups of interest to your organization in the needs assessment study. Also decide if a professional firm or individual consultant are needed to help you develop your research methodologies.

7. **Conduct your planned study** articulated in the prior step and compile an easy-to-read report of your findings.

8. **Involve all of the participants in articulating an implementation proposal** (sponsoring organizations, fathers that you have met in focus groups, funding agency, etc.). Develop this proposal by first supplementing and revising the earlier versions of your problem definition and goals. Then develop a set of general strategies and specific program proposals that could be implemented to achieve your goals. Be sure to develop a realistic time line for implementing your proposal.

9. **Be sure to consider** all of the following levels of intervention in your general strategies: counseling services to fathers and their families, group services, mediation services to fathers and their families, community education, and new family agency policies.

Source: From *Fathering at Risk: Helping Nonresidential Fathers,* 2001 (pp. 176–177), by J. Dudley and G. Stone. New York: Springer. Reprinted by permission.

The illustration offers a general outline for how a needs assessment was conducted with one at-risk group—nonresidential fathers. With minor modifications, this outline could be used with other at-risk populations, such as teenage parents, adults who were adopted as children and wish to find their biological parent, recent immigrants from the Middle East, cancer survivors, older lesbian women who are socially isolated, homeless people.

Feminist Research

Feminist research uses a theoretical perspective informed by feminist theories. However, feminist researchers do not agree on all issues and draw on different feminist theories. **Feminist research** is defined both by the research methods feminists researchers prefer and the research topics they choose to study. Most feminist researchers prefer qualitative over quantitative research methods because of the flexibility of this method and the value it places on uncovering new knowledge at deeper levels of meaning.

Feminist researchers are also concerned with the focus of their studies. In large part, these researchers seem to be primarily concerned with studying the relative positions and experiences of women in relation to men and the effects that gender issues have on both sexes (Deem, 2002). Examples of possible feminist research topics are gender discrimination in hiring, the low representation of women in administrative and other leadership roles, salary inequities based on gender, the roles of men and women in parenting children and assuming household tasks, family-supportive policies of employers, and numerous other topics. Among students, feminist research topics could include gender discrimination in the classroom, body image issues, domestic violence, and gender biases in selecting social work careers. Two examples of feminist research are described in the following examples; one study uses quantitative methods, and the other uses qualitative methods.

Example of Feminist Research: A Study of Women's Salaries

Gibelman (2003) explored the issue of women's salaries in the human services by analyzing existing data from the Bureau of Labor Statistics. By analyzing these data, she found that salary disparities continue to exist between men and women. She attributes these disparities to the result of discrimination patterns. Gibelman recommends several strategies for combating such discrimination, including public and professional education and advocacy. She also draws parallels between gender discrimination experienced by both social workers and client groups that are served.

Some feminists suggest that feminism and qualitative methods are well suited to each other, because both are guided by similar principles (Skeggs, 2001). Both feminism and qualitative methods have a concern that respondents gain something from their involvement in the research. Both are sensitive to power relations between researchers and respondents and want the experience of research participants to be taken seriously. Also, both assume a responsibility and accountability not only to the research participants but also to the wider community. Note that many of these principles are also important to PAR, which suggests that all three of these research approaches have much in common. Many feminist researchers actually use the participatory action approach.

Example of Feminist Research: A Qualitative Study of Welfare Recipients

Karen Seccombe (1999) conducted a qualitative study of forty-seven women on welfare. She developed her study based on a theoretical perspective that welfare reform is flawed because it is based on patriarchal views of women and their roles in families. She coupled this perspective with a view that a capitalist economy needs a cheap labor force, which women on welfare can fill. She documented the personal stories of these forty-seven women related to trying to raise a family on a welfare budget, confronting the problems of dependency and stigma fostered by the welfare system, and the trials and tribulations of finding satisfactory employment opportunities.

Afrocentric Research

Various ethnic perspectives on research have been emerging over the past several years, most of them strongly identified with a particular ethnic group or heritage. This **ethnic-based research** is rooted in the history of these ethnic groups, the group's unique values, and concern for the current needs of the group and culture.

Afrocentric research is probably the most developed ethnic-based research perspective. To understand Afrocentric research, we must understand the term *Afrocentricity.* The concept of Afrocentricity is linked to some well-known African American concepts such as black consciousness and black awareness as well as to an African worldview (Resnicow & Ross-Gaddy, 1997). Afrocentricity has been defined as a philosophic orientation that places African ideals at the center of any analysis that involves African culture and behavior. These ideals include the importance of family and giving more emphasis to communal than individual values. An Afrocentric perspective is offered as an alternative to the Eurocentric perspective, which we often assume incorrectly to be the perspective common to all groups (Asante, 1987).

Afrocentric researchers have a special awareness of their culture as African Americans, their history of slavery in the United States, and their African roots. The U.S. Census Bureau and other sources remind us that African Americans are more likely than white Americans to be poor, unemployed, have higher infant mortality rates, and to suffer from many other adversities that require greater attention (www.census.gov). Afrocentric and other researchers focus their studies on both the problems and the strengths of African Americans. Such findings provide greater understanding of this group's needs and offer implications for effectively helping.

While there is a growing body of written material that defines Afrocentricity and highlights the issues of importance to people with this perspective, Afrocentric research in social work seems to be in an earlier stage of development. While few research articles in social work are identified as being Afrocentric, an increasing number are focusing on cultural diversity and political issues that directly concern African Americans. These studies are a valuable resource for all social workers and can sensitize and inform social workers about the strengths and problems of their African American clients. An example of such a study emphasizing African and African American cultural and political issues follows:

Example of an Afrocentric Research Study

Wendy Haight (1998) conducted an ethnography of a group of African American families who were members of an African American Baptist church with a rich 100-year history. An ethnography is a special type of qualitative research that provides a detailed description of a case. Haight describes a Sunday school project that was part of the church. She focused on the beliefs of African American adults manifested in their socialization of their children within this Sunday school project. This study provided valuable information about the indigenous socialization beliefs and practices of this group. The findings were also used to help shape a computer club that, among other things, instilled cooperative social relationships, spiritual themes, and storytelling by mentors.

Chapter Reflections

Critical Thinking and Social Work Research

Critical thinking is another recent development of importance to social work and social work education. **Critical thinking** involves a careful examination of beliefs and actions (Gibbs and Gambrill, 1996). It requires giving attention to the process of reasoning and considers alternative points of view, being genuinely fair-minded in presenting these varied views. Critical thinking is based on standards of clarity, accuracy, relevance, and comprehensiveness and is not concerned with such things as obtaining social approval or being politically correct.

While critical thinking may be a familiar term in many aspects of our lives, this concept has recently become an important development in social work circles (e.g., Gibbs & Gambrill, 1996). This recent development has also become one of the mandates identified in the accreditation standards for social work promulgated by the Council on Social Work Education. Because of this, critical thinking is now stressed throughout the social work curriculum, and students are taught how to think critically in courses in practice, policy, human behavior and the environment, research, and fieldwork, among others.

Gibbs and Gambrill (1996) identify several types of problems that social workers experience in their practice when they fail to be critical thinkers. These problems include misclassifying clients, focusing on irrelevant factors, selecting weak or inappropriate interventions, increasing client dependency, and continuing an intervention either too long or not long enough.

Scientific reasoning and critical thinking share many common values. Both provide a special way of thinking about the assumptions we make, our explanations and their sources, and our decisions. Several attributes that are important in critical thinking are also important in research, including the following:

- distinguishing between questions of fact and value
- using caution when inferring what may have caused improvement
- being cautious when making generalizations
- stating problems and goals in measurable terms
- continually asking, "Does this intervention work?"
- generally being a skeptic

These and other attributes are discussed throughout this book because they are important attributes needed by consumers and producers of research. As a consumer of research, you are expected to be "critical" in your review of how researchers frame the research topic or problem they are studying, how they use research methods in gathering their data, how they present their findings, and whether they base their recommendations on their findings. You are also encouraged to be critical thinkers in the producer role—for example, when you are involved in defining your own focus for a study, conducting a literature search, collecting data, presenting your findings, and proposing recommendations to others.

Discussion Questions

1. Identify a research study based on PAR (participatory action research), feminist research, or an ethnic perspective. How does this study seem to be different from other studies you have read? Are there differences in the research methods used or the emphasis given to findings and recommendations?

2. Review some Websites on African Americans to find out more about the needs and problems of African American people. Some sources are www.census.gov (click on "A," then click on "African Americans") and www.lenzine.com/census/index.php. Then identify one research topic that you may be interested in studying. How might an Afrocentric researcher investigate this topic differently than other researchers?

References

Asante, M. K. (1987). *The Afrocentric idea*. Philadelphia: Temple University Press.

Deem, R. (2002). Talking to manager-academics: Methodological dilemmas and feminist research strategies. *Sociology, 36*(4), 835–856.

DePoy, E., Hartman, A., & Haslert, D. (1999). Critical action research: A model for social work knowing. *Social Work, 44*(6), 560–569.

Dudley, J. (1983). *Living with stigma: The plight of the people who we label mentally retarded*. Springfield, IL: Charles Thomas.

Dudley, J., & Stone, G. (2001). *Fathering at risk: Helping nonresidential fathers*. New York: Springer.

Gibbs, L., & Gambrill, E. (1996). *Critical thinking for social workers: A workbook*. Thousands Oaks, CA: Pine Forge Press.

Gibelman, M. (2003). So how far have we come? Pestilent and persistent gender gap in pay. *Social Work, 48*(1), 22–32.

Haight, W. (1998). "Gathering the spirit" at First Baptist Church: Spirituality as a protective factor in the lives of African American children. *Social Work, 43*(3), 213–222.

Liebow, E. (1967). *Talley's corner: A study of Negro streetcorner men.* Boston: Little Brown.

McCarthy, C. (1994). Sociologist leaves a gift for the forgotten (obituary for Elliot Liebow). *National Catholic Reporter, 30*(41), 2.

Owens, S. (2003). African American women living with HIV/AIDS: Families as sources of support and stress. *Social Work, 48*,(2), 163–171.

Resnicow, K., & Ross-Gaddy, D. (1997). Development of a racial identity scale for low-income African-Americans. *Journal of Black Studies, 28*(2), 239–255.

Sanks, T. H. (2001). *Salt, leaven, and light: The community called church.* New York: Crossland.

Seccombe, K. (1999). *So you think I drive a Cadillac: Welfare recipients' perspectives on the system and its reform.* Boston: Allyn and Bacon.

Siebert, D., Mutran, E., & Reitzes, D. (1999). Friendship and social support: The importance of role identity to aging adults. *Social Work, 44*,(6), 522–533.

Skeggs, B. (2001). Feminist ethnography. In P. Atkinson, A. Coffey, and S. Delamont (Eds.), *Encyclopaedia of ethnography.* London: Sage.

Tutty, L., Rothery, M., & Grinnell, R. (1996). *Qualitative research for social workers.* Boston: Allyn and Bacon.

The profession of social work is based on the values of service, social and economic justice, dignity and worth of the person, importance of human relationships, and integrity and competence in practice. (Council on Social Work Education, 2002a)

Research Ethics and Social Work's Mandates

Along with consumer and producer roles, social workers have other supportive roles regarding research activities in their social agencies. These roles include being

- a gatekeeper to ensure that any new study to be conducted in the agency meets professional standards
- an advocate for clients' protection and privacy
- a promoter of research that is beneficial to the clients' well-being

To carry out all of these roles, social workers need to know the ethical standards and other mandates of the social work profession pertinent to conducting agency research.

This chapter focuses on several different types of ethical problems that occur in research and some of the more common safeguards that can be instituted to address and prevent these problems. The chapter also describes the special mandates required of all social workers by our professional associations and looks closely at how these mandates pertain to the research process. These mandates are revisited throughout the book because of their importance.

Let's begin by clarifying these social work mandates. Social workers are committed to both a code of ethics and several other important mandates. This chapter looks closely at these mandates and their relevance to research. The two primary organizations responsible for promulgating these mandates are

1. the **Council on Social Work Education (CSWE)**—social work education's agency that accredits BSW and MSW programs and promulgates standards for BSW and MSW programs, including the mandates described in this chapter
2. the **National Association of Social Workers (NASW)**—a national association that represents all professional social workers and sponsors the Code of Ethics for Social Workers

Three mandates of CSWE that are directly relevant to research are highlighted in this chapter, namely (1) adhering to the values and ethics of social work, (2) promoting an interest in diversity, and (3) promoting social and economic justice, with special attention to at-risk populations.

Before examining the social work mandates pertinent to social workers, let's examine some of the ethical problems and dilemmas that could confront social workers who are connected in some way to research activities. This examination is followed by a description of the ethical safeguards that can be used to prevent these ethical problems from occurring.

Ethical Problems in Research

Why are the values and ethical safeguards provided by the NASW Code of Ethics and the ethical code of science so important? Research studies can be conducted in such a way that they are harmful or pose serious problems for research participants. These problems often occur inadvertently because the researcher has not given enough forethought to possible negative consequences. In other cases, researchers have given some thought to these problems and may decide that the potential contributions that could result from a study outweighed the potential dangers or intrusions experienced by the research participants.

Several types of ethical problems could happen in a study, including physical harm, psychological harm, invasion of privacy, deceiving the research participants, and misrepresenting or fabricating findings.

Physical Harm

Numerous studies have been known to harm their research participants. The Tuskegee study conducted in the 1930s is a classic example. This experimental study was conducted to find out what the adverse effects of syphilis would be on humans if the disease was left untreated. In that study, African American men were deliberately deceived and denied effective treatment so that the researchers could find out what syphilis could do to people if allowed to run its course. CNN has an Interactive Tuskegee Study Website (http://cnn.com/HEALTH) that can be visited on the Internet to find out more about the ethical problems of this study.

The Tuskegee Experiment

Beginning in the 1930s, 399 men signed up with the U.S. Public Health Service for free medical care. The Public Health Service was conducting a study on the effects of syphilis on the human body. The men were never told that they had syphilis. They were told they had "bad blood" and were denied access to treatment even for years after penicillin came into use in 1947. By the time the study was exposed in 1972, 28 men had died of syphilis, 100 others were dead of related complications, at least 40 wives had been infected and 19 children had contracted the disease at birth.

(Retrieved online from http://cnn.com/HEALTH/9705/16/nfm.tuskegee/index.html.)

Another example of a study causing serious physical harm is the research conducted in the 1940s during the early testing of the atomic bomb. The study's sponsor, the U.S. government, wanted to find out if there would be adverse effects on humans from the fallout of radiation. They did this by allowing people to observe the testing of atomic explosions without informing them of any dangers.

Numerous drug studies have also been conducted with research subjects who were not fully aware of what drug they were injecting. At times, these subjects were deceived into believing that they were taking a new drug in experimental studies when they were actually taking a placebo (sugar pill). Other subjects took potentially dangerous new drugs without being aware of the likely adverse consequences. Often, these studies were conducted in prisons and mental institutions and targeted uninformed and unsuspecting inmates or institutional residents. Such studies are no longer conducted because of regulations enacted by the federal and state governments, universities, and others requiring researchers to follow strict ethical standards and procedures that prevent such abuses.

Psychological Harm

Some studies also have the potential of causing psychological harm. Psychological harm can be as or more serious than physical harm and is often less tangible to detect. Such studies can have the greatest adverse effect on people who are particularly vulnerable, such as people with mental illness or mental retardation, frail older people, the very young, or those who are physically ill. Examples of studies that could impose psychological harm on particular groups are

- divorce studies that ask children sensitive questions, such as which parent they prefer
- asking people with mental retardation or mental illness about their past experiences of being victims of sexual abuse
- asking a child, teenager, or an emotionally vulnerable woman if they have been sexual abused
- asking a person with a mental illness, particularly someone with psychotic episodes, about their dreams
- casually asking older adults to share their feelings about loved ones who have been lost through death

Psychological harm, as mentioned above, can be difficult to detect unless it is carefully assessed and monitored. Such harm could become manifested not only during the time of a study but also much later in the subject's life. It could become manifested as difficulty in coping, withdrawal from existing social supports, or even suicide. Self-esteem issues could also be provoked, particularly if the person was already having serious doubts about self-worth or identity.

Invasion of Privacy

Sometimes studies are inappropriate because they are an unnecessary invasion of privacy. A study that invades anyone's privacy without providing extensive information

TEST YOUR KNOWLEDGE

An Ethics Exercise

Assume you work for a family service agency that provides families with help on various types of problems. In discussing your caseload with other social workers, you have discovered that some of your cases include children whose parents are either divorced or separated. You want to conduct a study of the effects of divorce and separation on these children. You decide to ask several personal questions of the children and want to consider any possible negative effects from these questions. Answer the following exercise questions:

- What ethical issues seem evident as you prepare to do this study?
- How will you address these issues?
- What types of questions, if any, would you decide not to ask these children as one way to protect them?

about the study beforehand could be unethical. Such a study should be avoided unless there is a very strong justification and provisions are introduced to address any problems. It is also possible that invasion of privacy resulting from a study could lead to psychological harm. Vulnerable people (e.g., children, many teenagers, older people, people with mental illness, etc.) and those who have difficulty saying no to participating in studies may be among the most likely to be susceptible to harm. **Informed consent** could address many of the concerns raised about studies that invade the participants' privacy. Informed consent means that the participants are thoroughly informed about the study before they are expected to consent to participate. Informed consent is described in greater detail later in the chapter.

Studies that could be an invasion of privacy include those that ask questions that people may feel uncomfortable answering. Examples include

- asking about the person's sexual practices
- asking about alcohol or drug (legal or illegal) practices
- asking parents to share their feelings about their child who has a disability
- exploring marital status issues
- exploring a person's sexual orientation
- exploring a person's diagnosis, whether a mental illness, cognitive disability, or physical condition

Since a number of topics associated with privacy comprise a significant portion of the topics of interest to social workers, does this mean that many of these topics should not be explored? Studies that are likely to invade a person's privacy can still be legitimate if informed consent is provided and there is adequate justification for the study. Informed consent gives people an explanation for the study and the explicit option to participate or not. An example would be a study of parents of children with Down syndrome. A study focusing on these parents' feelings about their children would be clearly justified if informed consent is given and the results are used, for example, to set up parent training workshops for raising a Down syndrome child. The important thing is to balance the concerns about invasion of privacy with the justification for the study. Informed consent and careful assessment of the vulnerability of people to the research topic are important steps to take in addressing such ethical issues.

Deception of Participants

An ethical problem is also evident when people are deceived about a study or not informed that they are being studied as research subjects. Deceiving a person into participating in a study could be harmful and is surely an invasion of privacy. Examples of such practices, mostly in past decades, are studies of residents of mental institutions, such as those described in Goffman's *Asylum* (1962). Goffman was a sociologist who received approval from the superintendent of a mental hospital to conduct a participant observation study. No one else in the institution was informed that he was conducting research. Goffman disguised himself as an "assistant recreation director" and then wandered freely throughout the institution for a two-year period, conducting his study. At the time of this study in the late 1950s, such procedures were not illegal. However, a federal law currently prohibits such studies, particularly if researchers or their sponsoring agencies are receiving federal funding.

Researchers usually have good intentions when they may deceive their research participants. For example, when informed consent is provided, researchers may decide that it is important to avoid sharing too many details about the study's purpose, because this could create **reactivity,** or an interference to what is being studied. For example, if a researcher is testing a hypothesis and the participants know what the hypothesis is, they may be inclined to provide information the researcher wants to hear rather than what the participants actually feel or think. Studies that attempt to measure the positive effect of a movie or a workshop that confronts racist or sexist attitudes must conceal their study's purpose to some degree as well; otherwise, participants may catch on to what the study is about and respond with comments that indicate less prejudice than they actually have.

The "60 Minutes II" undercover episode described below is an example of deception of the administration and staff of a psychiatric facility. Yet this secretive investigation led to reform in a facility that was knowingly harming its patients. The dilemma imbedded in this example is obvious. While using deception in an investigation is wrong, so are unsound professional practices. A decision had to be made about whether the intent of the study and the deception needed to conduct it outweighed the professional agency's right to privacy. What do you think?

"60 Minutes II" Reveals Abuse in a Psychiatric Facility

A popular TV news magazine program, "60 Minutes II," hired a social worker as an undercover investigator to observe life in a psychiatric facility. The social worker

(continued)

concealed a video tape recorder in his shirt and a camera in his unusually thick eyeglasses while working as a mental health technician at a private psychiatric hospital in 1999. CBS was motivated to initiate this undercover story after hearing of the death of a sixteen-year-old boy who was restrained at one of facilities owned by the same company. This undercover investigation documented many appalling conditions in this institution, including fraudulent reporting of cases (some of which were bogus), an understaffed facility, neglect in giving potentially dangerous drugs, juveniles being placed in restraint by staff without training, and so on. Two facilities owned by this company were quickly closed after the airing of this episode on "60 Minutes II." This episode also led to renewed activities by Congress and mental health advocates to reform options available for using restraints.

(O'Neill, 1999)

This "60 Minutes II" episode illustrates something else: that television, newspapers, magazines, and other media outlets often cover topics of interest to social workers and frequently examine these topics using research tools. The research tools used by the media include participant observation, in-depth interviewing, questionnaires, analysis of existing documents, and other types of observation. The use of these research tools may not fulfill all of the criteria of scientific research covered in the previous chapter, but they are a form of research.

Misrepresentation of Findings

Another serious ethical problem is the misrepresentation in reports and presentations of the research methods or the findings of a study. Dishonesty is one underlying cause of this problem. A possible scenario might be that researchers are disappointed with their findings and so modify them slightly to their favor or advantage. Researchers may be tempted to make a dramatic impact with their recommendations although their findings may not support it. This can lead a dishonest researcher to fudging the results.

Ignorance by a researcher is another, although less likely, cause of misrepresentation. Some researchers may not fully understand the methods they have used

TEST YOUR KNOWLEDGE **Media and Research**

Look for such investigations covered by the media and bring them to your reserach methods class for discussion. In class discussions, discuss whether or not a particular media inquiry is scientific research. Consider any ethical issues evident in the investigation and how they could be handled.

and may innocently misrepresent them in their reports. Or they may use statistical tests in data analysis incorrectly, which leads to incorrect results and conclusions.

Misrepresentation is an ethical problem that may not have an immediate effect on research participants, but it can have long-term adverse implications. For example, social workers and other professionals who are consumers of such studies could institute a major policy or practice change based on these misrepresented findings. If dishonest reporting of research exists and is tolerated, it is difficult to fully imagine the adverse impact that it can have on the science enterprise. Consumers of research must be able to trust the honesty and accuracy of research reports if these studies are to be taken seriously. If the integrity of the researcher cannot be assumed, this will likely lead to the gradual demise of some areas of science and their contributions.

Examples of misrepresentation of studies could include

- A sample of research participants is claimed to be "representative" of a larger population when it was actually selected by a nonprobability sampling approach.
- Program evaluators for a social agency exclude the negative findings of their study in a progress report sent to their funding agency. Their motive is to avoid jeopardizing the agency's continued existence.
- The results of one statistical test that found a significant relationship between two variables is reported, whereas other appropriate statistical tests that found no significance are not reported.
- The responses to an open-ended question in a survey are forced into predetermined categories and presented as if they were the results of a forced-response question.
- Staff members fabricate a lower rate of recidivism of clients returning to their agency after discharge by leaving out returning clients who are classified in some other way.

Balancing Risks and Gains

A final note is important to mention: the balancing of risks and gains. The vast majority of research studies conducted in the United States at present are not conducted to harm people; the opposite is true. In most cases, they are primarily intended to benefit people in numerous important ways. Medical studies, for example, often test the effects of a new medical intervention or medication therapy on a small group of people before these interventions are made available to the general population. Any harm that may occur from such studies is likely to be a side effect that is considered to be worth the risk. Generally, considerations given to risking harm to people must be balanced by considerations given to the potential gains that can come from a study. Studies that follow strict ethical standards, including informing the participants of the possible risks of being harmed and obtaining their explicit consent, should, in most instances, address the balance that is needed between risks and gains.

Ethical Safeguards of Research

It can be discouraging to realize how many ethical problems can arise in studies. It is important to realize, however, that these problems can be prevented. This is where both the ethical standards of research and the values and ethics of social work become important. Let's look at the safeguards that can prevent these ethical problems from occurring.

Researchers are obligated to incorporate several safeguards into their research to prevent ethical problems like the ones mentioned above from occurring. Such ethical safeguards are required by all government-sponsored and government-funded studies, including all studies sponsored by academic institutions. The Department of Health and Human Services (HHS) (formerly referred to as the Department of Health, Education, and Welfare) promulgated one of the first policy statements on ethical principles and guidelines for the protection of human subjects of biomedical and behavioral research in 1979. It was referred to as the Belmont Report and can be reviewed on the Website of the Department of HHS (http://ohrp.osophs.dhhs.gov/humansubjects/guidance/belmont.htm).

The most important ethical safeguards to consider in social work research include

- confidentiality
- informed consent
- monitoring the effects of a study on the participants and offering assistance if necessary
- involving research participants in decision making about the study
- selecting researchers without a conflict of interest

Confidentiality

A primary ethical safeguard is to protect the privacy of all research participants by ensuring confidentiality or anonymity. **Confidentiality** is the circumstance in which the researcher knows the names of each participant but promises not to disclose these names to anyone outside the research team. Confidentiality also includes ensuring that data that are presented cannot identify any participants. Data in this case would be in qualitative form, since numbers are not likely to identify anyone. Examples of data identifying someone could be a peculiar set of behaviors or circumstances that are so unusual that they could be traced to a participant or a controversial incident involving a participant that has been reported in the newspapers. Fictitious names can be one way to protect the identity of participants in case studies. Arrangements must also be made to restrict access to narrative research material and to destroy these data in a reasonable amount of time after the study is completed.

A federal law known by the acronym HIPAA is an important example of the increasing importance being placed on confidentiality in professional practice as well as research. HIPAA mandates increased security measures for ensuring confidentiality of all health records of patients. In part, these increased security measures have been approved to secure confidentiality in the use of electronic files. Researchers, among others, who need access to health care data must comply with the standards of this law.

What Is HIPAA?

HIPAA is an acronym for the Health Insurance Portability and Accountability Act of 1996. This law protects the confidentiality and security of health data of all patients. HIPAA has called on the Department of Health and Human Services to publish new rules that will ensure, among other things, security standards protecting the confidentiality and integrity of the "individually identifiable health information" of all health care patients past, present, or future.

   Who is required to comply? Virtually all health care organizations—including all health care providers, health plans, public health authorities, health care clearinghouses, and self-ensured employers, as well as life insurers, information systems vendors, various service organizations, and universities.

(Retrieved online from www.hipaadvisory.com.)

Anonymity is the circumstance in which the researcher does not know the names of those who have participated in the study, which in itself ensures that the participants' names will not be known to others. Anonymity is usually achieved when a questionnaire is distributed to a group of people and they complete the instrument and return it unnamed. There are, of course, exceptions to ensuring anonymity even in a questionnaire study. For example, if the value of a participant's "ethnicity" indicates he or she is a Latino and there is only one Latino in the sample or population studied, then you would know whose questionnaire it is.

   The researcher must make every effort to ensure that confidentiality is honored in a study. While anonymity is typically not a requirement for a study, assurance of anonymity can sometimes be helpful in encouraging participants to respond to a questionnaire study as openly and honestly as possible. There is also a drawback to anonymity. If researchers do not know which participants filled out the questionnaires that have been returned, they cannot follow up individually to remind those participants who did not return their questionnaires. Of course, researchers can send reminders to everyone in the study, both those who participated and those who did not, urging the latter group to fill out and return their questionnaires and informing those who have already responded to disregard the message.

Informed Consent

A necessary ethical safeguard to build into a study is an informed consent procedure. Research participants should give informed consent before they participate in any study. The information provided in an informed consent form must be clearly communicated and presented at the level of the participants' understanding. It has been suggested that informed consent information should always be written no higher than a sixth-grade level to ensure that it is simple enough to understand.

Informed consent means that the participants are fully informed about the study before they are expected to consent to participate. Several types of information should be explicitly covered in an informed consent, including

1. general purpose of the study
2. qualifications and organizational affiliation of the researcher
3. expectations of the research participant (e.g., how many times they will be interviewed, when and where interviews will occur, what kinds of questions will be asked, how long interviews will last, etc.)
4. assurance of confidentiality (and if this is not possible, an explicit explanation about how the participants' identities will be revealed and to whom)
5. identification of any possible negative effects the study might have on participants
6. identification of any potential benefits resulting from participation
7. an explicit reminder that participants can stop participating at any time and that stopping participation will not result in any negative consequences
8. the name of someone who can be called if participants have any questions or concerns

The amount of information to be shared about the study in an informed consent protocol is also important to consider. For example, though the purpose of the study needs to be explained, giving too much information about the study could create a reactive effect. In this instance, if the participants realize the hypotheses of the study and respond to what they think is wanted by the researcher, this will interfere with their giving valid responses. On the other hand, giving too little information about the purpose of the study could be perceived as being deceptive and unethical.

Informed consent can be presented in either written or oral form. The advantages of written form are important to consider. Information provided in written form can be more easily studied by the participants, thus making it easier to understand. In addition, information provided by the researcher in writing cannot be easily questioned at a later time, particularly if there are any legal issues raised. Another advantage is that a research participant's signature on the informed consent form is clear evidence that consent was provided. Most universities and social agencies require written consent for many of these reasons.

Nevertheless, informed consent in written form has some limitations. Such a form can still be misunderstood if the participant does not understand what it says. For example, the participant may be illiterate, blind, or have cognitive limitations. Therefore, a written explanation of the study should also be thoroughly discussed with the participants to make sure that it is fully understood. Such a discussion is particularly helpful with people who have limited cognitive skills or distorted thinking processes related to mental illness. Also, people who are especially vulnerable to others who have a power advantage, such as involuntary clients, will likely need a thorough discussion to ensure that they are fully informed. They may also need to hear more than once that participation is voluntary. In the special case of children or clients who have legal guardians, the parents or guardians must become involved and give informed consent. However, even though the children or clients without guardianship are not legally responsible, they still need a thorough explanation of the study and the option of not participating.

An example of a informed consent statement that was read is presented below. The statement was made to a group of adults diagnosed with mental illness and mental retardation and recently discharged from a mental hospital. In this example, limitations were imposed on confidentiality by the service provider, a state agency. Note how these limitations are described in the statement.

Example of a Consumer-Informing Statement

My name is _____. I work with the University of X. I would like to find out how you have been doing since you left (mental hospital). I would like to talk to you because you were part of a court case. The case is over now, but we still want to know how you are doing. I will be asking you questions but you do not have to answer if you do not want to. You can quit whenever you want. Everything that you tell me will be given to the people who are in charge of your services. Your opinion is important and may help you get better services. If you tell me that you are in some kind of danger, I will have to tell someone who can help. It is possible that some of what you say may be published in a journal for other people to read but your name will be kept a secret. If you have any questions about what I say, you can call my supervisor _____ or people at the university. I will give you the phone number if you want it. Do you want to talk to me about how things are going? It is okay if you say no and it is okay if you say yes. Nothing bad will happen if you don't want to talk to me.

Verbal statements of informed consent can also have advantages. Verbal statements can be clarified as they are being stated. They can also be more personable than a written form. Discussion and questions about informed consent can also be more freely initiated if the consent is provided verbally.

In the special case of studies involving questionnaires, the informed consent information can be included in a cover letter or in the introductory paragraphs of the questionnaires. Usually, it is presumed that participants accept the informed consent provisions if they voluntarily fill out the questionnaire and return it to the researcher.

Institutional review boards, or IRBs, are a group of people at an institution who have been designated to promulgate ethical standards and approve and

TEST YOUR KNOWLEDGE

Critiquing Two Informed Consent Letters

Two informed consent letters that were used in different studies are presented below. One of these letters is an example that generally meets the standards of informed consent, whereas the other does not. What are the strengths in the first letter? What are the limitations in the second? For each of these letters, you may also want to figure out what is missing, based on the eight types of information required in a consent form listed on page 46.

Informed Consent Letter 1

Dear Parent/Guardian,

The research team at _____ continues to have a state contract to interview designated class members for the _____ Research Project Study. The research team includes Drs. _____ and _____ and a group of trained field researchers.

The purpose of the study is to follow the changes in the lives and satisfaction of designated class members who are at least 18 years of age. Even though the class action suit was dismissed by the court in 1998, the state office is still interested in following this group of people whom they serve. The study will continue through June 30, 2001. A randomly selected group of 240 people have been identified to continue to participate in the annual interview. As the parent/guardian, we are informing you that (consumer name here) has been selected to participate.

The interview includes a review of the records, discussions with staff, and discussions with (consumer name here). We collect information such as background information (e.g., age, gender, diagnoses), adaptive behavior, social adjustment, medical status, current service plan, work/day program, and daily routine. (He/She) will be asked his/her opinion about things such as where (he/she) lives, staff, food, and friends. If (consumer name here) feels a question is too personal, (he/she) does not have to answer it.

This information will be used to learn more about designated class members and measure their progress. Participating in the interview can benefit (him/her) by allowing (him/her) to voice opinions that may lead to better services. Interview information will be given to the state office and local mental health authorities that are responsible for

monitor the ethical provisions of all studies sponsored by the institution. All researchers are legally required to submit a formal statement to their IRB that describes their study and its procedures, benefits, and how it protects research participants from risks like those described earlier in the chapter. IRBs can also serve as a training center to inform researchers of specific requirements related to informed consent. Many IRBs also require annual training for all investigators on the ethical issues of research. Virtually all universities and governmental agencies have an IRB. Many social agencies have their own IRBs as well. Agencies that sponsor research and do not have an IRB should institute a formal way to establish ethical standards and procedures, protect research participants, and making sure this group of people receive the services they need. Annual reports about the group of 240 participants may be distributed to other interested parties as well. In order to share this information with other professionals, some of our findings may be submitted for publication in professional journals. The annual reports and research publications will keep the identity of the participants confidential.

Participation in the study is voluntary, and you may withdraw from the study at any time. Everyone is strongly encouraged to participate, but it is not required in order to continue to receive services. If you have any questions or want to withdraw from the study, please call _____ at _____. We will accept collect calls. If we do not hear from you by August 15, we will assume that you have agreed to participate in the study. Thank you for your assistance with this project.

University X is eager to ensure that anyone in a research study is treated fairly and with respect. If you have any concerns or questions about how you are being treated in this project, contact _____ who is affiliated with research services at (phone number).

Informed Consent Letter 2

Dear Fellow Licensed Social Workers:

My dissertation work is directly related to the licensing requirements in the state of _____. I hope that you will be willing to give a few minutes of your time to contribute to this important work. The following are some of the individuals that have already given some of their time.

(*Several high-level social work people are listed here.*)

Please complete the enclosed survey and return it in the self-enclosed envelope by February 1.

All individual's responses will be kept completely CONFIDENTIAL. The envelope will be coded to organize mailing, but the surveys will not be coded to identify individuals.

Thank you for your time and cooperation.

prevent ethical problems. Excerpts of the informed consent of an IRB of one academic institution are described below.

Information Required in a Typical Informed Consent Form

All informed consent statements must be written on appropriate letterhead stationery.
    The following is a list of minimum information that should be provided for all types of research including anonymous surveys or questionnaires:

- general purpose of the study and that it involves research
- name(s) of the principal researchers and sponsor(s), where appropriate

(continued)

- description of procedures
- statement that participation is completely voluntary and that participation may be discontinued at any time without prejudice to the subject
- number of subjects involved
- duration of subject's participation
- description of reasonably foreseeable risks
- statement that confidentiality will be maintained to the extent possible by law
- description of procedures for maintaining confidentiality and protecting subject privacy
- statement that procedure may involve risks that are currently unforeseeable
- statement that participants are at least 18 years of age
- an explanation of whom to contact for answers to questions about the research along with this statement: "University X is eager to ensure that anyone in a research study is treated fairly and with respect. If you have any questions or concerns about how you are being treated in this project, contact (provide name of primary investigator and appropriate phone number) or (staff person) in the Office of Research Services at (phone number)."

Monitoring Study Effects and Offering Assistance

Researchers have a responsibility to protect the participants in their study. Confidentiality and informed consent procedures provide some protection. Special provisions are needed if the participants of a study are vulnerable in some way or if participation in a study could result in any physical or psychological harm. In these instances, the researcher needs to monitor the effects of the study on participants and build in mechanisms for participants to be referred to appropriate agencies for treatment or other assistance when harm is a possibility.

A study of a new drug can serve as an example. Prior to beginning the study, extensive efforts should be made to explore any potential harm or inconvenience caused by the drug. During the course of the study, researchers should introduce medical procedures that can detect any evidence of harmful effects. For example, a physician can provide periodic physical exams. Also, the research team should build in periodic observations of the participants. Questionnaires filled out by the participants could also be used to help detect any possible harm or hardship. Finally, a follow-up interview and exam should be conducted after the study is completed. Possibly, periodic follow-up interviews should be conducted at different intervals (e.g., at three months, six months, one year, etc.).

Involving Participants in Decision Making

An innovative way of increasing protection for research participants is to involve them in some or all of the steps of the study as it progresses. The participatory action research (PAR) approach is designed to do this. For example, when the researcher is working on step 2 of the research process (focusing the study), prospective research participants could be encouraged to share their ideas about a focus. Or they could be asked to give feedback on a focus that has already been developed by the researchers in draft form. Questions that they could be asked related to ethical concerns are

- Is this a focus that is relevant and meaningful to you?
- What aspects of this focus, if any, may be difficult for you and other participants to discuss?
- What special privacy issues may need to be addressed related to this focus?
- What specific cultural and gender issues may need more attention in the proposed focus?

Prospective participants could also be consulted during the designing of the study. For example, they could be asked to suggest survey questions or to react to questions that have already been developed. Their feedback could be obtained through either a focus group approach or individual interviews.

Selecting Researchers without a Conflict of Interest

Misrepresentation of the findings of a study and other actions that compromise the study's integrity and the safety of the participants must be addressed. One important way to do this is to hire or appoint qualified outside researchers who have no stake in the results of the study. Program evaluations, for example, are often administered by a staff member who works in the agency sponsoring the program. In these instances, researchers are likely to be placed in a conflict-of-interest position because they are staff members. If agency-based researchers, for example, gather results that are negative or potentially damaging to the agency, they may be inclined to minimize or even ignore these findings in their presentations. They may also be instructed by their supervisor or administrator to suppress such findings.

In contrast, if qualified outside researchers are hired who have the autonomy and freedom to report all findings of significance, misrepresentation can be avoided. Similarly, when research reports are submitted to professional journals for publication considerations, a peer review panel of experienced professionals can provide a valuable safeguard for preventing misrepresentation of findings and methods.

Mandates of Social Work

The remaining portion of the chapter is devoted to these three mandates of the Council on Social Work Education that directly impact research: (1) adhering to the values and ethics of social work, (2) promoting diversity, and (3) promoting social and economic justice, with special attention to at-risk populations.

Adhering to Values and Ethics of Social Work

The Council on Social Work Education (CSWE) mandates that social work programs must provide comprehensive coverage of the values and ethics of social work in their courses. The values and ethics of social work are identified, in large part, in the Code of Ethics promulgated by NASW (National Association of Social Workers, 1999). The ethical standards of the Code of Ethics can be found in the back of the book in Appendix B. Our personal beliefs, which can also be considered some of our personal values, were mentioned in Chapter 1. We are also expected to adhere to professional values. The core professional values of social workers are referred to broadly as service, social justice, dignity and worth of the person, the importance of human relationships, integrity, and competence (NASW Code of Ethics, Preamble, 1999).

Ethical principles are attempts to operationalize general values into action statements. These statements point to some behaviors that are important to follow and other behaviors to avoid. For example, if the value is "service," the ethical principle, according to the Code, is that "social workers' primary goal is to help people in need and to address social problems." We could develop even more specific ethical principles related to service to specific types of people we are expected to help.

The NASW Code of Ethics (hereafter referred to as the "Code") has many sections describing ethical principles for social work practice that are also relevant to research. These sections cover issues such as:

- privacy and confidentiality (section 1.07)
- informed consent (section 1.03)
- clients who lack decision-making capacity (section 1.14)
- dishonesty, fraud, and deception (section 4.04)
- misrepresentation (section 4.06)

All of these sections describe ethical standards expected of social workers while working with clients in professional practice. Even so, these issues also sound very similar to the ethical standards of a researcher. As an example, let's look more closely at Informed Consent (NASW, *Code of Ethics,* section 1.03). *Inform* and *consent* are coupled together, as clients must be informed about what they and the social worker will be doing together before they are asked to consent to it. Thus the phrase *informed consent* means that the consent is preceded by being informed.

Informed Consent

- Social workers should provide services to clients only in the context of a professional relationship based, when appropriate, on valid informed consent.
- Social workers should use clear and understandable language to inform clients of the purpose of the services, risks related to the services, . . . clients' right to refuse or withdraw consent, and the time frame covered by the consent.
- Social workers should provide clients with an opportunity to ask questions.
- In instances when clients are not literate or have difficulty understanding the primary language used in the practice setting, social workers should take steps to ensure clients' comprehension. . . .
- In instances when clients lack the capacity to provide informed consent, social workers should protect clients' interests by seeking permission from an appropriate

> third party, informing clients consistent with the clients' level of understanding. In such instances social workers should seek to ensure that the third party acts in a manner consistent with clients' wishes and interests. . . .
>
> (NASW Code of Ethics, section 1.03)

NASW Code of Ethics: Evaluation and Research Standards   One entire section of the Code is devoted to social workers' ethical obligations to research. Section 5.02 is titled "Evaluation and Research" and can be found with the ethical standards of the Code of Ethics in Appendix B. Note that many of these specific standards can be used to prevent the ethical problems described earlier in the chapter. Actually, these standards are almost identical to the five ethical safeguards mentioned earlier in the chapter. These ethical standards can be paraphrased as follows:

- follow available procedures (IRBs) for protecting research participants (section 5.02d)
- the need for informed consent and identification of what to cover in a informed consent procedure (section 5.02e)
- the need to protect individuals who are incapable of giving informed consent (section 5.02f)
- exceptions in using informed consent when the importance of the research justifies it (section 5.02g)
- the research participant's right to withdraw from a study (section 5.02h)
- providing participants with access to appropriate support services (section 5.02i)
- protecting participants from distress, harm, danger, and deprivation (section 5.02j)
- ensuring confidentiality or anonymity (section 5.02k, l, m)
- obligation to report findings accurately and to avoid fabrication (section 5.02n)
- avoid any conflicts of interest (section 5.02o)

In the beginning of the chapter, we mentioned that social workers have several roles that they should be prepared to carry out as professionals in a social agency. They can be *gatekeepers,* who ensure that all studies conducted in their agency meet professional standards. They can be *advocates* for clients' protection and privacy. Additionally, they can be *promoters* of research studies that are beneficial to the clients' well-being. To carry out these three roles, social workers should know and be able to follow the ethical standards of the Code.

Promoting an Interest in Diversity

CSWE also mandates that social work programs provide sufficient content for understanding, affirming, and respecting people from diverse backgrounds. Because social workers typically work with a widely diverse population of clients, this mandate

TEST YOUR KNOWLEDGE

Ethics and the Gatekeeper Role

Assume that a social work professor whom you do not know contacts your agency, a health department, and wants to conduct a study on domestic violence. She wants to interview clients of your agency who are victims of domestic violence to find out more about the adverse effects of their experiences on their parenting, employment, and general well-being. Assume that you are designated by your agency as the "initial gatekeeper" who determines whether or not this research should be supported. You know that the agency is concerned about domestic violence and could benefit from the results. You want to make sure that all of the ethical issues are addressed. How would you answer the following questions:

1. From an ethical standpoint, what kinds of information will you need to know about the purpose of the study and the affiliation of the researcher?
2. How can you be an advocate in protecting clients without unnecessarily interfering with the study?
3. What will you expect the researcher to say or do in providing "informed consent"?

becomes critical to effectively meet the needs of people in a culturally relevant way (CSWE, 2002a). Promoting diversity in research is clearly part of this mandate.

The term *human diversity* can refer to an almost unlimited number of characteristics that distinguish people. The Code of Ethics highlights twelve characteristics of diversity that are particularly important in preparing social workers with cultural competence and sensitivity to social diversity:

> *Social workers should obtain education about and seek to understand the nature of social diversity and oppression with respect to race, ethnicity, national origin, color, sex, sexual orientation, age, marital status, political belief, religion, and mental or physical disability.* (NASW, *Code of Ethics*, 1999)

While the Code has helped to narrow the list of human diversity characteristics considerably, the list is still rather long. Yet, we know that most of these characteristics are associated with serious human needs, hardships, diseases, and oppression.

So what does it mean to give special attention to diversity in research? Historically, most research studies conducted in the United States have limited their focus to white men of middle- and upper-class backgrounds. Many sources of knowledge and theory currently used by social workers are largely based on such limited samples of people. The theories of Freud, Erikson, and Jung, for example, are still popular explanations for understanding the human life cycle, yet these theories have been developed based on studies of predominantly white middle- and upper-class European people.

Fortunately, diversity has become a more normative aspect of social work research in recent years. Studies have expanded their focus to include women, people of color, and people of different social classes, sexual orientations, disabilities, and age. Also, theoretical perspectives have expanded to include feminist and Afrocentric perspectives and, to a lesser extent, perspectives emphasizing the cultural needs of Latinos, Asian Americans, other recent immigrant groups, gays and lesbians, disability groups, and others (Anderson & Carter, 2003). International issues are also becoming more important as we increasingly realize that we are living in a global community and dependent on a global economy.

A Study of Attitudes toward Older Adults

Philip Tan and colleagues (2001) investigated the attitudes of BSW students toward older adults, based on an instrument that measures attitudes toward twenty distinct characteristics of older people. Overall, the students' attitudes were neither positive nor negative but in the neutral range. The relatively small group of students in this sample who had more positive attitudes toward older adults were more likely to have taken a gerontology course and/or had close relationships to older adults.

A large number of journals have recently sprung up that focus on diversity and international issues, including *Affilia: The Journal of Women and Social Work, Ethnic and Racial Studies, Indian Journal of Social Work, Journal of Gay and Lesbian Social Services, Journal of Gerontological Social Work, Hispanic Journal of Behavioral Sciences, Human Services in the Rural Environment, Journal of Multicultural Social Work, International Social Work, Journal of Immigrant and Refugee Services,* and *European Journal of Social Work.*

Internationally Focused Research

In investigating the features of a good death, Mak (2002) interviewed thirty-three Chinese patients to understand their perspective. Her qualitative study uncovered seven elements or themes: (1) being aware of dying, (2) maintaining hope, (3) being free from pain and suffering, (4) experiencing personal control, (5) maintaining connectedness to others, (6) preparing to depart, and (7) accepting the timing of one's death. Accepting the timing of their death, the last element, was reported to be easier under four circumstances: (1) they had completed their social roles (e.g., parenting), (2) they died at an old age when it is good and natural, (3) they had a religious faith to help facilitate a hope in a better life after death, and (4) they had experienced meaningful lives.

While the general diversity characteristics proposed by CSWE (e.g., race, ethnicity, social class, gender, sexual orientation, disability, age, national origin, etc.) are vitally important to consider in conducting research, additional types of diversity are also important when investigating specific populations. These characteristics are referred to as "group-specific diversity characteristics" in this book. For example, if a researcher is interested in studying a population of people with mental illnesses, developmental disabilities, or a combination of these labels, some of the more subtle aspects of individual diversity could be overlooked. Studies of people with developmental disabilities, for example, should include different levels of disability (mild, moderate, severe, and profound) and different etiological or causal factors (e.g., Down syndrome, cerebral palsy, environmental factors). Similarly, studies of people with mental illness should consider a wide range of diagnoses. People with substance abuse are widely diverse based on the type of substance used, their history of substance abuse, and their prognosis for treatment. People who are victims of physical and psychological abuse can vary widely based on their current family arrangement, environmental factors, whether there is a history of abuse in their family of origin, and so on. These examples are introduced to emphasize that both the general characteristics of diversity mentioned by CSWE and the diversity characteristics inherent in particular groups must be taken into account in planning research. Ultimately, it is up to researchers to determine which diversity characteristics are most relevant and important to consider.

Diversity Issues and Research Steps   Let's look at how diversity issues can be incorporated in all of the steps of the research process. During step 1 (understanding and defining the research topic) and step 2 (focusing), the researcher is building the foundations of a study, so it is absolutely critical to consider the diversity issues that are most important at these stages. This is the time when the researcher should be encouraged to take a broad, diversified perspective on the research topic. For example, a literature review should include articles with diverse viewpoints about the research topic. Previous studies should be found that focus on samples with diverse characteristics. From there, a focus should be crafted (step 2) that takes into account the important diversity characteristics pertinent to the research topic. An example is given below of a homeless study that gave central attention to diversity issues but also overlooked an important diversity point.

A Study Addressing Diversity in Homelessness

Two social workers conducted a study of homeless people in St. Louis (North & Smith, 1994). They wanted to focus on the varied ways that white and minority men and women were thought to be experiencing homelessness. These authors' sensitivity to diversity issues was commendable in the way that they compared the participants' homeless circumstances based on race and gender. Essentially, they compared the circumstances of four subgroups (nonwhite men, white men, nonwhite women, white women). Unfortunately, they grouped all people of color together under the category of "nonwhite" and neglected to differentiate African Americans, Latinos, and Native Americans.

Diversity is also important when the research design is being developed (step 3). For example, a data collection approach should be selected that does not exclude any important groups or viewpoints. Some possible diversity questions to consider when selecting a data collection approach include: `

- Can the participants read? (related to considering a questionnaire)
- Are there any language barriers?
- Will any group have discomfort or difficulty participating in an interview study?
- Will any group have difficulty sharing their ideas on a questionnaire for any reason?
- Will some groups be more likely excluded if an observational approach is used?

Deciding on a sampling approach raises other diversity issues. An important question to ask is whether the sample is diverse. There was considerable debate about this issue when a new sampling approach was being considered to supplement the U.S. Census Bureau's approach in the U.S. census of 2000. Some groups thought that a special effort should be made to involve groups of people who were known to be difficult to reach; otherwise, they would be underrepresented in a census count. These groups included racial minorities, those with very low incomes, undocumented workers from other countries, and those who did not speak English.

Several questions could be asked that could help a researcher develop a diverse sample. These questions should take into account both general and group-specific diversity characteristics, as follows:

1. *General characteristics:* Is there adequate representation of the population by race and ethnicity, gender, age, social class, sexual orientation, national origin, and ability/disability?
2. *Group-specific characteristics:* Is there an adequate representation of group-specific diversity characteristics reflected in the particular population of interest? Examples include:
   - If it is a study of university students, are students at all levels and statuses of the university included (freshman to graduate students, full-time and part-time)?
   - If it is study of families, are different family arrangements considered, such as married, unmarried, single, and cohabitation; or is there an interest in a particular type of arrangement?
   - If it is a study of people with mental illness, are the range of diagnoses of mental illness included, or is there an interest in focusing on a particular diagnosis?

Diversity issues are important to consider in the remaining steps of the research process as well. Many of these issues will be discussed when the book focuses on each of these steps.

Promoting Social and Economic Justice

A third special mandate promulgated by CSWE is that social work programs give special emphasis to social and economic justice issues. One section of the CSWE

TEST YOUR KNOWLEDGE

A Diversity Scenario

You have been assigned to conduct an assessment of the needs of older adults in a community surrounding your agency, a senior center. You want to find out if older adults in the community would like to utilize some of the center's existing services as well as some new services being considered. New services include exercise classes, conversation groups, intergenerational support groups, a lunch program, and nutritional workshops. You are planning to conduct a phone interview with a representative sample of households in this community.

Questions to consider in designing your interview could include:

- Can you think of groups of older adults that could be overlooked by using a phone interview? If so, how will you attempt to involve these groups?
- What will you do if some people say that they do not respond to phone interviews, or if they want to know more about your legitimacy?
- What will you do if the person who answers the phone only speaks Spanish or another foreign language?
- What will you do if the person who answers the phone is not an older adult, although older adults are known to live in the household? For example, what if the older adult is hesitant to speak or the person answering the phone is determined to speak for the older adult? What can you do to ensure that the older adult's voice is heard?

accreditation document describes three objectives for fulfilling this mandate. These objectives are stated as expectations of graduates (CSWE, 2002b). Social workers are expected to

- *practice without discrimination and with respect, knowledge, and skills related to clients' age, class, color, culture, disability, ethnicity, family structure, gender, marital status, national origin, race, religion, and sexual orientation*
- *understand the forms and mechanisms of oppression and discrimination and apply strategies of advocacy and social change that advance social and economic justice*
- *function within the structure of organizations and service delivery systems and seek necessary organizational change*

These mandates are important to address in research activities as well as social work practice. Social work research is concerned with more than just generating knowledge. The values and ethics of the profession encourage us to develop knowledge that promotes the welfare of people and empowers disadvantaged groups. In other words, research can be an empowering process for social work clients. Let's look at some of the ways that this can be done.

One way we can promote social justice is to implement aspects of the participatory action research (PAR) approach. PAR was introduced as a special research approach in Chapter 2. PAR promotes a set of principles that promote social justice. PAR can be used to place research capabilities in the hands of disenfranchised people so that they can use them to transform their lives (Park, 1993). This approach is used to focus on topics relevant to the research participants and to actively involve them in the steps of the research process. In PAR research, the relationship between the researcher and the research participants is a "just" one in which there is more equality than usual and the participants have some influence and power over what happens. Some of the key PAR principles that support social justice are (DePoy, 1999):

- Collaborate with those affected by the problem to clearly articulate their views about what the research problem is.
- Determine if the purpose of a research study can bring about social change or improvement for the participants.
- Involve lay researchers as collaborators with professional researchers. In this case, lay researchers can be research participants, clients, community leaders, and other lay experts.
- Train lay researchers with skills in designing, conducting, and using research.
- Involve the research participants in ways that will benefit them by seeking their suggestions on recommendations and other next steps.

Example of a PAR Study Used to Support Social Action

Donna Reese and colleagues (1999) initiated PAR research and other activities that resulted in improved access to hospice services for African Americans. Collaboration occurred with research participants and practitioners throughout the study. The researchers' activities began with a small qualitative study of African American pastors. This pilot study was followed by a larger quantitative study of African American hospice patients documenting their access barriers to hospice. Finally, a social action effort was initiated to engage local health care providers in addressing these access barriers. The findings of their studies were used to facilitate this social action effort.

Traditional research methods can also be used to help bring about positive changes in policies and practice. The focus of studies can be crafted to be responsive to the needs and problems of client populations and to improving their environmental conditions. Studies using traditional methods can and often do focus on empowerment and social change. Examples include

- promoting equity in salaries by investigating whether the salaries of women and minorities are equitable with the salaries of white males
- advocating for improved employment opportunities for people with disabilities by documenting ways they are discriminated against in hiring practices

- advocating for improved jobs and higher incomes for homeless people by documenting how many homeless people work but cannot afford decent housing
- studying the problem of stigma from the viewpoints of various groups that are adversely affected by this problem
- advocating an improved quality of life for people who are difficult to reach by interviewing them directly rather than relying on more accessible secondary sources

Giving Priority to At-Risk Populations   CSWE's social and economic justice mandate is intentionally linked to another CSWE mandate. This mandate states that social workers should give priority to specific populations that are "at risk" in some way. At-risk groups are those that are more vulnerable than others to serious health and social problems. Each geographic area of the United States has particular groups that are more at risk than others. Groups at greater risk are likely to reflect one or more of the general diversity characteristics mentioned earlier in the chapter (e.g., race, gender, sexual orientation). Families living in poverty, for example, are an important group to help, but some poor families may be more at risk than others. Groups in poverty at greater risk could include teen- or single-parent families, the homeless, substance abusers who use illegal drugs, intravenous drug users who share needles, young gay men who do not practice safe sex, older adults on limited pensions, people with Alzheimers, older lesbians who are socially isolated, and so on. The groups with the greatest need will likely vary from one geographic area to another. Based on the general mandate to give priority to these at-risk populations, researchers as well as practitioners should increasingly focus on ways of improving their well-being. An example of a study that focused on an at-risk group is described below.

Research Focusing on Empowerment Issues with an At-Risk Group

Linhorst and colleagues (2002) reviewed existing documents and conducted focus groups with clients and staff of a public psychiatric hospital to identify barriers to client empowerment. They focused on the conditions necessary for empowerment to occur in their participation in treatment planning. Several empowerment issues were reported, such as preparing clients with decision-making skills, providing them with a range of treatment options, ensuring enough time for client participation in treatment planning, and promoting staff attitudes that are respectful of clients' ability to participate in treatment planning.

Journals are also springing up that focus on specific at-risk groups. These journals often offer a more in-depth examination of the needs and concerns of these groups, as follows: *Child Abuse and Neglect, Journal of Child and Adolescent Substance Abuse, Journal of Family Violence, Journal of Research in Crime and Delinquency, Journal of Palliative and Hospice Care,* and *Suicidal and Life Threatening Behavior.*

Chapter Reflections

Attending to Social Work Mandates throughout the Book

Social work's mandates—social work values and ethical standards, diversity issues, at-risk groups, and social and economic justice concerns—will be explored throughout the book. A short section will be included at the end of the remaining chapters to highlight the concepts, issues, and illustrations that were covered within the chapter relating to each of these four mandates. These sections can be useful in reintroducing particular issues to the reader for further exploration. Many of the discussion questions at the end of each chapter are intended to help the reader address these mandates as well.

Discussion Questions

1. Visit the Internet and find out more about one of the following three studies that are known for violating people's rights. Identify a Website describing one of these three studies by going to a search engine such as Google and typing in the phrase in parentheses listed below for the study you select. The search engine will identify a list of Websites addressing this topic. Find one that focuses on this study. Read the information on this Website. Then report what you found to the class. These three studies are:
   - The Milgram studies, in which an electric shock was administered to a "learner" for each mistake he made during the experiment (Milgram studies)
   - Bandura's jail studies (Bandura jail studies)
   - Studies of radiation fallout on people exposed to the testing of the atomic bomb in the 1940s (radiation studies and atomic bomb testing)

2. Select one of the following sections of the Code of Ethics found in Appendix B (pages 310–325)
   - clients who lack decision-making capacity (section 1.14)
   - dishonesty, fraud, and deception (section 4.04)
   - misrepresentation (section 4.06)

   These sections describe ethical standards to be followed in social work practice. Explain how the ethical principles in this section apply to research as well as practice.

3. Social workers can be agency gatekeepers, advocates for clients' protection and privacy, and promoters of research that is beneficial to the clients' well-being. If you are working in a social agency or currently have a field practicum, give examples of how you could participate in each of these roles.

4. Review the Test Your Knowledge: Ethics Exercise on page 40. Besides answering the first three questions listed in this Ethics example, answer the following questions:
   - What will you include in an "informed consent" procedure?
   - How will you initially plan to address any unanticipated negative consequences of the study?
   - How can you implement any of the aspects of participant action research approach?

5. Construct an informed consent form and other ethical provisions of a study that could be conducted at your field agency. Complete each of the following steps for this task:
   - Check to see what is required by your field agency for protecting research participants when studies are conducted.
   - Consider all of the following information in your consent form: the purpose of the study, how the results will be used, the expectations of research participants, your affiliation, any possible harmful effects from participating in the study, possible benefits of participating, ensuring confidentiality, and making participation voluntary.
   - Would you add arrangements for monitoring any harmful effects from the study? (e.g., a sensitive topic could stir up difficult emotions)
   - Explain how you would protect the privacy and confidentiality of the research participants when you collect the data and present the findings.
   - Describe your plans for protecting and storing the data.

6. Review the case of deception in the CBS undercover investigation ("60 Minutes II" Reveals Abuse in a Psychiatric Facility) on pages 41–42. Identify the ethical issues that favor such an investigation. Identify the ethical issues against such an investigation. Debate the issues in class, with some students taking one side and others taking the other side. How would you balance the risks and gains of doing such an investigation? Can you think of an alternative way to conduct such an investigation without deception?

7. Select an at-risk group in your community and craft two research questions that you could explore in learning more about the needs of this group.

8. Select a social justice issue in your community or state. Then in general terms, describe a study you could conduct that provides useful information for addressing this justice issue.

9. Several recent journals have been devoted to diversity issues and at-risk groups. Examples have been given on pages 55 and 60. Select one of these journals, identify and read a research article in this journal, and report to your class what you have learned.

References

Anderson, J., & Carter, R. (Eds.). (2003). *Diversity perspectives for social work practice*. Boston: Allyn and Bacon.

Council on Social Work Education (CSWE). (2002a). *Educational policy and accreditation standards*. (Sections renumbered December 2001.) Alexandria, VA: Author.

Council on Social Work Education (CSWE). (2002b). *Educational policy 3.0: Foundation program objectives*. Alexandria, VA: Author.

DePoy, E., Hartman, A., & Haslert, D. (1999). Critical action research: A model for social work knowing. *Social Work, 44*(6), 560–569.

Goffman, E. (1962). *Asylum: Essays on the social situation of mental patients and other inmates*. Chicago: Aldine.

Linhorst, D., Hamilton, G., Young, E., & Eckert, A. (2002). Opportunities and barriers to empowering people with severe mental illness through participation in treatment planning. *Social Work, 47*(4), 425–434.

Mak, M. H. J. (2002). Accepting the timing of one's death: An experience of Chinese hospice patients. *Omega, 45*(3), 245–260.

Marlow, C. (2001). *Research methods for generalist social work* (3rd ed.). Stamford, CT: Thomson Learning.

National Association of Social Workers (NASW). (1999). *Code of ethics of the National Association of Social Workers*. (Approved by the 1996 NASW Delegate Assembly and revised by the 1999 NASW Delegate Assembly.) Washington, DC: Author.

North, C., & Smith, E. (1994). Comparison of white and non-white homeless men and women. *Social Work, 39* (6), 637–649.

O'Neill, J. (1999). Advocacy takes a new tack. *NASW News, 44*(8), 4.

Park, P. (1993). What is participatory research? A theoretical and methodological perspective. In P. Park, M. Bryden-Miller, B. Hall, & T. Jackson (Eds.), *Voices of change: Participatory research in the United States and Canada*. Westport, CT: Bergin & Garvey.

Phoenix Health Systems. (2003). *What is HIPAA?* (Health Insurance Portability and Accountability Act of 1996). Retrieved online at www.hipaadvisory.com.

Reese, D., Ahern, R., Nair, S., O'Faire, J., & Warren, C. (1999). Hospice access and use by African Americans: Addressing cultural and institutional barriers through participatory action research. *Social Work, 44*(6), 549–559.

Tan, P., Hawkins, M., & Ryan, E. (2001). Baccalaureate social work student attitudes toward older adults. *Journal of Baccalaureate Social Work, 6*(2), 45–55.

chapter 4

Understanding the Research Topic

If we were to probe deeply and honestly, we might find that our work is populated by voices and interests of which we were unaware—by agency procedures and routines, by interpersonal dynamics on our team, by local politics, by cultural biases—that have become the invisible boundary of our world making, policing from within the kinds of worlds we construct, the cases we see, the roles we inhabit, the way we engage our clients with our knowledge. (McKee, 2003, pp. 404–405)

The remaining chapters provide detailed descriptions of the steps in the research process introduced in Chapter 1. These steps are presented in the order that they occur, with each step being presented within the context of the overall research process. Each chapter focuses on either one or more of these steps. The presentations of the steps are intended to be read with two overall purposes in mind—to help the reader become a critical consumer of research studies and a producer of agency research.

Step 1—understanding the research topic—is the focus of this chapter. The topic of a research study can focus on almost anything. A study could focus on a social problem, a practice issue, an exploration of the strengths of a particular group, a controversial public policy, or numerous other things. Often, a research topic is identified as a problem to be solved. Because this is so, the research topic is often described in the text as a "problem." Keep in mind that this does not preclude the likely possibility of the topic having a nonproblem focus.

Steps in the Research Process

1. **Understanding the research topic to be studied**
2. Focusing the study
3. Designing the study
4. Collecting the data
5. Analyzing the data
6. Preparing a report

Social workers often find themselves dealing with problems from which other professions have already chosen to walk away. Whether it is dealing with the rippling effects of welfare reform or the long-term consequences of institutional racism, the profession of social work may be the best overall resource for helping oppressed populations in this society. Whether we are considering social work practice or social work research, our profession has a value-based and ethical commitment to explore problems and controversial issues that others may choose to ignore.

The issue of problem identification in research is by no means a value-free process. Although many researchers and research texts would present it as a purely scientific endeavor, there are opportunities for numerous personal, political, and social issues to affect problem identification. In this chapter, the various steps in problem identification are explored, along with the various factors that can influence this process. An important point in all of this is that the way in which a research problem or topic is defined will affect the way in which the researcher pursues the other steps in conducting the study.

What Issues Affect Topic Selection?

There are many issues that affect which topic a researcher chooses to investigate. Often, researchers must set research priorities that are influenced by both personal interests and factors evident in their environment. Ultimately, researchers must decide which gaps in knowledge are of greatest importance to them. Various factors are likely to push and pull researchers from one issue to the next. This section identifies some of the factors that may impact topic selection.

In general, many factors influence how researchers identify and define the research topics that they decide to investigate. A sampling of these factors include the researchers'

- political perspective, whether it be a Republican, Democrat, or Independent; ideologist or pragmatist; conservative, liberal, or radical; and so on
- sociocultural perspective such as Eurocentric, Afrocentric, feminist, and so on
- professional discipline, whether it be sociology, anthropology, psychology, social work, and so on
- specialization within social work, whether it be clinical, social change, administration, policy analysis, and so on
- personal life experiences of the researcher
- funding, employer mandates, and other external influences

Political Perspective

First, a researcher's political perspective can influence how the research topic is defined. For example, conservatives may choose to view a social problem like homelessness by considering whether the personal characteristics of homeless people could explain their circumstances. Examples are a lack of motivation to find employment, the existence of a mental health problem, or an inability to sustain a marital or family relationship. A liberal may look more to the social causes of homelessness, such as inadequate mental health services available to assist homeless people in finding a job or maintaining their household. A radical may consider the impact of a capitalist society and its economic policies that allow homelessness to increase during times of economic crisis. Obviously, each of these political perspectives will influence how researchers will investigate homelessness and other problems.

It should be noted, however, that these varying perspectives (e.g., conservative versus liberal, or Republican versus Democrat) do not have to be mutually exclusive. A researcher who primarily uses a liberal perspective, for example, could also be interested in many of the issues identified by a conservative or a radical perspective.

Sociocultural Views

Another set of influences may come from the researchers' sociocultural views, if these are of central importance. Most researchers base their research primarily on a Eurocentric perspective. It is likely that the majority of researchers in American universities have a European heritage, whether from a recent immigrant family or from several generations back. Their heritage is likely to encompass, to some degree, such values as democracy, individualism, religious freedom, and capitalism. These deeply rooted, often unconscious values influence the directions taken by many researchers' investigations. Afrocentric researchers, a small but growing group, are likely to be keenly conscious of their African heritage and its values related to kinship, community, and the collective good. Though feminist researchers are likely to vary in their political persuasions, they tend to examine the impact of societal conditions on women and the ways in which women may be victims of discrimination. Generally, it should be noted that these perspectives are not mutually exclusive. A researcher who uses Afrocentric ideas, for example, could also use Eurocentric ones. Feminist and Afrocentric perspectives were discussed more fully in Chapter 2.

Example of Feminist Research

A research study by McQuillan and Ferreuse (1998) titled, "Importance of Variation Among Men and the Benefits of Feminism for Families" is an example of feminist research. Their overall research question was to examine why so many men do not accept influence from their wives. They suggest that this problem is associated with marital dissatisfaction. One theoretical explanation they offer in explaining this problem is that there are structural inequalities in marriage in that husbands tend to be older, more educated, have higher prestige jobs, and have more authority at work.

Professional Discipline

Another factor likely to influence how researchers identify and define the research topic is their professional discipline. Each discipline in the social and behavioral sciences usually teaches a particular theoretical perspective and a preferred set of theoretical constructs for studying social phenomenon. Also, each discipline tends to emphasize a primary research methodology or approach to collecting data.

Sociologists, for example, are taught to study the impact of societal forces on people. They may investigate how societal definitions of social class and social status within groups determine how individuals function. The focus of sociologists is usually on larger social units such as a school system, a corporation, or an occupational group, and how these influence the attitudes or behavior of the members. Also, most sociologists use a survey approach in conducting their data collection. Frequently, sociologists focus on the attitudes and beliefs of people related to social factors, and they often use structured research questionnaires.

Example of a Sociological Study

Lawless and Fox (2001) pointed out the difficulty in conducting studies that attempt to understand the political participation of urban poor people. Then they proceeded to investigate some of the factors that influenced the political participation of a sample of 462 low-income men and women living in New York City. One of their central findings was revealing. Severe economic hardship and having routine contact with government agents (welfare workers and the police) served as significant experiences that bolstered this group's willingness to participate in the political system. Their experiences with welfare workers were mixed. Welfare offices encouraged many of the welfare recipients to register to vote, which was positive. But it seemed that the recipients who experienced more negative treatment in their encounters with welfare workers were also more willing to participate in the political system to improve services to the poor generally.

Psychologists who conduct research, in contrast to sociologists, usually focus on individuals, examining such things as their motivations, belief systems, attitudes, and knowledge. Psychologists often favor experimental research, including experimental designs with control groups. Clinical psychologists often focus on research topics that are similar to the focus of clinical social work researchers. Both groups are interested in understanding people who have various psychiatric diagnoses and how interventions can be effective in helping them.

Anthropologists have a macro focus like sociologists, but their primary interest is in culture. They investigate how cultural patterns (e.g., cultural symbols, world view, behavioral patterns and customs) originate, evolve, and are sustained and how they impact the members of a cultural group. Anthropologists usually conduct their research using a qualitative approach. A popular specific method that they use is called an ethnography. An ethnographic approach is used to obtain vividly descriptive accounts of different cultural groups, including how the culture's values, rituals, networks, communication patterns, and other elements impact the members. Ethnographic studies are good examples of purely descriptive studies. Ethnographic studies are similar to participant observation research. Both use a qualitative approach that involves both participation and observation within a social context that is being investigated. More will be said about participant observation in Chapter 10.

Specializations within Social Work

Another set of factors that influences how social work researchers define a research topic are the methods of social work practice. These methods include individual practice, group and family practice, community organization and social action, administration, and social policy. Social work researchers are actively conducting research in all of these specialized areas. For example, clinical researchers are primarily concerned with examining and strengthening clinical practice. They have recently given attention to such issues as cognitive behavioral approaches, Gestalt, short-term therapies, and outcome evaluations of various types of clinical interventions (e.g., Reid, 1997).

Other researchers are interested in administrative issues in social work. They are concerned with enhancing the organizational environment in which social workers practice. Their studies have focused on various organizational and policy issues, leadership styles, cooperative staff team models, how to promote greater productivity and efficiency, and innovative ways to promote ties with the community. A professional journal, *Administration in Social Work,* is devoted to research that focuses on administrative topics. Similarly, *Social Service Review* is a good source for research studies on social policies affecting clients and social work services.

Research interest groups can also, to a lesser extent, focus on other methods of social work practice such as community organizing and practice with small groups. For example, *Social Work with Groups* is a journal that reports on research in group practice. Research interest groups also exist related to the various fields of practice, such as public welfare, family services, marital therapy, child welfare, mental health, and aging. Most of these fields have their own journals, which report on a variety of topics of practice research in these settings. An example of a study that focuses on practice issues is reported below.

Example of a Study Focusing on the Helping Relationship

Ribner and Knei-Paz (2002) interviewed eleven female clients from multiproblem families about the social worker–client helping relationship. Their focus as social work researchers was on how these clients perceived a "successful helping relationship" based on past experiences. This qualitative study used narrative research techniques. Several valuable findings were presented from this study. One set of findings focused on the clients' perceptions of the working styles of the social workers. Qualities of their working styles that were important to these women were an enabling atmosphere created by the social worker, a sense of equality within the working relationship, and working together in partnership.

Personal Life Experiences

Finally, the personal life experiences of researchers often influence their choice of a research topic and the ways in which they define a research problem. In part, personal experiences derive from the personal characteristics of researchers, such as their gender, race, age, sexual orientation, religion, and many other characteristics. Women, for example, sometimes concentrate their research on women's health care issues or parenting concerns. Gay and lesbian researchers may take a special interest in the problem of discrimination against gays and lesbians, and older researchers may gravitate toward critically examining the policies of nursing homes and the non-institutional alternatives. Keep in mind that researchers who do not have these personal characteristics can be just as likely to conduct studies in these areas as well and that people with these personal characteristics also do investigate numerous other topics. The topics mentioned here are merely cited as examples of tendencies.

The personal characteristics that can influence how researchers choose research topics are not to be confused with the sociocultural perspectives noted earlier. Researchers may be African Americans, for example, and their ethnicity may influence their desire to investigate adoption policies for African American children but they may not use an Afrocentric perspective. Similarly, a female researcher may choose to study the social supports needed by women with breast cancer without using a feminist perspective.

The personal circumstances of researchers can also influence their research focus if these circumstances have had an important impact on them. Examples include being a single parent or a noncustodial father, having a disabled child, serving in the military, being a recovering alcoholic, having been raised in a foster home, growing up with a sibling having schizophrenia or mental retardation, or being a recent immigrant from Pakistan.

> ### A Social Work Researcher's Illustration
>
> A social work colleague has focused a considerable amount of her research on the challenges and problems experienced by step-families. Her parents were divorced when she was very young and she ended up living with her mother until the age of 13. At that time, this colleague's mother remarried and she became a member of a blended family that included a new step-father and three step-brothers. Unsurprisingly, the dynamics of her family changed dramatically and have left a very strong impression on her up to the present time.

Whatever the reasons are for why researchers choose a particular focus, it is important for them to understand these reasons and recognize that their personal views can interfere with the conduct of their study. They must have an ability to identify any personal biases and take the necessary measures to prevent these biases from interfering with the study. Needless to say, it is especially incumbent on researchers to take appropriate measures to avoid designing a study so that it simply produces the results they set out to obtain.

Funding, Employer Mandates, and Other External Influences

Several other factors beyond the researcher's control also influence the selection of the research topic. Funding opportunities are one such factor. Researchers tend to be influenced by the funding opportunities that are available to support their research. Funding sources include governmental agencies at the federal, state, or local levels; private foundations; and smaller funding sources available through universities, social agencies, and the United Way. For example, the federal government has recently funded research addressing crime and drug-related issues and military and internal security concerns as well as research on AIDS, cancer, mental illness, and other health matters. Foundations usually have identified very specific research concerns that are directly related to why they are in existence, such as preventing child abuse, strengthening families, understanding end-of-life issues, and promoting racial and ethnic justice. The Institute for the Advancement of Social Work Research is a nonprofit organization charged with finding and developing funding sources for social work research. Their listserv offers extensive information on research opportunities for social workers on a monthly basis. Their Website is www.iaswresearch.org. Also, a United Way agency exists in most local communities and usually provides research funds for documenting that the services of their member agencies are effective.

Another factor that influences topic selection are the employers of social work researchers. Universities employ the majority of social workers who regularly conduct research. Universities designated as research universities, usually the larger state universities, expect their faculty to regularly conduct research and to seek funding for these investigations. Usually, these universities offer small grants of $5,000 or less to assist their individual faculty in conducting pilot and other preliminary studies. These studies provide preliminary findings that are usually important in the researcher's being successful in obtaining larger amounts of money from governmental agencies and private foundations. Also, some universities identify a list of general topics of research as part of their mission statement; this list influences the selection of research topics by individual faculty. For example, an urban university could have four or five multidisciplinary research areas they want to emphasize. Examples include children, their families, and the schools; health care policy and practice; or various kinds of engineering technology.

Another factor that influences topic selection is the level of development of a given field. Many research areas have received extensive attention and generated considerable research knowledge. These areas are likely to be popular to individual researchers. Such areas include the impact of divorce on children, adoption policies and practices, and the impact of poverty. Other research areas have recently been given more national attention and are beginning to generate important knowledge in such areas as AIDS, breast and prostate cancer, the impact of a global economy, and provisions for the frail elderly. These areas are luring other researchers into investigations. Still other research areas have been grossly neglected and need more public attention.

Research Topics and Social Work

As noted in Chapter 1, the first step in the research process is to identify and define a research topic. Although this may sound fairly straightforward, it can sometimes be one of the more complicated tasks for a researcher. It is similar to the challenge that social work practitioners face when they meet with a client and begin to explore the issues that are causing problems for the client. Practitioners ask such questions as "Which is the 'real' problem?" "Which problem or issue is worth addressing?" "Which problem is most amenable to the solutions your agency has to offer?" "How can the client and I narrow down the focus of the problem to the point that it makes sense?" "What is working in a client's life?" While these questions may appear to apply solely to the practice life of social workers, they can also apply to a researcher's efforts to define a research topic. As was mentioned before, good research and good practice share common concerns and skills.

The Research Topic and the Producer Role

Let's assume that you will be conducting your own research or assisting someone else with their study. The initial step of identifying the research topic becomes very important to consider. When social workers conduct their own research, they need to consider several important questions. Some of these questions are:

1. *Is the topic you want to address important?* The time and cost of conducting research are often scarce, so it's wise to consider the importance of the research topic. Is it important to your agency? To your clients? To your effectiveness as a social worker? Hopefully, you will be able to say yes to at least one of these questions before you proceed much further.

2. *Is the topic too large?* Often when a research topic is initially identified, it can be too broad or complex to address in one study. Thus, the first thing you would do is to "pare down" or narrow the topic to get to a specific dimension of the larger topic or to a point where only a few general research questions would be asked.

3. *Is the topic interesting to the researcher?* This question is important to you. It may determine whether you succeed or not or whether you can maintain enough interest to stay with the project until it is completed.

4. *Are the important concepts related to the topic "measurable"?* Much more will be said about measurement in Chapter 5, but for now just consider whether the concepts you choose to study are easy to define and describe. Further, do you have concrete ideas about how you will measure these concepts? Can they be measured by asking specific questions or observing particular behaviors? If it becomes too challenging to find a way to measure these concepts, then they may be beyond the scope of the current study.

5. *Do you have the requisite skills and knowledge to conduct the research?*

6. *Will you be able to gain access to the required data?* This becomes a logistical question. Maybe you have all of the above questions answered to your satisfaction but for ethical reasons or due to other constraints placed on you, you may

not be able to get access to the people whom you want to involve as research participants.

A practice research topic is described next to illustrate some of the questions to ask in the initial step of research. In this example, Maria is the program director for children's mental health services in a large comprehensive mental health center. She is concerned about the availability of psychiatric consultation for children served by the agency. Several social workers serving children have complained that the waiting time for psychiatric consultation is extremely long. It is the job of Maria to explore the causes of this long wait. In essence, she has a research project to develop. In doing so, she asks these questions:

1. *Is the topic important?* This is one of the first questions Maria needs to address. In doing so, she also considers what difference having this information would make and to whom. Maria is constantly faced with the challenge of how to prioritize her time. Engaging in research is only a part of her duties. If Maria is to devote time to a research question, it must be an important topic—one that will make a difference in her work and in her agency. After Maria listened to worker after worker complain about the waiting time problem, she became increasingly convinced that exploring this issue was important and that it would make a difference if she were able to gain knowledge that could lead to a resolution of the problem.

2. *Is the topic too large?* It may not be practical to pursue some research topics because they are too expansive for one research project. In this case, the topic may need to be broken down into smaller, more researchable topics. In Maria's case, she decides that her topic is not too large, since the scope of the topic is limited to her agency practices. However, it would probably be too much for her to consider researching the topic of child psychiatric care on a broader scale, such as exploring psychiatric care for her entire city.

Is the Research Topic Too Large?

Many social work students who begin to plan their own studies may identify a global research topic like American education or the public school system. The research topics in these instances are too large. It will need to be pared down to a more manageable topic, such as communication problems between teachers and minority students at their school.

3. *Is the topic interesting for the researcher?* It can be difficult to pursue a research topic that holds little interest. Maria definitely has an interest in the research topic, since she cares deeply about the children served by her agency and also has a driving motivation to ensure that there is equity in services provided by her agency.

4. *Is the topic "measurable"?* There are some problems that may be difficult or impossible to measure. (A considerable amount of time will be spent talking about measurement issues in the next chapter, so not much time will be spent on this topic now.) For example, it may be easier to count how many times a parent and child argue while meeting with them than to evaluate just how much love or anger they actually feel toward each other. In one case, we are measuring behaviors that are somewhat easy to measure; whereas in the other example, we are attempting to measure feelings or attitudes. The latter types of phenomena are difficult to measure. Maria felt that her research focus would lead to exploring issues that could be measured. For example, one of the measuring issues would likely involve an exploration of the waiting time for children versus adults to obtain psychiatric consultation.

5. *Does the researcher have the requisite skills and knowledge to conduct the research?* This is the same type of question practitioners might ask themselves when they are taking on a new client. The NASW Code of Ethics requires that we not practice in areas in which we do not have expertise. Why should it be any different for research? Fortunately, social work education provides students with the fundamental knowledge and skills to investigate many research topics. (That's why you are in this course reading this text!) Of course these skills will vary from person to person. These differences may be based on whether you have an undergraduate degree in social work or a graduate degree. The differences may also be based on whether you have a particular expertise in one type of research over another. Throughout the book, research is categorized as either quantitative or qualitative. Based on the research topic, one of these approaches might be more appropriate. Maria decides that she has the fundamental knowledge and skills to explore the topic in her agency. Her BSW course work in research methods and statistics has been adequate to prepare her to address this agency topic.

6. *Will the researcher be able to gain access to the required data?* Maria will be able to access the data needed to complete her study, and therefore her research topic can be explored. However, some research topics cannot be pursued because it is not possible to collect the data. An example of this would be a social work student who was interested in the attitudes toward violence held by teens detained in a local detention center. This is a fascinating topic that is underresearched. There are several good measurement devices available to assess these attitudes. The researcher is very interested in the topic, and she has the skills to conduct the research. The topic is not too large to explore, and it is an important topic. This topic meets all the requirements discussed to this point, but there was one major barrier. It is against the policy of the facility to allow research to be conducted with the youth in the facility. So despite meeting all the other criteria, this research cannot be conducted because the researcher would not be able to access the data because of the agency's policy. Of course, agencies are free to do what they feel is necessary to protect the rights of their clients. The point is that before researchers move too

far along in the research process, they need to be sure that they can collect the data needed to explore the topic.

The Research Topic and the Consumer Role

Let's look briefly at the research topic and your role as a critical consumer who reads and utilizes research studies. When you read a research study, it is important to pay close attention to the author's definition of the research topic or problem. This should be described in the introductory section of the article. Questions you will want to ask are:

* Is this research problem or topic relevant to social workers? How is it relevant? Is it relevant to your interests? How can this study help you?

* Do you understand what the research topic or problem is? Can you explain it to others in an understandable way?

* Do you think the research topic is clearly and concisely stated? If not, what is not clear? What important information is missing? Is the terminology or subject matter largely foreign to you? In this case, you may want to go back and read more about this topic. Or possibly is the article written poorly? Don't hesitate to consider this latter possibility, as researchers are not always the best writers.

* Do you detect any biases in how the research topic is described? It might favor one view and leave out another. If so, can you identify the viewpoints that are left out? Or are important groups of people left out or omitted from the problem description? This could indicate an important diversity issue to consider. For example, if unemployment was the focus, were all races of people considered?

* Another important component of a research problem will be a description of any explanations given for the causes. These explanations can be referred to as theories. Can you detect any theories, whether they are identified as theories or not? At this point, you may want to refer back to Chapter 1 for a definition of a theory and for the criteria of good theory.

* Finally, do you think the review of the literature was adequate?

The Literature Review

The literature review is presented to help describe the research problem. Some of the articles in a literature review are studies conducted on the topic, whereas others may be conceptual or theoretical contributions. It is almost impossible to know whether the literature review is adequate without being familiar with the literature on a particular topic. The four criteria that follow below offer a starting point for evaluating a literature review when you are not familiar with the topic.

Criteria for Judging Whether a Literature Review Is Adequate

A simple way to begin to determine the adequacy of a literature review is to consider four criteria:

1. Are there a reasonable *number of references* cited? Usually about eight to ten references is reasonable, even though this number will vary with the topic.
2. Are these references *fairly recent,* such as within ten years of when the study was conducted? Count back ten years from the date that the study was likely conducted, not ten years from today. Keep in mind that the study was probably conducted about two years before the publication date of the study.
3. Does the literature *focus on the research topic* and not on some peripheral or unrelated topics?
4. Did the researchers attempt to describe *differing viewpoints* that were cited in the literature? Any views that are different from the researchers' may be easy to identify, because they are not usually presented as persuasively as the researcher's.

These four criteria are likely to vary in importance in various professional journals. Some journals expect authors to provide extensive literature reviews, while others prefer brief reviews. Many issue-oriented journals, for example, assume that the reader is familiar with the literature and prefer short introductions. How much is already known in a particular field will also determine the length of the review. Reviews of the more developed fields will have more literature to be reviewed, whereas those in newer fields will not.

The importance of having fairly recent references in a literature review can also have exceptions. While most references should be within a period of ten years or less, some references that are older may also be important to include because they are seminal articles that have provided foundational understanding of a topic or offer a method still pertinent.

Tips on Completing Literature Searches

You as a research consumer will want to evaluate the quality of the literature review of a research article. A quantity of eight to ten references in a literature review is a good starting point. Of course, this is a somewhat arbitrary number; it can be common for a researcher to cite many more articles. Rather than thinking strictly "by the numbers," we need to consider whether the review of the literature gives an adequate understanding of the nature of the problem, including how it has been explored and researched by others.

The literature review has a vital purpose to the producer of social work research. Once you have completed a thorough literature review as a research producer, you should have a fairly comprehensive understanding of the nature of the research problem and how much is known about it from previous research. It is conceivable that a literature review may lead you to conclude that you don't even need to complete your proposed research! Maybe someone else has already explored the issue. However, you may find that there are gaps in the knowledge base and that your particular view on the problem has not been addressed. Either way, the literature review is critical.

A literature review can be thought of as a search and evaluation of the available literature in a given subject area relevant to a research problem. It commonly involves the following elements:

- *surveying* (searching and obtaining) the literature relevant to your research topic
- *synthesizing* the information that is gathered into a summary
- *critically analyzing* the information gathered, which can involve (1) identifying areas of controversy surrounding the issue, and (2) crafting questions for further research
- *presenting* the literature

Purposes in Completing a Literature Review

Bourner (1996, p. 8) states that prior to starting a research project the first step is to review the literature in the field. He provides a number of reasons for conducting a literature review, including:

1. *Identify gaps in current knowledge.* A comprehensive literature review can help us see what areas are unknown, unexplored, or less specified. This information can be vital to the researcher who is trying to add to the knowledge in an area.

2. *Avoid reinventing the wheel.* As stated earlier, someone may have explored the research problem already in a way that addresses your concerns. At the very least, the literature review can save you some time and may stop you from making the same mistakes as others.

3. *Carry on from where others have left off.* This idea is consistent with not reinventing the wheel but also speaks to how reviewing the literature can allow you to build on the platform of existing knowledge and ideas. In the perfect world, we like to think of science as a building process whereby each new finding builds on pre-existing knowledge in a progressive manner.

4. *Identify other people working in the same and related fields.* It can be helpful to identify and even contact others who are working in the same area. A researcher network is a valuable resource, and the availability of e-mail provides for easy access to others, both near and far. Actually, that is how many researchers end up being coinvestigators and coauthors of published articles, even when they live thousands of miles apart.

5. *Increase your breadth of knowledge of your subject area.* A thorough literature review provides you with a broad and expansive understanding of the research problem that you are exploring. This can be helpful when you are determining the

particular gaps in knowledge that might exist as well as identifying some of the key consistent findings related to your topic.

6. *Identify the seminal works in your area.* Most areas of research have highly original works that were instrumental in the creation and exploration of a research problem. It is vital to the completion of a thorough literature review to identify those works that laid the critical foundation for subsequent research in an area.

7. *Identify methods that could be relevant to your project.* A literature review can also serve as a means of exploring how other researchers have approached the research problem. It can be helpful to you to see how other researchers have designed their studies. You might decide to use a similar research design or data collection strategy, or you might see where the problems arose in other researchers' efforts and thereby avoid the same mistakes they made. Various data collection strategies and techniques are discussed later in the book.

Marlow (2001, p. 51) suggests that the literature review can be used in formulating the overall research questions. Specifically, it can be helpful in (1) connecting the research questions to preexisting theory, (2) identifying previous research relevant to the research question, and (3) giving direction to the research project.

Strategies for Gathering Information

Hopefully, you are now convinced that it is important to conduct a thorough review of the literature relevant to your research topic. The next step is to explore the sources where the literature is located. Likely, you will find that your university library is an excellent resource for finding research relevant to your research topic. There are at least four major search strategies available for locating references related to your issue (White, 1994). These include (1) consultation, (2) searches in subject indexes, (3) browsing, and (4) footnote chasing.

1. *Consultation* involves locating references by simply communicating with others. It tends to be a low-recall strategy, since it is limited by the knowledge, memory, and biases of correspondents. On the other hand, it can be high in relevance, because the references provided have been prescreened for pertinence. A major advantage of this type of consultation is the ability to locate unpublished materials. Internet technology (e.g., e-mail, discussion groups) has greatly increased the utility of consultation as a search technique. Professional listservs can be one effective way to contact experts in the field.

2. *Subject indexes* are a familiar tool for most researchers. These indexes are explored using computer technology. Subject indexes are used to search bibliographic descriptions, which generally include the title, abstract, and authors of a document in addition to controlled-vocabulary terms (e.g., subject headings, index terms), which are added by the producer of the data base. Subject index searching tends to be high recall and low precision, since a large amount of irrelevant information is

often retrieved. The precision of subject index searching can be improved by combining keyword searches of abstracts and titles with controlled-vocabulary searches (e.g., locating documents by subject heading). In addition, many data bases offer search-refining capabilities, such as the ability to combine multiple searches and to limit searches by type of publication, year, language, or other characteristics. Most social work researchers will find indexes—such as *Social Work Abstracts, PsycInfo, Sociological Abstracts, Social Science Index, ERIC,* and *Ageline*—to be helpful indexes for searching articles relevant to their research topic.

3. *Browsing*—that is, browsing through materials (e.g., library shelves, journal indexes) to find relevant information—can be another way to find information pertinent to your research topic. Browsing is a high-recall strategy, since the amount of information collected is limited only by the researcher's willingness to continue searching. However, browsing generally results in low-precision retrievals, since quite a bit of information must be assessed for relevance (White, 1994). As with other search strategies, technology is improving the efficiency and effectiveness of browsing. For instance, *Current Contents,* an electronic data base, simplifies and enhances the browsing strategy by indexing the tables of contents of selected journals.

4. *Footnote chasing* is the process of locating useful information by searching the reference or bibliography sections of papers that focus on the topic of interest. Footnote chasing tends to have high precision, since other authors have reviewed the material and found it to be pertinent to the content domain. However, this technique is only as effective as the quality of the source materials. The *Social Science Index (SSCI)* provides the capability to conduct electronic footnote chasing, since it indexes the cited references for data base entries. The combination of citation searching and footnote chasing using *SSCI* is an extremely powerful search technique. On a humorous aside, in order to engage in footnote chasing, you will need to copy all of the pages of a research article, including the reference pages. Sometimes students want to cut costs by not copying the reference sections at the end of articles. Don't make this mistake as you embark on your literature review. The reference section of an article is akin to a roadmap; it gives directions as to how the authors of articles arrive at their destination. So make sure you copy the reference section as well as the article.

Writing Up a Literature Review

Writing up a summary of the literature review often comes next. This summary should be prepared with a specific audience and purpose in mind. Several steps are important to consider in preparing this summary.

1. *Critical review of each article.* As a first step, the various types of literature that you have found on a topic need to be carefully and critically examined. What are the key concepts, findings, and/or methodologies that are highlighted in each article or report? What viewpoints do they stress? Are varying views considered? If the literature review is primarily focusing on a particular topic of interest, how

does each of these articles and reports contribute greater understanding about this topic?

2. *Comparing the articles to each other.* Once each article or report has been carefully reviewed, the next step is to begin organizing them into a meaningful summary. It is important to compare the various articles at this stage. How are these articles similar and different from each other? If they are reporting on research studies, what findings are similar and which ones are different? Perhaps two studies on the same topic, for example, focus on research participants who have important demographic differences based on race, gender, or age. Given this, how are the findings of these studies different, and how might the differences in the research participants explain the differences in findings?

3. *Prioritizing the articles in terms of their relative importance.* By this point in the process, it should become clear that some articles or reports are more useful to the literature review than others. Their relative importance can be determined, in part, by deciding which articles are most directly relevant to the topic of interest. It may be important to prioritize the importance of each article as a means of sorting out which ones are most useful. This exercise may lead to a decision to discard some articles that offer little if any value to the literature review.

4. *Preparing a summary of the literature that has been reviewed.* Finally, the articles need to be organized into an integrated summary that is clearly and succinctly written. This summary should be in a form that is most meaningful to those who intend to use it. An outline of the summary will help begin this process. If there are several dimensions to the topic, sorting the articles out by these dimensions may come next. Also material on concepts, theories, and other theoretical perspectives may need to be discussed separately from findings of studies that have been conducted. Brief summaries must be prepared that describe the important contributions of each article related to the topic of interest to the literature review. Weaving these summaries into an integrated overall summary will come next. This summary includes discussing how these various articles are similar to and different from each other. Varying viewpoints should be evident in this review, and gaps or missing information about the topic can be highlighted as well. Overall, this summary of the literature should succeed in informing the reader about the current state of knowledge on the topic of interest.

Chapter Reflections

Values and Ethics, Diversity, At-Risk Groups, and Social Justice

Understanding the research topic or problem has many implications for the four social work mandates. Several ethical issues surface related to this step of the research process. When you are conducting your own research and doing a literature search, it is important to become as knowledgeable as possible about your research topic. While your time is limited, you have several resources at your disposal to conduct a broad search of the literature. Also, don't forget to consider all of the important viewpoints about the research problem rather than just settling on the one you like most. Also try not to overlook the research participants' views in the planning of the research. These ethical issues are also pertinent when consuming the research reports of others. Critically consume their review of the literature to make sure it is extensive enough, reflects varying views about the research topic, and seems balanced when controversies exist. An ethical question to ask is "Are important viewpoints, theories, and research findings existing in the literature intentionally omitted?"

Diversity and at-risk groups are particularly important to consider when examining the research problem. Many of the examples of research described in the chapter have purposely focused on groups that have urgent needs and are considered at risk. Urban dwellers in poverty, multiproblem families, and nonresidential parents are examples. Also, this first step in the research process is the time to decide whether you want to focus on an at-risk group to study.

The chapter also discusses the many perspectives that influence the researcher in selecting a problem or topic to investigate. Many of these perspectives relate to the diversity issues that can be evident in research. Examples that have been given in the chapter include a feminist and Afrocentric perspective, different specializations in social work, and varying political perspectives.

Social and economic justice issues are evident in many of the examples in the chapter as well, such as the discussion about welfare reform and the political participation of urban poor people. Also don't forget that the participatory action approach to research and the principles that it uses are a powerful way to conduct research and promote social justice at the same time.

Discussion Questions

1. Interview a faculty member in your social work program (or in the sociology, psychology, or anthropology departments) who conducts research. Pick a topic they are researching currently or have researched recently. Ask them what motivated them to pick this topic to study. Explore with them whether any of the factors influencing topic identification mentioned earlier in the chapter (e.g., political perspective, sociocultural perspective, professional discipline, personal life experiences, etc.) were important to them. Share your results with your classmates as a way of getting to know the social work faculty.

2. Conduct a literature search for one of the following topics: older adults and AIDS, child sexual abuse, or blended families using Allyn and Bacon's Research Navigator. How many articles are selected in the search? Limit the search to the last five years and find out how many articles are selected. Attempt to identify five of these articles you think may be the most important to read. No need to read these articles at this time.

3. Read the introductory section of a research article on a topic of interest to you. Does it help you understand the research topic? How would you explain the topic to others in a form that is understandable? What biases, if any, did you detect in how the research topic is described? Did this introduction seem to emphasize one viewpoint and leave out other viewpoints? What are the other viewpoints that were left out?

4. Select a research topic of interest to you. Use Allyn and Bacon's Research Navigator to identify relevant articles. What words did you select in your online search that provided the most helpful links to relevant articles on your topic?

References

Bourner, T. (1996). The research process: Four steps to success. In T. Greenfield (Ed.), *Research methods: Guidance for postgraduates* (pp. 7–11). London: Arnold.

Lawless, J., & Fox, R. (2001). Political participation of the urban poor. *Social Problems, 48*(3), 362.

Marlow, C. (2001). *Research methods for generalist social work* (3rd ed.). Stamford, CT: Thomson Learning.

McKee, M. (2003). Excavating our frames of mind: The key to dialogue and collaboration. *Social Work, 48*(3), 404–405.

McQuillan, J., & Ferreeuse, M. (1998). Importance of variation among men and the benefits of feminism for families. In A. Booth & A. C. Crouter (Eds.), *Men in families: When do they get involved? What difference does it make?* Mahwah, NJ: Erlbaum.

Reid, W. J. (1997). Long-term trends in clinical social work. *Social Service Review, 71*(2), 202–216.

Ribner, D., & Knei-Paz, C. (2002). Client's view of a successful helping relationship. *Social Work, 47*(4), 379–387.

White, H. (1994). Scientific communication and literature retrieval. In H. Cooper & L. V. Hedges (Eds.), *The handbook of research synthesis* (pp. 41–56). New York: Russell Sage.

chapter 5

Defining and Measuring Concepts

Measurement constitutes a powerful discourse that has important consequences for the lives of the people with whom we work. To participate in measurement discourse, we need to understand its language . . . if we are to be effective interpreters, resources, and advocates. (Witkin, 2001)

The previous chapter focused on the topics researchers investigate. These topics are often referred to as research problems to be solved. That chapter describes a wide range of factors that have an influence on the selection of the research problem and explores the widely different ways in which researchers are likely to understand a particular problem. In this chapter, we will explore how the research problem is more fully understood and described through definitions and measurement.

Concepts, Variables, Values, and Constants

First of all, a research problem is understood by the **concepts** that give it form. Concepts are ideas or thoughts about which we have a mental image. Concepts are usually in an abstract form and are not readily observable. Because there is often no widely agreed-on measure of a particular concept, it can mean different things to different people An example is the concept of crime, which can refer to any or all of a long list of illegal acts, such as robbery, burglary, assault, rape, murder, use of narcotics, fraud, and so on. It can refer to either misdemeanors or felonies or both. Crime could also be viewed by some as any type of infraction or transgression by one person against another, regardless of whether it is illegal. The important point here is that different people have different definitions of crime. Therefore, if you were to conduct a study about crime, you would initially be faced with the task of deciding what you mean by crime. This involves creating a definition and measure of crime so that other people will be able to understand it the way you do.

Consider the example below on how another concept, research-related anxiety, is defined in a study conducted by two social work researchers.

Is Research-Related Anxiety a Fear or Eagerness to Do Well?

Nora Gustavsson and Ann MacEachron (2001) explored the anxiety of social work students related to math, use of the library, and computers. They explored two alternative perspectives on the concept of research-related anxiety—as a "fear" and as "eagerness to do well." Anxiety from both perspectives was measured and found to be evident in a sample of social work students. These authors concluded that viewing anxiety about research as "eagerness to do well" emphasized the students' anxiety as a strength that could facilitate their learning.

What are your reactions to the concept of research-related anxiety described above? Do you think this concept is evident in the real world? If you have research-related anxiety, do you think your anxiety is more of a fear or an eagerness to do well or maybe a little of both? Or would you describe it in a different way? How would you want your research instructor to respond to any research-related anxiety you have?

Let's look at another concept that is relevant to social work practice—substance abuse. Consider the varied ways this concept can be described.

The Concept of Substance Abuse

The images we associate with substance abuse can vary in numerous ways, including someone staggering along or leaning against a building and hanging onto a liquor bottle or a college student involved in binge drinking at a party (Schutt, 2001). Other images could include a recovering alcoholic drinking one beer, a school-age boy drinking a bottle of beer out of sight of his parents, or a school-age French boy openly drinking a glass of wine with his family over a meal. If you were to conduct a study of substance abuse, you would have to decide which images reflect your definition of substance abuse. Based on the above examples, we can see that such things as the social situation, cultural issues, physical tolerance, age, and individual standards may need to be considered in a definition.

Another factor important in defining and measuring research problems are variables. Variables are a central aspect of any research study. For example, if you don't understand what the most important variables in a study are, you will probably not be able to understand other aspects of the study. A **variable** is defined as a concept that has two additional properties. First, it varies, or changes. Second, it is measurable. A variable adds something important to a concept: it provides a means of measuring it.

Poverty, for example, may be a concept of interest in a study, but it cannot be measured unless it is developed into a variable. Let's say that the researcher decides to measure poverty as a gross annual income of $14,000 or less for a family of four. By arbitrarily setting this income limit, a variable has been created for poverty. Now poverty is not only measurable but also meets the other property of a variable—it varies. It varies from a value of no income at all to various incomes below $14,000 annually. Any annual income of $14,000 or less (for a family of four) would be considered poverty. Any family income above $14,000 would not be considered poverty. Actually, many alternative measures of poverty could be used as well.

A **value** is an important aspect of a variable. Don't confuse this term with social work values; they are altogether different. A value is one specific measure of a variable. For example, the variable, gender, has two values—female and male. Each participant is assigned to one value or the other. Another example is the variable, level of education. If the highest level of education completed by a person is a high school degree, this would be this person's value of this variable.

A **constant,** unlike a variable, is a concept that doesn't change. Since constants do not change or vary, there is little reason to give attention to them in research studies. An example of a constant is "people" in the statement "People communicate with language." In other words, all people, not just some, communicate in some way using language. "Language," however, can be turned into a variable, which then could take values such as English, Spanish, Russian, and so on. As another example, in many studies we focus on an identified population of people, such as homeless people, teen parents, infants, or Haitians. In these instances, everyone in the population is the same in terms of why they were selected. For instance, in a study of homeless people, everyone is homeless. Thus, homelessness is a constant, as it is assumed for all participants.

Constructing and Measuring Variables

Variables usually need to be constructed and measured to fit the needs of each study. Variable construction is a process of shaping an abstract concept into a measure. This process is also sometimes referred to as operationalizing a concept or providing an operational definition of a concept. Constructing variables usually involves several sequential steps. These steps include first identifying the key concept and then defining, describing, and developing a measure of the variable.

1. *Identifying the key concept.* A concept that is important to a study needs to be initially identified. The concept is then constructed into a variable that provides a measure of it. As was explained in the last chapter, understanding and defining the research problem is the first step in the overall research process. Defining the research problem also helps in identifying the key concepts to be studied. These concepts are usually embedded in the researchers' definition of the problem.

In a study about poverty, for example, the researchers begin their study by articulating such things as their view of poverty and its causes, who are the poor with whom they are especially concerned, and how poverty can be overcome. Once these views are articulated, the important concepts usually can be identified, and variable construction can be addressed. Seccombe's study offers an example of how key concepts were initially identified.

A Study of Welfare Recipients

Seccombe's (1999) perspective of poverty influenced her choice of the important concepts to be studied. As a feminist researcher, she decided to focus on the impact that the welfare system had on welfare recipients; these recipients were mostly single mothers who were divorced or unmarried. Her perspective took into account explanations for poverty based on the individual's role, restrictions imposed by the welfare system, the influence of a culture of poverty, and fate. Yet, she was most interested in understanding how poverty was different for women in particular. Her understanding of the problem led her to focus on such concepts as the stigma associated with being on welfare, dependency issues fostered by the welfare system, the difficulties in managing a welfare budget, the importance of social supports, and the lack of satisfactory employment opportunities for women on welfare.

2. *Defining the variable.* The next step involves defining the variable. A good way to approach this step is to develop a straightforward but simple definition of the variable. Writing definition statements may take some practice. Researchers often write the definitions of their variables over and over until they are concise and accurate. For example, in a study focusing on the assertiveness of social workers, assertiveness would need to be defined. In this case, being assertive could be defined as "being able to express your feelings, stand up for your rights, and those of others, and state your opinions without abusing or taking advantage of others" (Sundel & Sundel, 1980, p. 10).

3. *Describing the variable.* The third step in variable construction is to elaborate on the definition, or give it more description or detail. This step may involve setting the outer limits for the variable and differentiating it from other variables. Describing the variable, assertiveness, offers an example. Assertiveness can be clarified beyond the above definition by stating what it is not. Sundel and Sundel (1980) suggest that assertiveness needs to be distinguished from being underassertive and overassertive. Underassertive could be considered passive, submissive, and meek. Underassertive people frequently make excuses for themselves, are apologetic for what they say, and often blame themselves when things go wrong. Overassertive people could be described as aggressive, hostile, and arrogant. They often attempt to control or manipulate, blame, dominate, and intimidate others and sometimes use verbal or physical violence.

4. *Developing a measure of the variable.* Finally, the variable would be developed into a specific measure. Measurements can be developed easily for some variables but may be more difficult for others. First, let's consider a couple of examples of variables in which a measure is easy to develop. Age is a variable, and it could be measured by asking participants to fill in their age in a blank space following the question "What is your age?" Another fairly easy variable to measure is satisfaction with various aspects of your job. A question could be asked, such as "How satisfied are you with your current job responsibilities?" with these measures: very satisfied, satisfied, dissatisfied, very dissatisfied.

Let's look at an example of a more complicated variable like assertiveness. Because this variable has multiple dimensions and is reflected in varied types of behaviors, it will likely need to be measured by asking several questions, not one or two. A standardized scale by Sundel and Sundel (1980) offers one way to measure assertiveness (see Table 5.1). In this case, their scale measures assertiveness within the context of social work activities. Each question identifies a particular behavior that can be important to social workers related to whether they are assertive or not.

If you review the assertiveness scale in Table 5.1, you will see that it measures several dimensions of assertiveness based on different types of relationships. These authors decided that a comprehensive measure of assertiveness needs to take into account five different types of relationships on an equal basis. The first subset of five items (1–5) of this scale covers relationships with clients; the second subset (6–10) covers relationships with coworkers; the third subset (11–15), with subordinates; the fourth subset (16–20), with superiors; and the fifth subset (21–25), with professionals of other disciplines.

Also note that some items in this scale are stated in a way that is favorable to assertiveness, and other questions are stated in the opposite way, as unfavorable. You will see that the unfavorable statements can be easily identified, because they end in an asterisk. This mix of positive and negative statements is helpful in discouraging the research participant from getting into a pattern of answering all of the questions in the same way (e.g., answering all of the statements as being always or almost always true of me). This problem is referred to as a response pattern and does not accurately reflect the participants' views. During the data analysis step, the scores for the unfavorable statements must be reversed so that these scores have the same meaning as the favorable statements. Then all of the items are stated in the same way, favorable to assertiveness, and a total score can be calculated for each participant by adding up the score for each item. This total score is a summary measure of each respondent's assertiveness. A summary score that takes into consideration the responses to several statements on the same overall topic can also be referred to as an index of each respondent's assertiveness.

You may want to fill out the assertiveness scale in Table 5.1 to determine how assertive you are. Do this by answering all of the items on the scale. Then, calculate your total assertive score in two steps. The first step is to change the values of reversed items that end with an asterisk (*). For example, change your responses on these items from 1 to 5; 2 to 4; 5 to 1; and so on. A value of 3 would not change. The second step is to add your numerical responses to get your assertiveness score. As you can see from this assertiveness scale, questions 11 to 15 are questions for those who supervise. A perfect assertiveness score is 100 for nonsupervisors (who do not respond to questions 11–15). A perfect assertiveness score for supervisors is 125. The lowest possible score for nonsupervisors is 20, and 25 for supervisors. You can decide for yourself whether your score reflects enough assertiveness. For example, a score of 75 or over for nonsupervisors could be viewed as very assertive. A score of 50 or less for nonsupervisors may suggest a need to give serious attention to improving one's assertiveness skills. Incidentally, social workers should either have or work on developing strong assertiveness skills to be effective in their practice.

| TABLE 5.1 | **How Assertive Are You?** |

Indicate the extent to which you would behave in the manner described by the following statements. Next to each statement, write the number that best corresponds to your behavior, according to the following code:

    1 = never or almost never true of me

    2 = rarely true of me

    3 = sometimes true of me

    4 = usually true of me

    5 = always or almost always true of me

————   1. When a client arrives more than five minutes late for his/her appointment, I end the session on time.

————   2. When a client asks me how I handle my personal problems and I don't want to divulge this, I refocus the client on his/her difficulty.

————   3. When a client tells me that s/he didn't have time to do an assignment that s/he had agreed to do, I accept that and go on to the next issue.*

————   4. If a client failed to pay his/her fee for services, I would discuss this matter with him/her at the first available opportunity.

————   5. If a client calls to cancel an appointment, I say something to try to make him/her feel bad.*

————   6. In a staff meeting, I will voice my opinions when I think I should, even if it disagrees with my peers.

————   7. When a coworker asks me personal questions, I answer them because I'm too uncomfortable to refuse.*

————   8. When a colleague asks me to serve on a committee, I agree to even if I don't want to serve.*

————   9. If a coworker borrowed money from me, I would ask him/her to pay it back.

———— 10. When a coworker repeatedly asks me to cover for him/her so that s/he can conduct personal business, I refuse.

———— 11. When a worker that I am supervising arrives late for our supervisory session, I end the session on time.

———— 12. When a worker is late in handing in reports, it irritates me and I lose my temper.*

———— 13. When a supervisee uses agency time to conduct personal business that interferes with his/her responsibilities, I become anxious and do not discuss this with him/her.*

———— 14. When I observe a supervisee being rude or providing incorrect information to a client, I call him/her aside at the first available opportunity to discuss the situation.

(continued)

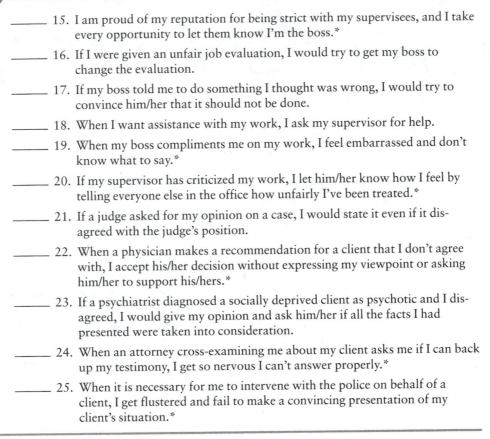

TABLE 5.1   Continued

_____ 15. I am proud of my reputation for being strict with my supervisees, and I take every opportunity to let them know I'm the boss.*

_____ 16. If I were given an unfair job evaluation, I would try to get my boss to change the evaluation.

_____ 17. If my boss told me to do something I thought was wrong, I would try to convince him/her that it should not be done.

_____ 18. When I want assistance with my work, I ask my supervisor for help.

_____ 19. When my boss compliments me on my work, I feel embarrassed and don't know what to say.*

_____ 20. If my supervisor has criticized my work, I let him/her know how I feel by telling everyone else in the office how unfairly I've been treated.*

_____ 21. If a judge asked for my opinion on a case, I would state it even if it disagreed with the judge's position.

_____ 22. When a physician makes a recommendation for a client that I don't agree with, I accept his/her decision without expressing my viewpoint or asking him/her to support his/hers.*

_____ 23. If a psychiatrist diagnosed a socially deprived client as psychotic and I disagreed, I would give my opinion and ask him/her if all the facts I had presented were taken into consideration.

_____ 24. When an attorney cross-examining me about my client asks me if I can back up my testimony, I get so nervous I can't answer properly.*

_____ 25. When it is necessary for me to intervene with the police on behalf of a client, I get flustered and fail to make a convincing presentation of my client's situation.*

Source: From _Be Assertive: A Practical Guide for Human Service Workers_ by G. Sundel and M. Sundel, 1980. Newbury Park: Sage. Reprinted by permission of the authors.

In summary, concepts and variables are a central focus of most research studies. Concepts are measured by first developing them into variables. Variables are then measured by the values assigned to them.

Understanding Measurement

Since measuring the concepts of interest to a study is central to the research process, the topic of measurement is introduced next. **Measurement** is defined as the process of determining the values of a variable for the people being studied. For example, the measurement of the educational level of the participants in a study would amount to finding out the highest educational level obtained by each person. The values could be the following: some high school, high school diploma, some college, undergraduate degree, and so on.

Measurement is a concept of central importance to research, as it offers valuable tools for conducting the steps in the research process that follows. Social workers encounter measurement issues in many daily activities. We frequently ask questions that beg for a measured response. For example, we may ask about the potential achievement level of an underachieving child with whom we work in a public school. Or we may question how likely a mother or father can parent adequately if child neglect is evident. We may inquire about the potential earning power of a welfare recipient who has neither a high school diploma nor any work history. Or we may find ourselves wondering about the intellectual ability of a adult with severe retardation when she seems to understand most of our nonverbal cues even though she has difficulty dressing herself. We may question whether adult abuse exists for a ninety-year-old woman who sleeps on the floor and turns on her stove to heat her apartment. And we may question whether we can help someone with schizophrenia if he is unwilling to take his medication regularly. These questions and countless others require answers that we need in our jobs. If we could come up with accurate answers, we might be able to make a difference in the lives of our clients.

Social workers are known for getting involved in "messy" situations that do not seem to have easy solutions. Many social work educators say that if you can't stand ambiguity, you probably won't survive as a social worker. These messy situations often involve complicated social circumstances that are described by ambiguous concepts. Many of these concepts have not had widespread agreement about their definition or measurement. Examples include poverty, happiness, well-being, racism, a woman's right to choose and the right to life, love, gender equality, spirituality, employability, optimum levels of immigration, and so on. We use many of these concepts to describe the social problems our clients are experiencing or the solutions for their problems, and we plead for public policy responses that will effectively serve the greatest number or help those with the greatest need.

Let's consider for a moment why the concepts just mentioned are so difficult to measure. In part it is because they are so abstract. The concept of happiness, for example, can vary, based on numerous factors. Many of these concepts are also rather nebulous and easily misunderstood by many people. Gender equality is an example of a misunderstood concept. Does it mean, for example, that males and females should be treated equally on everything? If this is so, how do we take into account factors like childbirth, breast feeding, and differing levels of physical strength that are gender related?

Some of these concepts are also politically laden, because they provide advantages to some people and disadvantages to others once we give them measures. Poverty is an example. A definition of poverty can determine how many people are perceived to experience it (based on this definition) and what can be done to help them. A definition of poverty is used by federal and state governments to determine who is eligible to receive welfare benefits, food stamps, Medicaid, subsidized housing, and other essential resources. We need to remember that when politics become evident, ethical dilemmas are also present. So a lot can be at stake in measurement.

Hopefully, you are now aware that a lot of the needs and problems of our clients are manifested in abstract concepts. Actually, much of our world is evident in abstractions. Unless we understand this abstract world, we won't be able to understand how it affects our clients and the problems that confront them. This is another reason why research studies and measurement are so important and often so challenging. If we are to understand and address our clients' needs and problems, we must first attempt to measure these abstract concepts. We must also investigate the relationships among these concepts.

How Knowledge Is Generated

An unusual term to consider at this point is *epistemology*. Epistemology refers to the science of how knowledge is generated. Epistemologists provide standards for knowing how to generate knowledge in our field, particularly when we must move from the abstract world of ideas to the observable world where measurement can occur.

Consider the example of human intelligence as our abstract concept. Intelligence is a central dimension of our humanity and an important concept for social workers to understand. While intelligence consists of a complex array of cognitive functions, it is essentially beyond our observation and not directly measurable. As Figure 5.1 indicates, we must make a leap of "calculated" faith to develop a measure of it. Thus, we devise either an intelligence test or an adaptive behavior scale that is intended to reflect human intelligence in the observable world.

This leap of faith is how knowledge is generated. Although an abstract concept like intelligence cannot be measured directly, other standards are used in developing a measure of it that is accurate and consistent. These standards are referred to as validity and reliability and will be discussed later in this chapter.

Quantitative and Qualitative Measurements

Two overall approaches for conducting social research, the deductive and inductive, were introduced in Chapter 2. It was pointed out that the deductive approach

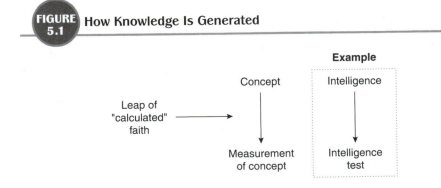

FIGURE 5.1   How Knowledge Is Generated

uses quantitative methods and the inductive approach uses qualitative methods. Deductive research begins by crafting a theoretical explanation for why something is happening in the real world (e.g., a hypothesis proposes that women tend to be Democrats and men, Republicans) followed by a second step of attempting to find support for it in the real world (e.g., a study could be conducted to determine the political affiliation of a group of women and men). In contrast, inductive research begins without any theoretical explanations. The first step is to immerse yourself in the real world and study something (e.g., find out why so many people are homeless by talking with homeless people on the street) and generate possible theoretical explanations from what you learn (e.g., possibly coming up with several explanations, such as some homeless people have a mental illness and are not being treated by the mental health system, while others are currently employed in a low-skilled job but cannot afford to pay for decent housing, and still others are suffering from substance abuse, and so on).

Deductive research usually involves measurements in the form of numbers and inductive research involves measurement in word form. Let's first discuss how measurement can be created using quantitative indicators. This leads us to a familiar term, *numbers*.

Numbers

When we think of measurement, we usually think of numbers or numerical scores. For example, weight is measured by a numerical score of pounds, and height is measured by feet and inches. We use numbers to measure many things that we encounter. One advantage of such a measure is that it can be standardized and the scores can be comparable for several people who are studied. We often refer to numerical scores or responses as "quantitative data." Quantitative data also have an advantage over qualitative data; they can be analyzed using statistics. Many researchers have a strong tendency to develop measures that are in numerical form because statistical analysis becomes possible.

One potential disadvantage, however, is that quantitative measures can be weakened by a problem called *reductionism* (discussed in Chapter 2). Reductionism results whenever an effort to create a numerical measure of a concept results in losing some of the properties of the concept. An example would be success in school being determined solely by a grade-point average. Other properties of success in school that would be overlooked in this measure would include development of interpersonal relationship skills, establishing a socially oriented values system, and developing confidence and skills for employment. Overall, measures using numerical scores have many advantages but also have limitations.

There are many questions that elicit a numerical response. Some of the questions raised earlier in the chapter could be answered with a numerical measure. For example, the question "What is the potential achievement level of an underachieving child?" can be answered with a numerical score if a school achievement test is administered. A school achievement test may produce a numerical score, such as the upper 25 percentile of all who have taken the test, or score 355 out of total of 425. Similarly, the question asking about the "potential earning power of a welfare recipient who has neither a high school diploma nor any work history" could be measured by the salary that she earns at different points in time. A salary is in dollars, which is a numerical expression. Neither of the above numerical measures (test score or salary) offers a totally satisfactory answer to these questions, but at least they provide a partial one that is standardized and comparative. Other examples of pertinent concerns that can be answered numerically are as follows:

- The size of a social worker's workload is measured by the *number* of cases assigned.
- The clients' eligibility for services is determined by their *salary and other assets*.
- The severity of aggressive behavior exhibited by an emotionally disturbed child can be determined by the *frequency* with which he fights or bullies others.
- The success of a student's course work (as you well know!) is measured as a *numerical* grade or a letter grade that is usually based on a numerical range of scores from 0 to 100 percent.

We have many quantitative measures at our disposal in social work. We can ask people numerous questions, such as their age, salary, number of children in their family, their educational level, and miles of travel from home to work or school. All of the answers are in some kind of numerical form. Note that most of these questions refer to demographic or background characteristics that may be of interest to a researcher or a social worker during an intake process.

Researchers could also ask other questions of a quantitative nature that may be important indicators of client progress or improvement. Examples include the number of times that someone

- is absent from school
- completes homework on time
- takes their medications
- verbalizes anger (rather than physically fights) when a conflict arises
- compliments or praises a spouse for any contribution to the family
- talks in a class discussion
- invites other residents living at a retirement village to lunch

Words

We can also use words to measure many things we encounter. We could ask, for example, several demographic questions that elicit a word response. Examples include What is your gender? (female or male) Race? (European American, African American, Latino, etc.) Nationality of birth? (Ireland, Poland, Kenya, Haiti, United States) Religious affiliation? (Protestant, Catholic, Jewish, Muslim) Neighborhood of residence? (in Philadelphia—West Philadelphia, South Philadelphia, Center City, and so on).

We can also ask other questions eliciting word responses that can be important indicators of a client's attitudes, feelings, needs, or interests. Examples of such questions, with possible answers in parentheses, include:

- Do you like your courses? (yes, no)
- How do you feel today? (happy, OK, sad)
- Who is your best friend? (name)
- What is your favorite sport? (football, baseball, volley ball, soccer, tennis, track)
- How serious is this problem? (very serious, serious, somewhat serious, not serious)

We could also ask questions eliciting a word response that could be important indicators of a client progress, improvement, or increased knowledge. For example:

- How much of what you have learned from this training session can you use in your job? (a lot, some, very little, none)
- How satisfied are you with the supervision you are receiving? (very satisfied, satisfied, somewhat satisfied, not satisfied)
- How often are you aware of how you are feeling? (frequently, often, occasionally, almost never)
- Is having multiple sex partners an example of unsafe sex? (yes, no)
- Is a pattern of drinking alcohol in the morning one characteristic of alcoholism? (true, false)

Note that some of the above examples use a Likert scale. A **Likert scale** is a set of response categories that proceed in order from one extreme to the opposite extreme, such as strongly agree, agree, not sure, disagree, strongly disagree. Likert scales are discussed later in the chapter. It is also important to point out that all of the word-response questions discussed so far have a common feature: they elicit a forced response. **Forced-response questions** restrict the respondent's answer to a predetermined list of response categories. Forced-response questions are also sometimes referred to as closed-ended questions in social work.

Longer Word Forms

The questions that have been discussed so far have been forced-response questions that can be answered with either a number or word. In addition, measurement can be evident in longer word forms, such as phrases, sentences, or more extended comments. When such open-ended questions are asked, they are likely to elicit responses in a longer word form.

Open-ended questions do not provide a restricted set of response categories from which respondents must choose their answers. Instead, respondents answer these questions in their own words. While open-ended question can elicit single-word responses, they are more likely to involve several words, a sentence or two, or lengthier comments. As an example, if we ask a group of adolescents in a residential program if they like their residence, we could ask them to respond by selecting one of the following responses: yes, maybe, or no. This is a forced-response question; respondents are forced to choose one and only one response from the list. However, let's say we want to find out more information about why these adolescents like or dislike their residence. We could ask a follow-up question that is open ended, such as "What do you like about your residence?" Also, to elicit any negative responses, we could ask "What do you dislike about your residence?" If we recorded their responses to these two questions in the adolescents' own words, we could easily have as many different responses as we have people who are interviewed. Also, some responses may be short and limited to a word or two, and other comments may be much longer.

In one study, a sample of people with developmental disabilities were asked an open-ended question: "How do the staff members assist you in getting together with your best friend?" (Dudley, 2001). Some of their responses follow:

> Drive me in car.
> Helps me to find my way there.
> They tell me to go and talk to (my best friend) when I'm upset.
> They talk to me about who I need to get together with.
> Remind me.
> Staff lets friends come here.
> They arrange visit.
> I live with her (best friend).
> They take me to see him.
> I do it on my own.
> Will help with phone calls to friends if needed.
> Helping me get to church. Tell me about Jesus.
> By doing stuff when you ask them.
> Give me cigarettes.

As you can see, these responses reveal a wide variety of ways that staff assist clients in making contact with their best friend. Each response is expressed in an individualized way. Some of the responses indicate that transportation helps. Others suggest helpful directions for getting to a friend's home. Discussions, encouraging visits, and other types of support are also mentioned. Also, one comment—"Give me cigarettes"—seems, at least on the surface, to be unrelated to the question.

Some researchers do not believe that longer word forms offer a measurement of something. These reservations are largely based on the view that the results are not standardized. In contrast, the viewpoint taken in this book is that measurement can be manifested in many different forms, including numbers, one word, or longer word forms. Measurement should not be limited to findings resulting from forced-response questions just because they are quantitative and can be analyzed by statistics.

Levels of Measurement

Next, let's explore levels of measurement. **Levels of measurement** can be defined as the degree to which the values of a variable can be quantified. Levels of measurement are important to understand because they provide guidelines for constructing measurements of variables and determine how a variable can be analyzed. As Table 5.2 below indicates, there are four levels of measurement.

Let's look more closely at each of these levels of measurement. **Nominal variables** have values that are categories. These categories must meet three properties: being distinct, mutually exclusive, and exhaustive. Being distinct means that the label assigned to a category clearly identifies what it means. For example, "Catholic" is a distinct category for the variable, religious affiliation, while "doubter" may not be. Second, nominal variables have values that are mutually exclusive or do not overlap. For example, Catholic, Protestant, Jewish, Muslim, and other would be categories of religious affiliation that don't overlap. In other words, no one is likely to select more than one of these categories. Third, nominal variables have an exhaustive set of categories, which means that there is one category that fits the circumstances of each of the respondents. The earlier set of categories for religious affiliation (Catholic, Protestant, Jewish, Muslim, and other) is an example. If a respondent was a Buddhist or agnostic, for example, she could still select "other." The "other" category is a miscellaneous category that can be included to ensure a choice for every respondent.

TABLE 5.2   **Levels of Measurement**

Level of Measurement	Definition	Examples
1. Nominal	Values are in two or more categories that are distinct, mutually exclusive, and exhaustive of all possibilities.	Race, gender
2. Ordinal	Values are in two or more categories, have all of the properties of nominal variables, and have a sequential order to them.	Social class, Likert-scale questions on attitudes
3. Interval	Values have a sequential order to them, and there is an equal distance between the different values. There is no true zero value.	Temperature
4. Ratio	Values have a sequential order to them, and there is an equal distance between the different values. Also, zero is a true zero value that represents an absence of the variable.	Income, age, weight

Diversity Issue and Nominal-Level Variables

Diversity is often important to consider in developing response categories for nominal variables. When categories are identified, we should ask if we have considered the characteristics of all of the respondents in a study. For example, if you are studying a group that is most likely to be made up of divorced and separated parents, an appropriate list of categories for marital status would be married, separated, divorced, and other. However, if you are conducting a study of parents with more diverse backgrounds, you would add to your list other categories, such as single, engaged, widow, and cohabitation.

Ordinal variables have all three properties required of nominal variables. An additional property for ordinal variables is that these categories can be listed in sequential order, from higher to lower or greater to lesser. Likert scales are ordinal variables because they have an order to them. A set of Likert categories (e.g., strongly satisfied, satisfied, dissatisfied, and strongly dissatisfied) are listed in degree of satisfaction. Examples of other variables that have values in a sequential order are social class (upper class, middle class, lower class) and severity of a behavior disorder (severe, moderate, minimal, none). Note that it doesn't make sense to talk about the distance between categories of ordinal variables.

The values of **interval variables** do not have response categories. They have individual numerical scores based on a standard unit of measure, which has numerical values along a continuum. With interval variables, we can compare distances between points meaningfully. Temperature in degrees Fahrenheit is an interval variable, because the values are numbers along a continuum. If it is 90 degrees on a particular day, it is 2 degrees warmer than 88 degrees; if it is 70 degrees, it is also 2 degrees warmer than 68. In other words, the distance between 90 and 88 is equal to the distance between 70 and 68. Other examples of interval variables are IQ (intelligence) scores and GRE (Graduate Record Examination) scores. With interval variables, we not only know that one value is higher or lower than another, but we also know how much numerical distance there is between values.

Ratio variables are similar to interval variables, except that zero is a true zero value. In other words, zero represents a true absence of the variable. The true zero makes a ratio variable meaningful in a special way. You can say one value is twice as great as another, for example. Income is a ratio variable. An income of 0 is a true zero. And it makes sense to say that someone who earns $30,000 earns three times as much as someone who earns $10,000. Temperature, on the other hand, is at the interval, not ratio, level, because 0 degrees is not a true absence of temperature. It doesn't make sense to say that if it's 100 degrees outside, it is twice as warm as if it's 50 degrees. Most numerical variables used in research are ratio variables—for example, income, education, age, weight, height, number of children, and so on. These variables have a standard unit of measure, such as dollars and cents for income; years of school completed for education; years, months, and days for age; pounds for weight; feet and inches for height; and so on. In addition, zero for all of these variables represents a true absence of the variable.

Another way to distinguish the levels of measurement is to say that nominal and ordinal variables are categorical in nature; their values consist of discrete categories that are discontinuous from one another. For example, the values of gender—male and female—are discrete or distinctly different. In contrast, the values of interval and ratio variables are not categories. They are numerical scores deriving from a standard unit of measure. The values of interval and ratio variables are continuous, without interruption along a continuum. An example is age, which increases with each increment of time.

Because interval and ratio variables have properties that are very similar and use the same statistical tests, they will be combined together and referred to as interval/ratio variables. Interval/ratio variables have an advantage over the other levels of measurement because they can be analyzed using the most powerful statistical tests. More will be discussed on this advantage in Chapter 14.

Finally, we have **prenominal variables,** which refer to variables in qualitative studies that have not yet fulfilled the definition of nominal-level variables. Prenominal variables could have values that overlap. For example, we may ask participants of a study to tell us what activities they like to do. Their responses could include swimming, tennis, baseball, reading, hiking, skiing, watching TV, and so on. If we allow them to identify more than one activity, some participants will have more than one response. Therefore, a participant's values may fit into two or more categories rather than just one.

Often, variables are initially developed or constructed in a prenominal stage, which suggests how important this stage can be. In this case, if we were to measure something, it could be in longer word form. We could, for example, be interested in finding out the most important challenges of divorced parents. By interviewing several divorced parents, we could record narratives that describe their problems, pain, hardships, hopes, and so on. After analyzing these narratives, we may conclude that three or four types of responses were predominant in the interviews. For example, some of the types of responses could be complaints about a shortage of money for covering daily expenses, a strained relationship with their former spouse, feeling overwhelmed by assuming most of the child-raising responsibility, and a desire to start a new life. Each of these types of responses could be formulated into a new set of questions that could be asked in another study. Also, these responses could be left in narrative form and presented as examples of the different types of responses that divorced parents are experiencing. More attention will be given to analyzing prenominal variables in Chapter 15.

Validity and Reliability

Before leaving the topic of measurement, we must consider an important question: How "good" are the measures we are using? We are asking how much we can depend on a measurement instrument to be satisfactory in measuring something of interest to us. Actually, we are asking two important issues: Does the measure have both validity and reliability? Validity refers to whether the measure of the intended concept is an accurate reflection of the concept. Reliability refers to whether the measure of the intended concept consistently measures the same thing. Referring back to Figure 5.1, we are reminded that a leap of calculated faith is needed to develop a measure of a concept. This leap of faith involves using the standards of validity and reliability.

Validity

Validity is a standard that we use to determine whether an instrument measures what it is supposed to measure and whether it measures it accurately. Accuracy is the key issue here. For example, do the Federal Bureau of Investigation's *Uniform Crime Reports* (2002) measure the incidence of rape? The answer is yes, because the FBI compiles statistics on the incidence of rape reported by local law authorities in each state. Next, we should ask, how accurately do the FBI *Uniform Crime Reports* measure the incidence of rape? The answer to this question is less certain. We know that many victims of rape do not report it to local authorities for several reasons, including the difficulty involved in prosecuting rapists and the embarrassment incurred in sharing such a horrific experience. So we must conclude that the FBI *Uniform Crime Reports* on rape are only partially valid because so many incidences go unreported. This point reminds us that determining validity is a matter of degree. There is no such thing as complete or absolute validity. The more validity that a measure has, the better.

Validity can be a problem if the research participant does not know a lot about the topic of inquiry. For example, a traditional father who is employed every weekday away from his home will not be able to give accurate answers to questions about what the children are doing during weekdays, such as who they play with, how much TV they watch, what they eat for lunch, and so on. If the mother in the family is usually home raising the children, she will be a more accurate source.

How Is Validity Measured?   How do we know whether a measurement instrument is valid? There are many different ways of determining validity. Face validity is the simplest. **Face validity** means that the measure appears to be valid "on its face" (Babbie, 2001). In other words, as you look over the measure, it appears to be valid based on what you know about the concept or based on what your mental image is. If you are not sure, an additional way to consider face validity is to ask the same questions of an "expert," or someone else who knows more about the variable than you. You could also ask such experts what they would suggest adding or changing to make it a more accurate measure of a variable you are constructing.

For example, let's say you are attempting to develop a measure of active tenant participation in a neighborhood tenant council. Your goal is to achieve active participation in six months, and you need a measure of whether you have accomplished your goal. Initially, you decide to measure active participation as being at least eight tenants attending every monthly council meeting during the six-month period. Next, you can ask the tenant council for their opinions on this measure. They agree with your measure, except that they believe that active participation can only be achieved if at least one tenant comes from each of the three high-rise apartment buildings in the housing complex. If you add their suggestion, you will not only increase the number and diversity of people who agree with this measure. You may also get the tenants more involved in efforts to achieve the goal.

Face validity can be a commonsense test to use. It involves carefully reviewing the measurement instrument and asking yourself whether it appears to measure accurately what you want it to measure. You can conduct a check of face validity fairly easily. The steps are simple, as outlined here.

An Easy Way to Determine Face Validity

You can use the Leadership Comfort Scale (Table 5.3, page 105) or the Sundel assertiveness scale in Table 5.1 (page 87) to practice these steps:

1. Fill out the measurement instrument.
2. Determine or calculate your overall score.
3. Use the author's interpretation of what your score means if such an interpretation is provided. (It is provided with the Sundel assertiveness scale.)
4. Ask yourself if you agree with the results (e.g., Does your score reflect what you perceive to be your comfort level with group leadership? Or does your score reflect your understanding of how assertive you are?).

Three additional tests of validity can help determine a measure's validity in more rigorous ways. These three tests are content validity, criterion-related validity, and construct validity. Like face validity, these tests determine the degree to which a measure is valid, not whether or not it has absolute validity. Because each of these tests measures a different aspect of validity, it is preferable to use as many of these tests as possible in determining validity.

Content validity is the degree to which a measure covers the range of meanings included within the concept (Babbie, 2001). Content validity is particularly useful if you have developed an instrument that is to measure a multidimensional concept. Content validity would be used to determine if the questions you selected reflect all of the dimensions of the variable. An example would be a measure of prejudice. In order for a measure of prejudice to have content validity, it needs to reflect all types of prejudice, such as prejudice against women, older people, racial and ethnic minorities, religious minorities, and so on. If the variable was to be limited to prejudice against women, for example, content validity would be concerned with the measure covering prejudice in all of the important areas, such as in employment, family matters, financial opportunities, and so on.

The assertiveness scale in Table 5.1 is an example of a multidimensional variable that has content validity related to the different types of relationships that social workers encounter. The authors of this scale decided that an overall measure of assertiveness needed to take into account five different types of relationships, so they constructed a scale that has five items about assertive behaviors for each of five types: clients, coworkers, subordinates, superiors, and professionals of other disciplines.

Criterion-related validity is another test of the validity of a measure. Criterion-related validity means that a measure is valid if its scores correlate with the scores of another measure of the same construct (Babbie, 2001). The other measure of the same construct would be the external criterion. Perhaps the external criterion could be a behavioral indicator that correlates with a verbal response to an interview question. For example, you may want to find out if the research participants in a sample are religious. You decide to measure this variable by asking, "How religious are you?" Response categories include very religious, religious, somewhat religious, and not religious. You could also find out how frequently the participants attend religious services. This would be the external criterion, which is a behavioral indicator of how religious they are. You could claim that your measure ("How religious are you?") has criterion-related validity if the participants who indicate that they are religious also usually attend religious services regularly and those who indicate that they are not religious usually do not attend religious services.

Another example of criterion-related validity would be a correlation between a future behavior, such as actual future arrests, and a scale used to predict future crime recidivism. In another example, a correlation between a depression scale that you develop and a well-established measure like the Beck Depression Scale would be an example of criterion-related validity. Criterion-related validity is also referred to as predictive validity, because the external criterion predicts the new measure, and vice versa.

Construct validity is a third rigorous test of the validity of a measure. It is especially relevant to use when it is difficult to use criterion-related validity, because we cannot find a behavioral criterion of the measure (Babbie, 2001). In these instances, we can consider how the variable to be measured is logically associated to other variables. A hypothesis could be crafted that proposes that the variable in question is logically associated with another variable. For example, construct validity could be determined for an assertiveness scale by identifying other variables with which it has a logical relationship. In this case, it seems logical that assertiveness has a relationship to such variables as effective communication skills and success in salary negotiations. Construct validity would involve determining if measures of either of these two variables are correlated with scores of the assertiveness scale. Generally, construct validity provides less compelling evidence of validity than criterion-related validity, because the variable to which it is being compared is not another measure of the same variable but one that has a logical association with it.

Reliability

Reliability is the second key standard to be considered in determining if a measure is satisfactory. **Reliability** refers to the internal consistency of the measure. Does the instrument measure a concept consistently from one time to another? In addition, does the instrument measure a concept consistently among different people (i.e., is the measure consistently understood by different participants in the same way)? Several factors impact reliability, as follows:

1. *Ambiguous wording.* Reliability is weak if the questions asked in a measurement instrument use words that are ambiguous. Words are considered ambiguous if they are likely to be interpreted differently by two or more research participants or by the same participant at different times. Let's consider the phrase "social work services" in the question "How satisfied are you with social work services?" One person could associate this term with one image, while another person associates it with something altogether different. "Satisfaction with social work services" could be associated with "liking the social worker" by one participant, "not having delays in receiving services" by a second participant, and "receiving the help that was requested" by a third participant. Since the phrase "social work services" is so general and open to so many interpretations, it would be better to ask about specific aspects of service, such as:

- How satisfied are you with the availability of the social worker?
- How satisfied are you that the social worker listens to what you say?
- How satisfied are you with getting your needs met?

2. *Retrospective questions.* Reliability can also be a problem with retrospective questions. These questions ask for information about something that was experienced in the past. For example, a retrospective question could be "How many cups of coffee did you drink on average last month?" or "How many times did you visit a doctor last year?" Whenever a question asks for information requiring memory of the past, consideration needs to be given to how well participants will be able to recall. While people have widely varying capacities to remember things from the past, usually any question that asks about experiences a month or more in the past should be avoided.

3. *External factors.* External factors beyond the instrument could interfere with reliability as well. The characteristics of the people who administer the measurement instrument could influence reliability. For example, some participants' responses could be swayed by varying the interviewer's gender, race, age, accent used, attire, energy level, or interest level. Reliability can also be influenced by other external factors that influence the research participants. For example, the participants' fatigue, motivation, and depression, all of which may vary, can affect reliability. Although all of these external factors and others need to be carefully thought about before administering an interview, there are limits to what can be done to eliminate all such interference.

How Is Reliability Measured?   How do we know if a measure is reliable? Two simple methods are important to consider in determining the reliability of a measure: test-retest and interrater reliability. Both tests, like the validity tests, determine the degree to which a measure is reliable, not whether or not it has absolute reliability.

A **test-retest method** is the first means of determining reliability. A test-retest method determines whether a question is consistent by administering it to the same person at two different points in time. The two different responses to the question are then compared to see if the participant's responses are the same or similar. The second administration of the measure should be done fairly soon after the first measure to ensure that nothing has changed in the participant's life related to what is being measured.

A test-retest method can be conducted fairly easily to strengthen a survey instrument. The questions can be administered to the same person(s) at two different times within close proximity of each other. Next, the answers to the same questions are compared to see if they are the same or not. Finally, you can look more closely at the questions that have different answers from the same person to see if they have ambiguous wording, retrospective questioning, or other shortcomings that may have added confusion. An exercise involving test-retest reliability is provided here.

An Exercise Using the Test-Retest Method

You can conduct a test-retest of the assertiveness scale in Table 5.1 to practice determining how reliable a measure is. Proceed as follows:

- Complete the scale at two different times within close proximity of each other. Make sure that your first set of responses are concealed when you complete the scale a second time.
- Compare your first and second pairs of responses for each item to determine if they are the same or not.
- When the two responses to an item are different, consider whether the item has ambiguous wording, is retrospective, or has other problems that can be corrected.
- Revise the items with inconsistent responses to improve their reliability.

The second method is called **interrater reliability.** In a test of interrater reliability, two or more people, referred to as raters, measure the same episode independent of each other. Afterward, they compare their results to determine if they are the same or similar. For example, let's say you want to observe a client group session to determine who talks the most and the least. You want to make sure that the observational rating instrument you are using is reliable. You could have two raters observe the same group session independently of each other through a one-way mirror. They would be recording on the rating instrument how frequently each client talks. You would then compare the results of the two raters to see how much they are in agreement. Following is an example of how a researcher used interrater reliability in a study.

Example of a Study Using Interrater Reliability

Cheryl Waites (2000) conducted a study to determine if BSW students who completed their degree program gave better answers to the questions about a case vignette than BSW students enrolled in the introductory course. The case vignette illustrated problems and needs affecting one family and some issues that could be addressed by a social worker geared to a generalist approach. Students were asked to answer six open-ended questions related to the problems, goals, strategies, evaluation, and termination of the case. The six questions of this vignette were tested for reliability in a pilot study of ten social work students and graduates. The first rater scored how well each participant answered the six questions. For interrater reliability, a second rater scored four of these ten participants as well to provide comparative ratings. Reliability between rater 1 and 2 was the same 80 percent of the time. Therefore, interrater reliability was reported as 80 percent. The interrater reliability increased to 88 percent in the actual study, resulting from improvements suggested by the participants in the pilot study.

Two other more complicated tests of reliability can also be used. These are the split-half and the alternate form methods. The **split-half method** involves splitting the items of an instrument into two random groupings and finding out if there is a strong association between the responses to the two sets of items. The **alternate form method** involves administering two different forms of an instrument that are very similar and determining if the responses to one instrument are strongly associated with the responses to the other instrument.

Measures of reliability and some of the measures of validity are reported as correlation scores. These correlation scores provide indicators of how much validity or reliability are evident in a measure. Typically, measures of correlation range from -1 to $+1$, with a 0 being in the middle. Perfect validity or reliability would be a score of -1 or $+1$. No evidence of validity or reliability would be a 0. Also, a score of -0.3 or $+0.3$ is usually considered poor validity or reliability, -0.4 or $+0.4$ would be moderate validity or reliability, and -0.7 or $+0.7$ would be good validity or reliability.

Reliability should be considered in small, practical ways as you prepare your measurement instrument. You could, for example, include two identical questions in different places on a survey and determine if participants answered both questions with the same response. If not, you may have to consider the possibility that these and other questions are not reliable. Also, reliability can be checked by asking a forced-response and open-ended question on the same specific topic. If the responses to the open-ended question are consistent with those to the forced-response question for the same respondents, then you can have some confidence that these questions are reliable. For example, if most participants respond to the forced-response question "Do you like where you live?" with a yes but then respond to the follow-up question "What do you like about where you live?" with comments like "the staff don't like me" or "I wish that I had a different roommate," you may want to consider why there is an inconsistency between these responses. It could be that the respondents don't fully understand the questions or that possibly the forced-response question is problematic because it favors a normative response of yes.

The connections between validity and reliability can be summarized as follows: A measure of an intended concept

- can have neither validity nor reliability
- can be reliable but not valid
- if valid, must be reliable
- has both validity and reliability

A measure can be reliable but not necessarily valid. In other words, an instrument can be measuring something consistently but not measuring what it is supposed to measure. For example, the FBI *Uniform Crime Reports* may be a fairly consistent measure but not a valid measure of mental illness. In contrast, a measure must be reliable if it is valid. If a measure is not consistently measuring the same thing, it is logical that it will not be an accurate measure of it.

Triangulation is a method of ensuring that a measure has validity and reliability. **Triangulation** is a process of using multiple methods to measure one concept. If researchers determine that the results of one measure of a variable are similar to the results from another measure of the same variable, they are triangulating the findings. This process also adds confidence that these two measures are both reliable and valid, because they have similar results.

Social workers are often involved in triangulating the information they collect from clients to ensure that it is accurate. For example, a social worker may cross-check the self-reporting of a parent accused of abusing her children with her behavior and with other sources, such as family members, the children, and neighbors. Sometimes, the more sources used in triangulation, the better.

Triangulation is often thought of as a way of guarding against any biases of the researcher and research participants (Taylor & Bogdan, 1984). Such biases can present serious threats to the integrity of the data that are collected, because they lessen their authenticity and accuracy. Whenever the researcher's presence interferes with how people respond to a survey or how they behave when observed, a reactive effect is introduced. This reactive effect is often referred to as reactivity. *Reactivity* is a condition in which the researcher's presence interferes with how people behave. Reactivity can be extremely problematic in any study.

Standardized Scales

Before leaving the topic of measurement, it is important to give more focused attention to standardized scales. Standardized scales are structured data collection instruments and can be questionnaires, interview schedules, or observation rating scales. These instruments are composed of a set of questions or statements that measure important concepts that are otherwise difficult to measure. These scales have been used extensively in prior research studies and practice and have strong evidence of validity and reliability.

Scales are available that measure numerous concepts relevant for social work practice in assessment, evaluation of treatment progress, and determination of overall program effectiveness. Standardized assessment scales are currently being recommended to social workers as a means of addressing new accountability requirements of regulatory and funding agencies (Dennison, 2002). These scales measure such things as anxiety, depression, hope, loneliness, self-esteem, stress, contentment, abusive and neglectful parenting behaviors, social supports, and well-being. Examples of such scales can be found in Ginsberg (2001) and Royse and colleagues (2001). The *Mental Measurements Yearbook* (2001) is another source for information on standardized tests covering scales on educational skills, personality, vocational aptitude, psychology, and related areas. This source is updated every year. The *Mental Measurements Yearbook* also has an online version you may be able to access through your university library. Sometimes a fee is required to use a scale, based on who has copyright to it.

Standardized scales are also useful in helping social workers assess their knowledge and skills in particular areas of practice. For example, Toseland and Rivas (2001) offer a scale to measure a person's comfort with group leadership (see Table 5.3). This scale is intended to help people identify their strengths and weaknesses related to leading small groups, based on degree of comfort in ten different situations frequently experienced by group leaders.

 TABLE 5.3   **Leadership Comfort Scale**

Indicate your feelings when the following situations arise in the group. Circle the appropriate feeling.

1. Dealing with silence	comfortable	uncomfortable
2. Dealing with negative feelings from members	comfortable	uncomfortable
3. Having little structure in the group	comfortable	uncomfortable
4. Dealing with ambiguity of purpose	comfortable	uncomfortable
5. Having to self-disclose your feelings to the group	comfortable	uncomfortable
6. Experiencing high self-disclosure among members	comfortable	uncomfortable
7. Dealing with conflict in the group	comfortable	uncomfortable
8. Having your leadership authority questioned	comfortable	uncomfortable
9. Being evaluated by group members	comfortable	uncomfortable
10. Allowing members to take responsibility for the group	comfortable	uncomfortable

Source: From *An Introduction to Group Work Practice,* 4th ed., by R. W. Toseland and R. F. Rivas, 2001. Boston: Allyn and Bacon. Copyright © 2001 by Pearson Education. Reprinted by permission.

Sometimes scales are suitable to use in studies, and other times they are not. One obvious reason for using a scale is that it may be the only way to validly measure a central concept in a study such as depression or self-esteem. However, standardized scales also have their disadvantages. As was mentioned earlier, a fee may be required for using them. The language used in a scale may not be compatible with the language used by the participants, or the scale itself may not quite measure a concept of interest. Furthermore, scales can be viewed by some research participants as too impersonal, and they can be difficult for some participants to fill out if they are not fully literate or have an inadequate command of the English language.

Likert Scales

Several specialized scales also exist. A few of them will be briefly introduced because they can be used in developing instruments for social work research. Likert scales are the most familiar. Likert scales give primary attention to the response categories used in a measurement instrument. As mentioned earlier in the chapter, a Likert scale is a set of response categories that proceed in order from one extreme to the opposite extreme, such as strongly agree, agree, not sure, disagree, strongly disagree. Note that Likert scales can be used as a set of response categories for a wide variety of statements, including statements that clarify values and attitudes and descriptions of behaviors. With a Likert scale, the respondent is presented with a statement in a questionnaire and asked to choose a response from one of the response categories given (e.g., "strongly agree," "agree," etc.). When identical response categories are used for several items or statements in a questionnaire, they can be scored and analyzed in a uniform manner.

Note that the measure of assertiveness in Table 5.1 (pages 87–88) is an example of a Likert scale. This scale consists of a questionnaire that includes several statements pertinent to assertiveness. Each of these statements uses the same set of response categories ("never or almost never true of me," "rarely true of me," "sometimes true of me," "usually true of me," and "always or almost always true of me") that fit the definition of a Likert scale (namely, proceeding in order from one extreme to the opposite extreme).

The general principal is that Likert items should have five to eight values or categories. There are two reasons for this. The first reason is that forced-response questions are criticized because they "force" a person to select a response. With at least five options available, chances are better that respondents can find one with which they can agree. The second reason is that five to eight options provide enough "spread" of answers to be able to detect small changes in attitudes or opinions.

Likert questions with less than five response categories are also permissible, particularly when there is a good rationale. For example, if a question is asked and there are only two, three, or four possible answers, then there should be only that many response categories. An example is "Are you satisfied with your salary?" The responses could be "yes," "sort of," "no," and "not sure." Or if the question is asking for the correct answer to a topic such as "Is having multiple sex partners an example of unsafe sex?" the only possible responses would be "yes" or "no." A "maybe" category would not make sense to include. Perhaps a "don't know" category could also be included to discourage respondents who don't know from guessing.

There are other considerations for determining which Likert scale categories to use, based on what you know about a particular sample of participants. You don't always need to spread out the scale evenly. For example, if you are surveying a specific group of senior citizens and you ask their age, you would not include any age categories below 60 or 65.

Thurstone and Guttman Scales

While the Likert scale is the most commonly used scale in questionnaires, other scales have special qualities that can be considered as well. Two scales in particular are the Thurstone and Guttman scales (Babbie, 2001). Because each of these scales adds important properties to the development of the items or statements that are used in a scale, they are briefly mentioned here. A **Thurstone scale** involves consulting a group of outside experts. The statements used in a Thurstone scale are selected by consulting a group of experts on a particular concept or topic and asking them to rate several statements in terms of how strongly each of these statements measures this concept. The statements that are consistently rated most strongly by most of the judges are included in the questionnaire, while the weaker statements are discarded. In this scale, the statements are likely to be more accurate or valid in measuring a concept because of the experts' input.

The **Guttman scale** has special qualities as well. This scale recognizes that the statements used in a scale can vary in degree of importance. This scale takes into account the fact that some statements of a scale may be more extreme indicators of a concept than others. Measuring political activism offers an example of this.

Measuring Political Activism

Political activism is an important stance to take in promoting social and economic justice for our clients. The principles of a Guttman scale can be helpful in constructing a scale to measure the degree to which a social worker is politically active. Some of the more *extreme statements* of such a scale might include:

- run for a political office
- become a local precinct captain for a political party
- present a policy position at a legislative hearing or a NASW-sponsored political event
- participate in a protest march or demonstration in Washington, D.C.

Some of the *weaker statements* measuring political activism might include:

- vote in an election
- discuss your political views with another person
- write a letter to a public official
- join PACE (the political action committee for NASW)

As this example suggests, statements like "run for a political office" and "speak at a legislative hearing" are more extreme measures of political activism than "vote in an election" or "discuss your political views with another person" even though all of these statements reflect political activism to some degree. Questionnaires that have such variability in their statements can treat the responses to the more extreme indicators as more important than the responses to the weaker statements. Also, the responses to such a scale might be expected to reflect patterns of interest to a researcher. For example, respondents with favorable responses to the more extreme indicators (e.g., "run for office") could be predicted to have favorable responses to the weaker indicators (e.g., "vote in an election"). However, the converse pattern would not necessarily be expected: those responding favorably to the weaker statements would not necessarily have favorable responses to the more extreme statements.

Diversity Issues and Standardized Scales

Diversity issues are important to consider when deciding whether or not to use a standardized scale. Witkin (2001) suggests some good diversity questions to think over when considering whether to use a standardized scale.

- To what extent are the cultural experiences of people of color, gay men and lesbians, people with disabilities, and other disadvantaged groups considered by the scale?
- What are the negative consequences of having clients complete a scale, if any? Do they get put into a category that stigmatizes them?
- What can this scale tell me about a client beyond what I already know?

A Goal Attainment Scale for Evaluating Social Work Practice

Scales are useful in social work practice as well as research. A **goal attainment scale (GAS)** is one such scale that has widespread use in practice and is a useful resource to consider when measuring clients' progress in reaching their goals. A goal attainment scale is presented in Figure 5.2. The first column of the scale in Figure 5.2 describes five points of measure: "most unfavorable outcome likely," "less-than-expected success," "expected level of success," "more than favorable success," and "most favorable outcome which is unlikely but plausible." Note that each of these points of measure are also assigned a quantitative score of 1 through 5. The second and third columns of the scale are left blank, to be filled in by the social worker and client. The second column is to be used for the first goal, and the third column for the second goal. Each of the cells in these two columns are to reflect a descriptor of the level of anticipated success of the respective goal at a follow-up date.

FIGURE 5.2 **Goal Attainment Scale**

Goal #1:_____

Goal #2:_____

Levels of Predicted Attainment	Scale 1	Scale 2
Most unfavorable outcome thought likely (1)		
Less than expected success (2)		
Expected level of success (3)		
More than expected success (4)		
Most favorable outcome, unlikely but still plausible (5)		

Goal 1

Date and rating at construction: _____

Date and rating at follow-up: _____

Goal 2

Date and rating at construction: _____

Date and rating at follow-up: _____

The steps involved in using a GAS are fairly straightforward.

1. Consider whether or not the GAS is the most appropriate design to use with a particular client. Usually, this design is appropriate if more than one client contact is expected and the client's goals are measurable.
2. Make sure that all of the pertinent issues of informed consent are covered and understood by the client (i.e., discuss with the client the purpose of the selected tool; how it works; how the client, worker, and agency can benefit; the expectations

you have for the client in participating in this evaluation; ways of ensuring confidentiality; options for the client to withdraw, etc.).

3. Help the client identify the problem.
4. Select a mutually agreed-on goal to overcome this problem.
5. Set a realistic date when the goal is to be achieved. Note that the form in Figure 5.2 provides space at the bottom for both the initial date when the GAS is constructed and the follow-up date when the goal is expected to be achieved.
6. Work with the client to construct specific predictions for a series of five levels of reaching the goal (most unfavorable, less than expected, expected level of success, more than expected, and most favorable outcome) by filling in the blank cells. Usually, the easiest way to do this is to first identify the "expected level of success," followed by the outer limits of the "most unfavorable" and "most favorable outcome." Finally the "less than expected" and "more than expected" levels can be identified. Now the GAS is ready to be used. As mentioned earlier, the form in Figure 5.2 can be used and provides space for two goals.
7. Measure the client's actual level of attainment in reaching the goal during the beginning session as a baseline measure.
8. During the final session after the service has been provided, measure the client's actual level of attainment in reaching the goal. Discuss the progress that has been made and how the GAS was helpful in measuring this progress.

Examples of how a few students and their clients have constructed goal attainment scales offer illustrations.

Specific Goal Attainment Scales for Three Different Client Goals

Goal 1: Stop Smoking
1 = no intention of quitting smoking and smokes more
2 = recognizes need to stop smoking but does not
3 = recognizes need to stop and switches to a lighter brand
4 = recognizes need to stop and cuts back 50 percent
5 = fully recognizes need to stop and does

Goal 2: Get Employed
1 = remains unemployed
2 = employed part-time
3 = gainfully employed full-time and making $20,000/year
4 = gainfully employed full-time and making $30,000/year
5 = gainfully employed full-time and making $50,000/year

Goal 3: Improve Parenting Skills
1 = ignores parenting skills altogether
2 = reads a book on parenting skills
3 = learns one new parenting skill
4 = applies one new parenting skill
5 = applies two new parenting skills

The goal attainment scale has many special features that make it a useful evaluation tool, such as:

1. While this is scale is standardized in terms of the five levels of success, it can also be described in an individualized way related to the needs of each client's personal circumstances in the blank cells.
2. The GAS can be used in a participatory way with a client, involving the client in identifying and thinking about personal goals, defining measures of success in meeting the goals, and measuring progress. When the tool is used in this way, it can be a great motivator in getting clients to work on their goals. Also, when discrepancies become evident between the worker and client about the scale or measures of it, they can be brought up for useful discussion.
3. It can be used as both a qualitative and quantitative measure.
4. It measures degrees of progress (five levels) rather than simply two levels (yes or no).
5. Each point on the scale can be multidimensional or include more than one variable (e.g., note how the goal to stop smoking in the above example can include recognizing the need to stop, switching brands, cutting back, and stopping smoking at each of the five levels).
6. It is a good tool for visualizing progress.
7. It can serve as a formal or informal contract with the client.
8. The qualitative aspects of the scale can be standardized and used with a group of clients with similar circumstances.
9. It can be used as an assessment tool as it is being constructed, which can facilitate greater understanding about the goal.
10. It can be used in almost any form that works for the client. For example, the tool could be simplified by reducing it to a three-point scale.

The GAS has limitations to consider and external barriers that sometimes need to be overcome. These limitations and barriers include:

1. It does not work well when only one session of service is provided.
2. It is difficult to use when there is a language barrier.
3. The agency may not encourage goal setting.
4. It is easier to use with some problems than others. For example, some counseling goals may be more complicated and difficult to operationalize into a five-point scale.
5. It does not work as well in a context other than a face-to-face interview.
6. The client may have a cognitive barrier.
7. It may not have meaning to the client or could be an unnecessary distraction.
8. Some clients may be suspicious of how it will be used beyond the worker-client relationship. This issue may need extensive discussion and assurance of confidentiality.

Chapter Reflections

Values and Ethics, Diversity, At-Risk Groups, and Social Justice

Values and ethics are important to consider when it comes to measurement issues. The chapter has emphasized the ethical importance of developing measures that fit the people being studied. Validity, reliability, and triangulation offer important standards to use in doing this. Actually ethics may come into play when a decision is to be made about having either numerical or word forms of measurement. While some concepts can be easily measured using numerical scores, other relevant concepts cannot. Qualitative measures often need to be considered when addressing some of the more complicated and controversial concepts relevant to social work. An important question to ask in a critical consumer role is "Is important meaning manifested in the data lost by forcing qualitative findings into numerical or statistical formats?"

Diversity issues are also important in selecting concepts and measures of them. Several concepts were mentioned in the chapter that reflect some of the diversity evident in our clients' social circumstances. Poverty, substance abuse, and crime were three such concepts discussed. Seccombe (1999) reminds us that we also need to listen to the voices of the research participants as we decide on concepts to study. The concepts that Seccombe investigated were evident in these voices—concepts like the stigma associated with welfare and the difficulties of managing a welfare budget.

Diversity comes into play when developing measures as well. For example, the wording used in measures should be in a form that is readily understood by the participants. Also, when response categories are identified, we should ask if we have considered the characteristics of all of the respondents in a study. For example, to what extent are the cultural experiences of people of color, gay men and lesbians, people with disabilities, and other disadvantaged groups considered when selecting a standardized scale or developing a new one?

The illustration about political activism in this chapter may help you to think more about this concept and its implications for social justice issues. As the illustration suggests, this concept is a challenging one to measure. The political activism of social workers is also a pertinent topic to explore, since participation in the political process is one of the important ways in which social and economic justice can be promoted. Hopefully, some will feel that this is a topic that could be more fully researched in social work circles.

Discussion Questions

1. A researcher decides to measure the variable "marital status" by asking the participants "What is your marital status?" This forced-response question is followed by the following three response categories: married, unmarried, and single. Identify two things that are problematic about this set of response categories. Base your response on whether or not they fulfill the three properties of nominal-level variables.

2. What is the level of measurement of each of the following variables?
   * race
   * social class
   * sexual orientation
   * age
   * number of children in the household
   * distance in miles from home to work
   * a Likert scale (strongly agree, somewhat agree, somewhat disagree, or strongly disagree)
   * numerical grade-point average
   * letter grade for a course

3. How would you define and measure the complex multidimensional concepts listed below? Identify three or four interrelated questions (or statements) that collectively could measure each of these concepts. Note that an answer is already provided for the first concept on stereotypes about welfare recipients.
   * stereotypes about welfare recipients held by people generally—Answer: Measure this variable by asking if the participants strongly agree, somewhat agree, somewhat disagree, or strongly disagree with each of the following statements: (1) Most welfare recipients misuse their money, (2) Most welfare recipients choose not to work, (3) Most welfare recipients neglect their children. (All of these statements are stereotypes.)
   * knowledge about safe sex held by teenagers
   * nutritional meals provided to children by their parents
   * a variety of play opportunities available for children under 12 years of age in a neighborhood
   * children provided adequate protection from physical harm in their homes
   * adequate child care available for preschool children so a parent can go to work
   * adequate transportation available so a parent can go to work

4. Assume that you want to determine if the staff members of your agency are satisfied with their jobs. You have defined job satisfaction to include the following dimensions of satisfaction: work assignments, salary, medical insurance, relationships with coworkers, and quality of supervision. Develop one Likert scale question for each of these dimensions of job satisfaction.

5. Determine the reliability of the assertiveness scale (Table 5.1) using the test-retest method. Do this by taking the test. Then two hours later conceal your first set of answers and take the test again. Afterward, compare your first and second answers for each question to determine if they are identical or no more than one score apart. Select one question in which your scores were quite different. Check to see if the question has ambiguous wording. Rewrite the question so that it is no longer ambiguous to you.

6. Develop a scale of political activism for social workers. Do this by crafting twelve political behaviors that describe various levels of political activism. Craft four behaviors that reflect an extreme level of political activism, four that reflect a moderate level, and four that reflect a weak level. Feel free to use the information in the example (page 107), which identifies some of the behaviors that could be used in a scale that measures political activism. Also develop a set of response categories that can be used (e.g., a Likert scale, a choice of yes-no categories, etc.).

7. Find a measure of anxiety with at least moderate reliability in the *Mental Measurements Yearbook*. What types of evidence are used to evaluate the validity of this measure of anxiety?

8. Weight is a ratio level of measurement. What values of weight could you use if you wanted to measure it as an ordinal variable? What values could you use if you wanted to measure it as a nominal variable?

9. Help a client to identify a goal. (If you are not currently seeing clients, identify a goal for a family member or friend and complete the rest of the exercise.) Next, construct a goal attainment scale with this client that delineates five levels of progress toward achieving a goal. If possible, return to the goal attainment scale during a later follow-up interview to measure and discuss the client's progress.

10. Create or make up a worker-client scenario that could be relevant for using a goal attainment scale. Have two students role-play this scenario in class, both during an initial interview when the GAS is being constructed and during a follow-up interview when progress toward the goal is being measured. In the initial interview, have the social worker concentrate on explaining the goal attainment scale and involving the client in constructing levels of achievement for the follow-up interview. At the follow-up interview, have the social worker concentrate on discussing how both the worker and client rate the client's level of achievement and discuss any differences in opinion about the level that the client has achieved.

R e f e r e n c e s

Babbie, E. (2001). *The practice of social research,* 9th ed. Belmont, CA: Wadsworth/Thomson Learning.

Dennison, S. (2002). Integrating standardized measures into social work practice: An exploratory study of BSW, MSW, and continuing education curricula. *Professional Development: The International Journal of Continuing Social Work Education, 5*(2), 38–45.

Dudley, J. (2001). Gaining more understanding of the friendships of people with a dual diagnosis. Unpublished research report, University of North Carolina, Charlotte.

Federal Bureau of Investigation (FBI). (2002). *Uniform Crime Report.* Retrieved online from http://fbi.gov/ucr/ucr.htm.

Ginsberg, L. (2001). *Social work evaluation: Principles and methods.* Boston: Allyn and Bacon.

Gustavsson, N., & MacEachron, A. (2001). Perspectives on research-related anxiety among BSW students: An exploratory study. *Journal of Baccalaureate Social Work, 7*(1), 111–119.

Mental Measurements Yearbook. (2001). New Brunswick, NJ: Rutgers University Press.

Royse, D., Thyer, B., Padgett, D., & Logan, T. (2001). *Program evaluation: An introduction,* 3rd ed. Belmont CA: Brooks/Cole.

Schutt, R. K. (2001). *Investigating the social world,* 3rd ed. Thousands Oaks, CA: Pine Forge Press.

Seccombe, K. (1999). *So you think I drive a Cadillac: Welfare recipients' perspectives on the system and its reform.* Boston: Allyn and Bacon.

Sundel, S., & Sundel, M. (1980). *Be assertive: A practical guide for human service workers.* Newbury Park, CA: Sage.

Taylor, S., & Bogdan, R. (1984). *Introduction to qualitative research methods: The search for meanings,* 2nd ed. New York: Wiley.

Toseland, R. W., & Rivas, R. F. (2001). *An introduction to group work practice,* 4th ed. Boston: Allyn and Bacon.

Waites, C. (2000). Assessing generalist topic-solving skills: An outcome measure. *Journal of Baccalaureate Social Work, 6*(1), 67–79.

Witkin, S. (2001). The measure of things. *Social Work, 46*(2), 101–104.

chapter 6

Focusing a Research Study

This is the pivotal step in a study. It's the time when researchers have to specify what they want to study. Their personal values, priorities, and biases begin to emerge. And the stage begins to be set for what is to follow.

Let's examine the next step in the research process. This is the time to focus on a specific aspect of the larger research topic, since it is not feasible to conduct a study of the entire research topic. That would be much too much to do. Focusing involves crafting a set of general research questions to answer or a set of hypotheses to explore. Note the word *craft* is used, because this step involves a creative response. Keep in mind that this is step 2 of the research process, as you can see.

Let's begin with an example to point out the challenges of crafting the focus for a research topic. Note in the example how the process of focusing involves choosing to give attention to some issues and possibly putting other issues aside for now.

Steps in the Research Process

1. Understanding the research topic to be studied
2. **Focusing the study**
3. Designing the study
4. Collecting the data
5. Analyzing the data
6. Preparing a report

Focusing a Study about the Impact of Divorce on Children

Let's consider the impact that divorce may have on children as our topic of interest. While at first glance it may seem to be a simple task to identify the research questions we want to ask, this step can become very complicated, very quickly. Often, the most difficult challenge facing the researcher at this point in the process is how to narrow the focus of the research problem. In our example with children of divorce, to simply ask "What is the effect of divorce on children?" would leave us with a rather broad research focus. While it may seem like it is a focused question at first, there are ways to narrow it even more to make it easier to study. For example, a more focused research problem might be to explore the differential effect of divorce on children, based on the degree of animosity and conflict in the parents' relationship. This effort to further focus research questions helps identify particular issues that may affect children's adjustment in divorce. Other important

(continued)

issues affecting their adjustment, such as the influence of nonfamilial social supports, may need to be left for another study (Glenn Stone, Miami University).

As we explore step 2, it is important to introduce and distinguish two general types of studies—exploratory and explanatory. An important issue to consider initially is the intent of the study. Is the study intending to discover new explanations about something? If so, this will be an **exploratory study.** Or is it to find support for explanations that have already been crafted by the researcher? In this case, it will be an **explanatory study.** Following are some of the differences between the two:

Exploratory studies	Explanatory studies
• discover new explanations	• find support for existing explanations
• focus on research questions	• focus on exploring explanations
• use qualitative and quantitative methods	or hypotheses
	• use quantitative methods only

In exploratory studies, we do not know a lot about the research topic. These studies are often largely descriptive in nature. In these cases, step 2 mostly involves asking general questions that will produce more information about the topic. Exploratory studies often have up to five general research questions that provide a focus for what will be studied. In contrast, if the study is intended to be explanatory, step 2 involves crafting very specific explanations that need to be explored in the real world. Explanatory studies may have as many as three or four explanatory statements or hypotheses to be tested.

If the study is exploratory, an additional question to be asked is "How exploratory will it be?" In other words, there are gradations of exploratory studies. Some studies are more openly exploratory than others. One way to answer this question is to ask if the study will use mostly qualitative or quantitative methods. As Figure 6.1 indicates, exploratory studies could use qualitative or quantitative methods. However, qualitative methods offer a wider exploration, because their inquiries are open-ended by design and have more flexibility.

If the study is explanatory, we will likely be testing a set of hypotheses. Explanatory studies, as is evident in Figure 6.1, use only quantitative methods because of their measurement advantages. Explanatory studies, like exploratory ones, also have degrees of explanation that are important to consider. In explana-

 Distinguishing Exploratory and Explanatory Studies

tory studies, researchers could be only testing whether the variables in the hypotheses are associated with one another. Or they could be testing whether or not there are causal relationships among these variables. The answers to these questions will help determine how the research design will be developed.

Exploratory Studies Ask General Research Questions

Let's look more closely at exploratory studies. Exploratory studies are conducted when we do not know very much about the research topic and we want to learn more. We begin by crafting general research questions, which are broad in nature and open-ended. These general research questions are not to be confused with the specific questions that are asked of participants in a study. Each general research question, when delineated further, should generate numerous specific questions that can be asked of the participants. A general research question would likely be too broad if the number of specific questions it generates seems almost endless. Similarly, a general research question would likely be too narrow if it generates only one or two specific questions.

An example of a good general research question is "How important are friendships to people with disabilities?" Notice that the topic reflected in this question is too broad to be answered in a meaningful way by just asking this one question. Most likely, several specific questions need to be explored with research participants to answer this general question. We could begin by finding out some background information about their friendships. We could ask, for example, "Do you have close friends?" "How many friends do you have?" "Are your friends people with similar disabilities?" "Are they other people outside the service delivery system?" "How culturally diverse are your friends?" "What do you do with your friends?" "How often are you in contact with your friends?"

Once we find out some of the background details about these friendships, we could ask several additional questions that would help us determine how important these friendships are. We could ask, for example, "How satisfied are you with your friendships?" "What would you like to do with your friends that you don't currently do?" "Do you want more friends?" "What kinds of new friends do you want?" We could ask these specific questions in interviews, or we could have the research participants respond to a set of questions on a questionnaire.

Research Questions for a Study on Employment Interests

Ellen Csikai and Kathleen Belanger (2002) conducted a study to find out about the employment interests of their students. Their overall research questions were:

- Which fields of practice are social work students most interested in entering?
- Are these interests significantly different for BSW and MSW students?
- Do certain attitudes about a particular field influence students' interest in entering that field?

Note that each of Csikai and Belanger's research questions could be further delineated into several specific questions to be asked of research participants. For example, the last question about the influence of "certain attitudes" of students could be further delineated into several specific types of attitudes.

Let's consider how general research questions are chosen. First, anyone wanting to craft research questions related to a particular topic of interest needs to be familiar with the topic and the pertinent literature that is available. It is important to complete a literature search before embarking on this step. Also, the "crafter" can benefit from having conversations with some of the people directly experiencing the problem. This can occur in a small pilot research study on the topic, in informal conversations with individuals, or in a few focus group sessions.

Several other factors are likely to influence the crafting of general research questions. One factor is the researcher's motivations for choosing a topic for a study. For example, someone who decides to investigate the social supports of older people with dementia may be an employee or volunteer in older adult services who has observed a relative absence of social supports for their clients. Alternatively, they may have a relative or close friend who has dementia. Or they may have a special interest in the social supports for clients generally, which is a popular social work research topic.

In summary, the best research questions to ask have several notable characteristics. They identify an important topic to study. They focus on only a few specific issues or aspects of a larger research topic. Each research question generates several specific questions to be asked of research participants. Previous studies on the topic have been taken into account, and some of the people who are personally affected by the problem have been consulted. Finally, these questions are well written and reflect clarity and succinctness.

Examples of General Research Questions

A group of scholars at the National Conference on Family Relations recommend several general research questions on the topic of welfare reform (National Council on Family Relations, 2002). Each of these questions can be the focus for a different study. These research questions include:

1. What aspects of welfare reform have led to improvements in the well-being of parents and their children?
2. Have welfare reform promarriage policies been effective?
3. What dimensions of well-being have been affected by welfare reform (e.g., physical and mental health, quality of family relations, achievement and educational attainment)?
4. How do economic cycles like recession affect the effectiveness of welfare reform?

Each of these four research questions focuses on specific aspects of welfare reform, not the entire topic. While these questions are still general in nature, each of them provides enough of a focus for a study to be feasible. Note also that all of these questions are interested in investigating the effectiveness of welfare reform interventions. In other words, all of them are concerned about program effectiveness, an important topic of social work research.

Exploratory studies can use either quantitative or qualitative methods, as discussed earlier. Between the two, qualitative methods provide more of an open exploration than quantitative methods. First, let's look at how these studies can use quantitative methods. Studies that ask specific questions with forced-response answers are quantitative. For example, a study may use a questionnaire with a list of true/false statements to explore how much the participants in a training program understood the material that was taught. This set of questions would be quantitative, because the responses would be standardized (asked the same way for everyone) and the responses could easily be converted to numbers. For example, the results of a question that uses a set of true and false response categories could easily be converted into numbers for computer entry and analysis (true = 1 and false = 2).

Exploratory studies could also use qualitative methods. In this instance, the specific questions that would be asked would be open-ended. In the earlier example of a study on the friendships of people with disabilities, the specific questions could include "What do you like about your best friend?" and "What do you dislike?" In this case, the responses could be in the form of a simple word or phrase or even several sentences of explanation, all of which are qualitative.

Explanatory Studies Test Hypotheses

Research studies could also be explanatory in nature. "Explanatory" means that these studies begin with a hypothetical explanation or hypothesis that is to be tested in the real world. As we learned in Chapters 1 and 2, a hypothesis is a statement that describes the relationship between two or more variables in the real world. Measurements are created for each variable to test the hypothesis. Then data are collected in the real world using these measurements to find support for the hypothesis or to cast doubt on it. Explanatory studies use quantitative methods (see Chapter 2).

Hypotheses are not used exclusively in research studies. Hypothesizing is something that people sometimes do in their personal lives without even thinking about it. In addition, social workers sometimes hypothesize as they plan the interventions they will use in helping their clients. Even though they may seldom use the word *hypothesizing*, social workers often hypothesize about how they plan to help a client. For example, a social worker might say "If I intervene by doing X, my client will respond by doing Y."

Examples of Hypothesizing

Hypothesizing in our personal lives

1. The more often I floss my teeth, the fewer cavities I will have.
2. The more hours that I study each week throughout the semester, the fewer all-nighters I will have in preparing for the final exam.
3. If I carry bottled water with me during the day, I will be less likely to become dehydrated than if I don't carry bottled water.

Hypothesizing in social work practice

1. The more attentive I am to what my client is saying, the more information my client will share.
2. The more options I offer my clients for solving their problems, the greater the likelihood that they will make decisions about what to do.
3. If I call each of the board members to remind them about the next board meeting, attendance will be higher than if I don't.

Like research questions, hypotheses should be concise and clearly stated. They should also be based on the findings from prior studies and professional experiences. For example, we could hypothesize that "Younger children in the public schools are more likely to have interracial friends than older children." This explanation could be based on findings of previous studies or personal experiences that suggest that race becomes more important to a child's identity as the child grows older.

Hypotheses must also make common sense. Examples of hypotheses that don't seem to make much sense are "People with hairy ears are more likely to have heart attacks" and "People who do not regularly brush their teeth will have hearing loss later in their life." Of course, we know that having hairy ears has nothing to do with the functioning of the heart; neither does brushing teeth affect hearing.

Constructing Hypotheses

Let's look at the specific construction of a hypothesis. A hypothesis is a hypothetical explanation describing the relationship between two variables. Hypotheses are proposed so that they can be verified or refuted in a study. An example of a hypothesis would be "Women are more likely to be affiliated with the Democratic Party than men." This hypothesis could also be stated conversely as "Men are more likely to be affiliated with the Republican Party than women." The two variables are gender (values: women or men) and political party affiliation (values: Democrat or Republican). The hypothesis is suggesting that there is a special relationship between the two variables, gender and political party affiliation.

Essentially, a hypothesis proposes that an association exists between the two variables. Let's refer to these variables as variable 1 and variable 2. What this means is that the different values of variable 1 are associated in some way with the different values of variable 2. Put another way, research participants who have a particular value of variable 1 are also likely to have a particular value of variable 2. In the above example, we see that women (a value of gender) are more likely to be Democrats (a value of political party).

In some cases, the relationship between the two variables in a hypothesis has another property: it can be a positive or negative relationship. This special property exists only when both variables in the hypothesis are at the ordinal or interval/ratio levels of measurement. A *positive relationship* exists when the values of both variables increase or decrease together. An example of such a hypothesis would be "The more years you work, the higher your salary becomes." In this case, as the number of years of a person's work increases, so does the person's salary. Likewise, as the number of years of work decreases, so does the salary. A positive relationship in a hypothesis is also sometimes referred to as a *direct relationship*.

If a hypothesis has a *negative relationship,* the values of one variable increase while the values of the other variable decrease, and vice versa. A negative relationship is also sometimes referred to as an *inverse relationship*. An example of a hypothesis with a negative or inverse relationship would be "The higher the educational level of a person, the fewer children he or she is likely to have." As you can see in this explanation, as either variable increases, the other variable is expected to decrease. When educational level increases, the number of offspring decreases; conversely, when educational level decreases, the number of offspring increases.

Types of Variables

As was stated earlier, hypotheses contain two variables. In some cases, these hypotheses are claiming that a causal relationship exists. This relationship could also be described as the "cause" and the "effect." If a hypothesis is stated as a causal relationship, the variables are referred to as independent and dependent variables, respectively. The **independent variable** is presumed to be the cause and is referred to as a causal variable. It is usually the variable of interest being introduced in the study, and it often is a practice or program intervention in social work research. As it changes, it is presumed to cause a change in the dependent variable. The independent variable is referred to as a *presumed* cause because this cause has not yet been verified in the real world.

A **dependent variable** is the effect variable, or the variable that is changed by the independent variable. In social work circles, this variable is also sometimes referred to as the client outcome variable. While the independent variable is the variable being introduced, the dependent variable is the variable being measured to determine if it changes.

Example of a Study That Explores Hypotheses

Hodge (2003) conducted a study to explore whether the values of social workers and their clients are different. He tested two hypotheses:

1. MSW social workers affirm value positions to the left of (more liberal than) working-class and middle-class clients.

(continued)

2. BSW social workers affirm value positions in between those of MSW social workers and clients.

Both hypotheses were supported by his study.

While independent and dependent variables are the focus of a hypothesis, other variables are also likely to have an influence on the dependent variable. If they are not identified in the hypothesis, they are referred to as extraneous variables. **Extraneous variables** are variables that have not been considered in the hypothesis. These variables are often viewed as confounding or interfering with the relationship between an independent and dependent variable. These variables may also be overlooked because the researcher may not be aware of them. They may appear superfluous or unimportant during the initial construction of a hypothesis but on further examination be suspected of contributing some influence over the dependent variable. Extraneous variables are also sometimes referred to as *control variables*.

A Hypothesis Exploring a Link between Maltreatment and Pregnancy

Smith (1996) attempted to find out if there is a link between maltreatment during childhood and teenage pregnancy. Maltreatment was defined as sexual, emotional, and physical abuse and neglect. She had to take into account several *control variables,* such as participants' income level, race, and family structure, as well as several *indirect* or *mediating variables* that maltreatment may be associated with, such as participants' school performance, lack of close relationships with conventional friends, lack of supportive adults, and self-esteem. In addition, the study was longitudinal to avoid retrospective data gathering about childhood maltreatment that could introduce error. Controlling for all of these variables, maltreatment was found to be a significant predictor of teenage pregnancy. Some of the mediating variables were also associated with maltreatment and teenage pregnancy.

Sometimes extraneous variables help in clarifying the association between an independent and dependent variable, particularly when this association does not seem to be totally evident or logical. Let's revisit, for example, our earlier hypothesis that gender is associated with political party affiliation. This seems like an overly simplistic explanation for choosing a political party. It does not seem logical that gender would be the sole or even primary basis for selecting a political party. This explanation could be further clarified by investigating the influence of other extraneous variables as well, such as income level, race, or age. As Figure 6.2 reveals, it may be easier to understand how gender, in combination with some of these other variables, could influence choice of political party. For example, it makes sense that women of color and women who are poor would prefer the Democratic Party, because this party strongly supports social programs these women need (e.g., job training, child care, and adequate housing).

FIGURE 6.2   **An Example of Multiple Variables of Influence**

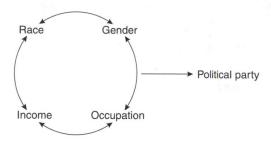

Some extraneous variables exist or are evident prior to the introduction of the independent variable and may have a prior influence over both the independent and dependent variables. For example, let's hypothesize that divorcing couples who experience considerable unresolved conflict are less likely than couples without such conflict to share legal custody of their children. A study actually found that the greater the conflict between divorcing couples, the less likely the parents ended up with shared custody (Dudley, 1991). But we may not want to stop our exploration here. We may want to know what might have caused these conflicts. Suppose we find out in the literature that the type of divorce proceedings two parents choose (e.g., litigation in court, adversarial attorneys out of court, or divorce mediation) influences the degree to which these parents experience conflict once they obtain a divorce. If that is so, we may want to gather data on the type of divorce proceedings chosen that would be a prior variable. Going back in time farther, we may even want to consider the couple's communication patterns in their marriage prior to their marital separation as another important variable to consider.

Let's also consider the influence of prior extraneous variables when conducting studies in social work settings. A social worker introduces a clinical intervention (the IV, or independent variable) with a client who is abusing other family members. After several sessions, the client discontinues abusing family members. In this instance, while the clinical intervention may have had a major influence in reducing the abuse, other prior factors, such as the client's communication skills or level of self-esteem, may have had some influence as well. Figure 6.3 diagrams this possibility. This discovery suggests that this clinical intervention may only help clients with good communication skills or high self-esteem and not clients with problems in these areas.

Extraneous variables are also likely to have a current influence, or occur during the time that an intervention (IV) is being implemented. These variables could be associated with the independent variable but would not have to be. For example, let's say that a client with a substance abuse problem participates in family therapy to rebuild his estranged relationships with other family members. After several family therapy sessions, this client demonstrates improved communication

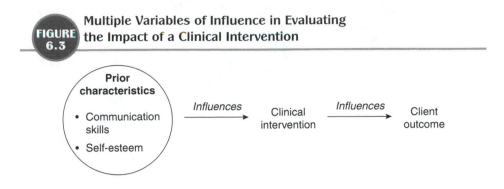

FIGURE 6.3 Multiple Variables of Influence in Evaluating the Impact of a Clinical Intervention

with some family members. Meanwhile, while the family therapy is being offered, the family social worker encourages this client to attend an Alcoholics Anonymous (AA) self-help group, which he attends weekly. In this instance, while the family therapy, which is the independent variable, may be responsible for the improved communication, the AA group, which was not identified in the hypothesis, could also have an influence.

You may wonder what can be done about extraneous variables. Once these extraneous variables are identified, they can be controlled so that they will not have any influence on the variables in a hypothesis. Specific sampling strategies, statistical tests, and experimental designs, for example, can be introduced to control the influence of these variables. These strategies will be discussed in Chapter 11. It is also possible that a variable previously considered extraneous can become an important variable to investigate in a follow-up investigation. In this case, an extraneous variable could become the independent variable in a later study. Let's look at this in our earlier example involving the abusive client receiving family therapy. The social worker may decide not to offer family therapy; instead, the client could be referred to an AA group to explore whether AA alone can help him improve his communication with his family. In this case, the AA group, which had been the extraneous variable, becomes the independent variable.

Three Conditions of Causal Relationships

In review, hypotheses are proposed explanations for something the researcher attempts to find support for in the real world. The mechanics of constructing a hypothesis have been described, and the different types of variables (independent, dependent, extraneous) involved in an explanation have been identified. Let's look more closely at the nature of the relationship between the two variables in a hypothesis. For example, if the social worker's intervention is introduced as an independent variable and the extent of progress made by the client is the dependent variable, how can we determine if the intervention is responsible for the client's progress? Stated another way, is there a causal relationship between the intervention and the client's functioning? If the relationship is a causal one, we have made a very important discovery.

The independent variable is the presumed causal variable, but we cannot be sure that it actually causes a change in the dependent variable unless it meets certain conditions. A causal relationship must meet three necessary conditions (Marlow, 2001).

1. *The independent variable must precede the dependent variable in time.* This condition makes common sense. If the independent variable is introduced after the dependent variable changes, it cannot be considered an explanation for why the dependent variable changed. Let's consider this point in an example in which our independent variable is a group service. This service will be introduced to ten clients with substance abuse problems who have been on a waiting list for approximately three months. Before beginning the group service, we determine that these ten clients have reduced their substance abuse problems on average by about one-half since being on the agency's waiting list. What could have caused this improvement? By no means can we claim that the group service had anything to do with this improvement, because it has not yet been introduced. We would have to look for other factors that may have occurred during this three-month waiting period to explain their improvement.

2. *The independent variable must have a statistically significant association with the dependent variable.* A statistically significant association means we are fairly confident that the relationship actually exists in the real world. In this case, there is an association in which the values of one variable are associated with the values of the other. A statistical test would be used to determine if a statistically significant association exists. Statistical significance is explained more fully in Chapter 14.

The second condition can be illustrated in our example of a group service for substance abuse clients. Let's modify our earlier example and say that the group service was offered before, rather than after, the clients showed improvement. In this case, the first condition is now met, because the independent variable preceded the change in the dependent variable in time. In order for the second condition to be met, a statistical test would have to reveal a statistically significant association between these two variables.

3. *The change that occurs in the dependent variable must be due to the independent variable and not to any extraneous variable.* Ideally, an experimental design involving both an experimental and control group would be used to determine if the group service alone was responsible for improvement in these clients' substance use. However, another approach would be to use statistical techniques to control all of the extraneous variables that could be identified. Experimental and quasi-experimental designs will be discussed in Chapter 11, and statistical strategies will be discussed in Chapter 14.

In our example, let's assume that the ten substance abuse clients have reduced their use of substances by one-half during the time that the group service is offered. (Condition 1 is met.) Also, a statistically significant association is found between the group service and the clients' reduction in substance use. (Condition 2 is met.)

The third condition would be to prove that no other factors besides the group service were responsible for this reduction.

To address condition 3, extraneous variables would need to be removed from having any influence. Extraneous variables could include numerous things, such as other professional services provided, changes in the clients' family circumstances, a dramatic religious experience, personal growth unrelated to the group, involvement in a self-help group like Alcoholics Anonymous, and so on. An experimental design would be needed to determine whether or not the group service was responsible for the reduction in substance use.

The following list shows how these three conditions are met. In this list, X symbolizes the group service, O represents various measures of the group members' substance use, O_1 is a measure of the group members' substance use prior to the group service, and O_2 is a measure of their substance use after the group service.

- *Condition 1:* X precedes O_2 in time. (The group service precedes in time a measure of the client outcome variable that reveals a reduction in substance use.)
- *Condition 2:* After X is introduced, O_2 reveals a statistically significant improvement over O_1. (After group service is provided, the reduction in substance use is found to be statistically significantly better than it was prior to the group service.)
- *Condition 3:* X is found to be a cause in the change from O_1 to O_2. (The group service is found to be a causal factor in reducing the clients' substance use, because other variables are controlled.)

Practical Uses of Hypotheses

Phenomena that are important to social work can only partially be understood by examining the relationship between two variables at a time. A systems framework, which is emphasized in many social work courses, provides a useful context for understanding the relationships between variables. A system can be considered a collection of variables that are interrelated and bound together by a common purpose. As Figure 6.4 illustrates, the real world is more likely to look like world A than world B.

We begin an investigation with a two-variable hypotheses, because it simplifies our inquiry. However, to understand what is going on in the real world, we often need to consider the interrelatedness of several variables. Testing a hypothesis with two variables at a time provides, at best, a partial investigation. In actuality, several interrelated hypotheses often need to be investigated to develop a fuller explanation with a larger systems context. As was pointed out in Chapter 1, a meaningful theory is a collection of interrelated hypotheses on one overall topic.

Hypothesis construction in sociological research often explores independent variables, which can be measures of social problems such as poverty, racism, segregated schools, sexism, and crime. The negative effects of these social problem are selected as dependent variables. For example, sociologists may hypothesize that

A System Framework for Viewing the World

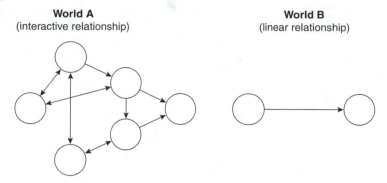

people living in poverty are likely to have more health problems than those not living in poverty. Or they could hypothesize that segregated schools are more likely to offer an educational experience that is inferior to integrated schools.

Hypothesizing to Evaluate Social Work Practice

Hypothesis construction can also be very useful in social work practice. Social workers sometimes hypothesize that a specific intervention (e.g., a special interviewing technique, a new program, policy change, etc.) will lead to a desired outcome for clients. (You may want to refer back to some examples of hypothesizing in social work practice in the example on page 120.) A social work intervention is a good example of an independent variable, because it is within the social worker's control. Introducing an intervention is also a good choice for an independent variable, because it has the potential of creating positive changes in a client's life. Isn't it gratifying to be able to introduce something into our clients' lives that can improve their circumstances?

Example of a Hypothesis-Driven Study Using a Social Work Intervention

Deana Morrow (1996) investigated the effects of a ten-week educational experiential group intervention on thirteen adult lesbians. The group intervention was referred to as the "Coming Out Issues Group," and it addressed issues pertinent to lesbians, such as lesbian identity development, homophobia and heterosexism, religious concerns, career concerns, family issues, sexism and racism, and assertiveness skills development. The impact of this group intervention was found to be associated with modest gains in ego development and lesbian identity development and major gains in disclosure and empowerment.

Generating Hypotheses

So far we have discussed the importance of testing hypotheses in explanatory studies. Hypotheses can also be generated within exploratory studies. In exploratory studies, the researcher conducts a holistic investigation that takes into account many different issues related to a topic. Within the context of such an investigation, potential hypotheses can be discovered from the relatively few people that are studied. Such hypotheses can then be tested in follow-up studies that are more explanatory.

For example, let's say we are attempting to understand why some people with disabilities are successful in developing friendships and others are not. We decide to interview a number of people with disabilities, and we ask several open-ended questions to find out more about their experiences with friends. In the course of these interviews, we discover that about half of them developed close friendships with nondisabled people, and most of the disabled people with these friendships belonged to a local community center or YMCA/YWCA in their neighborhood. We can generate a new hypothesis: People with disabilities can develop friendships with nondisabled people by joining various neighborhood groups like the YMCA/YWCA. We can attempt to confirm this new hypothesis by conducting a follow-up study suggesting that whether or not they have membership in such neighborhood groups becomes the independent variable and new outside friendships is the hoped-for outcome or consequence.

In brief, hypotheses provide a revolving link between exploratory and explanatory studies. The best hypotheses to be tested may be those that are generated from the findings of exploratory studies. Yet, hypotheses that are tested in explanatory studies may not be confirmed from the data, leading the researcher back to exploratory investigations as illustrated in Figure 6.5.

Focusing a Research Study and the Consumer Role

Let's look briefly at what a critical consumer needs to consider about step 2, focusing a research study, while reading a research report. The emphasis of this chapter so far is more pertinent to the producer than the consumer role. As you read a research study, it will be important to pay close attention to how the author focuses the study. After all, the research questions or hypotheses that are selected are pivotal to understanding the rest of the study.

Once the research topic is described in the introductory section of a research report, a statement about the focus comes next. Usually the focus (research questions or hypotheses) is located immediately prior to the section of a study that describes the research design. That section is easy to find, because it is introduced by such subheadings as "Research Design," "Method," or "Methodology."

Interrelatedness of Exploratory and Explanatory Studies

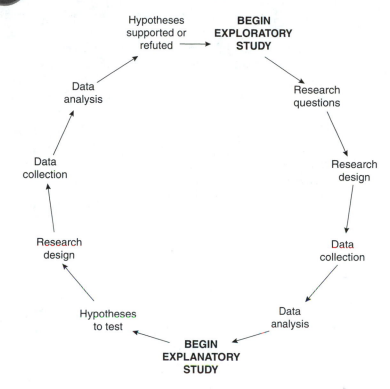

As a consumer, you will have several questions and concerns about step 2, including the following:

1. Can you identify the research questions or the hypotheses that were explored in the study? Usually, a study focuses on either research questions or hypotheses, but occasionally a study will include both.
2. If research questions are identified, what seem to be the most important concepts and variables in the study? These are usually identified in the research questions.
3. If hypotheses are being explored, can you identify the independent and dependent variables of each hypothesis? Also, are any extraneous variables identified, and if so, are they controlled by the researcher? In addition, can you detect any important extraneous variables that are not identified?
4. Are the research questions or hypotheses stated clearly? Anticipate the possibility that they are unclear or confusing. For example, often researchers do

not describe the general research questions in a question format. Instead, they write them as a purpose of the study. While this can be confusing, it can be fairly easy for you to convert a purpose statement into a question format.

5. Do you detect any biases in how the research questions or hypotheses are described? The researchers may leave out an important group or an important concern of some groups. If so, can you identify the groups or issues that are left out? Diversity issues are most important to consider during this step of the study, since concerns important to some groups can be overlooked. These omissions could be biases, intentional or inadvertent, of the researcher.

6. Is this research focus relevant to social workers? How is it relevant? Is it relevant to your interests? How can these research questions or hypotheses help you as a social worker? If the focus does not have much relevance to your work, you may want to discontinue reading this study and move on to one that is more relevant and useful to you.

C h a p t e r   R e f l e c t i o n s

Values and Ethics, Diversity, At-Risk Groups, and Social Justice

Focusing a study has relevance to all four mandates. Selecting the most important variables can be an ethical matter as well as one of relevance to diversity issues. Is the focus of the study relevant to social work? Does it address the people most affected by the problem? For example, are the groups at greatest risk included? Does the focus of the study truly help our clients and promote their justice in some way?

Hypothesis construction and the three conditions for claiming causality are introduced and provide a helpful framework for evaluating social work practice. Evaluating our practice is a topic of extreme importance, partially because it is an ethical obligation evident in the NASW Code of Ethics. Another ethical issue evident in this step of the research process is the importance of considering and possibly consulting our clients as we craft a focus. They may be able to help us focus on what is most relevant to their needs. If the focus of a study is not relevant to them, then an important question to ask is why they should even participate.

Diverse and at-risk groups continue to be mentioned in illustrations in this chapter to highlight their importance to social work. People with disabilities, pregnant teenagers who have been abused in childhood, and people with alcoholism are among the groups that are highlighted. Focusing research on such groups and involving them in the development of a study as consultants can further social justice issues.

Discussion Questions

1. Examine the two general research questions described below. What is problematic about each of these research questions? Are they too focused? Not focused enough? Explain your answers.
   - What are the problems facing teenagers in residential care?
   - Why do intravenous drug users share the same needles when injecting drugs?

2. Craft two general research questions you could explore on a topic of importance to you. Next, write two hypotheses that could be tested on the same topic.

3. Develop a hypothesis that identifies an intervention for the independent variable and a client outcome for the dependent variable. Next, develop another hypothesis in which the dependent variable in the previous hypothesis becomes the independent variable for the new hypothesis.

4. What are the independent and dependent variables in the four hypotheses listed below? Decide whether the relationships in each hypothesis are positive, negative, or have no direction.
   - The more hours students take to prepare for an exam, the higher their exam grades are likely to be.
   - Women are likely to have more close friends than men.
   - If the general purpose of a group session is stated at the beginning of the session, more people will participate in the discussion.
   - The more knowledge social workers have about AIDS, the more comfortable they are in helping people with AIDS.

References

Csikai, E., & Belanger, K. (2002). Fields of social work practice: Social work students' attitudes and interests. *Journal of Baccalaureate Social Work, 8*(1), 33–49.

Dudley, J. (1991). The consequences of divorce proceedings for divorced fathers. In C. Everett (Ed.), *The consequences of divorce: Economic and custodial impact on children and adults.* New York: Haworth Press.

Hodge, D. (2003). Value differences between social workers and members of the working and middle classes. *Social Work, 48*(1), 107–119.

Marlow, C. (2001). *Research methods for generalist social work.* 3rd ed. Stamford, CT: Thomson Learning.

Morrow, D. (1996). Coming-out issues for adult lesbians: A group intervention. *Social Work, 41*(6), 647–656.

National Council on Family Relations (NCFR). (2002). *NCFR 64th annual conference program.* Minneapolis: Author.

Smith, C. (1996). The link between childhood maltreatment and teenage pregnancy. *Social Work Research, 20*(3), 131–141.

chapter 7

A research design has similarities to the plan of intervention worked out between the social worker and client. Both are plans for action. The research plan describes the what, how, when, and why of data collection, while the social worker's plan describes the what, how, when, and why for helping clients solve their problems.

Designing the Study

Once researchers have an understanding of the research topic and have crafted a few research questions or hypotheses as their focus, they are ready to plan their research design. A research design is a plan that describes how the research will be conducted. The research design is in some ways similar to the intervention plan that is worked out between the social worker and the client. You may want to refer to Table 1.1 to review the steps in social work practice and how they are similar to the research steps.

As you can see in the following listing, the research design involves three major steps, which are introduced in this chapter. These involve deciding who will be studied, how the data will be collected, and whether causal relationships will be explored.

> **Steps in the Research Process**
>
> 1. Understanding the research topic to be studied
> 2. Focusing the study
> 3. **Designing the study**
>   a. Selecting the participants
>   b. Selecting a data collection approach and measuring concepts
>   c. Exploring causal relationships
> 4. Collecting the data
> 5. Analyzing the data
> 6. Preparing a report

Review of Prior Steps

Let's review what we have covered so far that will have a direct influence on how the study will be designed. As discussed in Chapter 4, we begin a research study by learning as much as we can about the research topic or problem that has been selected. During this first step, we are likely to be thinking about a group of people who are faced with this problem. For example, we may be interested in a group of children in a low-income neighborhood who are challenged with underachievement. Or we could be concerned about whether or not a group of pregnant mothers are satisfied with the prenatal services they are receiving from a local health care agency.

As discussed in Chapter 6, the next step is to focus the study on something of interest that is feasible to study. We do this by crafting a set of research questions, or hypotheses. We focus the study because we cannot examine the entire research topic all at once. Let's say, for example, we decide to craft some general research questions we want to explore about the satisfaction of young mothers with their health care services. We may decide on three general research questions: (1) How satisfied are these mothers with the services that they are receiving from the physicians, nurses, and social workers? (2) What is most satisfying to them? (3) What is least satisfying? Or we may test a hypothesis such as "The more satisfied these mothers are with their social work services, the more likely they are to use the services provided by the physicians and nurses." Note how this hypothesis goes a little further than the research questions in that it offers a possible connection between satisfaction with social work services and utilization of other health care services. Now we are ready to tackle the research design.

Considering Secondary Research

A good question to begin with is to ask whether new data are needed. They may not be needed if data already exist to answer the research questions. **Secondary research** is research that analyzes data already collected in another study. The important point to remember is that secondary research should not be overlooked if relevant data are already available. An example of a study using secondary data from another study is summarized here.

Example of a Study Using Secondary Analysis

John O'Donnell (1999) conducted a secondary analysis of data from an earlier federally funded research and demonstration project on casework practice in kinship foster care. Kinship foster care refers to the placement of children in the home of a relative approved by the agency as a foster parent. The data were collected in this prior study from caseworkers in two private child welfare agencies. O'Donnell reported on a subset of the original data set that focused on the involvement of African American fathers. His findings documented the lack of father involvement in the caseworkers' assessment and planning of foster care services for the children. While useful secondary data were available for several of these fathers, the data emphasized their problems, not their strengths. Further, the data did not explore some issues of importance to O'Donnell, such as why more fathers of children in paternal kinship homes participated in casework services than fathers of children in maternal kinship homes.

Research firms and academic groups that have conducted large-scale studies may offer their data to interested people without a charge or for a reasonable fee. Such firms can offer extensive data on large representative samples that can be generalized to an even larger population. Reports on some of these large-scale studies can also be found on the Internet. A few good examples of research organizations that have Websites reporting on large-scale studies are:

- Child Trends—a nonprofit, nonpartisan research organization dedicated to improving the lives of children by conducting research and providing science-based information to improve the decisions, programs, and policies that affect children (www.childtrends.org)
- The National Center for Policy Research (CPR) for Women and Families—a nonprofit, nonpartisan organization that promotes the health and well-being of women and families by gathering and analyzing information and translating that information into clearly presented facts and policy implications that are made widely available to the public, the media, and policy makers (www.cpr4womenandfamilies.org)
- The Institute for the Advancement of Social Work Research—a Washington, D.C.–based nonprofit organization that advocates for research to strengthen the social work profession's capacity to address complex social needs and to contribute to improved prevention and treatment interventions, services, and policies (www.iaswresearch.org)
- The National Opinion Research Center (NORC) at the University of Chicago—conducts national studies in an interdisciplinary framework across several substantive areas (www.norc.uchicago.edu)
- The National Center on Addictions and Substance Abuse at Columbia University—reports on surveys of teenagers and family members about cigarette, alcohol, and drug attitudes and use (www.casacolumbia.org)
- The National Archive of Criminal Justice Data at the University of Michigan—preserves and distributes computerized crime and justice data from federal and state agencies (www.icpsr.umich.edu/NACJD/).
- The National Survey of American Families at the Urban Institute—provides a comprehensive look at the well-being of children and nonelderly adults and reveals differences among the thirteen states studied in depth. The survey provides quantitative measures of child, adult, and family well-being in America, with an emphasis on persons in low-income families (www.urban.org/Content/Research/NewFederalism/NSAF/Overview/NSAFOverview.htm)

Also, don't forget to consider numerous types of existing data from state and local health and social service agencies. These data come in various forms, such as client case records and summaries, client and staff logs, process recordings, annual reports, and minutes of staff meetings, to name a few. Pertinent data could also be available from studies conducted by a communitywide organization like the United Way, an interagency council, or an ad hoc group representing several agencies that meets together to collaborate on some task.

It is important to note that existing data, if they are available, usually have several limitations. For example, the questions a previous study investigated may not be the same questions you want to ask. Another limitation is that the data may not be accessible because of confidentiality issues. Or, the data may be too costly to purchase. Also, existing data that are available in social agencies may not be uniform or complete. For example, client records may not all include the same kinds of information, or such records may be inaccurate or incomplete in some instances. On the other hand, the costs and flaws of secondary data should be weighed against the realistic costs and likely flaws of new data. New data are costly to collect, and they too will suffer from flaws and other problems. Two examples of existing community data sets available to be analyzed by others are described here.

Examples of Two Community Studies Offering the Option of Secondary Research

1. *Community needs survey*
   The United Way and the county government of one city conduct a community needs survey every three years. They survey a representative sample of county households by phone. The survey gathers data on counseling needs, health care concerns, employment needs, the needs of children and the elderly, transportation needs, and many other areas. This study can be found on this Website: 164.109. 58.120/ Departments/ office+of+planning+and+evaluation/home.asp.

2. *Public opinion survey*
   An urban institute of a university conducts a public opinion survey of 850 randomly selected residents of a county on an annual basis. These surveys are conducted by phone on topics such as health care, education, public safety, quality of life, and so on. Other organizations are encouraged to add their own questions to the survey for a fee (e.g., $450 for a closed-ended question and $550 for an open-ended question). This urban institute also provides these organizations with analysis and interpretations of the results, along with the demographic characteristics of the respondents. More information on this study can be found on this Website: www.uncc.edu/urbinst/2002%20Annual%20Survey.pdf.

Is the Study Exploratory or Explanatory?

If existing data are unavailable to address the research questions, then data will need to be collected. A good place to begin in developing a research design is to ask "Will the study be exploratory or explanatory?" Once this question is answered, we can explore some of the components of a design, such as selecting the data collection approach and deciding which group will be the data source. Exploratory and explanatory studies were introduced in Chapter 6, and you may want to review that material.

There are numerous research designs that can be considered by the researcher. The most important point is to create the design that best fits the research questions or hypotheses crafted by the researcher. The way to begin thinking about a research design is to consider if it is an exploratory or explanatory design. Let's consider how the differences between these two types of studies are important when developing the research design.

Exploratory Research Designs

Generally, exploratory research designs are simpler than explanatory ones. Typically, these designs are *cross-sectional,* which means that the data are collected at only one point in time from research participants. Exploratory studies usually involve a relatively small sample of research participants. These studies are not usually concerned with whether or not the sample is representative of a larger population. Actually, the population may be difficult to identify and define (e.g., people with AIDS, gay or lesbian teenagers, Muslims in a city). Further, the data collection approach is likely to use a flexible instrument with qualitative properties. Data collection approaches used in exploratory designs are likely to be one of the following methods:

* semi- or unstructured interview
* unstructured questionnaire
* unstructured observation
* participant observation
* use of existing documents

Explanatory Research Designs

Explanatory designs, in contrast, have different features. Sometimes data are collected at only one point in time. These studies are referred to as **cross-sectional studies.** More often, explanatory studies collect data from research participants at two or more points in time. Such studies are referred to as **longitudinal studies.** Longitudinal designs are particularly important to use when investigating causal relationships between two variables or trends in social indicators from one time period to another. The U.S. census is an example of a longitudinal study that is conducted of the entire U.S. population every ten years, in part to document changes and trends in the population.

Explanatory designs also have larger samples than exploratory studies. In addition, their samples are likely to be representative of a larger population of interest, because the researcher intends to generalize the findings to people beyond the study. The measurement instruments used in explanatory studies are typically quantitative and meet minimal standards of validity and reliability. Data collection approaches used in explanatory designs include all of the following methods:

* structured interview
* structured questionnaire
* structured observation
* use of existing documents

Explanatory designs sometimes use experimental or quasi-experimental designs. Chapter 11 is devoted to these designs because of their importance in exploring causality.

A summary of what has been covered so far on research designs follows:

1. If the design is exploratory → How exploratory will it be? → Will it use qualitative or quantitative methods?
2. If the design is explanatory → Will it be cross-sectional or longitudinal → Is it investigating an association between variables or causality?

Three Key Questions

Once it has been determined whether the study will be exploratory or explanatory, three key questions need to be asked about the research design:

1. Who will be the source of the data?
2. How will the data be collected?
3. How will the important concepts be defined, measured, and analyzed?

These three questions are interrelated. The answers to each depends on how the other questions are answered, as described in Figure 7.1.

An Illustration of an Exploratory Study

A case example illustrates the importance of answering these three interrelated questions concurrently in the design of a study. Let's assume you are employed in an

FIGURE 7.1 **Three Key Questions and Their Interrelatedness**

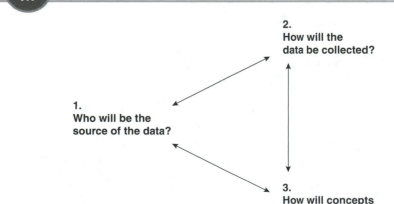

agency that serves families, particularly those coping with AIDS. Your agency wants to set up a program to help children who are HIV+ or have AIDS. In your study, you are interested in finding out the extent to which these children experience stigma problems, such as rejection, ridicule, and discrimination, in their schools and neighborhoods. This will be an exploratory study, since little is known about this problem. Three general research questions have been crafted for this study:

1. To what extent do these children experience rejection, ridicule, and discrimination?
2. How are these problems manifested? Are there particular patterns in terms of perpetrators and settings?
3. How well do these children cope with these problems?

Figure 7.2 presents an outline of this process. Let's consider in detail the three design questions.

1. *Who will be the source of data?* You could focus directly on these children, or you could find out about them through a secondhand source, such as their parents or teachers. If you study the children directly, several questions may need to be considered, such as:

• Are these children able to communicate about their stigma encounters?
• Are they willing to communicate about them?

FIGURE 7.2 **Planning an Exploratory Research Design for Children with HIV (Using the Three Key Questions)**

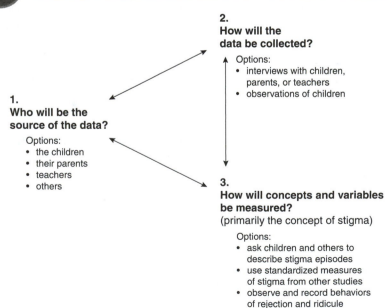

- To what extent is this study an invasion of privacy and possibly harmful to them? How can these ethical issues be satisfactorily addressed?
- Are their parents willing to permit such an investigation?
- Would observations be permitted to find out how the children are affected by these stigma problems? If so, where can they be observed (home, school, neighborhood activities, etc.)?

Possibly you will decide to interview their parents, other family members, or their teachers instead of the children, because of some of the ethical issues related to studying children. In this case, you will consider a secondhand source of data, which will pose limitations in itself. You may have to consider several questions, such as:

- Will the parents and/or teachers be willing to be interviewed?
- Will these secondhand sources have enough of an understanding of these stigma problems?
- Will they have enough exposure to the places where the children experience stigma?
- Can they be objective enough to report what the children feel and experience rather than sharing their own views and feelings?

2. *How will the data be collected?* You will also need to decide how the data on the children's stigma problems will be collected. You have several choices. You could interview the children, observe them, or combine interviewing and observing. You could also interview their parents or teachers. These options raise another set of questions that could be asked about data collection. If you decide to study the children themselves, you would need to ask:

- If an interview is used, will it be structured, semistructured, or unstructured?
- Will you consider using a questionnaire?
- If you observe them, will you use a structured or unstructured approach?
- If you use an unstructured observational approach, will you use participant observation or strictly observation?

If you decide to interview the parents or teachers, you will need to consider other questions, such as:

- Will you use an interview approach or a questionnaire?
- If you decide to use an interview, will it be structured, semistructured, or unstructured?

It is probably becoming evident by now that the decisions about who you will study and how you will collect data need to be decided together. For example, if you choose to study the children, you can interview them. An interview approach can work if the children are able to share information about their stigma problems. They will need to have some understanding of their stigma problems to be able to describe these episodes. A questionnaire may not be as viable an option if the children have difficulty responding about such problems in writing or if they do not yet have proficiency in reading.

If many of the children cannot communicate adequately in an interview context, you may decide instead to interview their family members or teachers. However, they may not know much about what is happening in this aspect of the children's lives. Another possibility is to conduct an observational study of the children. You may decide to observe the children in their daily routines in various places and times. Observations, however, can create reactivity resulting from the researcher's presence. You may decide to conduct a participant observation study of these children, with the researcher becoming a fairly regular participant in their lives. However, this approach would take considerable time, beginning with a period of building rapport. Participant observation studies are also costly.

3. *How will concepts and variables be defined, measured, and analyzed?* While a data collection approach is being selected, you will need to consider how the data collection instrument will define and measure the concepts of interest to the researcher. Let's consider the central concept of stigma in this illustration, even though this study would have other important concepts to measure as well. In this example, you will have to find a way to define and measure stigma. Some of the questions you may ask about the concept of stigma are:

- How will the children's stigma problems be defined and measured?
- Are there any existing measures of stigma designed specifically for children who are HIV+?
- Are there any existing measures of stigma in general that could be used?
- If there are not valid and reliable measures of stigma, how will the researcher define and measure stigma?
- Can the children and their parents be the experts, defining stigma as they understand it?

Let's consider how measuring the important concepts like stigma are directly pertinent to the decision about who we will study and how we will collect data. The question about how stigma will be measured will have a direct influence on the decision about which data collection approach to use. If, for example, there is an existing measure of stigma that has been used with children, that measure could become the focus of one of the primary data collection instruments. Existing scales that measure stigma could possibly be found in sources like the *Mental Measurement Yearbook* and *Tests in Print*, which may be available in your university library.

In contrast, if there is not an existing measure of stigma, an unstructured approach would provide flexibility for a naturalistic search for understanding of stigma. These children may respond most effectively to an unstructured approach, whether it be an interview, observation, or a combination of both. You may or may not find that teachers and parents are a useful source of information about stigma. A pilot study of a few parents and teachers may help you find out both how much they know and how much they are willing to share.

An Illustration of an Explanatory Study

Now let's consider an explanatory study that addresses the three key design questions. Let's assume that you are employed in the agency that serves families described in the previous illustration of an exploratory study. Your agency wants to set up a program to help children who are HIV+ or have AIDS, and you have obtained several new insights about their stigma problems from conducting an exploratory study developed from the previous illustration. Now it is time to do something about this problem. A social work intervention is needed to help the children or possibly to educate others, such as their teachers, family members, or classmates, about AIDS. An explanatory study is needed as well to measure the effect of the intervention on the children and others who are significant in their lives.

Let's assume that you had decided to interview the children in the previous exploratory study. You found out that most of the children frequently experienced stigma problems, particularly at school. These problems included being called names, being pushed and spit on, and being ignored, beaten up, ostracized by peers, and left out of many peer associations and activities. From the previous study, you also discovered that the perpetrators were mostly other children at the school. You also found that most of the children with AIDS had little if any personal skill in coping with and combating these stigma problems. Further, none of them had opportunities to talk openly with others about these problems. Instead, they tended to withdraw and turn their fears, anger, and anguish in on themselves. Your research interviews were the first real opportunity for them to talk about these problems and what could be done. This exploratory study also revealed that these children were having serious academic problems in school, which appeared to be related to their stigma problems. At this point, let's assume that you want to use the findings from the previous study to find out if a social work intervention can help these children.

The three key design questions were asked for the exploratory study in the first illustration, and numerous options were identified for designing an exploratory study. Let's return to these three key questions and ask them again for this explanatory study. Figure 7.3 lists the three design questions that need to be asked and the options available. Let's assume that this will be an explanatory study that tests one hypothesis. The independent variable in this illustration will be a social work intervention that is introduced to address the children's stigma problems. The independent variable could be, for example, a support group for the children with AIDS and the dependent variable could be an outcome of importance to these children, such as their academic performance. As an alternative, the independent variable could be a psychoeducational group involving non-HIV children in the same schools, and the dependent variable could be a stigma outcome to reduce or eliminate, such as name calling. Let's primarily concentrate on how to measure the outcome variable in this illustration.

1. *Who will be the source of data?* In this explanatory study you can focus on the children with HIV and AIDS, their classmates, their parents and teachers, or perhaps another relevant group. Since it has already been decided that this will be a study that focuses on an intervention that helps a group of people, you will need to decide who will be the recipients of the intervention. Will you help these children by intervening with them directly? Or will you help them indirectly by intervening

FIGURE 7.3   **Planning an Explanatory Research Design for Children with HIV**

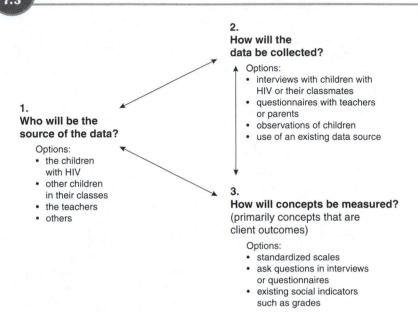

2.
How will the data be collected?

Options:
- interviews with children with HIV or their classmates
- questionnaires with teachers or parents
- observations of children
- use of an existing data source

1.
Who will be the source of the data?

Options:
- the children with HIV
- other children in their classes
- the teachers
- others

3.
How will concepts be measured?
(primarily concepts that are client outcomes)

Options:
- standardized scales
- ask questions in interviews or questionnaires
- existing social indicators such as grades

with their classmates, their parents and teachers, or others who can help them? The source of data will likely be clarified by answering these questions.

2. *How will the data be collected?* You will also need to decide how the data on the important concepts will be collected. The important concept we are focusing on in this illustration is the relevant client outcome. You have several choices. You could interview the children with HIV or their classmates, ask these children to fill out a questionnaire, observe them, or implement a combination of these approaches. You could also interview their parents or teachers. In addition, you could use existing data sources, such as the children's grades or attendance in school. These options raise a set of questions that could be asked about data collection. If you decide to collect data from the children, you could ask:

- If an interview is used, will it be structured, semistructured, or unstructured?
- If a questionnaire is used, will it be easy enough to understand and fill out?
- If you observe them, will you use a structured or unstructured approach to observation?
- If you use an unstructured observational approach, will you use participant or nonparticipant observation?

If you decide to interview the parents or teachers, you will need to consider similar questions, such as whether to use an interview approach or a questionnaire and if it will be structured, semistructured, or unstructured.

3. *How will variables be defined, measured, and analyzed?* As the data collection approach is being selected, you will also need to consider how it will define and

measure the important variables of interest to the researcher. In this case, the most important variables we will consider are the client outcomes. Some of the questions you may want to ask about measures of outcomes for the children are:

- What outcomes do the children, their parents and teachers, and the school administration want?
- Are there any existing measures of these outcomes that could be used?
- If there are no satisfactory existing measures of outcomes, how will you define and measure them?
- If interviews or questionnaires are conducted to measure the client outcomes, are these children willing and able to communicate pertinent information?
- If observations are conducted, will these observations provide information on the behaviors of the children that is meaningful to the study? Will these observations be permitted? Where can they be observed (home, school, neighborhood activities, etc.)?
- To what extent is this study an invasion of privacy and possibly harmful to these children? How can these ethical issues be satisfactorily addressed? Are their parents willing to permit such an investigation?

If problems are apparent in interviewing or observing the children, you may decide that the source of your data will be the parents or other family members or the teachers. You may have to ask additional questions that are similar to the questions asked in the first illustration, such as:

- Will their parents and/or teachers be willing to be interviewed?
- Will these secondhand sources have accurate information related to the concepts of interest?
- Can these secondhand sources be objective enough to report what they think the children feel and experience rather than sharing their own feelings?

Like the illustration for an exploratory study, the decisions about the three key study design questions need to be considered together. For example, if you choose the children as the data source, you could interview or observe them or ask them to fill out a questionnaire. An interview approach can work if the children are able to communicate meaningful information about the important concepts. A questionnaire will not be as viable an option if the children do not have reading proficiency or have difficulty responding about such concepts in writing.

If many of the children cannot communicate adequately in an interview context, you may decide instead to interview their family members or teachers. However, they may not know what is happening in their children's lives related to stigma problems. Another possibility is to conduct an observational study of the children. You may decide to observe the children in their daily routines in various places and times. Observations, however, can create a reactive effect resulting from the researcher's presence. Also, observations take a lot of time.

The questions about how to measure the outcomes for the children will have a direct influence on the decision about which data collection approach to use. If, for example, there is an existing measure of an outcome that can be used with children, that measure could become the focus of one of the primary data collection instruments. In contrast, if there is not an existing measure, an unstructured interview or observational approach would provide flexibility for an open, naturalistic search for understanding. Actually, in this case, there are several existing measures that could be considered as outcomes. For example, if you are interested in determining if the social work intervention will improve the children's academic performance, then the children's grades, attendance patterns, and reports of classroom behavior could all be considered as measures of academic performance.

As you can see, there are many different possibilities for designing an explanatory study. Here is one possibility. Let's say that you decide to develop a children's support group for ten children with HIV or AIDS who are 7 to 10 years old. This group will meet for one hour each week in the school throughout the academic year. It will focus on helping these children discuss their stigma problems and problem solve about various ways to cope with these problems. The group leader will also introduce some ways of coping with stigma that have been documented in the literature to be effective. Along with offering the children's group, you will conduct an explanatory study that tests the hypothesis "A children's support group that focuses on their stigma problems related to HIV will help the group members improve their grades in school." The children's school grades will be made available by school officials as an existing data source. These grades will be collected both before and after the group is implemented to determine whether they improve significantly during the period of time that the group is provided.

In conclusion, note that both the exploratory and explanatory studies are relevant to social workers. Social workers are professionally prepared to develop and deliver interventions that are effective in helping a client group. Here is where the research connection comes in. The exploratory study is beneficial in providing information that can be used in developing a relevant intervention. The explanatory study is valuable in providing the documentation that the intervention works.

Designing a Study and the Consumer Role

Let's look briefly at what a critical consumer needs to consider about step 3 (designing the study) when reading a research report. It will be particularly important to pay close attention to how the researcher addresses the three key questions covered in this chapter: Who will be the source of the data? How will the data be collected? and How will the important concepts be defined, measured, and analyzed? The specific questions for a consumer to ask about the research design are:

1. What sampling approach did the researcher use? Was it a probability or nonprobability type sampling approach? Can you describe the specific procedures that were followed in selecting the sample?
2. Is the population of interest of the researcher clearly identified? If not, what do you think the population is? Can the findings from the sample be generalized with any degree of confidence to this population?

3. Is the sample made up of a diversity of people? What relevant groups may be left out, if any?

4. What data collection approach was used (e.g., participant observation, interview, experiment, etc.)? Can you describe the specific procedures or steps that were followed in collecting the data? What are the advantages and limitations of the data collection approach for the topic being researched?

5. Does the data collection approach seem appropriate for the group that is studied? If not, what seems problematic?

6. Is there an adequate description of how each of the important variables is defined and measured? Can you explain what each of these definitions and measures are?

The next four chapters describe how these three questions can be addressed in the process of designing a study. Chapter 8 examines how sampling techniques can be used in selecting the sources of data. Chapter 9 examines how surveys are constructed and used in data collection. Chapter 10 focuses on observational designs, an emerging data collection approach in social work research. Chapter 11 focuses on exploring causal relationships in research designs.

Chapter Reflections

Values and Ethics, Diversity, At-Risk Groups, and Social Justice

Numerous ethical problems and issues are potentially evident in designing a study. For example, we need to ask how the research participants can benefit from the study. We also need to ask how they can be protected from physical and psychological harm if they decide to participate in the study. We should also ask how the participants can be protected from an invasion of their privacy. The informed consent procedure needs to be carefully planned and implemented to ensure that these and other ethical issues are given sufficient attention.

Diversity issues are also important in designing the study. The selection of a sample needs to give careful consideration to all of the pertinent diversity characteristics evident in the population of interest, whether obvious or subtle. Also the choice of a data collection approach requires giving thought to its appropriateness for all groups of interest. For example, are people being inadvertently left out because they cannot read a questionnaire in English or read at all? Are others left out because anonymity cannot be ensured?

At-risk groups are identified in many of the illustrations in the chapter to highlight their special needs. For example, African American fathers and kinship families are the focus of a study on page 133. Children who are HIV + or have AIDS are the focus of the two major illustrations of exploratory and explanatory studies. In addition, several Websites are identified in the chapter that describe large-scale studies that can be investigated further. Many of these organizations focus on groups that need considerably more research attention, such as women and families, clients with substance abuse problems, and clients in the criminal justice system.

Similarly, social justice issues are important to consider in designing a study. Possibly an exploratory design is called for in studying underresearched groups that may not be well understood or may be difficult to access, such as Bosnian immigrants, gay and lesbian teenagers, or men with cancer. Often, exploratory studies are empowering, because they offer such groups the opportunity to speak about their issues in their own voices. Participatory action research (PAR) designs and implementation of some of the steps of PAR can also promote social justice concerns.

The research design is the blueprint for conducting a study. The three key questions to ask are (1) Who will be the source of the data? (2) How will the data be collected? and (3) How will the important concepts be measured? How these design questions are asked will vary depending on whether the study is exploratory or explanatory.

Discussion Questions

1. Go online and access the Website of Child Trends (www.childtrends.org). Select a study of interest to you and identify the general research questions or hypotheses of the study. Also, attempt to answer the three key questions about the research design of the study. Give a brief report to your class.

2. The U.S. Census Bureau surveys the entire U.S. population every ten years. Access the bureau's Website (www.census.gov) and compare the demographic characteristics of the U.S. population in 1990 and 2000. What characteristics appear to have changed dramatically?

3. Plan your own exploratory research design for studying the stigma problems of children who are HIV+. Select the group of people (children, parents, or teachers) that you will study, select a data collection approach, and decide how you will define and measure their stigma problems.

4. Plan your own explanatory research design for children with HIV. Instead of identifying an intervention for children with HIV like the one highlighted in the illustration on page 142, develop an intervention addressing an environmental stressor as the independent variable and a stigma problem you want to eliminate as the dependent variable. An example was given in the chapter of a psychoeducational group for non-HIV children as the independent variable and a stigma outcome you would want to reduce or eliminate, such as name calling, as the dependent variable. Create a different environmental example.

5. Select a topic of interest to you, identify two or three general research questions, and then attempt to answer the three key questions discussed in the chapter.

Reference

O'Donnell, J. (1999). Involvement of African American fathers in kinship foster care services. *Social Work, 44*(5), 428–441.

Considering Sampling Techniques

One of the important questions to ask in designing the study is "Who will be the source of the data?" Social workers are actively involved in serving various client populations, so this may not be a difficult question to answer. However, sometimes the sampling question is not that easy. For example, what if the people you want to study are recent Haitian or Russian immigrants? In this case, language barriers may have to be taken into account. Or let's say you want to study five-year-old children. It may be difficult to communicate with them, depending on your topic. Also, parental and agency permission will be expected as part of an informed consent protocol. In another example, what about people with mental illness? You will have to find out if they can answer your questions, and this will likely depend on their diagnosis and the severity of their conditions. Selecting the participants of a sample is step 3a of the research process.

Steps in the Research Process

1. Understanding the research topic to be studied
2. Focusing the study
3. Designing the study
   a. **Selecting the participants**
   b. Selecting a data collection approach and measuring concepts
   c. Exploring causal relationships
4. Collecting the data
5. Analyzing the data
6. Preparing a report

Important Concepts about Sampling

Usually, researchers decide to study a sample of a larger population rather than the entire population because of time and budget constraints. The sample is a subgroup of the population. Let's define some important terms. The **population** comprises all of the people of interest to the researcher conducting a study. The **sample** is a subgroup of the population the researcher selects to study. For example, the sample of a study could be all of the people who reside in one homeless shelter, while the population could be every homeless person in an entire city. Or the sample could be a classroom of children in one school, and the population could be all of the children of that particular grade level in the entire school system.

Occasionally, researchers study the entire population of interest. Such a study is called a census. A census is a study in which all of the people in the population are included. The U.S. Census is the most familiar census study, as it involves a study of everyone in the United States. Often agency research studies are a census of all of their active clients, because the total number is small enough and there is an interest in including everyone.

A CNN Poll

The TV news programs often conduct polls to determine the opinions of their viewing audience on controversial issues. For example, in one poll the viewers were asked if they were satisfied with President Bush's handling of the war on terrorism. People were to respond by e-mailing their views to CNN. What is the value of this CNN poll for the viewing audience? What are the limitations of such a poll?

Another important concept in sampling is representativeness. In some cases samples are intended to be representative of the population, and in other cases they are not. A **representative sample** is a sample in which the characteristics of the sample accurately reflect the characteristics of the population. Mathematical techniques can help in selecting a representative sample. These techniques will be discussed later in the chapter. For now, consider the advantages of a representative sample. If you interview a representative sample, you will have a fairly good idea about how the entire population thinks on the same topic without interviewing everyone.

When we have a representative sample, we can generalize the findings to the entire population. When we generalize, we are claiming that the findings of the sample apply to the population as well. However, some degree of sampling error needs to be expected when generalizing. So when findings are generalized, the degree of sampling error is also calculated. **Sampling error** is the degree of error to be expected when generalizing from a sample to the population. We may claim that the findings of a sample are the same for the population, with the possibility of a small percent of sampling error.

For example, a study was conducted of 240 people with mental illness and mental retardation (Conroy, Fullerton, Dudley, & Ahlgrim-Delzell, 2001). These 240 people were a representative sample of a larger group of 1,094 people with a dual diagnosis. The degree of potential sampling error in generalizing the findings from the sample to the larger group of 1,094 was calculated to be up to ±5 percent. As an illustration, a score of 61 (out of 100) on a vocational behavior scale for the sample could be generalized to the population of people with mental illness and mental retardation as a score between 58 and 64. (Five percent is calculated as $0.05 \times 61 = 3.05$ or rounded off as a score of 3. So $61 - 3 = 58$ and $61 + 3 = 64$.)

Selecting a Sample

Let's assume that we will study a sample of people because we do not have the time to interview the entire population. We must first consider the unit of analysis we are studying. The *unit of analysis* is the level of the system we are comparing in the study. Usually, we study individuals as the unit of analysis. A study using the unit of analysis of individuals is comparing the responses of individuals on a particular topic. However, we could also study larger units, such as families, groups, neighborhoods, cities, and so on. In these cases, we would be comparing families, groups, neighborhoods, and cities and not individuals. For example, we may want to investigate how different cities experience homelessness. In this case, we would gather relevant data on homelessness for each city and then compare the cities on the problem of homelessness. Note that while data on individuals who are homeless would be collected in this example, individuals would not be the focus of comparison.

Example of a Study with a Larger Unit of Analysis

Reporters with a city newspaper conducted a study to find out if supermarkets, which have lower prices and larger selections of food and household goods than small neighborhood stores, were equally distributed in their city. They were particularly interested in whether there was a fairly equal distribution of supermarkets among white and African American residential areas and low- and high-income neighborhoods (Purvis, 2003). The unit of analysis that was used for this study was census tracts. The findings revealed, among other things, that only 8 percent of African Americans lived in census tracts with at least one supermarket, while 31 percent of whites lived in census tracts with at least one supermarket. The study discussed some of the difficulties that low-income and minority residents endure in obtaining their groceries. These difficulties include a low income, a lack of access to good transportation, diet restrictions, and limitations based on disabilities and age.

The next step in selecting a sample is to obtain or compile a sampling frame. A **sampling frame** is a list of all of the units in the population. Sometimes a sampling frame is easy to obtain from an existing list. For example, if we wanted to select a sample of clients to study, we could obtain the list of all of the clients served by the agency as a sampling frame. Sometimes, a sampling frame might not exist and would have to be compiled or developed. For example, let's say we want to conduct a study of all of the children in a large city. Most likely, there is no available list of every child residing in the city. While there may be partial lists of children, these lists are likely to have major flaws. For example, a list of all public school children would exclude children in private schools, schools outside the city, home schools, and children not in any school.

As mentioned earlier, representative samples depend on mathematical techniques. Probability theory is an important mathematical concept to consider. *Probability* is defined in the Webster dictionary as "the chance that a given event will occur." Probability theory is useful in telling us how likely something could happen. For example, could something be likely to happen 50 percent of the time, 95 percent, 99.9 percent? Probability theory is not used to inform us that something absolutely will or will not happen 100 percent of the time. *Likely* is not the same as *certainly*. If we are certain of something happening, we do not need to be concerned with probability theory.

Flip a Coin

If you flip a coin ten times, for example, you will most likely get the coin to fall heads half of the time and tails the other half of the time. But try to do this and see what you get. You will probably find out that it does not always come up 50 percent heads and 50 percent tails. The most likely result is 50:50. You may get a 40:60, 60:40, or even a 30:70 or 70:30 split. If you have time, try flipping the same coin 100 times. Your results will probably come closer to a 50:50 split. The empirical results are likely to be closer to the expected proportion (50:50) as the number of flips increases.

Probability and Nonprobability Sampling

There are two general kinds of sampling approaches—probability sampling and nonprobability sampling. **Probability sampling** is sampling in which every person in the population has an equal chance of being selected. In other words, based on probability theory, it is probable that anyone in the population can be selected to be in the study. A sample that is selected by probability sampling is considered a representative sample and can be generalized to its population with some small degree of error. **Nonprobability sampling** is sampling in which we do not know if every person in the population has an equal chance of being selected. Nonprobability sampling is often used, because the intent of the study is not to generalize the findings. Both probability and nonprobability sampling have specific approaches or strategies, as summarized here:

Probability Type	Nonprobability Type
(Each unit in population has an equal chance of being selected.)	(Chance of being selected is unknown.)
1. *Random*—selected by chance	1. *Convenience*—whoever can be found
2. *Systematic random*—selected systematically	2. *Quota*—stratified into subgroups before selection
3. *Stratified random*—stratified then random selection	3. *Criterion*—based on specific criteria
4. *Cluster*—multiple stages involved	4. *Snowball*—participants identify other participants

Types of Probability Sampling

Random Sampling   If you were to conduct a study in which you intended to generalize your findings to a larger population, you could choose from four types that are available. The first type is **random sampling.** Random sampling is a sampling approach in which each person in the population has an equal probability of being selected based on chance. A lottery, for example, uses a random approach in selecting the winner. A lottery can be visualized as a fish bowl filled with ping pong balls, each with a number of a person in a population. The ping pong balls are tossed around so that each one has an equal chance of being selected. If you were to randomly select a sample using the lottery approach, you would randomly select the number of ping pong balls you want in your sample. Random sampling can also be performed by using a table of random numbers. In this case, numbers are taken from a table consisting of columns of randomly assigned numbers. One key point about random sampling is important. This sampling approach is easy to do if you have access to everyone in the population at the same time. If not, then one of the other three approaches would be preferred.

Systematic Random Sampling   The second type of probability sampling is referred to as **systematic random sampling.** Systematic random sampling is distinguished from random sampling in that each person has an equal chance of being selected by systematic choice, not by random chance. Systematic random sampling is often used when random sampling is not feasible. Systematic random sampling is usually dependent on a list of every person in the population. From this list, every *n*th person can be selected systematically. The *n* is determined by the percent of the population in the sample. For example, if you wanted a sample that is 10 percent (10/100) of the population, you would select 1/10 of the list, or every tenth person. In a sample of 5 percent (5/100) of the population, you would select 1/20 of the list, or every twentieth person from the list.

Let's say you want to systematically select 10 percent of the social work students in your department. Assume that the social work department provides you with such a list. The steps to take are as follows. First, you would select one person on the list randomly. You could easily do this by blindfolding yourself and pointing to a name on the list. This would be the first person for your sample. Next, you would count down the list to the tenth name after the first name. This will be your second person. Then you would count down the list ten more names to pick the third person, and so on.

Here's another way of explaining it. Let's say you randomly picked the fifteenth person on the list. Next you would select the twenty-fifth name, then the thirty-fifth name, and so on, until you have selected 10 percent of the list. Once you get to the bottom of the list, you would go back to the beginning of the list and continue until you reach the randomly selected starting point. This should end up providing you with 10 percent of the list. To be truly random, the list should be in no particular order (i.e., by class standing—freshman, soph, junior, senior—etc.).

Systematic random sampling is often used when the population can be identified on one available list (which is the sampling frame). Telephone directories, client lists, and directories of members of professional associations are examples of sampling frames if they are representative of the population of interest. However, the frequent problem with some of these lists is that they may be far from complete. A telephone directory, for example, does not include people who have either an unlisted phone or none at all. Also, some people might be underrepresented using systematic sampling because they have the same name and are clustered together on a list. This could be an important concern, for example, if you want to be sure to have full representation of some minority groups (e.g., many Latinos have the name Hernandez, Fernandez, or Garcia).

Let's consider another example. You want to conduct a study of university students to find out their views on campus parking problems. You want to identify a representative sample of 10 percent of the students that can be generalized to the entire student body. You discover that a random approach would not be feasible because you do not have access to identifying information on all of the students at one particular time. (Can you imagine rounding up every student on campus at one specific time?) A systematic random approach might be a realistic choice. However, you discover that you cannot obtain a complete list of the students. For example, the administration of the university is not willing to give you a student list because of confidentiality. Neither will a telephone directory of students be useful, because many students have unlisted phone numbers or no phone at all. A creative alternative could be to use a systematic random approach in which you would have an interviewer stationed at each of the main entrances to the university. They could select and interview every tenth person coming through each of the entrances during one entire day. By the way, this approach has serious limitations, too, in that it would exclude those who did not come to school on the day of the study and would oversample those who came through more than once.

Stratified Random Sampling   A third type of probability sampling is called **stratified random sampling**. A stratified random sampling approach is useful when a study is comparing two or more subgroups of the population and you want to be sure to have a proportional representation of each subgroup. Let's assume that a study is comparing the viewpoints of male and female students on the topic of date rape. If a sample was selected randomly, you would not want to assume that there would be an equal number of males and females. While this is probable for larger samples, it is also likely that you could select more women or men by chance. (Remember the example of the coin flip.) A stratified random sample would overcome this possibility. First, you would stratify the population into two subgroups, in this case, male and female. Then you would randomly select an equal number from each subgroup. Stratified random sampling would be preferred for any study in which the subgroups are to be compared.

In some cases, you would want to select a proportional number from each subgroup rather than an equal number, because the subgroups are not equally represented in the population. For example, most social work programs have student bodies with three or four times more female students than males. Proportional sampling creates a sample that accurately represents the subgroups of the population.

The example of proportional sampling in Figure 8.1 consists of a population of 1,000 consisting of the three different income levels that make up 10, 60, and 30 percent of the population, respectively. As you can see from the proportional sample, each subgroup in the sample has the same percentage it has in the population, even though the sample is much smaller than the population.

Cluster Sampling   A fourth type of probability sampling is called **cluster sampling.** Cluster sampling is an approach to consider when the people in a population of interest cannot be identified in any direct way. Cluster sampling usually involves several stages. One of the most common uses for cluster sampling is research conducted in the schools. In this case, selecting individual students is not usually feasible. As an alternative, schools can be selected randomly, followed by classrooms being selected randomly. Finally, children are randomly identified in the randomly selected classrooms.

Another example of cluster sampling would involve a study of adults 65 years and older in a city. If there is not a complete list of older adults, then cluster sampling can help create a representative group by randomly selecting large clusters of the population, followed by randomly selecting subclusters until the sample can be identified.

A representative sample of adults 65 years and older is created by cluster sampling in the example in Figure 8.2. Eight voting precincts or districts are randomly selected from a total of thirteen precincts in stage 1. In stage 2, three streets are randomly select from each of these eight precincts. In stage 3, four households are randomly selected on each of these streets. Stage 4 involves interviews with the first older person available in each of these households. If there are no older adults living in a household, other households are randomly selected until the desired number of adults 65 years and older are identified and interviewed.

Even though cluster sampling is based on probability theory, samples that are selected by using this approach are less likely to be representative than samples produced by the previous three probability sampling approaches. This is because more than one stage is needed to identify the sample, and each of these stages poses a likelihood of error in selection.

FIGURE 8.1   Example of Stratified Random Sampling

Population of 1000 by Income Level		Randomly selected	Sample of 20% (200) by Income Level	
High income	10% (100)	⟶	High income	10% (20)
Middle income	60% (600)	⟶	Middle income	60% (120)
Low income	30% (300)	⟶	Low income	30% (60)

FIGURE 8.2   Example of Cluster Sampling

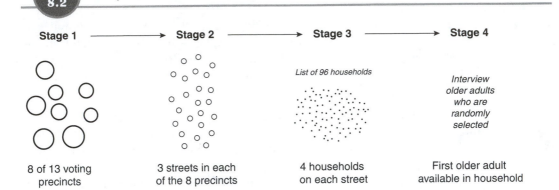

Stage 1	Stage 2	Stage 3	Stage 4
8 of 13 voting precincts	3 streets in each of the 8 precincts	List of 96 households 4 households on each street	Interview older adults who are randomly selected First older adult available in household

Example of Cluster Sampling

The National Opinion Research Center at the University of Chicago (www. norc.uchicago.edu) uses cluster sampling techniques in their studies. They identify research participants by randomly selecting geographical areas, then neighborhood blocks, then families, and then an individual within the family.

Types of Nonprobability Sampling

Nonprobability sampling is sampling in which we do not know if every person in the population has an equal chance of being selected. Nonprobability sampling is often used in exploratory studies when we do not intend to generalize the findings. In exploratory studies, the interest is almost exclusively in gaining insights from the people in the sample.

Nonprobability sampling is also used in studies in which we do not know much about the population, such as how large it is or its demographic characteristics. Examples of such populations in the United States include Native Americans, Muslims, and immigrants from El Salvador or Peru. Other groups may not be easily identified because of intentional concealment to protect themselves. Examples could include gays and lesbians, people who are HIV+ or have AIDS, and illegal immigrants.

Convenience Sampling   There are several specific types of nonprobability sampling to consider when conducting an exploratory study. The simplest type of nonprobability sampling is **convenience sampling,** which is also referred to as availability sampling. Convenience sampling is simply selecting people for a sample who are the easiest to find. Such people are often those who are known to the researcher, are in close proximity, and are easy to recruit for participation. Obviously, findings from such a sample cannot be generalized to a larger population. Most likely, a convenience sample has been selected based on some bias, such as that those within easy access are people who are similar in views or characteristics to the researcher. Nevertheless, such a sample can provide useful data on topics that have not been researched. Convenience or availability sampling is a good approach to use in preliminary or pilot research, when a few people from a sample are needed and specific selection criteria are not important.

Quota Sampling   Another nonprobability sampling approach is **quota sampling.** This approach is used when the intent is to compare two or more subgroups. Like the stratified random approach, the intent is to have either equal or proportional numbers of people in each subgroup. However, quota sampling differs from stratified random sampling in that it does not use a random selection from a known population. Quota sampling often is used when the population is not easily identified or known. An example of quota sampling would be to select ten students from each of the four levels of undergraduate education—freshman, sophomore, junior, and senior—in an exploratory study in which limited time is a factor in completing the study.

Criterion Sampling   A third approach is referred to as **criterion sampling.** This approach is also sometimes called a purposive approach. In this case, a study has particular criteria to follow in selecting a sample. For example, research participants are needed who meet certain criteria related to the purpose of the study. This approach is often used because a study is interested in the views or experiences of people with a certain status, diagnosis, experience, or set of circumstances. An example of a community study that used a criterion sampling approach is described here.

Example of Criterion Sampling

Beverly Stoner (2001), a social work student, conducted a study at her field placement agency, a community center in a geographic area with a high recent influx of Mexican immigrants. Many of these immigrants had come to the United States illegally to find employment. She conducted a needs assessment to determine the needs of the Latino population for free dental services. Her sample was selected based on four criteria identified by a local dental clinic task force that requested the study. Participants were to (1) be a Latino, (2) be a resident of the local county, (3) have a low income, and (4) be uninsured for dental services.

Criterion sampling is also evident in several specific sampling approaches that depend on specific criteria of importance to a community, social agency, funding agency, or the researcher. These specific types of criterion sampling approaches include key informants, typical case, exemplar case, focus groups, and community forums (Marlow, 2001).

Key informants are people who have special knowledge and experience on a topic. An example is a study of gangs in a specific neighborhood. Key informants who know the most about these gangs could be selected to be interviewed. These key informants may include former and current gang leaders, gang workers and others who work with these gang members and their families, and leaders of neighborhood groups who represent neighbors who have been adversely affected by gang problems.

A **typical case** would be a case (individual, family, agency, neighborhood, etc.) that seems to have many of the characteristics evident in other cases of a larger group. For example, a typical case in a social worker's caseload would be one that reflects a typical profile of most of the clients. A typical client case could be considered an important client system to study in some depth to learn more about the issues that are possibly facing other similar clients.

An **exemplar case** is another type of criterion sampling. In this instance a case would be selected that exemplifies or personifies what is most desired or preferred. For example, an exemplar client case could be one that has most effectively used a particular service. This case stands out among other cases that did not have such success. A study of this case could reveal insights about what worked well in utilizing this particular service and why it worked so well.

Focus groups are used in studies to find out the views of several people on an issue. Members of focus groups are selected because they have knowledge or expertise about a particular topic. A focus group is conducted as a group interview in which the participants are invited to discuss a particular topic, such as the legal problems faced by undocumented families. The leader facilitates a group discussion by asking several general questions on this topic. Focus groups are discussed in more detail in Chapter 12.

Community forums, like focus groups, are instances in which a selected group of people come together to discuss a topic of interest to all of them. They are likely to belong to the same community or neighborhood, and the topic is likely to be an an issue that has communitywide implications affecting all of them. Participants attending community forums could be selected by personal invitation, or an open invitation could be extended to all potential participants in the community.

Considerations in selecting people for small samples could be based on other criteria as well. Many of these criteria could be relevant for program evaluations in human service agencies. Examples include dramatic cases, unusual cases, variations in cases, and those that are the easiest to study (Patton, 1980).

Snowball Sampling   A fourth nonprobability approach is **snowball sampling.** This approach is appropriate to use when it is difficult to identify or locate the kinds of people who are the focus of a study. Such groups may be "hidden" or difficult to identify because they are a small group that is isolated from the mainstream or a group that is stigmatized. The first step in snowball sampling is to select and interview people who are known to fit the study's criteria. Next, they are asked to identify others who fit the criteria. Each time new people are identified to be interviewed, they are asked to identify others. This continues until enough research participants have been found. Sometimes, participants who identify other people can also assist in reaching them or may offer their name as a referral source. Examples of groups that might be most easily identified using a snowball approach are people with HIV+ or AIDS; a nationality group such as Poles, Russians, Kenyans, or Haitians; transsexuals; nonresidential unmarried fathers; people of the Muslim faith; or women with breast cancer.

Example of Snowball Sampling in Social Work Practice

A family social worker working in a high-rise public housing project began working with a Puerto Rican (PR) family. This family informed the social worker that English-speaking classes were needed by other PR residents. The social worker asked the family to identify other PR families. When they were contacted, they were also asked to identify additional PR families until virtually all of the PR families in the project were identified. Almost all of them eventually chose to participate in English-speaking classes. They also used these classes for mutual support and to become more informed about tenant issues.

Using Combinations of Sampling Approaches

Researchers sometimes use more than one sampling approach in their studies. A combination of sampling approaches are actually used in snowball sampling, for example. Snowball sampling usually begins with purposive or criterion sampling to identify people with a particular set of characteristics. Such a group of people are often difficult for the researcher to find, so snowball sampling techniques are used as well.

Example of a Study Using a Combination of Sampling Approaches

North and Smith (1994) conducted a study of homeless people that included a representative sample of people in shelters and those living on the street. A representative group of homeless people on the street was difficult to obtain, because they are often moving from place to place and sometimes are hidden from public view. First, these researchers asked key informants from shelters and other agencies to identify the areas in the inner city frequented by homeless people. Next, they surveyed these areas at various times to see how many frequented these locations. Based on this information, four street sampling routes were developed, with each route being a loop circuit that included these locations (bus station, library, parks, alleys, parking lots, etc.). Next, routes and starting points were randomized using a computer program. Then, homeless people were selected using a systematic random approach.

Sample Size

How many people should be included in a sample? The size of a sample is a complicated question and varies depending on the purpose of the study. Some general rules are to sample at least 10 percent of a population or at least thirty people for a sample. Thirty is considered the minimum number of participants needed for employing most statistical methods.

Probability Samples

Probability samples are larger than nonprobability samples, because they have different purposes. Probability-type sampling is used to generalize to a larger population. The larger the sample, in this case, the more confident the researcher will be that the sample is representative of a population. For example, a random sample of 10 BSW graduates will be less likely to represent the characteristics of a population of 500 BSW graduates than will a random sample of 100. Similarly, the larger the population, the larger that the sample should be.

Other factors are be considered with probability samples. Diverse populations will need larger samples to ensure an adequate representation of all of the varied characteristics in the population. In other words, selecting a sample from a population of 100 white, middle-class females will not have to be as large as a sample that includes both women and men and various racial and ethnic groups. While it is difficult to recommend an exact sample size for all populations, once a sample has been selected, the researcher can examine whether or not it is adequately representative of the important diversity characteristics of the population. If not, the sample can be increased.

Nonprobability Samples

Nonprobability sampling has different issues to consider in sample size. Because nonprobability samples are usually used in exploratory studies, the sample is not intended to be generalized to a larger population. Actually, the size of the population may not even be known. Exploratory and qualitative studies are mostly interested in gaining insights from the sample and may have no immediate interest in a larger population. Interest in the population may come in a follow-up study, when exploratory findings are ready to be tested with a larger group.

Nonprobability samples can be as small as one or as high as ten or more. These samples are naturally small because of the relatively large amount of time required for data collection. The more in-depth the investigation, the smaller the sample may have to be. A sample as small as one could be used when very little is known about a particular group and data collection involves several interviews. A sample of two or three may be warranted if important differences are noticed in a group and there is an interest in considering how these differences may vary in expressing themselves. As an example, an exploratory study of interracial adoptions may include two arrangements: one adoption arrangement in which the adopted parent and the child are of a different race, and a second adoptive arrangement in which they are of the same race. These two arrangements can then be compared to discover salient differences in what seems most important to each of these families.

Another reason why a sample of more than one is a good idea is that people tend to intentionally omit things, stretch the truth, or forget details. Figuring out what is actually happening in a social situation often involves investigating more than one source. In this case, it could involve getting several people's stories about a social situation, all of which may be distorted, and combining them to get an approximation of what is really happening.

The next step in the research process is to select a data collection approach, a topic that is covered in the next two chapters. Survey studies are described in Chapter 9 and observational studies in Chapter 10. Don't forget that decisions about a sampling approach are related to decisions about a data collection approach.

Chapter Reflections

Values and Ethics, Diversity, At-Risk Groups, and Social Justice

Numerous ethical problems and issues are potentially evident in selecting a sample of people to study and in preventing harm and other abuses to those who are studied. Examples of ethical problems include physical and psychological harm and using deception when explaining what the research is about. A well-thought-out informed consent procedure is critical to have in addressing such issues and in alerting researchers to prospective participants who may be more vulnerable to harm than others. An informed consent procedure should be carried out in an especially sensitive way with vulnerable groups such as children and those with chronic medical or mental conditions. It may also be wise to include a screening device to anticipate the need to exclude prospective participants from the study who may be particularly vulnerable to the questions that will be asked.

Diversity issues are also important to consider in selecting a sample to study. Several questions could be asked, such as "What are the aspects of diversity that are most evident in the characteristics of a population to be studied?" "Which of these characteristics could be easily overlooked?" "Can special efforts be made to ensure their inclusion in a sample that is selected?" Having a low-income or an ethnic minority status are examples of diverse characteristics that are often overlooked or underrepresented in studies. Examples of studies in the chapter that were successful in selecting people with diverse characteristics include Puerto Ricans (page 157) and homeless people (page 157). An especially creative way was devised to select a representative sample in the homeless study.

At-risk groups, in particular, are often not selected to be studied because they may be personally unfamiliar to the researcher or especially difficult to locate and involve. Specific sampling approaches could be selected that have features that can overcome some of these barriers. For example, ensuring an adequate representation of older people without phones may call for a cluster approach over a systematic random approach that uses a phone directory. Nonprobability sampling approaches are especially relevant in reaching many at-risk groups. For example, a snowball approach may be effective in selecting illegal immigrants from Mexico or Central America. Similarly, social justice issues are important to consider when selecting a population to study. Including at-risk groups in a study promotes social justice by virtue of drawing attention to their special needs. Specific sampling approaches may also lend themselves to furthering social justice issues. Focus groups and community forums, for example, are likely to assist participants in disenfranchised groups to talk with one another about mutual concerns and to further bonding and solidarity.

Discussion Questions

1. Assume that you work for a family service agency and will be conducting an exploratory study to find out more about the social supports of a recent immigrant group of Laotian families. You are interested in finding out how your family service agency can help them. You personally know only a few Laotian families, but you know that there are up to fifty such families in your city. Select three of these fifty families to study. Give your reasons for selecting these particular types of families.

2. Assume that you are interested in studying a diverse population of families. One subgroup consists of Central Americans who, in most cases, do not have listed telephone numbers. How can you make sure that these families are represented in your sample?

3. You are planning to conduct a client satisfaction study of former clients of the Department of Social Services (DSS) to determine their level of satisfaction with the services they received from DSS. These former clients represent all racial groups (white, African American, Hispanic, Asian, etc.). You work at DSS and have access to a list of their addresses and phone numbers. Your supervisor wants to be able to generalize the findings to all recent former clients. Select a sampling approach you could use and give your reasons for selecting this approach. In the process of contacting these former clients, you discover that a lot of the addresses and phone numbers you were given are no longer correct. How could this problem affect the representativeness of your sample?

4. You are planning to conduct a needs assessment of older adults in a low-income housing complex that has approximately 200 older adult households and another fifty households occupied by younger families. Virtually all of the older adults are either white or African American. Your needs assessment will be used to find out their interests in social clubs, educational programs, field trips, medical supports, and so on. Your population of interest is the 200 older adult households. The manager of the housing complex will provide you with a list of all of the residents but does not know their ages. You will be conducting interviews and asking several open-ended questions. You have a large budget to conduct this study. Select a sampling approach(es) and describe the specific sampling procedures you will use.

5. You are planning a new family support program and want to select and interview teen mothers who are on welfare, because you have decided that they have the greatest need for this program. How will you identify them?

6. A researcher is in the early stages of planning a comprehensive research project and is faced with a major sampling problem. She wants to obtain a random sample of

children in the state of New York between the ages of 3 and 18 years. What would you suggest to her?

References

Conroy, J., Fullerton, A., Dudley, J., & Ahlgrim-Delzell, L. (2001). The progress made by *Thomas S.* consumers: First visits to 2001 visits. Monograph 27 of the *Thomas S.* Longitudinal Research Project, University of North Carolina, Charlotte.

Marlow, C. (2001). *Research methods for generalist social work,* 3rd ed. Stamford, CT: Thomson Learning.

North, C., & Smith, E. (1994). Comparison of white and non-white homeless men and women. *Social Work, 39*(6), 637–649.

Patton, M. (1980). *Qualitative evaluation methods.* Newbury Park, CA: Sage.

Purvis, K. (2003). Nowhere to shop. *Charlotte Observer, 134*(40), 1.

Stoner, B. (2001). A needs assessment for free dental services for the low-income and uninsured population of North Mecklenburg County. Student research project, University of North Carolina, Charlotte.

chapter 9

Constructing Surveys

When you gather data directly from people, you only have a few basic options. You can ask them questions or observe their behavior. You could also do a combination of questioning and observing.

Another important question to ask in the development of a research design is "How will the data be collected?" As you can see in the listing, deciding on a data collection approach is step 3b of the research process.

When researchers collect data directly from people, they have two basic choices. They can either ask people questions or observe them in their environment (discussed in Chapter 10). Many social work studies collect data through **surveys** that ask questions of research participants. Two specific types of surveys are interviews and questionnaires. **Interviews** are inquiries in which an interviewer asks questions of an interviewee and records the responses. **Questionnaires** are inquiries in which the questions, either recorded on paper or on an electronic computer file, are given to the participant to answer. As Table 9.1 indicates, interviews and questionnaires vary based on the degree to which they are structured.

> **Steps in the Research Process**
>
> 1. Understanding the research topic to be studied
> 2. Focusing the study
> 3. Designing the study
>   a. Selecting the participants
>   b. Selecting a data collection approach and measuring concepts
>   - **Surveys**
>   - Observations
>   c. Exploring causal relationships
> 4. Collecting the data
> 5. Analyzing the data
> 6. Preparing a report

Using Interviews in Research

Types of Interviews

The first type of survey is the interview. Interviews can be conducted in a wide variety of ways. One way of describing the variations in interviews is to classify them as structured, semistructured, or unstructured (Marlow, 2001). All three types of

| **TABLE 9.1** | Survey Approaches Based on Asking Questions |

Interview	Questionnaire
• Structured interview	• Structured questionnaire
• Semistructured interview	
• Unstructured interview	• Unstructured questionnaire

interviews are familiar to social work practice because they are used in various social work situations. **Structured interviews** are interviews with questions that are formulated before the data are collected and that are asked in predetermined order. Little if any variation is permitted in how a structured interview is conducted. The responses to the questions are recorded on an interview schedule, which is a list of all of the questions to be asked, with places to record the responses to each question. Interviewers are trained to ask the questions so that every interviewee hears the same questions in the same way and order. Since a structured interview asks all of the participants of a study the same questions in exactly the same way, one major advantage is that the responses to each question can be compared to one another. A disadvantage of structured interviews is the lack of flexibility to vary questions to the needs of each participant.

Example of a Study Using a Structured Interview

Gellis (2003) used a set of structured interview schedules to examine the relationship between the social supports of seventy-nine Vietnamese immigrants and the likelihood of their having depression. These immigrants were receiving mental health services from a public psychiatric hospital. This study asked several demographic and background questions and used scales that measured depression, size of kinship and nonkinship networks, and satisfaction with these supports. Satisfaction with supports was measured by the question "How satisfied are you with the overall support you have?"

Because this longitudinal study asked standardized questions of everyone, statistical analysis was used. It was determined that nonkinship networks were associated with reduction in depression over time, and kinship networks were associated with greater depression. Limitations of this structured interview approach were noted in the study. One limitation was that the measures of the networks were restricted simply to the number of people in the kinship and nonkinship networks and the degree of satisfaction with these networks. This interview schedule did not measure other characteristics of these networks that could have provided therapeutic value, such as what the research participants did with and received from their networks.

Semistructured interviews use a more flexible format. Most of the questions are already formulated, but they can be asked in a different order. Also, additional questions can be added to probe or follow up on hunches. Many of the questions in these interviews can be open ended. The flexibility built into semistructured interviews makes them a useful tool for exploratory studies. A disadvantage is that the questions may not be asked in exactly the same way, resulting in more difficulty in comparing the responses. An interview schedule for semistructured interviews includes a list of the questions to be asked and a place to record each of the responses.

Example of Semistructured Interviews in Research

Kruzich and colleagues (2002) used a semistructured group interview approach to investigate family members' perceptions of the involvement of their children in residential treatment. These children were in placements for emotional disorders. Four different focus groups were convened to respond to five open-ended questions.

Flexibility was evident in the researchers' decision to add the fourth focus group, composed entirely of African American family members, after discovering that the two African American family members in the first three focus groups shared some unique concerns. Some of the unique concerns of the African American families included fears about using medications, the cultural dissimilarities of staff and clients, and staff stereotyping.

Unstructured interviews, also referred to as in-depth interviews, use a very flexible format. While the interview has a purpose and there may be some predetermined questions that the interviewer wants to ask, the interview is most characteristic of a conversation. However, it is different than a normal conversation in several ways (Taylor & Bogdan, 1984). The unstructured interview is private and confidential, and the flow of information mostly comes from the interviewee. An interview guide typically includes a list all of the topics to be explored and possibly some questions. The interview guide essentially is used to remind the interviewer of the topics to be covered. This guide, however, is quite different from the interview schedule used in structured and semistructured interviews, which lists specific questions to be asked. With unstructured interviews, it is usually up to the interviewer to formulate the specific questions and to decide when to ask them.

While semi- and unstructured interviews are usually conducted with individual interviewees, group interviews are also an option. A group interview has advantages, such as the group dynamics, that can be used to facilitate discussion among all of the participants. One interviewee, for example, might say something that stimulates or encourages another interviewee to express a similar or opposing idea. Participants in a group can often be a helpful catalyst in stimulating discussion on a topic of common interest. Yet, participants in group interviews may be reluctant to express certain opinions, thus producing a false homogeneity of views. They may be hesitant to recount events that might bring disapproval from others in the group, thus suppressing information. Focus groups (see Chapter 12) are a special type of group interview approach that is sometimes popular among social work researchers.

Ways to Conduct Interviews

Interviews are usually conducted in one of two ways: face-to-face interviews or phone interviews. Most interview studies seem to be conducted face to face. However, increasingly interviews are being conducted by phone. Anyone with a home phone is familiar with telemarketing, which often conducts phone surveys and sales promotions. Phone interviews can also use computer-assisted interviewing technology (Babbie, 2001). In this case, the interviewer types each response onto an electronic file when it is being stated. The responses are saved on an electronic data file that is automatically prepared for data analysis.

Using Questionnaires in Research

Questionnaires are the second type of survey. Questionnaires, like interviews, also elicit responses to questions, but an interviewer is not needed. Questionnaires are different from interviews in that the respondents read the questions to themselves and record their responses. Questionnaires are usually filled out on paper. Increasingly however, questionnaires are being filled out electronically on a computer file sent via e-mail or a Website.

Types of Questionnaires

As Table 9.1 indicates, questionnaires can be either structured or unstructured. More accurately, they can be constructed at different levels of structure. However, the researcher is not readily available to offer assistance in clarifying questions on a questionnaire, in contrast to an interview. Therefore, it is strongly advised to construct a questionnaire so that it is as self-explanatory as possible. **Structured questionnaires** are questionnaires with forced-response questions that are easy to answer without any assistance from the researcher. The initial instructions on a questionnaire are usually all the guidance that is needed. Structured questionnaires, being self-explanatory and easy to fill out, are preferred to unstructured questionnaires for this reason. Structured questionnaires are similar in format to structured interviews.

While questionnaires typically use forced-response questions because they are simple and easy to fill out, they can also include open-ended questions if these questions are self-explanatory. However, one drawback to including open-ended questions is that they require more time to fill out. Usually, one or two open-ended questions can be added at the end of a structured questionnaire without diminishing the rate of response.

An example of a structured questionnaire is a course evaluation instrument that students fill out to evaluate a course and the instructor at the end of each semester. While most of the questions in such an instrument are forced-response, a few open-ended questions (e.g., "What do you like about this course?") are often asked at the end. Many restaurant evaluation cards are another example of a structured questionnaire.

Although there is no standard type of unstructured questionnaire, a questionnaire composed entirely of open-ended questions would be an example of one. However, most respondents may be discouraged from completing a questionnaire that has too many open-ended questions because of the perceived time involved in completing it. Thus, unstructured questionnaires tend to have a low rate of response and are less often used. Examples of unstructured questionnaires include

- a client satisfaction questionnaire with open-ended questions (e.g., What do you like about the services you received? What do you dislike? etc.)
- a questionnaire with a journal format that can be used by a client to document times and circumstances when depression is evident

Ways to Administer Questionnaires

Questionnaires can be administered in a face-to-face encounter, through the mail, or via computers. Face-to-face questionnaires, for example, can be administered to clients, students, and staff members during the times they meet. Mailed questionnaires are easy to administer; they simply require a mailing address, an envelope, and postage. Electronic or computerized questionnaires are the latest development in questionnaire studies. A computerized self-administered questionnaire can be sent via floppy disk or e-mail attachment, or it can be accessed on a Website or an electronic bulletin board (Babbie, 2001). The responses can be saved and maintained on an electronic file, which is automatically prepared for data analysis. Electronic questionnaires can also circumvent some of costs involved in postal service mailings, because there is no additional cost for sending a questionnaire via the Internet. In addition, most computer users find them more convenient to fill out and return; once a questionnaire is completed, it can be returned by merely clicking on a command button such as "submit now." However, a major disadvantage of electronic questionnaires is that they exclude anyone without access to a computer. Returning completed questionnaires electronically also reveals the sender's identity.

Table 9.2 is a structured questionnaire that measures vulnerability to stress. While it does not measure stress itself, these authors assume that vulnerability to stress influences how much stress a person actually experiences. Fill out this questionnaire to determine your score.

After you fill out the instrument, look more closely at the questions of the instrument. Notice that it is a multidimensional measure of vulnerability. Several behaviors, not just one or a few, go into measuring vulnerability. You may think that only some of these items are relevant to you and your vulnerability to stress. For example, you may need only five or six hours of sleep in an average night not seven or eight (item 2), or you may not have the need to pray or meditate (item 6). You may also want to add other items to the questionnaire that are more relevant to you and your vulnerability to stress. Nevertheless, the large and varied number of questions that are asked are intended to take into account a wide range of lifestyles of the people filling out the questionnaire; each person should find at least some questions that are relevant to them.

TABLE 9.2   Example of a Questionnaire: How Vulnerable Are You to Stress?

Score each item from 1 (almost always), 2 (usually), 3 (sometimes), 4 (occasionally), and 5 (never), according to how much of the time each statement applies to you.

_____ 1. I eat at least one hot, balanced meal a day.

_____ 2. I get seven to eight hours sleep at least four nights a week.

_____ 3. I give and receive affection regularly.

_____ 4. I have at least one relative within 50 miles on whom I can rely.

_____ 5. I exercise to the point of perspiration at least twice a week.

_____ 6. I pray or meditate.

_____ 7. I take fewer than three alcoholic drinks a week.

_____ 8. I am the appropriate weight for my height.

_____ 9. I have an income adequate to meet basic expenses.

_____ 10. I get strength from my religious beliefs.

_____ 11. I regularly attend club or social activities.

_____ 12. I have a network of friends and acquaintances.

_____ 13. I have one or more friends to confide in about personal matters.

_____ 14. I am in good health (including eyesight, hearing, teeth).

_____ 15. I am able to speak openly about my feelings when angry or worried.

_____ 16. I have regular conversations with the people I live with about domestic problems (e.g., chores, money, and daily living issues).

_____ 17. I do something for fun at least once a week.

_____ 18. I am able to organize my time effectively.

_____ 19. I drink fewer than three cups of coffee, tea, or cola each day.

_____ 20. I take quiet or rest times for myself during the day.

_____   Total Score

To calculate your score, add up the numbers and subtract 20. Any number over 30 indicates a vulnerability to stress. You are seriously vulnerable if your score is between 50 and 75, and extremely vulnerable if it is over 75.

Source: Adapted from _How Vulnerable Are You to Stress?_ by L. Miller and A. Smith, no date, Boston University Medical Center.

Similarities between Data Collection in Research and Social Work

A short digression is appropriate at this time to point out how the data collection tools in research and social work practice are similar. A large percentage of a social worker's job involves interviewing clients, family members, and agency personnel. The three types of research interviews described above are similar in format to interviews used by a social worker, as summarized in Table 9.3.

TABLE 9.3   Social Workers' Use of Interviews

Interview Format	Use in Social Work
Structured interview	Occasional use (e.g., structured intake form)
Semistructured interview	Frequent use (e.g., flexible intake interview, assessment, focus group)
Unstructured interview	Most often used (e.g., typical unstructured social work interview)

1. *Structured interviews.* Occasionally social workers use an interview format similar to a structured interview. An example is an intake interview with a new client. A typical intake interview may include forced-response questions about who lives in the household; their ages, health conditions, employment status, and sources of income; the age and gender of the children; information about the children's school arrangements; and so on. These questions vary, of course, depending on the type of intake information needed by a social agency.

2. *Semistructured interviews.* Social workers frequently use an interview format that is like a semistructured interview. Examples include
   - a flexible intake or assessment interview that allows for variations in how the questions are asked
   - a social history that includes an in-depth exploration of some topics
   - a client exit interview that is flexibly administered to find out how clients perceived their agency experience in retrospect
   - many exercises used in small groups (e.g., an introductory ice breaker in which members interview each other and then introduce each other to the group)
   - focus groups that are usually organized around several open-ended questions

3. *Unstructured interviews.* Social workers usually use an unstructured format in most of their interviews with clients. Examples include
   - a counseling session
   - most family interviews
   - most small-group sessions
   - any free-floating discussion with a client, with the social worker assuming such roles as broker, mediator, or advocate

4. *Questionnaires.* Social workers also frequently use a questionnaire format in their work. A questionnaire format can be used in a variety of ways, including
   - gathering information for an intake or assessment
   - a performance or evaluation test
   - a client satisfaction survey

- a client case record that outlines topics to be filled in
- an exam for a course

This review of some of the similarities between research and social work data collection methods suggests that people who have a predisposition to social work are also likely to have a predisposition to collecting research data. Both enterprises wish to learn more about people and their circumstances by employing interviews and questionnaires.

Importance of High Response Rates

The response rate in survey studies is an important factor to consider. The **response rate** is the proportion of people who complete and return a survey. Response rates of survey studies vary widely. While there is no absolute rule about what constitutes an adequate response rate, usually a response rate of 50 percent or higher is adequate for analysis and reporting, particularly in a professional journal (Babbie, 2001). Exploratory studies that are not concerned with generalizing to a larger population may be somewhat less concerned about the response rate. However, reports of the findings of such studies should note which subgroups have a low response rate and how this may influence the nature of the findings.

The response rate can be an important factor in determining if the sample of a survey study is representative of a larger population. If the response rate is low, there is a high chance of a response bias. In this case, there will be a large number of nonrespondents, and they may differ in important ways from the respondents who participate in the study. Studies about controversial topics, for example, are likely to draw a higher response from those who feel strongly about the topic, whether positively or negatively. Conversely, the people without strong views will likely be underrepresented.

Maintaining the diversity of a sample is important in most survey studies. In these instances, if one subgroup of people is underrepresented, the findings will be less useful in understanding this particular subgroup. For example, a study about interracial relations in a neighborhood that is composed of African Americans, Cambodians, Koreans, and Puerto Ricans will be most valuable if there is a high response rate from all four subgroups.

Several techniques are available to increase the response rate of a study. Both the cover letter of a questionnaire and the introductory statement of an interview need to clearly communicate the purpose of a study and its importance. Phone interview studies, for example, are likely to have a higher response rate if the interviewer can explain the purpose and benefits of the study clearly, quickly, and convincingly. Ethical standards also need to be emphasized in these introductory statements to address any fears or lack of trust evident in respondents.

Mail questionnaire studies usually ensure a higher return rate by sending a reminder letter or postcard a week or two after the questionnaire is sent. Respondents often forget to respond to a survey after it is received, but they are often more responsive if they are reminded a second time. Questionnaires and interviews that are administered face to face are likely to have the highest response rates, because the surveys can be completed while the respondent is present.

Validity and Reliability Issues

Validity and reliability are important standards to emphasize when constructing survey instruments. Validity refers to the degree to which survey questions measure what they are supposed to measure. Reliability refers to the degree to which these questions are interpreted in the same way by different respondents and by the same respondents at different times. Validity and reliability issues are covered extensively in Chapter 5, along with the tests that can be used to measure these standards.

Both validity and reliability are strengthened by survey questions that are written in a clear and understandable way. Valid and reliable questions are also free of ambiguous and biased wording. Some of the typical flaws evident in survey questions related to validity and reliability standards are described on page 174. For example, in a client satisfaction study, validity and reliability are threatened if clients are asked about information that is difficult to recall, such as satisfaction with services received several months before, or if they are asked about current services that are described in a vague or nebulous way.

It is also important to have rigorous record-keeping procedures when conducting survey studies to ensure that the participants' responses are recorded accurately and completely. In structured interviews, this requires that interviewers be trained how to ask and record questions correctly. Accuracy of recording is even more challenging with qualitative surveys, because the responses are recorded in narrative form. In these instances, responses need to be recorded in verbatim form or as close to what was verbalized as possible. Videotaping of qualitative interviews is often preferred over recording by hand to ensure that the responses are as comprehensive and accurate as possible.

Comparing Interviews and Questionnaires

Both interviews and questionnaires have advantages and disadvantages. These advantages and disadvantages are related to such things as the validity and reliability of a survey, the response rate, the cost, and the time involved.

Interviews

Interviews are preferred over questionnaires for the following reasons:

- The questions can be clarified by the interviewer.
- A higher response rate is likely.
- Interviews are better suited for qualitative methods.
- Probing questions can be introduced to obtain elaboration on a response.

Some of the disadvantages of interviews include the high cost and greater time involved, the need to train interviewers, the respondents' lack of privacy in answering questions, and possible biases introduced by the interviewers' personal characteristics and the ways in which they ask questions.

Face-to-face interviews have the advantages of observing and responding to the nonverbal behavior of respondents, which is usually not accesssible in phone interviews. Face-to-face contact also provides access to people at specific sites and generally makes it easier to convince people to participate. Phone interviews, in contrast, have other advantages, including easier access to people in the privacy of their home; a greater possibility of maintaining anonymity; interviewing from a location of choice, such as home or an office; and more flexibility in determining when to administer the interview.

Questionnaires

Questionnaires have advantages as well and are preferred over interviews for the following reasons:

- Questionnaires are less expensive.
- They take less time to administer.
- No interviewer biases are introduced.
- Questionnaires can be disseminated via postal or electronic mail.
- Privacy and anonymity are more likely to be assured.

Some of the disadvantages of questionnaires include a lower response rate, inability to offer clarification for questions, difficulties when using qualitative methods, no opportunity to ask probing questions, no access to nonverbal communication, and not being sure who fills out the instrument.

Questionnaires administered on site have advantages. Typically, they have higher response rates than mailed questionnaires because the respondent can be encouraged to complete the survey at the time it is handed out. Yet, mailed questionnaires have advantages as well. One major advantage is that they can be sent to any location where there is an e-mail or postal address. A large number of questionnaires sent via an e-mail message can arrive at a variety of locations in a matter of a few minutes, while those sent via the postal system can arrive in a few days.

How to Construct a Survey

Constructing a survey, whether it is an interview or a questionnaire, consists of several important steps. The nine basic steps are summarized in Table 9.4 and described below.

1. *Identify the general purpose of the survey.* The first step in constructing a survey is to develop an overall purpose statement for it. This purpose should be

TABLE 9.4	Steps in Constructing a Survey

1. Identify the general purpose of the survey.

2. Identify the specific dimensions of the survey's purpose.

3. Select the preferred type of survey instrument.

4. Formulate possible questions to ask.

5. Select the best questions.

6. Craft questions without flaws.

7. Decide on the response options.

8. Determine the order for the questions.

9. Pretest the survey.

consistent with the general research questions of the study and should succinctly summarize the survey's intent. Some of the concepts in this purpose statement may need to be defined as well. For example, let's assume that the purpose of an interview study is "to determine if the clients of an agency are satisfied with the services they receive." The term *satisfaction* will likely need to be defined. It could be interpreted in various ways, for example, as "no major complaints," "being acceptable," or "being preferred over the services of competing agencies."

Examples of a General-Purpose Statement for Three Different Survey Studies

- To understand how teen parents understand their parental roles.
- To determine the nature and extent of mental illness among homeless people.
- To determine how satisfied staff members are with their jobs

2. *Identify the specific dimensions of the survey's purpose.* The next step is to begin to break down this purpose statement into subpurposes, or dimensions that are more specific. This step is particularly important if the concepts in the purpose statement are abstract. Let's use the example mentioned in the previous step (to determine if the clients of an agency are satisfied with the services they receive). "Services" can refer to numerous things. There are many different aspects or dimensions of services of importance to clients in an agency. Examples include the social worker's capacity to listen, the social worker's ability to help find solutions to their problems, the agency's fee schedule, how quickly the agency initially provides services, the physical accessibility of the agency, the psychological accessibility of the agency, whether services are available at convenient times, the role of the re-

ceptionist, and so on. It would be up to the researcher to decide which dimensions are most important to the study, and it would be very important to consult with staff members and clients before making a decision.

3. *Select the preferred type of survey instrument.* This step refers to the different types of surveys introduced earlier in the chapter and summarized in Table 9.1 (page 163). The researcher decides which one is the best fit for the purpose of the study. Each of the types of surveys has advantages and disadvantages, as described earlier, that are important to consider in making a decision. Also, the source of data can be critically important in deciding which survey type to use. For example, the best fit for a study of people who are unable to read would more likely be an interview than a questionnaire, while a phone interview or a mailed questionnaire may be the best fit for a regional study of social work graduates who live some distance from the researcher.

4. *Formulate possible questions that could be asked.* This step involves brainstorming. Jot down as many specific questions as you can think of that could be asked for each of the above dimensions of the general purpose. During this step, do not worry about how well the questions are written. Using the example of client satisfaction with services, you could come up with a few questions for each dimension of the overall purpose. For example, questions such as "Was the receptionist courteous?" and "Did the receptionist provide you with information that you needed?" could be asked to measure the role of the receptionist.

Content of Questions

Questions can focus on several different things (Patton, 1987), including:

1. *Experience or behavior questions* asking what a person does or has done (e.g., What steps did you take in finding a job?)
2. *Opinion or belief questions* asking about someone's goals, intentions, values, or desires (e.g., What is your opinion about affirmative action?)
3. *Feeling questions* about emotional responses to what happens around or to the person (e.g., How do you feel about the loss of your parent?)
4. *Knowledge questions* asking about knowledge of factual information (e.g., What is one of the high-risk sexual behaviors associated with contracting AIDS?)
5. *Sensory questions* about what is seen, heard, touched, tasted, or smelled (e.g., What did you hear when your parents were fighting?)
6. *Background questions* about the identifying characteristics of a person (e.g., How much formal education do you have?)

---

5. *Select the best questions.* Next, pick out the best questions for addressing the various dimensions of the survey's purpose. Content validity is important here, as you will want to select a few questions for each dimension. Selecting the best questions involves a careful review of each question to determine whether it is important to the focus of the study. Questions that do not fulfill a specific

purpose should not be used. Here are some criteria for selecting the best questions (Taber, 1965):

1. Is this question necessary?
2. How will the responses to the question be used?
3. Are several questions rather than one needed to obtain the information needed?
4. Do the participants have the information that is being asked?
5. Will the participants be willing to share this information accurately?
6. Is the question so vague that the responses may not be comparable?
7. Is the question so specific that it unnecessarily limits the response?

6. *Craft flaw-free questions.* Now, refine the questions so that they are as free as possible of flaws. Numerous flaws can be created when formulating questions. They include five typical ones found in many questions (Bailey, 1994):

1. use of ambiguous wording
2. double-barreled questions (two questions asked together)
3. leading questions that favor a particular response
4. sensitive questions leading to normative responses
5. overlooking a time frame in the question

Such flaws as these are likely to threaten the validity of the survey, because they result in responses that are not accurate or honest. Flawed questions that illustrate each of these five problems are listed in the box below.

TEST YOUR KNOWLEDGE

Flawed Questions

Identify the flaw in each of the following questions. Then, rewrite the question to correct the problem.

Questions with Ambiguous Wording

What is your annual income?
When do you work?

Two Questions in One

Do you think that the social worker was friendly and sensitive to your needs?
Are you satisfied with your supervisor, or would you prefer someone else?

Leading Questions

Do you support the woman's right to choose what happens to her body?
Do you support the right to life of a fetus?

Sensitive Questions Leading to Normative Responses

Do you drive when you drink?
Do you beat your child?

Overlooking a Time Frame

Have you been dating anyone?
Are you satisfied with your school experience?

7. *Decide on the options for response categories.* After refining the questions, the next step is to decide the response options for each question. The first consideration is to decide whether you want open-ended or closed-ended questions (see Chapter 5). Open-ended questions are advantageous if

- you want the response to be in the participant's own words
- you do not know enough about how participants will respond to set up a set of response categories

Closed-ended, or forced-response, questions also have advantages, which include:

- You are interested in comparing the responses that participants give to the questions.
- You want to analyze the responses using statistical analysis.
- It is too difficult or too much to expect the participants to respond to open-ended questions.

If closed-ended questions are chosen, various types of response categories can be considered. The levels of measurement described in Chapter 5 provide important conceptual understanding for describing them. The various types of response categories will be referred to as nominal, ordinal, and prenominal. Let's first consider *nominal response categories*. These categories fulfill all of the characteristics of nominal variables, including that each category be distinct, have no categories that overlap, and have a complete or exhaustive list of categories from which to choose. *Ordinal response categories* have all three of the nominal characteristics, and the categories are grouped in an order.

While ordinal response categories must be listed in a logical order (e.g., upper class, middle class, lower class), nominal categories have no order to them. Sometimes the order in which these categories are listed may influence which one is most likely to be selected. For example, respondents may have an inclination to select the first category. To avoid such a bias in the ordering of the categories, you could list them alphabetically or randomly. For example, a question asking which candidate you prefer for president of the United States could have the candidates listed in alphabetical order. Examples of nominal and ordinal response categories are described in Table 9.5.

Some questions have response categories that do not meet all of the requirements of the nominal level of measurement. These are *prenominal response categories*. For example, a question has several response categories, and the respondent is instructed to check all that apply, not just the most preferred response. In prenominal response categories, the intention of the question is not to "force" the best response but to permit multiple choices of responses. Another prenominal response approach would be for the respondent to add other response categories that are not included.

Questions with prenominal response categories are particularly useful in exploratory studies, when a forced-response is not that important. Here the intent is to give the respondent several choices, some of which could be new topics identified by the respondent. An example of a prenominal set of responses is shown in Table 9.6.

TABLE 9.5   Examples of Nominal and Ordinal Response Categories

Types of Response Categories	Examples of Types of Response Categories
Nominal • Each category is distinct. • There are no overlapping categories. • List of categories is complete.	*Nominal* Are you in favor or against the death penalty? _____ favor _____ against What is your political affiliation? _____ Democrat _____ Green Party _____ Independent _____ Republican _____ other (please identify) _____
Ordinal • Each category is distinct. • There are no overlapping categories. • List of categories is complete. • Categories have an order.	*Ordinal* Do you agree or disagree with the following statement: "Teenagers should be provided information about birth control in the schools"? _____ strongly agree _____ somewhat agree _____ not sure _____ somewhat disagree _____ strongly disagree

Closed-ended questions could also have responses at the *interval/ratio level of measurement*. In this case, categories would no longer be needed, as the response would be an exact measure. Examples would be questions that ask someone their age or the number of children that they have. The response would be an exact number, thus precluding the need for response categories.

8. *Determine the order for the questions.* This step sets up an order for the questions, particularly if it is a structured interview or questionnaire. The order in which questions are asked can be important, because some questions may influence how an interviewee will respond to other questions. Several issues are important to consider when establishing an order.

Sensitive questions can usually be handled by locating them at the end of the survey or by eliminating them if they are not necessary. Whether or not questions are sensitive may depend on who the research participants are. For example, asking participants their age may be a particularly sensitive matter for older

TABLE 9.6	Examples of Prenominal Response Categories	

Types of Response Category	Examples of Types of Response Categories
Prenominal	*Prenominal*
• fulfills only some of the characteristics of nominal response categories	What do you like to eat for breakfast? (Check all that apply.) _____ eggs _____ potatoes _____ bacon _____ sausage _____ bagels _____ toast _____ cereal _____ cheese _____ grits _____ Identify other foods _____

adults and also for young people in some circumstances but not for many others. While the age question can be asked at the end of the survey, another way to handle this sensitive issue would be to ask participants to identify their approximate age by having ranges of ages as response categories (e.g., under 21 years, 21–30, 31–40, etc.).

Example of a Sensitive Question

In one study of people with a dual diagnosis of mental illness and mental retardation, participants were asked a sensitive but important question that had not been asked in previous studies. The question was "Have you ever been forced to have sex with someone?" The researchers decided to ask this question because there were suspicions that some of these participants had been victims of sexual abuse. The researchers suspected that this question might stir up anger or other emotions that may discourage the clients from continuing the interview, so it was asked near the end of the interview. (Ahlgrim-Delzell & Dudley, 2001)

Another consideration in deciding on the order of questions is to cluster all of the questions on one topic together. In other words, avoid asking questions on the same topic in two or three different places in a survey. Clustering assists the research participant in considering one topic at a time. In an intake interview, for example, it is easiest to answer all of the questions about housing before covering employment issues or questions about the children's schools, day care, and so on.

Another consideration relates to the specificity of questions. Specific questions should follow general questions on the same topic. This order can assist the research participant in considering questions on one topic at a time. Also, asking general questions first encourages the respondents to share their own views on the general questions before responding to the specific questions formulated more to the researcher's views. General questions that introduce a new topic are sometimes referred to as *stem questions* in that they lead to specific questions on the same stem or topic.

An example would be a series of questions on evaluating a course. One of the general questions on a topic could be "What did you learn from this course?" Specific questions could follow on the specific dimensions of the course (lectures, readings, discussions, assignments, etc.). For example, a question could be asked about the class discussions—"What did you learn from the class discussions?" If even more specific questions are to be asked about the discussions, they would logically come next. For example, "What did you learn from the class discussions about ethical issues?"

Contingency questions are also a consideration in the ordering of questions. *Contingency questions* guide the respondent to the next question to answer when one answer to the prior question leads to one next question and another answer leads to a different next question. Setting up contingency questions provides a road map that has different routes for the respondents to follow, depending on how they respond to questions along the way. An example of a contingency question is described below. This example was used in a survey in which the purpose was to identify possible employers for BSW graduates.

"Do you hire BSW graduates at your agency?"
___ yes → If "yes," go to the next question.
___ no → If "no," go to question 23.

9. *Pretest the survey.* A pretest is a valuable step in the construction of a survey. Unfortunately, this step is often overlooked in the hastiness to begin data collection. A *pretest* is a rehearsal or role-play in which the survey is administered to someone posing as an interviewee. Pretests are helpful in resolving misunderstandings and ambiguities in the survey. For example, the instructions for completing a questionnaire may not be complete, a question may be unclear or leading, or the respondents may not know how to record their responses on the questionnaire. Also, a pretest can help determine the approximate time involved in completing the survey, which is a piece of valuable information to mention in the instructions. If it does takes too long, the survey should be shortened. Pretests are most useful if they are conducted with people who are similar to the people to be studied. In most cases, rehearsals with two to five respondents are sufficient for obtaining helpful information about the survey.

After having respondents complete the survey, you could ask them additional questions, such as:

- Was the survey too long, too short, or just right?
- Are there any questions that are unclear? Explain why the question(s) is unclear to you.
- Are there any questions you think should be asked that are not in the survey?
- Are there any questions that seem unnecessary or inappropriate?

Pretests can be conducted in various ways. One type of pretest is the "talk out loud method" (Ahlgrim-Delzell, personal communication, 2003). This approach is particularly useful in pretesting a questionnaire. As respondents rehearse their responses, they talk out loud about how they are answering each question, which helps the researcher determine whether or not they are understanding the questions as they are intended.

Constructing Qualitative Surveys

The steps used in constructing surveys are somewhat different based on whether quantitative or qualitative methods are used. The steps in constructing qualitative surveys are a more flexible variation of the steps involved in constructing quantitative surveys, as summarized in Table 9.7. Note that steps 2, 4, and 5 have more

TABLE 9.7 **Constructing Qualitative Surveys versus Quantitative Surveys**

Steps for Quantitative Surveys	Steps for Qualitative Surveys
1. Identify the general purpose of the survey.	1. No variation
2. Identify the specific dimensions of the survey's purpose.	2. No variation, except additional dimensions may be discovered during data collection.
3. Select the preferred type of survey instrument.	3. No variation
4. Formulate possible questions to ask.	4. No variation, except some questions could be refined and modified after data collection begins.
5. Select the best questions.	5. It is not as important to restrict the number of questions to be asked prior to data collection.
6. Craft questions without flaws.	6. No variation
7. Decide on the response options.	7. Open-ended questions, which do not have response categories, are primarily used.
8. Determine order for the questions.	8. The order is often less important.
9. Pretest the survey.	9. No variation

flexibility. These steps can only be defined to the extent that is possible. Also note in step 7 that the questions in qualitative surveys are typically open ended, in contrast to the more typical use of forced-response questions in quantitative surveys. While it is generally important to follow a logical order in asking questions in qualitative surveys (step 8), flexibility is often permissible, particularly in following the lead of the interviewee in discussing topics that naturally come up in the flow of the conversation.

Qualitative surveys are intended to be exploratory, and the questions that are asked encourage an elaboration of a point rather than a standardized response that can be reduced to a numerical score. Response categories are not used, because they tend to restrict the nature of the participant's response. Also, qualitative questions do not have to be used in exactly the same way for every participant. Qualitative interviews are flexibly administered so that they can be responsive to each participant's circumstances and the unique dynamics of each interview.

Example of Flexibility in a Qualitative Study

In her qualitative study of women on welfare, Seccombe (1999) was interested in understanding poverty from a woman's perspective. Rather than developing measures of the major problems beforehand, Seccombe used qualitative interviews that had more flexibility. For example, she explored the concept of stigma related to being on welfare by asking the mothers to describe their encounters with stigma. Follow-up questions asked them to elaborate on these encounters. She also asked them what they had heard people say about welfare and then used their responses to delve into the topic of stigma more deeply. She also asked them to share how they felt they were treated differently or unfairly compared to someone not on welfare.

Chapter Reflections

Values and Ethics, Diversity, At-Risk Groups, and Social Justice

Numerous ethical problems and issues are potentially evident in deciding on a data collection approach. Is the data collection approach, for example, suitable to the population being studied? Will it facilitate open, honest, and accurate responses? Ethical issues are also associated with how the questions are crafted. Are the questions flexible enough to allow the participants to communicate adequately about their circumstances? Also, are the questions that are asked free of flaws? Leading questions, for example, have a bias inherent in them and should be avoided. Sensitive questions have ethical implications as well. A sensitive question should be formulated carefully so that it does not unnecessarily invade a participant's privacy or potentially contribute harm. Moreover, if a strong rationale cannot be made for asking questions on sensitive topics, such questions probably should be avoided altogether.

Another ethical issue in data collection relates to choice. An important social work value is self-determination, suggesting that survey questions should have as many response choices as are relevant to the group being studied. For example, Likert scales, which usually have five or more response choices, are preferred to a yes/no response set. Open-ended questions, of course, offer an unlimited number of options for responding to a question.

Diversity issues are also important in an approach to data collection. The choice of an approach entails giving thought to its appropriateness for all groups of interest. For example, will people be inadvertently left out of a study because they cannot read a questionnaire in English or at the level it is written? Will others be left out if they are not provided a mailed questionnaire that will ensure them anonymity? Diversity issues are also important in crafting questions. This is illustrated by the questionnaire on vulnerability to stress (Table 9.2). As discussed in the chapter, a strength of this instrument is the variety of items that take into account a diversity of lifestyles. In addition, the study about women on welfare (page 180) illustrates how flexibility can be built into qualitative data collection methods.

Diverse and at-risk groups are identified in other illustrations in the chapter to highlight their importance related to data collection. For example, a survey study about the social supports of Vietnamese immigrants is described on page 163, and another survey study focuses on African American children with emotional disorders (page 164). Further, when little is known about a group of people, including at-risk groups, qualitative approaches, such as unstructured interviews and unstructured observation, are important to consider.

Similarly, social justice issues are important to consider in developing a data collection instrument. The qualitative study dealing with the stigma problems of women on welfare (page 180) illustrates how data collection can be designed so that the participants can take an active role in examining the problems they are facing. Social justice issues can also be linked to how a survey is constructed. For example, a pretest is the final step in the construction of a survey. When prospective participants are actively involved in this step, they can have an important role in the construction of the survey. They can become, in essence, consultants who are partners in helping to prepare the study.

D i s c u s s i o n   Q u e s t i o n s

1. Each of the following questions has one or more flaws. Identify these flaws. How would you improve these questions if you were going to include them on a questionnaire? (Review the five typical flaws described on page 174.)
   - What is your annual income?____
   - Were you satisfied with your field experience? __ yes __ no
   - Are you in agreement with the NASW Code of Ethics and committed to abiding by it? __ yes __ no
   - Do you agree with faculty that all of the papers and exams assigned are necessary and valuable for your learning experience? __ yes __ no

- Do you feel you will be a mediocre social worker? __ yes __ no
- Do you have a disability? __ yes __ no

2. Review the instrument measuring vulnerability to stress in Table 9.2. Craft two questions that were not asked that would be relevant to you and could influence your vulnerability to stress.

3. Assume that you are a new social worker employed in a residential complex for retired people. In talking to one resident, you find out that he has complaints about the quality of the food, the limited variety of social activities, and the inadequate transportation to nearby stores and restaurants. Furthermore, he states that the administrators of the facility tend to ignore his complaints and those of other residents. Construct a questionnaire composed of six questions that will help you to find out the extent to which other residents feel the way he does. You can use quantitative and/or qualitative survey questions.

4. Divide your class into groups of three. Have each group complete the following steps:
   - Select a topic of interest. Examples of topics could include attitudes about binge drinking, date rape, abortion, the war on terrorism, affirmative action, and so on.
   - Craft three interview questions on the topic that could be asked of other students.
   - Prepare an informed consent protocol that explains to the people you interview who you are, your purpose (e.g., a class project in a social work research course), how you will use their responses (share in class), and your intention of confidentiality.
   - Have each student interview two students (a total of six students per group) using the three interview questions.
   - After completing these interviews, have the students share their results in their small groups and identify what they learned about the topic and their interview questions. Students could then revise their questions based on what they learned.

References

Ahlgrim-Delzell, L., & Dudley, J. (2001). Confirmed, unconfirmed, and false allegations of abuse made by adults with mental retardation who are members of a class action lawsuit. *Child Abuse and Neglect, 25*, 1121–1132.

Babbie, E. (2001). *The practice of social research,* 9th ed. Belmont, CA: Wadsworth/Thomson Learning.

Bailey, K. (1994). *Methods of social research.* New York: Free Press.

Gellis, Z. (2003). Kin and nonkin social supports in a community sample of Vietnamese immigrants. *Social Work, 48*(2), 248–258.

Kruzich, J., Friesen, B., Williams-Murphy, T., & Longley, M. (2002). Voices of African American families: Perspectives on residential treatment. *Social Work, 47*(4), 461–470.

Marlow, C. (2001). *Research methods for generalist social work,* 3rd ed. Stamford, CT: Thomson Learning.

Miller, L., & Smith, A. (n.d.). *How vulnerable are you to stress?* Boston: Boston University Medical Center.

Patton, M. (1987). *How to use qualitative methods in evaluation.* Newbury Park, CA: Sage.

Seccombe, K. (1999). *So you think I drive a Cadillac: Welfare recipients' perspectives on the system and its reform.* Boston: Allyn and Bacon.

Taber, M. (1965). *Criteria for questionnaire and schedule items.* Urbana: School of Social Work, University of Illinois.

Taylor, S., & Bogdan, R. (1984). *Introduction to qualitative research methods: The search for meanings,* 2nd ed. New York: Wiley.

chapter 10

Constructing Observational Studies

Observations can sometimes uncover what may never be openly shared in an interview format, for example, a teenager's discussion about sexuality with her mother, a mother's nurture of her newborn infant during nursing, a father's bonding with his children while playing with them, or an older adult telling a story as a way of passing on wisdom to young children.

The second major type of data collection is observation. As you can see in the listing, observation is one of the two basic choices for a data collection approach in step 3b.

Observational research is very relevant to social work research, since social workers regularly depend on their observational skills in practice. Social workers are taught to pay close attention to what they observe when meeting with their clients, particularly when visiting them in their homes. The nonverbal communication of clients, in particular, is often viewed to be as important as their verbal communication. Because social workers are often involved in home visits and community outreach, they find themselves in social situations that provide excellent opportunities for observational research.

Observational research is a process of using all of the senses, particularly sight and hearing, to collect data about something. Observation focuses on what can be seen or heard—the behaviors of people. Behavior can be any of a number of things, such as a verbal comment or nonverbal expression, a conversation between two or more people, body movements of people, and physical contact between people. Observations can also focus on physical structures or objects present in the environment and aspects of nature, such as trees and rain.

Observational research is not intended to collect data about many of the things that survey research investigates, namely people's attitudes, emotions, knowledge, beliefs, and viewpoints. The behavior of people is often more important to consider

Steps in the Research Process
1. Understanding the research topic to be studied
2. Focusing the study
3. Designing the study
a. Selecting the participants
b. Selecting a data collection approach and measuring concepts
• Surveys
• **Observations**
c. Exploring causal relationships
4. Collecting the data
5. Analyzing the data
6. Preparing a report

than viewpoints or attitudes. After all, what people do seems to be more important than what they say. This is frequently the case in social work practice. If you want to find out if you have been effective in helping clients, you will likely want to know what the clients are doing differently. You could attempt to find this out by asking them what they are doing, but their reports of their behavior may be less accurate and complete than observing it firsthand. For example, wouldn't you prefer to see improved communication occurring between a parent and child in a family in which child abuse has been a problem rather than being told about the communication improvement from the parent? And wouldn't it be preferable for a supervisor to learn more about the job performance of a staff member by observing the person rather than seeking secondhand sources of information?

Even so, observational research is not always feasible, even when it is the preferred approach. In many instances, the behavior of interest is beyond the reach of an observational researcher. For example, observing the behavior between a parent and child when child abuse is a problem is likely to only happen in the privacy of the family's home when no one else is present. The job performance of a staff member in helping a client can also be difficult to observe, because the observer's presence may interfere with the interactions between the social worker and the client or may not be permitted. Even in many episodes in which services are being provided, an outside observer is not welcome. One example of this is the meetings of Alcoholics Anonymous groups, which usually are closed to nonrecovering people. Generally, observational research is best suited to episodes or activities that are open to the public or permit the presence of outsiders.

Conducting Structured Observations

Observational research can be structured or unstructured. Structured observation is usually deductive in nature and attempts to find support for or cast doubt on something. Structured studies identify and develop measures of the specific behaviors of interest to the researcher prior to conducting a study. Like any deductive study, these behaviors are hypothesized to be evident in at least some of the people who are studied.

This approach uses quantitative methods usually in the form of an *observational rating scale* that records particular behaviors that are observed. A rating scale lists specific types of behaviors and a place on the scale for recording when these behaviors are observed. For example, children with Attention Deficit/Hyperactivity Disorder could be monitored in a classroom situation for disruptive behaviors such as getting out of their seats without permission, talking to other students, or hitting someone. Such behaviors could be observed over time to determine if the student is improving in these areas. The researchers who collect observational data are sometimes referred to as *observational raters*.

An example of a structured study that observed interruptions in conversations between males and females is summarized next.

Example of a Structured Observational Study

Two sociologists from the University of California (Pfeiffer, 1985) were interested in interruptions that occurred in conversations, particularly in two-person male-female conversations. They unobtrusively observed conversations in public places as part of a expanding field of language research on the role of gender in speech. One of their findings was that males accounted for 96 percent of the interruptions.

An example of another observational rating scale was developed by Bales (1950). In this classic study, Bales observed interactions in several types of task groups and found that these groups had to address two types of problems. The first type were instrumental problems related to tasks and goals, and the second type were socioemotional problems related to member satisfaction, coordination, and interpersonal difficulties. These two problem areas led to the identification of twelve specific behaviors observed in the groups, as seen in Table 10.1. By observing and recording these behaviors in small task groups, Bales was able to compile an overall assessment of how well a group was functioning. He believed that a group functions best when it has some behaviors addressing both instrumental and socioemotional issues.

The raters in observational studies need training to help them identify the behaviors that are the focus of a study because these may be difficult to identify. The Bales study is an example of this. Behaviors that involve "releasing tension" or "showing solidarity" are not fully self-explanatory. For example, if expressions of anger are considered manifestations of releasing tension, how would a rater know that a person was angry. Anger can be manifested in several different ways. Moreover, one observational rater may notice an angry behavior, while another rater may not. Training that offers video illustrations of such behaviors and exercises that involve identifying such behaviors can be part of the raters' preparation.

TABLE 10.1 **Example of an Observational Rating Instrument by Bales**

Behaviors Addressing Instrumental Issues	Behaviors Addressing Socioemotional Issues
• asking for opinions	• expressing agreement
• giving opinions	• expressing disagreement
• asking for information	• showing tension
• giving information	• releasing tension
• asking for suggestions	• showing solidarity
• giving suggestions	• showing antagonism

Another necessary component of a structured observational study is *inter-rater reliability* (see Chapter 5). Interrater reliability is useful in determining how consistently behaviors are observed and recorded. It involves two or more raters observing the same episodes or social situations independent of each other. The recordings of these raters' observations are then analyzed to determine the extent to which they are consistent with each other. For example, did both raters observe the same behaviors, and did they classify these behaviors in the same way (e.g., classify an expression of anger as releasing tension and not something else, as in the Bales study)?

Conducting Unstructured Observations

Unstructured observation is a data collection approach that is more inductive in nature and is useful in gaining new insights about something. Observations are recorded by the researcher without a structured instrument. Instead, topical areas of interest are often identified that provide a general focus for the observation. Recordings of such observations are usually in the form of detailed notes or narrative records that describe what is being observed.

Observational studies can actually be conducted using varying degrees of structure; they do not have to be either all structured or unstructured. For example, a researcher may want to observe teenagers in a shopping center to gain insights about their contacts with each other. This can be done without a totally structured instrument. For example, a researcher can use a combination of both some structure and a lot of flexibility to focus on such things as who talks with whom, who initiates the contact, what they talk about, when they meet, locations where they hang out, and other related topics.

Participant Observation

One important variation in unstructured observational studies has to do with whether or not the researcher participates in the activities being observed. Sometimes, unstructured observation involves the researcher as a participant, while in other cases the researcher remains solely an observer. Participant observation is an observational data collection approach in which the researcher participates to some extent with the people being studied. A participant role is used to help the researcher become more of an "insider" who observes people and their social context from the inside out. Examples of how one researcher (Dudley, 1983) took on the participant role in a study of the stigma problems of people with mental retardation included:

- dancing with the people being studied
- eating with them at restaurants
- riding public transportation with them
- joining them for visits at their home

- sitting with them at their workstation at a sheltered workshop
- double dating with a couple being observed
- talking with them or listening to their conversations at various social occasions

The participant role of the researcher must be introduced in such a way that it does not interfere with the behaviors being observed. This requires being able to participate enough to become an "insider" but not so much as to create unnecessary reactivity. Participant observers usually begin with a rapport-building period to gain acceptance as insiders before fully concentrating on data collection. This initial period is a time in which such things as informed consent issues and the researcher's role can be clarified and supported.

Participant observation is an approach that is similar to the traditional research approach used by cultural anthropologists in studying people within their culture (Ferraro, 2000). Participant observers are likely to emphasize unstructured or semistructured interviewing methods along with unstructured observation. When interviewing methods are used, these researchers essentially follow the same procedures for unstructured or semistructured interviews described in Chapter 9 on constructing surveys.

Nonparticipatory Unstructured Observation

Unstructured observation can also be conducted without a participatory role by the researcher. However, in such situations, researchers must take into account that their presence can affect the ways in which the people to be observed will interact with each other. In this regard, it is important for these researchers to minimize any reactivity created by their presence. Usually this is done by observing people through a one-way mirror or by using video technology or digital photography to minimize the impact of the observer's presence. In these instances, the people gradually forget that they are being observed or at least become more relaxed about it. A carefully developed informed consent protocol also helps participants gain more trust and comfort with what the researcher is doing.

Unstructured observational studies, like structured ones, must have a means of assessing interrater reliability. Interrater reliability is introduced to determine how consistently the behaviors of people are being observed and recorded. This can be done by assigning two researchers to observe some of the same episodes independent of each other. Their recordings can then be analyzed to determine the extent to which they are consistent with each other. Introducing interrater reliability with unstructured observations is also important in determining the extent to which the larger social context is observed and described comprehensively. In a study of gang behavior, for example, one researcher may recall a particular exchange between gang members and the police that was a catalyst in provoking violent gang activity in a particular community, while another researcher may have overlooked this exchange.

Table 10.2 summarizes the major characteristics of both structured and unstructured observation and how they are different in their purposes and strategies.

TABLE 10.2   Characteristics of Structured and Unstructured Observational Approaches

Structured Observation	Unstructured Observation
• The evaluator or researcher is strictly an observer; there is no participation or involvement in the observed activity to maintain objectivity.	• The evaluator or researcher has the option of becoming involved as a participant in the activities being observed, if it can help to blend in. Participation is possible as long as a participant role does not interfere with what is being observed.
• Research questions or hypotheses usually offer a theoretical explanation for something prior to data collection. Then attempts are made through observation to find support for or cast doubt on this explanation (e.g., determining how long clients wait to be seen by a social worker).	• The focus of research questions is usually broad and exploratory.
	• Theoretical explanations are usually not initially offered; instead, efforts are made to discover explanations through what is observed.
• The focus is usually narrow and not open to change once data collection begins.	• The behaviors of interest to the researcher are usually not well defined, and structured measurement instruments are usually not available.
• Variables are measurable behaviors (e.g., number of times a child cries).	• The focus is usually open and flexible enough to include unexpected observations of behaviors not initially identified.
• An observational rating scale is typically used to record data (e.g., a checklist of polite and impolite behaviors by a receptionist).	• Activities are usually observed in a natural environment (e.g., a field agency), not research labs.
• Ideally, two independent researchers observe at least some of the same activities to determine the reliability of the data that are collected.	• Several observational sessions (longitudinal) are often conducted, with the initial sessions being primarily used for rapport building and blending in.
• Activities are often observed in a lab setting. Video technology, digital photography, or one-way mirrors are helpful aids in collecting data, because they can minimize the reactivity caused by an observer's presence.	• Note taking is in narrative form.
	• Data are mostly in qualitative form and are descriptive and detailed. (See Patton, 1987, pp. 93–94, for examples.)
	• Quotes or near quotations of important topics or conversations are highly desired if they can be recalled.
• Either one observational session (cross-sectional) or several observational sessions (longitudinal) are possible.	• The evaluator's impressions and feelings are recorded separately from what is observed as a check and balance on the observer's biases. The evaluator's impressions and feelings can also be helpful in analyzing the data as they provide insights and interpretations for the data being analyzed.
• Data are in quantitative form and are analyzed using an electronic statistical program (e.g., SPSS).	• Data are mostly analyzed using qualitative techniques.

Ethical Problems in Observing Covertly

As in any study, a thorough informed consent protocol is very important to incorporate into an observational study. Informed consent, as explained in Chapter 3, is a requirement for all research funded by the government. This includes research conducted by all universities and most nongovernmental agencies. Many observational studies of state hospitals, prisons, and other large institutions in the past were conducted without the residents' awareness, because there was no informed consent. While such studies exposed many of the adverse conditions of institutions on their residents, they would not be permitted today because of strict informed consent requirements of all governmental agencies and other funding groups. Goffman's (1962) study of a state mental hospital, described below, is an example of a seminal study that was conducted in the early 1960s before informed consent procedures were required.

Example of Participant Observation Research without Adequate Informed Consent

Goffman, a prominent sociologist during the middle of the twentieth century, conducted a study of a state mental hospital prior to the deinstitutionalization movement (Goffman, 1962). His intent was to learn more about the adverse effects of large, impersonal institutional structures on the residents. Goffman was assigned a disguised role as an "assistant recreation director" so that he could wander throughout the hospital without anyone knowing what he was doing. The superintendent, who gave approval for the study to be conducted, was the only one who knew about it.

Goffman's findings portrayed this institution as highly routinized, impersonal, and rigid and designed to accommodate the needs of the staff, not the residents. This was a seminal study because it provided dramatic new insights into the defects of large institutional settings like state mental hospitals. The results of the study served as an important catalyst for discharging large numbers of people from institutions. Goffman did not follow any informed consent procedures, but he significantly contributed to the enhancement of the lives of people with a mental illness. This study would not be possible in its present form today because of the current laws and policies pertaining to informed consent.

Some principles related to informed consent need to be implemented in observational studies. These principles include the following:

- The rights and well-being of every research participant must always be respected and protected.
- Both the purpose of the study and the researcher's role must be disclosed to research participants in a general way at the very least. Nondisclosure of a study's research purpose and the researchers' identity is unethical and should not be considered.
- Researchers should consider sharing the findings of their observational studies with the people who were observed after the observations are completed, if

these participants can benefit from hearing about such findings. Seeking feedback from them on the accuracy of the recordings can also serve as a cross-check on their validity.

It is important to note that informed consent procedures may sometimes be in conflict with a competing consideration—how to minimize the reactivity of a research observer. It is often true that the more researchers disclose about the purpose of their study and their research role, the more reactivity they will introduce. In these instances, a general disclosure of the researchers' purpose and role can be provided. Specific information about the study (e.g., the hypotheses) that may inhibit or bias the behavior of those being observed can be withheld. Such specific information can always be shared after the study is completed if it is important for participants to know.

Advantages of Observational Research

Observational research has many advantages and benefits over other approaches such as interviews or questionnaires. These advantages include:

- Observations are the only way to document behaviors firsthand.
- Observing behavior is preferred over reporting about behavior on a second-hand basis.
- Observational research can be holistic—looking beyond an immediate research focus to other related factors or larger contextual issues.
- Sometimes observation can uncover what may never be openly shared in an interview format.

TEST YOUR KNOWLEDGE **An Ethics Scenario**

You are a supervisor and you want to evaluate the impact that counseling groups have on members or clients. As a supervisor, you have in mind such questions as "Is this group beneficial to its members?" "How is it beneficial?" "Are the members of the group benefiting from the help that members give to each other in the group?" You want a noninvolved social worker to observe the group, but you are concerned that this evaluation could be disruptive to the group and may inhibit the participation of the group members. Answer the following questions:

1. What ethical issues may need to be considered in this observational study? How would you address them?
2. What will you say to the group leader and group members to provide "informed consent"?
3. What can you do to minimize disrupting and inhibiting the group process while observing?
4. How can you implement any aspects of a participatory action research approach?

Validity and Reliability Issues

Validity and reliability are important standards to emphasize in observational research. Observational research typically has strong validity, because researchers are actually seeing firsthand the behavior of interest. As an example, if a social worker wants to monitor the quality of a client's participation in a group therapy session, observing the behavior directly in the group is preferred to self-reporting by the client or the group leader. Self-reporting is limited by such things as memory limitations, what the self-reporter chooses to emphasize and deemphasize, any attempts to provide misinformation, and other biases.

The record-keeping procedures in observational studies must be handled in a rigorous way to ensure accurate records of what was observed. Videotaping of the episode is the ideal way to recall observations, if it can be arranged. Otherwise, detailed handwritten records should be completed within a timely period following an observation to ensure adequate recall. Usually, a shorthand version of notes can be completed immediately after an observation; a detailed narrative recording can follow sometime later in the same day of the observations. Considerable memory loss usually begins to set in and significantly reduces recall by the day after an observation.

Reliability is a more difficult standard to ensure, especially in unstructured observational studies. Interrater reliability, described earlier in the chapter, is most important to introduce. Different observers often see different things or see things somewhat differently. Having two or more researchers recording observations of the same activities independent of each other helps to strengthen reliability and minimize observer biases. Similarly, reliability is strengthened in structured observational studies when two or more raters observe the same activities and fill out the same rating scales independent of each other.

How to Construct an Observational Data Collection Instrument

Constructing a data collection instrument for observational research is similar in many ways to constructing a survey instrument. A summary of the differences in how these steps are conducted is described in Table 10.3. Essentially, observational procedures emphasize measures of behaviors rather than measures of attitudes, beliefs, motivation, and other interior factors.

Structured and unstructured observational instruments are constructed differently. If researchers construct structured observational instruments, they will follow the steps described in the right column of Table 10.3. Unstructured observational instruments would involve a more flexible variation of these steps, since these instruments are not intended to be actual measures of behaviors. The purpose of unstructured studies is to gather new insights from the behaviors observed. Unstructured observational instruments may only be structured to the extent that they identify topics, general behaviors, or themes that may be evident in the settings in which they are observed. Steps 4, 5, and 6 in Table 10.3 would give more emphasis to identifying and defining behaviors of interest rather than measuring them. Since

TABLE 10.3   Comparing Construction of an Observational Instrument with Constructing a Survey

Steps in Constructing a Survey	Steps in Constructing an Observational Instrument
1. Identify the general purpose of the survey.	1. Identify the general purpose of the observation.
2. Identify the specific dimensions of the purpose.	2. Identify the specific dimensions.
3. Select the preferred type of survey.	3. Select the preferred type of observation.
4. Formulate possible questions to ask.	4. Formulate the possible behaviors to observe.
5. Select the best questions.	5. Select the most important behaviors.
6. Craft questions without flaws.	6. Succinctly define instructions for how the behaviors are to be identified.
7. Decide on the response options.	7. Add rating categories to check, if appropriate.
8. Determine the order for the questions.	8. Determine the order for behaviors to be recorded only if this is important.
9. Pretest the survey.	9. Pretest the instrument with two independent observers.

steps 7 and 8 focus on specific measurement issues, these steps may not even be appropriate for unstructured instruments.

Observing Social Artifacts and Other Nonhuman Entities

While observational research conducted by social workers primarily focuses on human behavior, it can also focus on nonhuman entities. Webb and colleagues (1966) present numerous opportunities to measure and analyze such phenomena without intrusion from a researcher. They refer to these observations as **unobtrusive measures.** Numerous nonhuman entities of interest to social work can be observed and measured unobtrusively, including social artifacts, deterioration or improvements in physical materials, and physical settings such as an office or home.

These types of observations could include investigating physical traces, such as the wear and tear on training materials or library books assigned to students for particular courses. In community settings, these observations could focus on such things as the types of vegetable gardens planted in available plots in the inner city or the conditions of a neighborhood playground (e.g., the extent to which it is clean and the play equipment is working). Such observations could also include investigating archive records such as historical documents, which might describe the contributions of a social work pioneer, or legislative records, which might describe the political processes involved in enacting landmark legislation.

Examples of Observations in Social Work Settings

Observational research can be conducted in social work settings in a wide range of ways. Some examples follow:

- the physical appearance of a program setting (e.g., a physical description of the exterior and interior of a DSS agency)
- program activities and the interactions within these activities (e.g., how clients participate with each other in a group activity)
- informal interactions and unplanned activities of clients or staff (e.g., informal discussions of staff during a break)
- the language used by clients or staff (e.g., terms staff use in referring to clients)
- emphasis on nonverbal communication (e.g., dress, expression of feelings, seating arrangements, etc.)
- what seems to be missing (e.g., discovering a critical program element that is not present, noticing a lack of diversity among staff or clients by age, gender, race, diagnosis, etc.) (Patton, 1987, pp. 82–92)

Observations of the waiting rooms of social agencies are another focus for observational research. Clients' experiences in waiting rooms can be an important determinant of their overall satisfaction with the services of an agency and their desire to continue receiving services. A summary of one student's observations of a waiting room is an example of what can be discovered.

A Waiting Room Experience

Bren Sane (2003), a social work student, observed the waiting area of a social service agency to identify any problems experienced by clients while waiting for service at this agency. The agency director and assistant director welcomed her project, as they had been planning to research this dimension of their agency. Her observations took place on one day only, for three consecutive hours. The focus of her observations was limited to worker-client interaction in the waiting area of the agency.

The clients who were observed were either applying for social services or following up on existing services. The employees observed were receptionists and caseworkers. She observed the frequencies of the workers' greetings, tone of voice, empathy, facial gestures (smile, frown, eye contact, expressions), noise, seating, waiting time, and special needs being met (translator, physical/mental disabilities) by race and gender.

She explained, "I observed immediately that the noise level and some signs were hampering my ability to hear and see the receptionists. I spoke with the assistant, who then removed the signs from the counter and turned the television volume very low. However, these obstacles had already impacted a few of my observations. I observed fifteen cases in three hours. Overall, my observation revealed that clients are treated pleasantly, respectfully, and timely at this agency. All cases were greeted with 'Hello' or 'May I help you.' All clients were spoken to

(continued)

politely and pleasantly. Workers smiled at the majority of the clients. Workers were distracted from clients by the phone/coworkers only twice, and this could have been related to the client being served. I did observe that when a caseworker came to the waiting area to call a client back for service, the caseworker stood in the doorway without entering the waiting area. I did not observe any caseworker greet the clients with a handshake. Most of the caseworkers verbally greeted the clients, smiled at them, and made eye contact. The waiting area was noisy 50 percent of the time (even with the television volume low), especially when there were six to eight children in the area at one time. I did note a positive aspect to the television volume being louder on a day-to-day basis, though. As clients interacted with the receptionist, the television muted their dialogue from everyone else in the waiting area. Clients waited an average of twenty-one minutes to see a caseworker. Clients needing a translator waited an average of ten minutes to see a translator. The majority of the clients were Caucasian, English speaking, and female. The doors, reception window, and seating area were wheelchair accessible.

Chapter Reflections

Values and Ethics, Diversity, At-Risk Groups, and Social Justice

Several ethical problems and issues are potentially evident when designing an observational study. On the one hand, some studies may be favored because they support ethical issues. For example, observing a person's behavior provides firsthand data about what the person is doing and is preferred over secondhand reporting, which could be inaccurate and even dishonest. On the other hand, observational studies may also raise ethical problems. For example, covert observations that do not provide informed consent are clearly unethical, even though many such studies continue to be conducted. All observational studies should require some form of informed consent in which the purpose of the study and the role of the observer are disclosed to those who are being observed. Otherwise, people's basic human rights can be violated. This may seem unfortunate in some cases, since it means that a study intending to uncover unethical behavior would have to be among the studies to be disregarded. Thus, ethical issues may be evident on both sides of an issue when designing a study.

Diversity issues are also important in the design of an observational study. While diversity abounds in our society, it can only be studied to a limited extent using a survey study. Observational studies of the communication of men and women, for example, can detect some of the distinct differences through observational studies. Asking them to describe their differences in communication through a interview study may be much less revealing and often is fraught with unnecessary bias. Observations can offer a "wider lens" on diversity in that they provide data about how people express themselves, particularly on a nonverbal basis. The cultural customs and lifestyles of a group of people can also be more easily understood using a participant observation design rather than a survey. Observational studies can also provide a wider lens by describing the larger social context of the lives of research participants. A participant observation study, for example, uses a holistic approach that can gather data not only on research participants but also on the larger social context within which the participants function. Data from this larger context are often invaluable in helping to explain why participants behave as they do.

At-risk groups are also often better understood if they can be observed. A variety of at-risk groups are mentioned in the chapter as examples, including people with mental retardation, children with Attention Deficit/Hyperactivity Disorder, and abused children. Other examples of at-risk groups that could be readily understood using various strategies of observations are homeless people, people suffering from dementia, people with hearing and visual impairments, and workers in a factory.

Social justice issues can also be furthered by implementing some types of observational studies. Participant observation, in particular, provides an "insider's" perspective on the problems people face. Implementing some or all of the steps in participatory action research (PAR) can also promote social justice concerns. For example, homeless people and gang members can assist a researcher in finding the best locations for observing their activities. Their participation in a study can also provide access to other research participants that are normally unavailable to survey researchers. Observing the larger social context of a phenomenon can also further social justice goals by offering greater insights and understanding about a topic than is possible with a more focused survey study.

Discussion Questions

1. Observe the interactions between two or more people without interfering with what they are doing. Select clients or staff members at your field placement agency or at an agency in which you volunteer. Or select classmates in your classes. Decide on the type of observation you will use (structured or unstructured, participant or nonparticipant). If possible, prepare an informed consent protocol that explains to the people you will observe such things as who you are, your purpose (e.g., class project in a social work research course), how you will use what you observe (e.g., share in class), and your intention to abide by confidentiality. Observe them for about twenty to thirty minutes if possible. Afterward, record what you observed as soon as you can. Then present your findings to your class along with your reflections on what you learned about conducting an observational study. Be sure to discuss any ethical issues you faced and how you handled them. Choose one of the following topics as a focus:
   - *Interruptions* in the exchanges between men and women—who interrupts whom. Instead of using gender as a comparison, you could observe the interruptions between people of different ethnic backgrounds, people of different ages, etc. Also observe how the interruptions occur and how they seem to affect the behavior of the person who is interrupted.
   - How much people *listen to each other* (e.g., whether or not they listen at all, who listens more, how they verbally and nonverbally communicate that they are listening, some of the special ways they listen, how listening affects the talker).

- The *content of conversations* when differences are expressed (e.g., the topics, the viewpoints that are expressed, how differences in views are treated, how far the parties progress in discovering and appreciating each other's position).

2. Find a busy location on the campus where a lot of people pass by. Sit in an inconspicuous place and observe them. Observe the types of clothing worn by different students, faculty, and others. Then try to organize what you observed into categories. Instead of clothing you could observe hair styles, facial expressions (smiling, frowning, blank expression), or the types of people that interact with each other based on their race, gender, age, or disability/ability.

3. This exercise involves pairs of students working together. Each pair of students is to observe the same social situation for a period of fifteen minutes independently of each other. Decide together what you will observe. It could be, for example, a student association meeting, a class discussion, a staff meeting at your field agency, a planned activity on the campus, and so on. Afterward, each student should record the most important things that he or she observed. Then share what each recorded to determine how much these observations are similar and different. This exercise is similar to an interrater reliability procedure.

4. Observations like the one described in "A Waiting Room Experience" on pages 193–194 could pose ethical problems. Assume that this observer fully disclosed the purpose of her observation to the director and assistant director and that they requested that her role and purpose be withheld from all the clients and workers, especially those being observed in the waiting room. If you were this student, could you both satisfy the request of these administrators and maintain ethical standards that protect the people observed? If so, how would you do this? If the administrator allowed you to introduce an informed consent protocol, how would you do this in a way that would not create unnecessary reactivity?

References

Bales, R. (1950). *Interaction process analysis: A method for the study of small groups.* Reading, MA: Addison-Wesley.

Dudley, J. (1983). *Living with stigma: The plight of the people who we label mentally retarded.* Springfield, IL: Charles Thomas.

Ferraro, G. (2000). *Cultural anthropology: An applied perspective.* St. Paul, MN: West.

Goffman, E. (1962). *Asylum: Essays on the social situation of mental patients and other inmates.* Chicago: Aldine.

Patton, M. (1987). *How to use qualitative methods in evaluation.* Newbury Park, CA: Sage.

Pfeiffer, J. (1985, February 10). Conversation piece: Who interrupts most, men or women? Who asks questions? Researchers are seeking answers. *Philadelphia Inquirer,* Sec. M, p. 1.

Sane, B. (2003). Observation of a waiting room: A student research project. Charlotte: University of North Carolina–Charlotte.

Webb, E., Campbell, D., Schwartz, R., & Sechrest, L. (1966). *Unobtrusive measures: Nonreactive research in the social sciences.* Chicago: Rand McNally, College.

Social workers practice within their areas of competence and develop and enhance their professional expertise. Social workers continually strive to increase their professional knowledge and skills and to apply them in practice. . . . [In this regard,] social workers should monitor and evaluate policies, the implementation of programs, and practice interventions. (*NASW Code of Ethics*, 1999, Sections 1.04 & 5.02)

chapter **11**

Exploring Causal Relationships

Social workers are expected to show evidence that their practice is effective in improving their clients' lives. In this chapter, we consider how such evidence can be provided. One important consideration in developing a research design is deciding whether or not causal relationships are to be explored. Exploring causal relationships is important in determining whether or not our social work interventions help our clients. This is step 3c in the research process.

Let's begin with an unfortunate and rather tragic story. It involves a social worker employed with the public schools who overlooked the need to document the effectiveness of his services to his clients.

An Apparent Success That Ended in Failure

A social worker shared a story of how he had once successfully helped numerous preadolescent boys overcome academic and social defeat by providing them with a group work service. This service was sponsored by the public schools of a large city and provided to these boys in small groups. These groups were established to address the boys' problems of underachievement and disruptive behavior and to prevent problems predicted to come later, particularly dropping out of school and committing serious crimes. Each of these groups of boys met with the social worker twice each week over a two-year period. The social worker's roles included building a strong support group, mentoring, counseling, and advocacy.

Steps in the Research Process

1. Understanding the research topic to be studied
2. Focusing the study
3. Designing the study
   a. Selecting the participants
   b. Selecting a data collection approach and measuring concepts
      • Surveys
      • Observations
   c. **Exploring causal relationships**
4. Collecting the data
5. Analyzing the data
6. Preparing a report

(continued)

As the boys became more engaged and involved in their groups, they began to reveal dramatic improvements in their school performance and interpersonal behavior. Indeed, the principal, teachers, and parents all raved about how successful the program had become in redirecting the boys' behavior, improving their school work, and fostering their maturation.

Unfortunately, this group work program had no evaluation plan to document its effectiveness. The social worker remained in touch with most of these boys for several years after the groups ended. He collected anecdotal data on their many successes, such as completing high school, avoiding crime, getting married, and actively parenting their children. However, without an evaluation plan to document their many improvements (including better grades, improved interpersonal relations in school, graduation from high school, successful employment, and a crime-free adulthood), this "successful" social work program became an early victim of public funding cuts and was never considered again.

This dramatic illustration reminds us that a successful program must have an evaluation component that documents its success. Otherwise, it will not be a success. How can social workers determine if their interventions are effective in helping clients? Several key questions need to be asked:

- Do my clients have measurable goals? Do I help them reach these goals?
- Can I clearly describe the interventions that helped my clients?
- Do I document how my clients have improved after receiving my interventions?
- Can I be sure that something else other than my intervention was not responsible for their improvement?

Relevance of Causal Relationships in Social Work Practice

As was suggested in Chapter 6, hypotheses can be useful tools for formulating a social worker's intervention plan with clients. A hypothesis is stated as a cause-and-effect relationship between an independent and dependent variable. When formulating an intervention plan, the independent variable (IV) becomes the worker's intervention and the dependent variable (DV) becomes a measure of the outcome or goal for the client. Examples are provided in Table 11.1.

Keep in mind that the relationship between the worker's intervention and the client's goal or outcome is presumed to be causal in a hypothesis. A hypothesis proposes that the intervention can produce (or cause) a positive outcome for a client. After proposing this hypothesis, however, the intervention must be implemented to determine if it actually improves the client outcome.

TABLE 11.1	**Using Hypotheses to Formulate an Intervention Plan**

Social Worker's Intervention (preferred value of independent variable)	**Outcome Desired for Client** (preferred value of dependent variable)
When the social worker . . .	the client . . .
a. acknowledges the client's understanding of the problem,	a. is more willing to work in a cooperative way.
b. provides information on all relevant resources,	b. chooses the best resource for him or her.
c. provides three sessions of family social work,	c. family members communicate better with each other.
(Now write two hypotheses of your own, based on your own experiences.)	
When the social worker . . .	the client . . .
d.	d.
e.	e.

Claiming That the Intervention Makes a Difference

How do we know if the intervention causes a desired outcome to happen? Three conditions were described in Chapter 6 that must be met before a causal relationship can be claimed. Let's review them.

1. *Condition 1. The intervention (independent variable) must precede in time the client's improvement in a goal (dependent variable).* When you think about it, this condition makes logical sense. Can you imagine the following scenario? A social worker decides to help a client improve her circumstances and even before the worker's intervention is introduced, improvement becomes evident. Can the social worker take any credit for this improvement? Not at all, because the intervention had not yet been introduced. Apparently, something happened prior to the intervention that led to the client's improvement. It would be unethical for the social worker to claim any credit for this improvement.

An example that was used in Chapter 6 illustrates this point further. Let's imagine that a clinical recovery group is introduced as our intervention to assist ten substance abuse clients who have been on a waiting list for three months. Just before the group is introduced, however, we determine that these ten clients have reduced their substance abuse problem, on average, by about one-half while on the waiting list. Obviously, we cannot claim that the recovery group was responsible for any improvement, because the group had not yet been introduced. We would have to look for other factors that may have occurred during this three-month waiting period that contributed to their improvement.

2. *Condition 2. An association must be found between the intervention and the client's improvement in the goal.* An association means that the client's improvement becomes evident after the social worker's intervention is implemented. To find out if improvement occurred after the intervention had been introduced, we must first obtain a measure of the goal before the intervention is introduced. This measure is referred to as a *baseline* or *pretest measure*. (Don't confuse "pretest measure" with the final step in survey construction, which involves "pretesting" a survey instrument.) In the above example, we could find out how much alcohol each of the ten clients consumed before introducing the recovery group (a pretest measure), and we could also find out their alcohol consumption after the group was completed (a posttest measure). Then we could determine how much their consumption reduced from pretest to posttest. However, an association should not be equated with the cause for this improvement. So far, we can only suspect that the intervention was a cause.

An important question to ask about the clients' improvement is "How much improvement is enough?" Using our earlier example, let's assume that the clients reduced their alcohol consumption, on average, from five bottles of beer a day to three. Is this enough improvement? While this may be a difficult question to answer in absolute terms, the concept of significance can help. In answering whether enough improvement occurred, we can consider two different types of significance:

- **Statistical significance.** One way to determine whether the intervention has enough of an association with the client's improvement is to ascertain if it is a statistically significant association. Statistically significant associations can be determined by applying a statistical test that determines if the probability of an association between two variable is high.
- **Clinical significance.** Clinical significance is another way to determine if enough improvement has occurred after implementing the intervention. Clinical significance is also sometimes referred to as practical significance. Clinical significance is based on clinical criteria established by a professional group or agency. In this case, we can conclude that the amount of improvement in a client's goal is enough if it meets the established clinical criteria. Clinical significance may be preferred over statistical significance in many circumstances because it is based on clinical judgment, not mathematical probability.

Let's return to our example of the recovery group for substance abusing clients. Let's modify our earlier example and say that the group intervention was introduced before rather than after the clients showed improvement. In this instance, the first condition has been met, as the independent variable preceded an improvement in the dependent variable. In order for the second condition to be met, we would have to claim that there is a significant association between the intervention and client improvement. This could be determined statistically by applying a statistical test or clinically by using professional criteria or both.

If statistical significance is the standard to be used, this means that there is a statistically significant difference between the substance use of the ten group members before and after the intervention was implemented. In our example, let's assume that the average number of beers consumed by the group members per day before the intervention was five and that the number was three per day after the intervention. A statistical test could tell us if these two measures were significantly different based on probability theory. Statistical tests are discussed in Chapter 14.

Next let's determine if these ten group members improved significantly based on clinical criteria. In our example, we know that the number of beers for each member per day, on average, decreased by two (five beers minus three beers). The agency offering this group intervention will have to make a judgment about whether or not this is enough improvement. It may seem to be considerable, but what if the literature suggests that a professional intervention is not fully successful until a person totally withdraws from the substance? In this case, the agency could claim that clinical significance has not been achieved until total withdrawal occurs.

3. *Condition 3. The cause of the client's improvements must be due, at least in part, to the worker's intervention.* This condition is the most difficult to achieve. We must remember that just because there may be a significant association between the intervention and the change in the client's goal (condition 2), we cannot conclude that the intervention is responsible for this change. Many other factors could have an influence.

In most cases, an intervention cannot be expected to be totally responsible for the client's improvement. Other factors often have an effect as well. We are interested in determining how much the improvement is due to the intervention. If we were to use statistical tools to determine the extent of its effectiveness, we may discover, for example, that the intervention was responsible for only 40 percent of the improvement. Nevertheless, this partial effect can still be important.

In our example of the recovery group provided to clients with a substance abuse problem, let's assume that the ten members actually made significant progress with their drinking problems after completing ten group sessions. At this point, we may suspect that the group sessions had something to do with their improvement, but we would also need to consider other factors. For example, how do we know that other circumstances in the clients' lives—such as reconciliation with a separated spouse; participation in an Alcoholics Anonymous group; or joining a new church, mosque, or synagogue—were not responsible for the reduction in their drinking? In addition, how do we know that normal maturation by these clients was not a factor?

We refer to these other factors as extraneous variables. *Extraneous variables* are variables that have not been considered in a hypothesis. These variables are often viewed as confounding or interfering with the relationship between an independent and dependent variable. Extraneous variables can encompass any source of influence the researcher is not studying, whether it is known to the researcher or not. In actuality, both the recovery group and extraneous factors have the potential of impacting the clients in this group.

In summary, the three conditions necessary for claiming that an intervention has been at least partially responsible for the improvement in the client's goal are:

1. The intervention *precedes* improvement in the client's goal in time.
2. The client's goal *improves* significantly after the intervention is implemented.
3. The intervention is found to be at least partially *responsible* for this improvement after controlling for possible alternative influences.

Documenting the Impact of Social Work Interventions

The next question is "How do we provide documentation that the intervention was responsible for changes in the client's goal?" In the discussion of research designs in Chapter 7, two design options were described: a cross-sectional design and a longitudinal design. A *cross-sectional design* collects data from participants at one time only, and a *longitudinal design* collects data from research participants at two or more times. Longitudinal designs, in particular, provide the most powerful evidence of a causal relationship between an independent variable (IV) and a dependent variable (DV).

Quasi-experimental, experimental, and some pre-experimental designs are longitudinal designs that can be used to explore a causal relationship between an independent and dependent variable. These designs are called **group designs,** because they measure the impact of an intervention on a group of clients, not one client. Five group designs are described below. They are presented in the order of their power, from weakest to strongest, in determining causality. Two pre-experimental designs are described first and are considered the weakest, followed by two quasi-experimental designs that have additional power in determining causality. Finally, an experimental design is described that has the most power. The five designs include:

Pre-experimental Designs
- one-group posttest-only design
- one-group pretest/posttest design

Quasi-experimental Designs
- pretest/posttest comparison group design
- time series design

Experimental Design
- pretest/posttest control group design

Several additional quasi-experimental and experimental designs are described in Campbell and Stanley (1963).

Keep in mind that all of these group designs can be used to explore the impact of a social work intervention on a group of clients, whether they are individuals, families, or small groups. All of these designs introduce an *intervention,* which is the independent variable (IV). All of these designs also include a *posttest measure* of a client goal, which is the dependent variable (DV).

Most of these designs also include a baseline measure or pretest score of the client's goal. A **baseline** is a measure of the client's goal prior to introducing an intervention. Also, many of these designs have two groups—one that receives the intervention and one that does not. The group that does not receive the intervention is referred to as either a comparison or control group. A **comparison group** is a group of clients that is similar but not identical to the group receiving the intervention. A **control group** is a group of clients that is considered identical to the group receiving the intervention, based on random assignment or matching.

Extraneous Influences

Extraneous influences are not fully controlled in either pre-experimental or quasi-experimental designs. A partial list of these extraneous influences is described under the following general categories:

- *External factors* present during the time that an intervention is being introduced can influence the client goal. These factors are likely to be present in other aspects of clients' lives. For example, clients could be receiving professional services from another agency, attending a self-help group, or receiving support from close friends in addition to receiving the intervention. *History* is the technical term used by experimental researchers to describe external factors(Campbell & Stanley, 1963).

- *Internal factors* that are unrelated to the intervention and external factors occur within the research participants and can influence the client goal. These internal factors are biological or psychological processes that systematically vary with time independent of specific external events (Campbell & Stanley, 1963). They could include, for example, a sudden burst of maturation, a gradual physical decline, the emergence of a depressive mood, or increased self-esteem in clients, all of which can happen independent of the intervention. *Maturation* is the technical term used by experimental researchers to describe internal factors. Generally, the longer that the intervention is implemented, the more likely that clients will experience internal growth or change. For example, a program intervention that involves twelve weeks of a group service is long enough for a number of internal changes to occur in clients, while an intervention consisting of a one-day training session will likely be too short a time for any internal changes to occur.

- *Differences between the research participants* receiving the intervention and those who are not receiving it could also influence the client outcome variable. In other words, participants in the intervention group may improve to a greater extent than participants in a comparison group for reasons other than the intervention. For example, they could have less severe problems or higher levels of motivation to succeed. The technical term used by experimental researchers in describing differences in the characteristics of the research participants is referred to as *selection error* (Campbell & Stanley, 1963).

• *Reactivity caused by the data collection instruments* used to measure the client outcome variable could also influence the client outcome variable. The technical terms used by experimental researchers in describing such reactivity include two types: testing interference and instrumentation interference(Campbell & Stanley, 1963). *Testing interference* refers to biases in the participants' test responses, based on their sensitivity to the outcome variable by taking the test. The pretest could increase or decrease the participants' sensitivity to the outcome variable and thus make the test results unrepresentative of the effects of the intervention. Put another way, if participants take the test a second time as a posttest, they may respond differently because they have become aware of the researcher's intent after filling out the test the first time in a pretest. *Instrumentation interference* refers to changes in how the measurement instrument is administered by the researchers from the pretest to posttest.

• *Loss of research participants* during the execution of the study could also influence the client outcome variable. It is quite possible that some participants will drop out for a variety of reasons before the study is completed, and their withdrawal will interfere in some ways with the measure of the impact of the intervention. The technical term used by experimental researchers in describing such reactivity is *mortality* (Campbell & Stanley, 1963).

Validity and Group Designs

Internal and external validity are important standards to use in evaluating the strength of a group design. **Internal validity** addresses the question of whether the intervention, rather than other factors, is responsible for improvement in the client outcome variable. Put another way, did the independent variable effect a change in the dependent variable? As was mentioned above, several extraneous variables could be responsible for the improvement in addition to or instead of the intervention. For internal validity to be strong, factors independent of the intervention that are present in the participants' lives, such as receiving service from another professional agency or joining a self-help group, must be found not to be responsible for improvement in the outcome variable.

External validity addresses the issue of generalizing the results of a group design to other people. In this case, if the participants in the group design were randomly selected from a large population (e.g., a client group of 100 or more), generalizing to this larger group is possible. However, if participants selected for the group design were drawn from a smaller population or were selected using nonprobability sampling, generalizing is not advisable.

Thyer and Meyers (2003) suggest that the most realistic way to generalize the results of a group design is to use the process of *replication*. Replication involves repeating a group design with different client groups and at various times. If the results of a group design reveal that an intervention works for one client group, it could be tried with a different client group with similar characteristics. If the same result occurs, a claim that the intervention is effective would be somewhat strengthened. This could be followed by further replication, for example, with similar clients in another agency or by other researchers with similar clients in different geographic areas. Also, if the results of the group design indicate that an intervention is effective with a group of men, it could be tried with a group of women. Or if an intervention works for young adult clients, it could be tested with middle-aged adults. Repeated replication of a group design can be extremely valuable in exploring the extent to which an intervention can be generalized to others. Such replication can also be used to determine the limitations of an intervention and the characteristics of clients with whom it may not work.

Group Designs for Exploring the Impact of an Intervention

The five general group designs are described next and summarized in Table 11.2. Typically, these designs are used in evaluations of programs serving a large number of clients rather than evaluations of an individual social worker's practice involving one client system. Diagrams of each design are also included in the table, with X symbolizing the intervention, O representing various measures of the outcome variable, and R indicating that the two groups were randomly selected and assigned.

One-Group Posttest-Only Design

Pre-experimental designs are often important to consider initially because they are easy to implement and take less time than more powerful designs. A one-group posttest-only design is a pre-experimental design that is the weakest of all. This design involves collecting data at only one point in time after the intervention is implemented. Consequently, this is a cross-sectional rather than a longitudinal design. However, if social workers want to find out if their interventions have had an effect on their clients, this design is a good one for beginning such an exploration. A posttest-only design is diagrammed in Figure 11.1. During time 1, the intervention is introduced, and the posttest score of the outcome variable is measured in time 2.

Let's take the example of support groups being provided to boys in the fifth and sixth grades who are underachieving and disruptive in their behaviors. These groups are sponsored by a child welfare agency that provides these and other social work services to several different schools in one city. Let's assume that one goal of these support groups is to help these children improve their communication skills. In this example, one measure of the children's improved communication can be a reduction in episodes of fighting. Research evidence is available suggesting that

TABLE 11.2   Pre-Experimental, Quasi-Experimental, and Experimental Designs

Diagrams

Diagram	Description
XO_1	1. *One-group posttest-only design*—an intervention followed by a posttest measure of the client goal or outcome
$O_1 \, X \, O_2$	2. *One-group pretest/posttest design*—an intervention preceded by a pretest measure and followed by a posttest measure of the client goal or outcome
$O_1 \, X \, O_2$ $O_3 \, O_4$	3. *Pretest/posttest comparison group design*—a pretest/posttest design that also has a comparison group that does not receive the intervention
$O_1 \, O_2 \, O_3 \, X \, O_4 \, O_5 \, O_6$	4. *Time series design*—multiple measures of the client outcome prior to and after the intervention
$(R) \, O_1 \, X \, O_2$ $(R) \, O_3 \, O_4$	5. *Pretest/posttest control group design*—a pretest/posttest design that also involves a control group that does not receive the intervention

communication breakdown occurs when children express their anger by fighting rather than verbal expression. In this example, the support group is the IV and the frequency of fighting is one of the DVs.

After three sessions of the group, let's assume that members of the support groups continue to fight about as often as ever. If this is the case, a causal relationship between the support group and frequency of fighting is not worth exploring any further, because it is already evident that the intervention is not improving their communication in this area (i.e., condition 2 is not met). In this case, the social worker has a few alternatives. These support groups can be continued for a longer time to determine if additional sessions can lead to improvement, or the social worker may decide to try an alternative intervention.

A one-group posttest-only design has several weaknesses. Most important, there is no pretest measure to determine if any improvement occurred during the

FIGURE 11.1   One-Group Posttest-Only Design

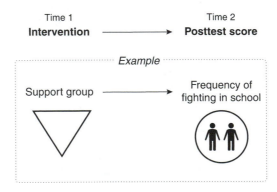

time of the intervention. Furthermore, none of the extraneous influences reported earlier in the chapter has been controlled.

One-Group Pretest/Posttest Design

The next design to be considered is a pretest/posttest design. This design builds on the previous one by adding a pretest or baseline measure prior to the initiation of the intervention. This design, like the first one, is pre-experimental. It is longitudinal because data are collected from the research participants at two different times, both before and after an intervention is introduced. This design is helpful in telling us how much improvement occurred between the pretest and posttest. The design is diagrammed in Figure 11.2. During time 1, the pretest score of the outcome variable is measured; during time 2, the intervention is introduced; and during time 3, the posttest score of the outcome variable is measured.

An illustration of this design clarifies its features. Using the previous example of the support groups, let's say that the social workers who lead these groups count (with the help of the teachers and principals) the number of times the children fight in school before the first session and after the third session. The worker determines that the frequency of fighting occurred five times per week, on average, before session 1 and five times per week after session 3. Next, the worker provides three additional support group sessions. During the sixth and final session, the boys have an average of three fighting episodes each week. In this case, they have reduced the frequency of their fighting episodes by two. The next step could be to determine if this is a statistically or clinically significant improvement.

With this design, we can only determine if improvement occurred during the time of the support groups. We are not able to claim that the support groups were responsible for this improvement because of several extraneous influences that could have also been responsible. The most important weakness of this design is that it does not have a comparison or control group to eliminate the influence of extraneous influences described earlier.

FIGURE 11.2   **One-Group Pretest/Posttest Design**

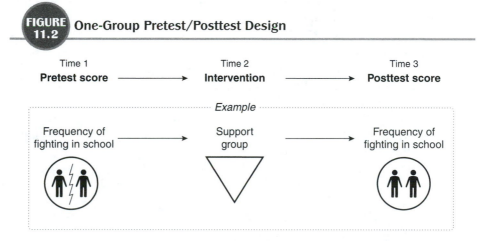

> ### Example of a Research Study with
> ### One-Group Pretest/Posttest Design
>
> Jeff Dongvillo and Jan Ligon (2001) investigated the levels of homophobia before and after a single lecture on the topic. They used a one-group pretest/posttest design. The research participants were students attending undergraduate and graduate social work courses. Homophobia was measured using the Index of Attitudes Towards Homosexuals.
>
> These researchers found no statistically significant changes in the scores from pretest to posttest. They concluded that the results may underscore the complexity of changing student attitudes. In other words, there may be a need for a more substantial training component than one lecture to change homophobic attitudes. They also noted that the students in their study had majors in fields other than social work, which involves another set of extraneous influences.

Pretest/Posttest Comparison Group Design

This is a quasi-experimental design that builds on the pretest/posttest design. It is a longitudinal design with data being collected on the clients' outcome variable both initially during a pretest and after an intervention is implemented as a posttest. In addition, this design adds a new feature. Another group with circumstances similar to the first group is selected as a comparison group. This second group does not receive the intervention. With this design, we are comparing the progress of both groups during the intervention period. As Figure 11.3 indicates, this design is diagrammed with two different groups, one that receives the intervention and the other that does not. During time 1, a pretest score of the outcome variable is measured for both groups; during time 2, the intervention is introduced for the group assigned to receive it and nothing happens for the comparison group; and during time 3, a posttest score of the outcome variable is measured for both groups.

A comparison group should be as similar as possible to the intervention group, particularly in the areas of importance to a study. For example, in our support group example, the comparison group should be made up of boys, not girls. Also, it should include those of similar age and with similar problems, if possible. A comparison group can be drawn from a larger pool of clients, such as those on a waiting list, those receiving traditional services, or former clients no longer receiving services. The most important weakness of this design is that the clients selected for the intervention and comparison groups, respectively, are likely to have many differences that have not been taken into account. These differences are likely to have a considerable influence over the outcome variable along with the influence of the intervention.

Let's consider this design using our previous example of the support groups. The boys who were assigned to participate in the support groups would comprise group 1. The frequency of their fighting would be counted both before and after participating in the support group. In addition, another set of boys in these schools

FIGURE 11.3 **Pretest/Posttest Design with Comparison Group**

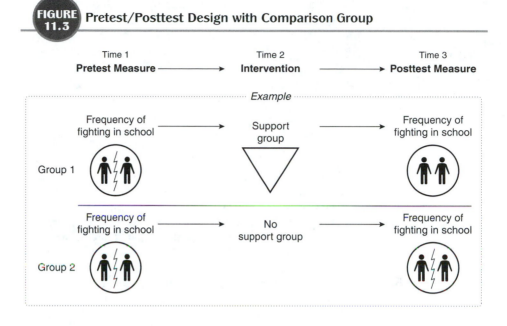

Time 1
Pretest Measure ———————→

Time 2
Intervention ———————→

Time 3
Posttest Measure

Example

Group 1

Frequency of
fighting in school ———————→ Support
group ———————→ Frequency of
fighting in school

Group 2

Frequency of
fighting in school ———————→ No
support group ———————→ Frequency of
fighting in school

with similar circumstances (if possible, fifth- and sixth-graders who are academically underachieving and involved in fighting) are selected as group 2. These boys would not participate in support groups. Possibly, they could be on a waiting list for such services, or they could be receiving a more traditional individual counseling service during the time that the boys in group 1 were participating in support groups. The fighting episodes of the boys in group 2 would also be counted during the same times that they were counted for group 1. Let's say that members of group 1 reduced their fighting, on average, from five to three fighting episodes from the pretest to posttest and that those in group 2 showed no improvement, having five episodes in both the pretest and posttest. We could conclude that the improvement in the boys in group 1 may have been the result of the support groups. Yet, other factors could also have been responsible for this improvement. For example, some of the boys in group 1 may have higher grades, better communication skills, or fewer family problems than those in group 2 (differences in research participant characteristics).

Ethical Issues   This design also creates a potential ethical problem that needs to be addressed. The boys in the comparison group could possibly be disadvantaged or harmed by not participating in the support groups offered to the boys in group 1. Let's say, for example, that some of the boys in group 2 have as much need for a support group as those in group 1. Further, group leaders are available to start additional support groups, but they are withheld to meet the features of this study. In this case, denying the boys in group 2 these group services would be unethical even if these boys were placed on a waiting list. It might also be unethical for them to receive a traditional counseling service instead of support groups, particularly if traditional counseling is not considered directly relevant to their needs. However, if the sponsoring agency does not have the resources to offer support groups to all of the children in both groups 1 and 2 at one time, then delaying these services for group 2 until the study is completed would not raise the same degree of ethical concern.

Example of a Study Using a Pretest/Posttest Comparison Group Design

David Royse and Holly Riffe (1999) conducted a study of BSW students to determine if their values changed after completing their first social work course, Introductory Social Services. A questionnaire with twenty-four items that reflected various social work values was used to measure their positions on twenty-four values statements. For each item, students could respond that they agreed, disagreed, or were undecided. These researchers used a pretest/posttest comparison group design. The comparison group, which was also administered the questionnaire as a pretest and posttest, consisted of social work majors, who were primarily juniors or seniors, and employed social workers. The comparison group did not receive the intervention, the first social work course.

The findings were revealing. One item, for example, stated "Many people on welfare don't deserve to receive it." While 57 percent of the students taking the introductory course disagreed with this statement before the course, 78 percent disagreed with this statement after the course, an increase of 21 percent. Also, students in the introductory course, on average, had overall scores in the posttest that were similar to the posttest scores of the comparison group.

Time Series Design

A time series design is another type of quasi-experimental design. This design has many of the features of the previous designs. It is also different from the other designs in that it has several pretest and posttest measures, not one of each. The design involves obtaining several measures of the client outcome variable prior to the introduction of an intervention and several additional measures after the intervention has been implemented. Figure 11.4 diagrams a time series design.

Let's consider the same illustration using a time series design. In our illustration, this design is used to investigate whether the support groups reduce the incidence of fighting in the schools. Note that there is no comparison group as in the last design. We begin by obtaining a baseline measure of the boys' frequency of fighting for each of the three weeks prior to the beginning of the support group. Assume that their fighting episodes on average are five times per week in week 1, four times in week 2, and six times in week 3. These three pretest measures suggest a fairly stable measure of fighting episodes in the pretest period, averaging five each week. Next, the intervention (the support groups) are introduced during weeks 4 through 23 for twenty sessions. Finally, after the support groups have ended, three weekly posttest measures

FIGURE 11.4   Time Series Design

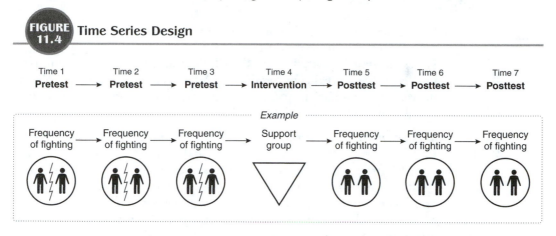

of their fighting episodes are obtained. Their fighting averages one episode in week 24, no episodes in week 25, and one episode in week 26. These three posttest measures, being very similar, average a little less than one episode each week. These boys have reduced their fighting from an average of five episodes each week before the support group was introduced to an average of one episode each week after participating in these groups.

A major advantage of a time series design is that it overcomes some of the ethical problems of designs that use comparison and control groups. A time series design does not use either a comparison or a control group. An important feature of the multiple pretest and posttest measures of this design is the useful data trends that are provided related to the intervention's effectiveness. These trends can help determine the extent to which the intervention, as opposed to other factors, is the causal agent. A few of these specific data trends are described, as follows:

1. *Stability of scores.* One of the data trends is stability. Are the pretest scores and the posttest scores stable, or are they widely varied? For example, if one pretest score in the support groups' example is five fighting episodes and another pretest score is one episode, further pretest measures are needed to determine which of these scores is more likely to be typical. The stability of the posttest scores is also important to consider. A consistently high improvement in posttest scores is most desired, while variability in posttest scores may suggest that improvement is somewhat evident but not sustainable. Variability in improvement scores in the posttest may also suggest that factors other than the intervention have had an influence.

2. *Changes from pretest to posttest scores.* Trends can also be evident in how the data change from the pretest to posttest scores. Many trends from the pretest to posttest scores reveal that the intervention is likely to be responsible for the improvement in a client's outcome. Some of these trends are:

- Pretest scores consistently reveal a lack of improvement, while posttest scores show consistent improvement.

- Pretest scores reveal gradual improvement over time, while posttest scores reveal substantial improvement over time.
- Pretest and initial posttest scores show little if any improvement, while later posttest scores reveal considerable improvement. These considerable improvements could be due to a delayed positive effect of the intervention or possibly an external influence.

3. *Improvements that are unrelated to the intervention.* Each consecutive pretest score shows improvement over the previous one, and the posttest scores simply continue the same pattern of improvement to the same degree. In this instance, the data may suggest that there is improvement but it is likely due to factors other than the intervention. For example, a group of children with behavior problems may have five screaming episodes during the first pretest in week 1, four episodes during the second pretest in week 2, and three episodes during the third pretest in week 3. In addition, this positive trend simply continues in the posttest scores after introducing a play therapy intervention, with two screaming episodes in the first posttest score, one episode in the second posttest score, and none in the final posttest score. In this example, we could not conclude that the play therapy intervention was responsible for the improvement, because this positive trend was manifested before the intervention was introduced and did not change in pattern after the intervention was introduced. These data trends are illustrated in Figure 11.5.

Pretest/Posttest Control Group Design

The fifth design is a pretest/posttest control group design. This is the classical experimental design and is a very powerful one for determining causality. It is similar to the pretest/posttest comparison group design, with one exception. Participants are randomly selected from a larger pool of prospective participants, and then randomly assigned to either the intervention or control group. In other words, each research participant in a larger pool of people has an equal chance of being selected to participate and an equal chance of being assigned to either the intervention group or the control group. Based on these two steps of random selection and assignment, the two groups of participants can be treated as if they are "identical." Generally, a combination of random selection and random assignment results in balancing out the extraneous factors between the two groups. With this design, pretest and posttest measures are obtained from both groups before and after the intervention group receives the intervention.

This design is diagrammed in Figure 11.6. Prior to time 1, participants are randomly selected and assigned to either an intervention group (group 1) or a control group (group 2). During time 1, a pretest score of the outcome variable is measured for both groups. During time 2, the intervention is introduced for the group assigned to receive it, and nothing happens for the control group. During time 3, a posttest score of the outcome variable is measured for both groups.

This design is quite powerful in determining the causal influence of a program intervention in improving an outcome for a client group. If we have a design in

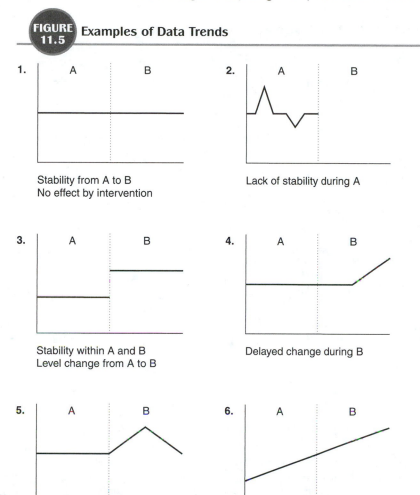

FIGURE 11.5 **Examples of Data Trends**

1.

A   B

Stability from A to B
No effect by intervention

2.

A   B

Lack of stability during A

3.

A   B

Stability within A and B
Level change from A to B

4.

A   B

Delayed change during B

5.

A   B

Short-term positive change in B
that later was reversed

6.

A   B

Positive change from A to B
but unrelated to intervention

which both groups are viewed as virtually identical in their characteristics and only one of them receives the intervention, we have created a situation in which all of the extraneous influences are virtually controlled. Note that both groups 1 and 2 are as identical as possible initially, because they are randomly selected and assigned. Both groups receive a pretest measure at the same time, and both receive a posttest measure after group 1 receives the intervention. Between the pretest and posttest, the only factor that is different for these two groups is that one receives the intervention and the other does not. Therefore, by using this design, we can logically conclude that any improvement occurring in group 1 would be the result of the intervention after subtracting any improvement evident in group 2 from pretest

FIGURE 11.6   **Pretest/Posttest Design with a Control Group**

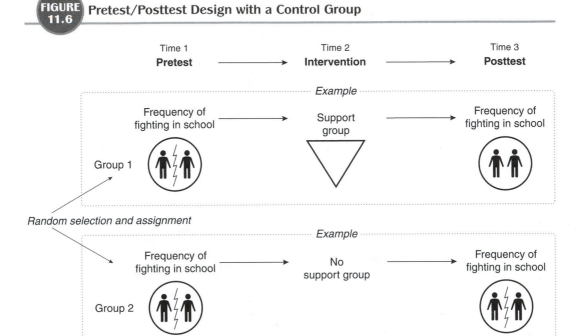

to posttest. The improvement in group 2 would take into account the influence of all of the extraneous factors that could occur for either group.

Our earlier example of the support groups can illustrate the use of this design. Let's refer to the boys who participate in the support groups as group 1 and the boys who do not participate as group 2. Both were randomly selected from a larger pool of boys with disruptive behavior and underachievement. Boys in group 1 were randomly selected to participate in the support groups, while boys in group 2 were randomly selected to receive no services. Further, let's assume that the average number of fighting episodes of the boys in group 1 during an initial point in time prior to the support group was six and the number of episodes of those in group 2 at the same point in time was also six. Later, after the support group is ended, the number of fighting episodes in group 1 is only two. At the same point in time, episodes for members of group 2 are five. We can now claim that boys in group 1 reduced their fighting from six to two episodes, while those in group 2 reduced their fighting from six to five episodes. Since group 2 reduced their fighting episodes by one episode without participating in a support group, the influence of factors other than the support group is taken into account by this one reduction in episodes. Since the boys in group 1 had a total reduction of four episodes, we would deduct one of those episodes to take into account factors of influence other than the intervention. This would leave a reduction of three (four minus one) fighting episodes for group 1 that we could conclude were the result of the support group.

Randomization or Matching   While participants are usually assigned to an intervention or control group using randomization, matching is an alternative procedure to consider. Matching is preferred over randomization when there are only a few participants involved in the study. With matching, participants are assigned to one or the other group based on matching the most relevant characteristics, such as the participants' age, gender, race, and other characteristics relevant to the study. Let's take the example of a study of people with physical disabilities that measures the impact of assertiveness training on their assertiveness skills. Relevant characteristics that could be matched are whether or not they are in a wheelchair and have any visual impairments. In this case, for example, if four of the participants who are randomly selected use wheelchairs, two would be assigned to one group and the other two to the other group. If two have visual impairments, one would be assigned to each group.

Sample Size   A note about sample size in group designs is important to mention when a sample is small, for example ten clients or less. With such a small sample it will be difficult to conclude with confidence that the desired improvement occurred because of the intervention. Generally, randomly assigning people to an intervention or control group tends to balance out the extraneous factors between the two groups. However, when there are just a few cases, differences between two groups cannot be balanced out so easily by randomization. In this case, we would need to be cautious in drawing any conclusions. Any improvements evident in the posttest in group 1 (the intervention group) that are not evident in group 2 could possibly be due to factors other than the intervention.

Ethical Issues   Unfortunately, this experimental design poses even more serious ethical challenges than the pretest/posttest comparison group design. It would be unethical to randomly select and assign clients to receive or not receive an intervention, particularly without their consent. Most likely, social workers would want this decision to be made based on professional criteria, not mathematical probability. Possibly this dilemma could be worked out by randomly selecting the clients from a waiting list and then randomly assigning one to receive the intervention and the other to continue to wait for services to be offered later. However, it would be important to explain this arrangement to both clients in an informed consent protocol. This modification could still pose ethical problems, because one client would be getting priority based on mathematical probability, not professional judgment. What if, for example, the second client who received services on a delayed basis experienced a life-threatening crisis during the waiting period?

Example of a Study Using a Pretest/Posttest Control Group Design

Alonzo Cavazos and Dolores Guerrero (1999) could not find any published studies that examined the relationship between assertiveness and field education. Therefore, they conducted a study of BSW students in their field placements to

(continued)

determine if assertiveness training would improve their assertiveness during the field experience. These researchers used a pretest/posttest control group design. They measured assertiveness using the Assertiveness Self-Report Inventory. Pretest and posttest measures of assertiveness were measured for members of both the treatment group that received assertiveness training and the control group that did not receive it.

The researchers were surprised to find out that assertiveness scores did not change in a statistically significant way for either group from pretest to posttest. In other words, the assertiveness training failed to raise their self-reported assertiveness scores.

Single System Designs and Practice Evaluations

You may ask, why is all of this so important to social work? Accountability and curiosity are two reasons. First, we must be accountable for what we do. This means that we must have the tools to evaluate our interventions and to determine whether or not they are working to help people. Funding and regulatory agencies, agency administrators, and our clients all have a right to demand this information. Second, we need to develop a curiosity about what our clients need, how they can be helped, and what we can do to make a difference in their lives. Single system designs are one powerful tool for addressing both of these concerns—accountability and curiosity—in our practice.

The five group designs presented above provide a conceptual framework for evaluating social work practice. Concepts such as a baseline or pretest measure, a posttest measure, and other strategies for controlling extraneous variables are all useful in evaluating practice. A time series design offers additional features, namely repeated pretest and posttest measures to determine whether the intervention impacts the client's goals. A multiple measure strategy can be used in place of comparison and control groups for controlling many of the extraneous influences. This is especially relevant because comparison and control groups often pose ethical problems that must be addressed.

A single system design, which is a by-product of these group designs, offers an effective way of evaluating a social worker's individual practice. A **single system design (SSD)** is a practice evaluation tool that measures whether or not there is a causal relationship between the practitioner's intervention and an outcome variable for a client system. This design is typically used with only one client system at a time, which is usually an individual, family, or small group. The SSD is a quasi-experimental design that uses a graph to visualize the progress clients are making. The graph is a user-friendly tool that can be easily understood by clients and doesn't require a strong statistical background by the worker.

A typical graph of a SSD consists of a baseline phase (phase A) and one or more intervention phases (e.g., phases B, C, D). This graph measures the client outcome variable along the vertical axis. A time line (e.g., daily, weekly) for recording measures of the outcome variable is designated along the horizontal axis. The phases are also designated on the graph. Essentially, the graph is used to plot the progress of the client outcome variable.

Different Types of Single System Designs

Several variations of a single system design are possible. These designs include an AB, ABC, ABAB, and other designs. The simplest design is an AB design, which consists of a baseline phase and one intervention phase. In this case, the client outcome variable is measured periodically along a time line (e.g., each day or week) during both the baseline phase (A) and an intervention phase (B). An example of a client case using an AB design helps illustrate how it can be used. A woman with serious depression wants to develop new friendships but is resistant to going out to meet people. The social worker is attempting to help her attend a variety of social occasions for meeting others. Because interacting with others in public is a problem for this client, an AB design is set up to encourage more social contact. The frequency of attending social occasions becomes the client outcome variable, and the social worker's intervention is a series of sessions of teaching interpersonal skills. The AB design can plot how many social occasions she attends as she is learning new interpersonal skills in phase B.

Another single system design is the ABC design. This design begins with a baseline phase (phase A). This phase is followed by the first intervention phase (phase B), which is then followed by a second intervention phase (phase C). The ABC design is particularly useful if the first intervention is not effective by itself. Using an ABC design, a second intervention can be introduced that can either replace or supplement the first intervention. Figure 11.7 illustrates an ABC design with three phases: a baseline phase, a phase when the first intervention is introduced, and a phase when the second intervention is introduced.

Using the example of the depressed client, teaching interpersonal skills could be the first intervention for encouraging more social contacts (phase B). If this intervention does not succeed, providing the client with a list of social events to meet people could be added as a second intervention (phase C). The ABC design can plot attending social occasions during phases A, B, and C to determine if attendance increases while the first intervention is being implemented as well as a

FIGURE 11.7 Graph of a Single System Design

	Phase A	Phase B	Phase C
Measure of outcome variable	(baseline)	(first intervention)	(second intervention)

Timeline

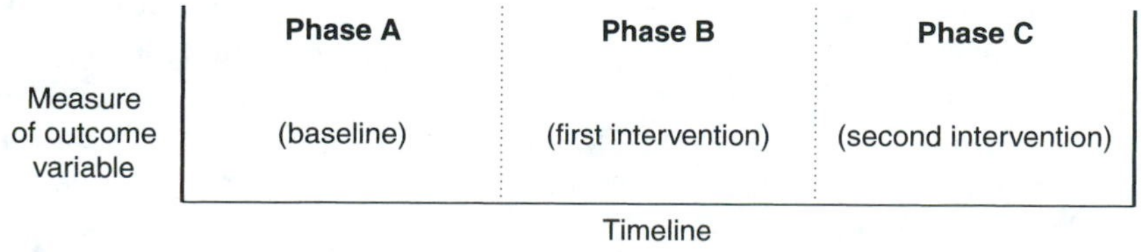

second intervention. Possibly combining the two interventions will promote greater social contact for this client.

Other variations of these designs are also possible. For example an ABCD design would introduce three different interventions. In the above example, let's assume that the combination of teaching interpersonal skills and informing the client of appropriate social events does not increase her social contacts. Perhaps the social worker could attend a social occasion with this client in phase D to see if the combination of all three interventions leads to greater social contact and ultimately to developing some friendships.

The ABAB design is another single system design used by many practitioners. This design consists of a baseline phase followed by an intervention phase. The intervention phase is followed by another baseline phase, at which time the intervention is removed. Finally, the intervention is reintroduced. This design can help you determine what happens to the client goal after the intervention is withdrawn. The withdrawal of the intervention can be used to explore whether other extraneous variables instead of the intervention are responsible for any continuation of client progress. If progress on the client goal declines during the reintroduction of phase A, this provides stronger evidence that the intervention and improvement are linked. Finally, the intervention can be reintroduced to find out if progress reappears.

While this design helps control for extraneous variables and can be an alternative to a comparison group, it can also pose ethical problems if the intervention is withdrawn while it is still being needed by the client. An intervention should not be withdrawn, for example, if a client explicitly requests its continuance because it is helpful or if the social worker feels that harm would be done by withdrawing it. However, sometimes an intervention is being offered to a client on an involuntary basis or as an agency mandate. In these cases, withdrawing the intervention when using a SSD may be less of an ethical concern. An example would be a school social worker who makes home visits to prevent further truancy. Let's assume that the parents of a truant child do not encourage these home visits but their son begins to attend school more frequently while home visits are occurring. After providing several home visits, it may make sense to temporarily discontinue them to find out how much these visits are responsible for the progress on truancy. If the truancy returns as a problem, this may be stronger evidence that the home visits had a causal influence and need to be resumed.

An ABAB design has another limitation in that it works only when the outcome variable can be reversed. If a client is taught a new set of behaviors, once these behaviors are learned, they may not be reversed in many cases. For example, if a parent is taught new assertiveness skills in phase B, withdrawing a teaching intervention will not likely lead to an immediate reversal of these newly developed skills.

Sometimes a design cannot begin with a baseline phase, because it is urgent to introduce the intervention during the first contact with the client. In this case, possibly a BAB design would work. With this design, the baseline phase is introduced after the intervention has been implemented for a while. Then the intervention can be reintroduced. However, like an ABAB design, withdrawing the intervention could pose ethical problems and may not work with outcome variables that cannot be reversed. Examples of these different types of SSD designs are shown in Figure 11.8.

FIGURE 11.8 Types of Single System Designs

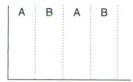

1. AB design

3. ABAB design

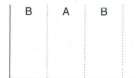

2. ABC design

4. BAB design

Implementing a Single System Design

The steps involved in using a single system design are as follows:

1. Consider whether or not the single system design (SSD) is the most appropriate design to use with a particular client system. Usually this design is appropriate if there are multiple contacts with the client, and the client's goals are measurable.
2. Make sure that all of the pertinent issues of informed consent are covered and understood by the client (i.e., purpose of the selected tool; how it works; how the client, worker, and agency can benefit; expectations you have for the client in participating in this evaluation; ensuring confidentiality; reminding the client of the option to withdraw; etc.).
3. Identify a goal or client outcome variable that you and your client will work on. Make sure that the goal is mutually agreed on. Also, make sure that the goal is measurable and that you and the client agree on a valid measure of it.
4. Decide how often the goal will be measured (e.g., every day, every week, etc.). Plan to measure the goal at equal time intervals if possible.
5. Decide on a specific intervention(s) that will be introduced to help the client reach the goal. Both the social worker and the client should understand and agree to the specific intervention that will be used.
6. Decide whether you will use an AB, ABC, or ABAB design, or a variation of one of them (e.g., BAB, ABCD).
7. Obtain as many measures of your goal as possible during both the baseline and intervention phases. Plot these measures along your horizontal axis, as follows:
   a. Plot three or more measures of your client's goal during a baseline phase (phase A) to establish a stable baseline measure. If you have major variations

in the baseline scores, add more baseline measures if possible until you have a fairly stable set of baseline scores.

    b. Next, plot several measures of your client's goals during the intervention phase(s) (phases B, C, etc.). Continue to measure your client's goal as many times as possible.

8. As you are implementing this evaluation tool, be sure to discuss the tool with the client, including periodically sharing the graph itself as a visual indicator of any progress.

9. Afterward, when the services are being terminated, assess the advantages and disadvantages of using this tool with the client.

An example of how one student used a single system design to work on a personal development issue is shown in Figure 11.9.

In summary, several important concepts introduced in this chapter describe the elements that are important in preparing various group and practice evaluation designs, as follows:

Longitudinal study—data collected from research participants at two or more points in time

Client goal—an outcome for a client

FIGURE 11.9   **Example of a Single System Design**

A BSW student wanted to address a problem that he was having and he used a single system design to do it (Gottel, 1996). He had picked up the habit of rushing through his meals and not taking the time to enjoy the "texture, flavor, and nutritional benefits" of what he was eating. His outcome variable was the amount of time he was taking to eat dinner; he wanted to increase it. After a baseline period of 10 days, he introduced his intervention for 20 days, which included a combination of four behaviors that he would follow concurrently: (1) Take five deep relaxing breaths before sitting down to eat; (2) Look at the food on the table and consciously recognize the healthy benefits that it offers; (3) Concentrate on the meal at hand; and (4) Concentrate on the food and those I am eating with, not the concerns of the past day. His SSD graph looked like this:

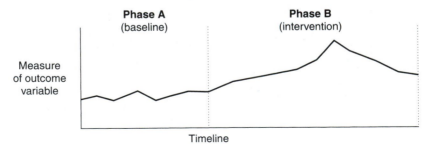

Measurable client goal—a client's goal that can be measured

Pretest—a measure of an outcome for a client prior to the intervention; also referred to as a baseline measure

Posttest—a measure of an outcome for a client after the intervention has been implemented

Well-defined intervention—an intervention that is defined clearly enough to be replicated

Statistical significance—a relationship between two variables that is considered significant, based on a statistical test (e.g., at the $p < 0.05$ level)

Clinical significance—a relationship between two variables that is considered significant, based on clinical criteria established by a professional group

Several pre-experimental, quasi-experimental, and experimental designs have been described in this chapter. Five are group designs that can be used to evaluate a program's effectiveness, and one is a single system design used to evaluate individual practice. Each of these designs can be used to explore the possibility of a causal relationship between a social work intervention and improvement in a client outcome variable. However, most of these designs have limitations that preclude making an unequivocal claim of causality. In addition, some of the more powerful designs have ethical problems inherent in them that must be addressed in some way. Other sources can be consulted for a fuller explanation of these and other evaluation designs (e.g., Bloom, Fischer, & Orme, 1999; Campbell & Stanley, 1963; Wuebben, Straits, & Shulman, 1974).

Chapter Reflections

Values and Ethics, Diversity, At-Risk Groups, and Social Justice

Several ethical issues can arise when exploring causal relationships. An especially important ethical question to ask is whether an intervention should be denied to any research participants because comparison or control groups are being considered. Above all, an informed consent protocol is essential to use with every evaluation study. In this regard, participants need to be informed that they may be assigned to a comparison or control group. They must also have a clear choice to decline participation without repercussions. In some instances, one of the pre-experimental designs may be preferred to using a design that withholds services from some groups. Also, ethical problems can surface when using single system designs that temporarily remove an intervention (e.g., an ABAB or BAB design). Such designs should only be used when there is strong justification. One guideline to consider in exploring these issues is to make every effort to provide the intervention to the participants with the greatest needs.

Also, several strategies can be considered to ensure a balance between the needs of research and ethical concerns. Perhaps some participants could be provided an intervention on a delayed basis if they are on a waiting list and not likely to be harmed by a delay. Another strategy could be to offer a traditional intervention, such as a counseling approach, to participants assigned to a comparison or control group. Also, when using a SSD, the timing for withdrawing an intervention may be arranged at opportune times when staff members (or field students) are unavailable because they are on vacation or otherwise away.

Diversity issues are also important to consider when exploring causal relationships. For example, it is important to have participants with diverse characteristics in evaluation studies so that we can learn whether an intervention works for people with different characteristics, not just for homogeneous groupings. Another diversity issue can emerge if some subgroups have difficulty understanding or accepting the more controversial features of evaluation designs, such as using comparison groups or withdrawing an intervention. In these cases, one strategy that is diversity sensitive is to devote substantial time with participants to explaining why these procedures are so important in evaluations.

An obvious issue of importance for both diversity issues and populations at risk is to select interventions and outcome measures for evaluation studies that are relevant to their needs. As in other chapters, at-risk groups are identified in many of the illustrations in the chapter to highlight their importance related to exploring causal relationships. For example, a recovery group for clients who are substance abusers and a support group for underachieving students with disruptive behaviors are the illustrations used to describe group designs. Also, the evaluation studies reported in the chapter focus on students' attitudes toward homophobia, social work values, and stress.

Social justice issues are also important to consider when exploring causal relationships. Justice is served, for example, when a study can convincingly document that an intervention works for a particular group. In this instance, the intervention has a greater chance of survival and expanded use. Social justice can also be served when social workers use "hypothesizing" as a tool in their practice, because it can be easily carried over to testing in evaluation studies. In this case, hypothesizing can link practice issues to evaluation studies. Justice is also furthered by actively involving clients in their evaluations. By encouraging them to participate in the development and use of a SSD when working with a social worker, we are empowering them to take more responsibility for their lives. The more that their lives are self-directed, the more that social justice is served.

D i s c u s s i o n   Q u e s t i o n s

1. Identify the advantages and limitations of each of the single system designs in Figure 11.8.

2. Find and read a research study that uses a quasi-experimental design. Use the Allyn and Bacon Research Navigator to find such an article. Identify the specific intervention and the measure of the client outcome variable(s) used in this study.

3. A probation agency asks you to prepare a pre-experimental design to find out if their former clients are involved in fewer street crimes after receiving a six-month probation service. Complete the following steps:
   - Develop a hypothesis that has the probation service as the independent variable and a dependent variable of your choosing as the client outcome variable.
   - Assume that you will use a one-group pretest/posttest design that will measure the influence of the probation service on this client outcome. Explain how you will measure this client outcome in the pretest and posttest (e.g., asking a particular question in an interview, using existing records, etc.). What will you be able to conclude from this design? What are the limitations of this design?

4. Using the same independent and dependent variables that you chose in question 3, assume instead that you will use a time series design that includes several pretest and posttest measures of the client outcome. What are the advantages of using a time series design over a one-group pretest/posttest design? What disadvantages are there, if any?

5. Use a single system design as an evaluation tool to work on a personal issue of your choosing. As a first step, identify a personal development issue that you want to work on and develop a measure of it. (Examples of personal development issues could be to stop smoking, talk more in class, increase study time, eat healthily, relieve stress, etc.). Next, obtain a stable record of your personal development issue by measuring it every day for seven days (seven baseline measures). At the end of this period, introduce an intervention you will use to address your personal development issue. Implement the intervention for fourteen days and obtain a measure of your personal development issue every day during this period. Afterward, bring the graph to class and share your work.

6. Design a single system design (AB) to plot the progress of the following case, which was developed by the BSW program at Siena College (Loudonville, NY). The client is Ralph, a fourteen-year-old male who is in the ninth grade. He has his family in an uproar. He neglects his homework every night, using excuses like "I just want to see who is going to be on next on MTV." As a result, his parents fight with him every night. According to his mom and dad, Ralph is flunking several courses. His father has punished him by taking away his CD player, but this doesn't seem to work. His mom has placed him on double restriction and has taken away his $175 pair of Nike sneakers with the little pumps on the front. Both parents are at a loss as to what to do next. Perhaps you can help the family by using a SSD and completing the three steps that follow:
   - Choose a client outcome variable to be addressed in the above situation and give an operational definition and measure of the variable.
   - Choose an intervention and give an operational definition and measure of the intervention. A measure of the intervention will tell you if it was introduced.
   - Using a SSD graph, chart a hypothetical relationship between your intervention and the outcome variable. Be sure to show on the graph the baseline and the intervention phases of your work with the client.

7. Use the single system design developed in question 6 to prepare a role-play in which a social worker meets with Ralph and his parents. In the first session the social worker helps the family work out a plan of action using the single system design as an evaluation tool. Both an intervention and a measurable goal need to be identified.

Also, a baseline measure of the goal needs to be obtained. In a later session, the SSD is used to explore progress or lack of it in reaching the goal.

8. A few years ago a *natural experiment* occurred in Helena, Montana. A natural experiment is an experiment occurring in natural events rather than in controlled laboratories. In this case, Helena's local council members executed the experiment by their actions. The council members enacted a "no smoking" ordinance for all public buildings that was in force for six months. An amazing thing happened; heart attacks dropped by 50 percent, being reported by the only hospital in this small town. This drop in heart attacks was explained to be caused by a reduction in secondhand smoking by people around smokers. The lung capillaries of people exposed to secondhand smoking are known to close up in 30 minutes. Unfortunately, six months later this ordinance was reversed and the rate of heart attacks in Helena returned to its previously high rate. What was the intervention in this natural experiment? What was the outcome variable? Diagram this quasi-experimental design using X for the intervention and O for the measures of the outcome variable.

References

Bloom, M., Fischer, J., & Orme, J. (1999). *Evaluating practice: Guidelines for the accountable professional,* 3rd ed. Boston: Allyn and Bacon.

Campbell, D., & Stanley, J. (1963). *Experimental and quasi-experimental designs for research.* Chicago: Rand McNally College.

Cavazos, A., & Guerrero, D. (1999). Assertiveness and field education: An exploratory study. *Journal of Baccalaureate Social Work, 4*(2), 85–94.

Dongvillo, J., & Ligon, J. (2001). Exploring the effectiveness of teaching techniques with lesbian and gay content in the social work curriculum. *Journal of Baccalaureate Social Work, 6*(2), 116–124.

National Association of Social Workers (NASW). (1999). *NASW Code of Ethics: Evaluation and*

Research, Sections 1.04 & 5.02. Washington, DC: Author.

Royse, D., & Riffe, H. (1999). Assessing students' values in an era of change. *Journal of Baccalaureate Social Work, 4*(2), 71–83.

Thyer, B., & Meyers, L. (2003). Linking assessment to outcome evaluation using single system and group research design. In C. Jordan and C. Franklin (Eds.), *Clinical assessment for social workers: Quantitative and qualitative methods,* 2nd ed. (pp. 385–405). Chicago: Lyceum.

Wuebben, P., Straits, B., & Shulman, G. (1974). *The experiment as a social occasion.* Berkeley, CA: Glendessary Press.

chapter 12

Collecting the Data

People who have a predisposition to social work are also likely to have a predisposition to collecting research data. Both groups are interested in learning more about people and their circumstances.

Collecting the data is the focus of this chapter. Collecting research data is a lot like collecting data as a social worker. This is good news, because it suggests that social workers already possess many of the skills that they can use as producers of social work research. This is step 4 in the research process.

Chapters 9 and 10 described how survey and observation instruments are constructed. Some of the material covered in those chapters is directly pertinent to this chapter. As we construct a data collection instrument, we inevitably introduce issues about collecting the data, which is the focus of this chapter. Thus, expect some overlap of material between those chapters and this one. This chapter focuses on topics of importance to both a producer and consumer of research during the time when data are collected. Most of the chapter is devoted to topics particularly pertinent to the producer role. These topics are:

> **Steps in the Research Process**
>
> 1. Understanding the research topic to be studied
> 2. Focusing the study
> 3. Designing the study
>   a. Selecting the participants
>   b. Selecting a data collection approach and measuring concepts
>   - Surveys
>   - Observations
>   c. Exploring causal relationships
> 4. **Collecting the data**
> 5. Analyzing the data
> 6. Preparing a report

- differences between collecting quantitative and qualitative data
- preparation for data collection
- considering the influence of the personal characteristics of the researcher
- the consumer role and collecting the data

Differences in Collecting Quantitative and Qualitative Data

Researchers collect data in varied ways. These variations are particularly evident in whether quantitative or qualitative methods are used. Quantitative and qualitative methods are introduced in Chapter 2.

Quantitative Methods

Quantitative inquiries are circumscribed and specific about what the data collector wants to know. These inquiries use structured questions or observations to measure variables of interest in the real world. A most important quality needed by these data collectors is to be object focused. Being object focused means being entirely focused on the object of what is being studied. An object-focused researcher collects data that reflect the perspectives and experience of the research participants without any interference from the data collector. Ideally, nothing within the data collector's control is allowed to interfere with the way in which the data are collected. Examples of behaviors of the data collector that could interfere with being object focused include any of the following:

- verbally or nonverbally communicating agreement or disagreement with the participant's responses
- contributing in any way to the participant's responses (e.g., giving hints about how the question could be answered)
- using special intonations in voice to emphasize some things and not others in a question
- asking questions differently for different research participants (e.g., probing to obtain clarity from one participant but not another)

Qualitative Methods

The purpose of using qualitative methods is to discover something that is unknown or not well understood by most people. Examples include new insights about someone's social circumstances or their reasons for not using an agency's services. Qualitative inquiries are much less focused and structured than quantitative inquiries. Qualitative data collectors are supposed to suspend their own beliefs, perspectives, and predispositions as if everything is happening for the first time and nothing is taken for granted (Taylor & Bogdan, 1984). No attempts are made to impose unnecessary restrictions or limitations on the search process before it begins. This means that data collectors have the flexibility to pursue hunches beyond what was initially prescribed, if these hunches are pertinent to the research topic.

The qualitative data collector has a broader role to play than one using quantitative methods. While being object focused, they also need several additional attributes and skills to be effective, such as:

- building rapport with key people and those that surround them
- being good listeners
- being able to identify pertinent cues for further exploration
- spontaneously formulating new questions that are relevant to the people being studied

- remembering in some detail what is being said and observed for later recording of data
- recording comprehensively and accurately what was said and observed

Overall, data collectors who use qualitative methods need to be subject focused as well as object focused. Being subject focused means being "in tune" with the research participants and making a special effort to "stand in their shoes" to understand them better. This often entails developing a close relationship with the participants, which includes communicating a special concern for them and their circumstances. Subject-focused involvement is a strategy for discovering the deeper meaning or reality imbedded in the lives of the people being studied.

Being subject focused, however, does not mean overidentifying with a research participant or losing one's objectivity. Overidentification is a state to avoid, because of its threat to the validity of the data. Preventive steps could include journaling regularly about what you as a data collector are feeling or thinking and keeping these recordings separate from what is observed and heard from the participants. Also, it would be a good idea to have a research supervisor available to discuss any such threats to data collection.

Going Native

Anthropologists have a term that they use to indicate when anthropologists have lost their sense of objectivity while conducting research in the field. It is referred to as "going native." Going native means overidentifying with the people being studied, losing one's own perspective, and forgetting one's purpose for being there. Social workers have a similar problem to guard against. They can also overidentify with their clients and their circumstances and lose the objectivity that is needed for helping them.

Subjectivity and *objectivity* are terms that have been deliberately left out of this discussion. Objectivity is replaced by *object focused* and subjectivity is replaced by *subject focused* to more accurately describe what is intended. *Subjectivity* is a term that is often used in a pejorative or negative sense. For example, a subjective person is often thought to be someone who has a bias or lack of objectivity. In qualitative research, an even better term than *subject focused* may be *fairness*. A qualitative data collector uses fairness in gathering data, which means making every effort to describe all perspectives that are observed and doing this accurately and without bias.

Marlow (2001) addresses the pejorative use of the word *subjectivity* by introducing an alternative term, *neutrality*, or being neutral. Someone who is neutral is free of bias. Data collectors who use both quantitative or qualitative methods are expected to be neutral.

Preparation for Data Collection

People who collect data using either quantitative or qualitative methods should be adequately prepared or trained. As the above descriptions of quantitative and qualitative data collection suggest, the expectations of the person who collects the data are distinctively different. In general terms, quantitative data collection requires a thorough understanding of the interview schedule (or observational rating scale) to be used and the specific ways in which the responses are to be recorded. Qualitative data collection, in contrast, requires a more comprehensive understanding of the research topic and much more familiarity with the specific research methodology used.

Preparation for Quantitative Methods

Data collectors preparing to use quantitative methods must be thoroughly familiar with the instrument that will be used. If they are preparing to conduct structured interviews, they will need to fully understand all of the questions to be asked. Data collectors must be able to ask each question clearly and with confidence. They will also need to know the amount of flexibility they have in clarifying any misunderstood questions. Any technical terms (e.g., particular medications or diseases) included in the questions need to be understood so that they can be explained, if necessary, to the interviewee. Guidelines are also needed for handling potentially difficult situations related to some questions. For example, if a sensitive question is asked and the interviewee responds by stopping the interview, the data collector needs to have some guidelines for what to do next. Quantitative data collectors also need to know how to correctly record the responses to each question on an interview schedule.

Understanding the Questions

A study of people with a dual diagnosis of mental illness and mental retardation involved interviewing agency staff members about their medical condition (Conroy et al., 2001). One question asked was:

> "Is there any evidence of tardive dyskinesia (which is a result of long-term use of certain powerful medications), such as involuntary facial twitches or tongue movements?"
>
> ___ 1. major evidence
> ___ 2. minor evidence
> ___ 3. no evidence of tardive dyskinesia

While the term *tardive dyskinesia* is partially described in the question, it is a technical term that may need further explanation. (Tardive dyskinesia is a neurological disorder that can result from taking medications prescribed to control seizures.) The interviewer must be able to explain this term to the interviewees if asked.

Similarly, a person conducting structured observations must be able to understand and detect the behaviors that are the study's focus. They must also detect variations in how these behaviors are manifested. These data collectors also need to know how to record these behaviors on a behavioral rating instrument.

Preparation for data collectors using quantitative methods will most likely consist of a training session involving all or part of a day. The length of time needed for training will depend on the length of the interview schedule and complexity of the questions. Preferably, this session is to be led by the researcher directing the study or someone else who is familiar with the instrument to be used. The trainer should provide an explanation for why each question is being asked. Ample time should also be allowed in the session for the interviewees to ask questions about the purpose and methodology of the study. They may ask about such things as strategies for asking questions, how to respond to a particular participant situation, and how to correctly record responses.

Babbie (2001) suggests that the training include conducting one or two demonstration interviews by the trainer in front of everyone. Afterward, the data collectors could practice conducting interviews privately in pairs, followed by a role-play of the interview by a trainee in front of everyone. Ongoing supervision of data collectors is also valuable, along with another training session or individual follow-up after fifteen or twenty interviews have been completed. By then, data collectors will have some interviewing experience and new questions to ask. Also, periodically, completed interviews should be reviewed to determine if they have been filled out correctly, including providing an adequate amount of data for the open-ended questions.

Preparation for Qualitative Methods

Those planning to collect data using qualitative methods will prepare themselves quite differently. These data collectors must have a good understanding of the research topic of the study and the specific questions that need to be asked, but they will also need to know much more. It helps if they know about other perspectives on the research topic and the findings of other studies. These perspectives and studies can enlighten them about how to collect the data. They will also need to understand the principles and strategies of qualitative research methods generally and the specific methods they will use, such as unstructured interviews, focus groups, or participant observation.

Taylor and Bogdan (1984, pp. 94–98), for example, offer several simple but helpful principles for conducting unstructured interviews. These guidelines include:

- *Being nonjudgmental:* It is important for the interviewer to create a safe atmosphere for the interviewee to openly disclose all kinds of information, including private thoughts and feelings. An important way of encouraging openness is to be nonjudgmental about what the interviewee says and does. Sometimes interviewees need to be reassured that what they are saying is accepted by the data collector, particularly when what they say is embarrassing or very personal. Nonverbal expressions of acceptance, such as a nod of empathy, go a long way in communicating acceptance.

- *Letting people talk:* An effective unstructured interviewer listens well and conveys this to the interviewee. Being comfortable with silence and allowing the interviewee to discuss things that are not relevant to the study often help in letting people feel comfortable talking. As the conversation flows, sympathetic gestures and relevant questions can bring the interviewee back to relevant topics.
- *Paying attention:* It is important to pay genuine attention to what the interviewee is saying and not let your mind drift. Good eye contact, supportive nods, and other gestures that reveal attentiveness are important. Attentiveness is also very important to ensure that comments are recorded accurately.
- *Being sensitive:* Being sensitive to how to behave and what to ask are also important. For example, be friendly but not ingratiating, sympathetic but not patronizing; ask probing questions but don't intrude into areas that should be left untouched.

These principles are familiar to social workers who follow similar principles in social work practice.

Preparation for Leading Focus Groups

A focus group is a special type of group that has been formed to help in planning a research study. Focus groups can also be used for developing a new program or numerous other service-related purposes. Because focus groups are increasingly used in both research and social work practice, more information is provided about these groups and how they are conducted.

Focus groups use qualitative data collection methods. A focus group in research is a special type of group interview that takes on characteristics of both semi- and unstructured interviews. It is designed to invite participants to discuss a particular topic by focusing on several open-ended questions on the topic. A focus group is usually composed of four to ten participants who have personal knowledge or expertise on a particular topic. The group is led by a facilitator who has skills in working with groups and a recorder who keeps detailed records of the information shared. Sometimes the group sessions are also tape-recorded. Discussion is relaxed, informal, and often enjoyable. The emphasis is on sharing what each participant knows about the topic. A focus group can be viewed as an opportunity to empower its participants, because it involves them directly in an open process of exploration and planning. Focus groups are a popular method that use some of the strategies of participatory action research (PAR) discussed in Chapter 2.

Focus groups used in research can be conducted in various ways. Some of the principles and procedures used in conducting these groups are as follows:

- General questions are introduced to provide a focus or purpose.
- All the participants share their views in response to the questions.
- Everyone has an adequate amount of time to share.
- No one debates each other.
- Differences are respected.
- The facilitator keeps the group focused on the topic and makes sure everyone has a chance to share their views.
- The recorder writes down everyone's comments.
- After everyone has shared, the recorder reads everyone's comments to make sure they are accurate and to encourage any additional clarification.
- The group looks for common themes among the views that have been shared.
- The results are organized into a report.

Caregivers of Family Members with Alzheimer's

A student conducted a focus group of four caregivers of family members with Alzheimer's disease (Gladora, 2002). The following questions were asked: "As a caregiver, what are your biggest needs?" "What do you wish you knew more about on assuming the caregiving role?" "How can the community be more responsive to your needs?" "What would help you provide the best care for your loved one?" The answers that were given were surprising and enlightening. The caregivers unanimously agreed that respite is their biggest need. (Respite services consist of having someone come in to care for their loved one for an allotted amount of time so they can have a break.)

What was interesting was what each caregiver wanted to do with their respite time. Because many caregivers often experience depression due to stress, people often believe they need to "get out" and engage in social interaction. Two of the participants wanted respite so that they could have solitude. They wanted to be alone with their thoughts, to run errands, or to go to the park and have quiet time with themselves. The other participants wanted respite to spend time with friends.

The participants also expressed the need for education for caregivers, especially when first assuming the caregiving role. Because their loved ones have Alzheimer's, these particular caregivers wished they had known more about Alzheimer's disease and the progression of symptoms associated with it. Had they known more, they said, they would not have been so shocked and felt so helpless as the disease progressed in their loved one. Also in terms of education, two caregivers wished they had more access to financial and legal information, such as how to get their loved one's essential paperwork and legal documents in order and what they needed to have. Finally, one caregiver felt that other people need to be more educated about long-term care insurance. She felt fortunate that she had invested in long-term care insurance. The caregivers felt that social services (free or cost-share) and church communities are the best way to help caregivers perform their caregiving role.

Other examples of studies using focus groups are described in various parts of the book, including page 60 in Chapter 3, pages 280–281 in Chapter 15, and pages 293–294 in Chapter 16.

Considering the Influence of the Personal Characteristics of the Researcher

Another consideration in collecting data is to select people who have characteristics that are compatible with the people being studied. *Demographic characteristics* are one such consideration. While gender, age, race, nationality, sexual orientation, and other demographic characteristics only partially define a person, they may be important in some research studies. For example, a study of gender-related topics, such as birth control, breast cancer, or prostate cancer, will be most easily conducted by an interviewer of the same gender as the interviewee. A study on racial issues, such as the views of minorities toward the majority culture, will likely be most effectively facilitated by an interviewer and interviewee of the same race or ethnic group. Similarly, a study about self-disclosure by lesbians would be more easily facilitated by a lesbian interviewer, just as a study of the Islamic faith may be most easily conducted by someone who is a member of the Islamic faith.

When the research topic of the study is not directly related to gender, race, or other demographic characteristics that are easily identified, such a match may not be relevant. For example, a study of the views of social work students toward their student association does not relate directly to issues such as gender or race. In this case, it may be important to have interviewers and interviewees who are different from each other to communicate the importance of diverse participation in the student association.

Another factor to consider in selecting data collectors is to find people who have some knowledge about the people being studied. For example, a study about children in the schools could benefit from having data collectors with some prior work or volunteer experience with school-age children. Similarly, a researcher conducting a mental health study may want to select their data collectors from a pool of professionals who work in this field.

People who personally know the interviewees are not usually a good choice for conducting interviews, particularly if private information is shared. In this case, ethical issues such as invasion of privacy and confidentiality could be violated. Or a conflict of interest may be possible. For example, if the research interviewers are also employed in the agency in which a study is being conducted, they will likely have a conflict of interest between their two roles. In addition, the clients who are studied may fear retribution if they reveal something critical about the agency.

Other issues may also need to be considered in selecting a data collector. If people have strong views about a research topic, whether for or against, they may be unable to remain neutral in their role of collecting data. For example, someone who has strong religious convictions, or is a devout atheist, may have difficulty collecting data for a study on diverse spiritual perspectives.

In review, some key questions to ask when considering who should be selected to collect the data are as follows:

- Will data collectors with demographic characteristics similar to the interviewee (age, race, gender, etc.) be able to elicit more openness and honesty in the responses than someone with different demographic characteristics?
- Are there other instances in which the characteristics of the participants (e.g., their diagnoses, type of disabilities, experience of abuse) may be important to consider in selecting an interviewer?
- Do prospective data collectors have other roles that could be in conflict with the data collector role?
- In these instances, would the interviewees perceive a conflict of interest even when there may not be one?
- Do data collectors have strong feelings or views about the research topic? If so, how easy will it be for them to set aside these views so that they will not interfere with data collection?
- Is there value in selecting data collectors who have characteristics that are different from interviewees? Could such differences facilitate more openness by the interviewee? Could such differences also promote a greater appreciation of diversity?

Collecting the Data and the Consumer Role

The step of collecting data is not covered extensively in most research reports, beyond the topics covered in this chapter. Nevertheless, it is important to find out how much care and rigor went into collecting the data. One aspect of this care and rigor can be found in the extent to which data collectors were well prepared for this task. The consumer of research reports has some important questions to consider, including the following:

1. If either interviews or observations are used as data collection approaches, is there any evidence in the research report that the data collectors were trained to collect data for this study? If so, what was the nature and extent of their training?
2. Was anything noted in the report about selecting research interviewers with particular demographic characteristics (e.g., race, gender, age, etc.) that match the characteristics of the research participants? If so, do you think that this was a good idea? Why or why not?
3. Does the report indicate that the data collectors have any special qualifications, such as research skills or knowledge about the topic, that could

facilitate data collection? If so, do you think this was helpful? Why or why not?

Chapter Reflections

Values and Ethics, Diversity, At-Risk Groups, and Social Justice

Values and ethics are continuously evident in collecting data. Several ethical issues are identified in the chapter related to data collectors. A training component for data collectors is paramount. Data collectors must be well trained and prepared for their roles, not only to effectively facilitate the research but also to protect the participants. For example, data collectors need to introduce an informed consent protocol in an effective way and ensure that the participants are thoroughly protected throughout the study.

Data collectors must also be object focused and able to monitor how they present themselves to avoid biasing the participants' responses. Qualitative evaluators must also remain subject focused and fair in what they observe and record. Being fair means being able to identify all of the perspectives evident in the phenomenon being studied and recording them accurately. Also, data collectors must be careful not to have a conflict of interest between their role as a data collector and other roles. For example, it is usually not a good idea for a data collector to be an employee working with the people who are the participants in a study.

Diversity issues are also important in collecting data. A data collector will often be different in some ways from the participants who are studied and will need to be sensitive to these differences. For example, heterosexual interviewers need to be sensitive to any biases or misunderstandings they have when interviewing a gay or lesbian. Also, sensitivity to diversity characteristics is important in the study of sensitive topics. The chapter suggests that some sensitive topics can be researched most effectively by matching people having some of the same characteristics. Such arrangements show respect and honor to participants who are sharing private material related to various diversity issues. For example, studies that focus on sexuality issues, such as breast or prostate cancer, should have a same-sex match of interviewer and interviewee.

At-risk groups may also need special considerations in data collection. An interviewer will need to create a safe, accepting environment for all interviewees to self-disclose openly and honestly. At-risk groups in particular need such an approach. For example, a teenage mother or father or parents who are ex-offenders are not likely to reveal their private thoughts and feelings about parenting in anything but a safe and nonjudgmental environment.

The research methods used in collecting data can be linked to social justice as well. Focus groups, for example, are often an excellent way to study a topic and at the same time empower the participants. Bringing participants together to discuss a topic of interest often fosters networking, bonding, and new insights about what can be done to help people. Qualitative methods generally can be empowering, because these methods encourage participants to speak in their own words and from their unique perspectives.

Discussion Questions

1. Interview another student about his or her views on a sensitive topic. Do this by first crafting three open-ended questions to ask. Then select someone who is noticeably different from you. For example:
   - If you are a female, interview a male on the topic of safe sex, abortion, sexual responsibility, or teenage pregnancy.
   - If you are a male, interview a female on any of the above topics.
   - If you are a "minority" person, interview a "majority" person on the topic of discrimination related to your minority status (e.g., based on race, homophobia, religion, social class, etc.).

   Next, discuss any difficulties you may have had in conducting the interview or that the interviewee may have had in responding to the questions. Also, discuss any advantages you may have discovered in being different.

2. Conduct a semistructured interview with another student who is culturally different from you. Ask at least two of the open-ended questions (McGoldrick, 1982) on family and culture listed below. Then share what you have learned with the class.
   - What characteristics of your ethnic/cultural group do you like the most? The least? Explain your answer.
   - Describe traditions and rituals in your family (e.g., celebrations of holidays, birthdays, dinner-time).
   - Describe the accepted roles of men and women in your family.
   - What signs of ethnic/cultural identity are in your home (e.g., art, books, toys, clothing, language, cooking)?
   - Describe the people who live in your neighborhood and your relationships toward them.
   - Describe the role that religion and spirituality plays in your family.

3. Assume you will be conducting an interview study of women who are inmates in a limited-security jail. The focus of your interviews will be their parenting roles with their children. How would you implement informed consent? Would you use a written or oral consent approach? What specific information would you cover in the informed consent procedure? What factors would go into your decisions? You may want to consult Chapter 3 in preparing your response.

4. Social workers can be promoters of research that is beneficial to the clients' well-being. If you are working in a social agency or currently have a field practicum, give examples of how you can promote research that is beneficial to the clients' well-being.

5. If you developed a scale of political activism for discussion question 6 in Chapter 5, conduct a study of social work students to find out how politically active they are. If time permits, survey a group of freshmen, sophomores, juniors, and seniors to find out if they are noticeably different in their political activism. Feel free to use some of the behaviors that are mentioned for a scale on "political activism" on page 107.

R e f e r e n c e s

Babbie, E. (2001). *The practice of social research,* 9th ed. Belmont, CA: Wadsworth/Thomson Learning.

Conroy, J., Fulerton, A., Dudley, J., & Ahlgrim-Delzell, L. (2001). The progress made by *Thomas S.* consumers: First visits to 2001 visits. Monograph 27, *Thomas S.* Longitudinal Research Project, University of North Carolina, Charlotte.

Gladora, A. (2002). Caregivers in DSS's caregiver support program focus group. Student research project, University of North Carolina, Charlotte.

Marlow, C. (2001). *Research methods for generalist social work,* 3rd ed. Stamford, CT: Thomson Learning.

McGoldrick, M. (1982). Ethnicity and family therapy: An overview. In M. McGoldrick, J. Pearce, and J. Giordano (Eds.), *Ethnicity and family therapy* (pp. 3–30). New York: Guilford.

Patton, M. (1987). *How to use evaluative methods in evaluation.* Newbury Park, CA: Sage.

Taylor, S., & Bogdan, R. (1984). *Introduction to qualitative research methods: The search for meanings,* 2nd ed. New York: Wiley.

13

Analyzing Data

The purpose of analyzing data is to transform them into useful information. Such information can be used to make critical decisions, such as determining if a practice intervention works, an existing program is effective, a new program is needed in the community, or an agency's funding should be renewed.

Data analysis is an important step in the research process, particularly for the producer role. **Data analysis** is defined as a process of transforming data into useful information. The multifaceted process of data analysis is covered in this chapter. Planning for data analysis is also covered in this chapter, even though it should begin when the study is being designed. As you can see, analyzing the data is one of the last steps in the research process.

The data analysis process is often misunderstood. Some people (including many students) think, for example, that research and statistics are synonymous. When they hear "research course," they associate it with an overwhelming math course they had to take. Others may think you need to be an expert in statistics to do research.

Let's clear up some of these misunderstandings. "Research methods" is much more than "statistics." Statistical tools are used in only one step of the research process, and statistics may not even be used at all if the research only involves qualitative methods. Also, you do not have to be a statistician to do research. In fact, very few social work researchers are experts in statistics. They know statistics generally, but they also know when to consult an expert. It is often wise to consult a statistics specialist when addressing some of the more complicated statistical steps of data analysis. Every social worker can be prepared, in an introductory way, to conduct research and analyze the data. Several aspects of data analysis are covered in this chapter, including what

Steps in the Research Process

1. Understanding the research topic to be studied
2. Focusing the study
3. Designing the study
   a. Selecting the participants
   b. Selecting a data collection approach and measuring concepts
      - Surveys
      - Observations
   c. Exploring causal relationships
4. Collecting the data
5. **Analyzing the data**
6. Preparing a report

data analysis is, planning for data analysis, quantitative and qualitative data analysis, and analyzing data and the consumer role.

What Is Data Analysis?

As described in previous chapters, data collected in studies can take many forms. The data in one study, for example, could consist of the responses of fifty community residents to a lengthy questionnaire. Or the data could consist of fifty or more pages of narrative notes that describe the daily lives of only two or three clients in a residential setting. The data could also consist of numerous observational rating forms describing the classroom behavior of children or a lengthy description of one client's social circumstances based on several unstructured interviews.

Initially, the data collected do not exist in a form that is immediately usable. A distilling process must occur that refines and shapes the data into information that can be useful to its stakeholders, who can be policy makers, agency administrators, other professionals, or a group of clients.

Example of a Study Using Qualitative Data Analysis

Longres and Scanlon (2001, p. 452) conducted a study of the views of social work faculty on how they prepare their students to promote justice through research. Two of their overall research questions were "Are social work research courses informed by concepts of social justice?" and "Does the infusion of justice into the research curriculum require that we promote certain research topics, theoretical frameworks, or research methodologies?" Semistructured interviews were used, and they elicited qualitative responses. The analysis of the data initially involved an identification of key themes. Then the data were reviewed again to find additional evidence of the themes that were identified. Finally, the researchers presented the themes as their findings, along with quotes from the data to illustrate each theme.

Data analysis takes many forms. While data analysis often uses statistical tools, particularly if the data are quantitative, data collected in a narrative or word form use other strategies. Examples of just a few of the varied techniques that could be used in analyzing data are

- identifying themes frequently evident in a set of case records (qualitative)
- construction of a set of general categories that summarizes a long list of individual responses to an open-ended question (qualitative)
- calculating a frequency distribution of the responses to a forced-response question using a Likert scale (quantitative)
- preparing a detailed case description of one person's circumstances based on several unstructured interviews (qualitative)
- conducting a bivariate statistical test to determine if there is an association between two variables (quantitative)

- conducting a content analysis of key words that are frequently expressed in a community report (qualitative)
- calculating mean (average) scores summarizing some of the background variables of a group of clients studied. These background characteristics could include the clients' age, annual income, number of children, length of time using services, and so on. (quantitative)

Planning for Data Analysis

It is very important to plan ahead for data analysis! This planning should usually begin during step 3 when the study is being designed. Once the general research questions or hypotheses are identified, a research design is developed to explore or test these propositions. Along with selecting a data source, a data collection approach, and measures of important variables, step 3 begins to consider how the data that will be collected are to be analyzed. You may want to refer back to the beginning of this chapter to recall all of the steps in the research process that precede data analysis.

Let's assume, for example, that you are going to conduct a study that asks one overall research question, "Why do students select social work as their major?" A survey would likely be the best way of finding out the students' reasons. A survey could be either a questionnaire filled out by the students or an interview conducted with each student. The purpose of the study will be to find out the answer to the overall research question, and the data analysis plan will be a means of doing this. A survey instrument could ask a variety of pertinent questions, such as the three types of questions that follow:

1. Did you choose a social work major because you want to help people?

     ___ yes   ___ no

2. On a scale of 1 to 5 (1 = extremely important, 2 = very important, 3 = important, 4 = somewhat important, and 5 = not at all important), how important are each of the following reasons why you selected a social work major?
   - ___ helping people
   - ___ solving social problems (such as family breakdown or teenage crime)
   - ___ contributing something meaningful to society
   - ___ having meaning in your life
   - ___ having a stable income

3. Why did you choose social work as a major?

These three types of questions vary from being very focused (question 1) to unfocused (question 3). They also elicit very different kinds of data. For example, questions 1 and 2 are forced-response questions that elicit a numerical or quantitative response, while question 3 elicits a qualitative or word response.

A data analysis question to ask at this point would be "Do you want quantitative or qualitative responses? Or do you want a combination of the two?" The answers to these questions depend on how much is known about the topic. For example, you could find out what is known from other studies about the reasons students select a social work major. If you decide to use questions 1 and 2, you should be fairly certain that some of the reasons found in other studies are included as choices in these questions.

However, you may conclude that you have no idea of the reasons why students choose this major. In this case you may want to ask open-ended questions like question 3. Or you could ask both questions 2 and 3 to explore the reasons you suspect are important as well as other reasons volunteered by the students. Generally, the important issue is whether you want to conduct an exploratory or explanatory study. A fuller discussion of some of the differences between exploratory and explanatory studies is found in Chapter 6.

Other issues related to data analysis are evident in the differences between questions 1 and 2 in this example. Question 1 asks for a response to only one reason ("to help people"), while question 2 inquires about several reasons. Another difference in these two questions is that the student has only two response categories to choose from in question 1 (yes or no) and five response choices in question 2. There can be advantages to question 1. If you are only interested in finding out if majors are motivated by the reason "to help people," why ask about any other reasons?

Question 2 has obvious advantages as well. If you inquire about several reasons for choosing this major, you will obtain answers to all of them, and you can find out which reasons are most frequently chosen. For example, several students might perceive "helping people" as "extremely" or "very important," while only one student might perceive "having a stable income" as "very important." Also, in question 2, if students are given five responses to choose from ("extremely important" to "not at all important"), they are likely to select a response category that more closely fits their perception than if they were forced into a yes or no response. Most people's opinions tend to be in gradations or degrees of certainty. In other words, many people see things more as being gray than as either black or white.

Quantitative versus Qualitative Data Analysis

Quantitative Data Analysis

Quantitative and qualitative methodologies are described in Chapter 2 and presented as being distinctly different. In review, quantitative methods, being deductive in nature, usually attempt to find support for theoretical explanations or ideas developed by the researcher. Quantitative inquiries are fairly specific about what they want to find out. They usually have measures of their concepts and ask questions or observe behaviors in such a way that the responses are in number form or can be converted to numerical scores. Questions are written to elicit an answer in a numerical form (e.g., "How old are you?" elicits a number of years) or to offer a set of response categories from which respondents are to choose the one most appropriate. These questions are forced-response questions. A question, for example, may be "What is your employment status?" and the answer could be one of several possibilities, such as working full-time, working part-time, working at home raising children full-time, looking for work, able to work but not looking, and disabled. While the responses in this case are all in word form, they can easily be assigned a number if each of the categories is distinct and does not overlap. In this case, the responses to this question can be coded and given a numerical score as follows:

1. working full-time
2. working part-time
3. working at home raising children full-time
4. looking for work
5. able to work but not looking
6. disabled
7. other

Based on this coding system, a respondent's employment status can be identified by a number. For example, a respondent who is looking for work would receive a value of 4. Assigning numbers to these response categories makes it possible to enter the data into a computer file and analyze them.

When it comes time to analyze the results of quantitative investigations, statistics can be used because the data are in number form. A further advantage of numerical data is that the computer can compute all of the mathematical equations much more easily than you could do it. Electronic statistical programs are used to compute these statistics. An electronic statistical program that is particularly popular in social work research is the Statistical Package for the Social Sciences (SPSS). SPSS is available in the computer labs of most universities, and a student version of SPSS can be purchased as well (SPSS, 2002).

Qualitative Data Analysis

Qualitative methods, in contrast to quantitative methods, usually attempt to discover something new or to more fully explain something not widely known. Qualitative inquiries have more flexibility inherent in them than quantitative inquiries. This flexibility allows these methods to be used to pursue ongoing hunches of the researchers, not just hunches initially identified in the research design. Qualitative methods usually involve semi- or unstructured data collection approaches. These methods ask open-ended questions, and such questions do not provide a set of response categories for the response. Instead, participants who are interviewed verbalize their response in their own words, and those who fill out a questionnaire write their response in the designated blank space on the instrument. A group of clients responded to the open-ended question "What do you think is the most important quality of a good social worker?" with the following responses:

- She listens to me.
- He calls me by my name.

- Helps me solve my problems.
- She is easy to reach when I need her.
- She gives me undivided attention.
- I like the way that he asks how I feel about my problem.

Unless the responses to an open-ended question are reduced to a smaller set of general categories, they remain in word form. Word form, in this case, would be preferred if the researcher wants to learn as much as possible about a topic from the respondents' perspectives. The analysis of the data would use some form of word analysis that preserves the meaning of each response. Some researchers use computer programs to help in conducting qualitative data analysis. Nud*ist N6 (2002) and NVivo (2002) are examples of such programs. In these instances, the computer is able to identify any repetition of specific words and phrases that are evident in the data. As an alternative, many social work researchers prefer to conduct a word or content analysis manually or without the use of a computer program. An explanation for how this can be done is provided in Chapter 15.

Analyzing Data and the Consumer Role

It is important for the consumer of a research report to have some understanding of how the data were analyzed. Some of the data analysis issues to consider are covered in the topics of the chapter. Consumers should be able to determine whether the data in a report are quantitative, qualitative, or both. They should also be able to identify the specific data analysis tools that were used, whether statistical or in word form. Some specific data analysis questions for the consumer to consider are:

1. *If quantitative data analysis was used, what specific statistical techniques were utilized to analyze the data?* For example, were any of the following statistics mentioned: percentages, mean scores, standard deviation, chi-square, *t*-test, correlation, or ANOVA? All of these statistics are described in Chapter 14.
2. *If qualitative data analysis was used, what specific data analysis strategies were employed?* For example, did the researcher prepare a case study, conduct a theme analysis, or construct general response categories to summarize responses to open-ended questions? All of these strategies and others are described in Chapter 15.

Social workers at the BSW level should be able to identify and describe the specific data analysis strategies used in a study. While it is beyond the competencies of a BSW to know whether the best data analysis strategies were used in someone else's report, it seems reasonable to expect a BSW consumer to have some general thoughts about whether or not appropriate strategies were used. MSW consumers are usually expected to know a bit more about the intricacies of data analysis strategies reported in a study.

In conclusion, when quantitative methods are used, the results are prepared in number form, making it possible to analyze the data using statistics. This is usually done with a computer program that does the statistical calculations. When qualitative methods are used, the results are mostly in word form and are reduced and summarized using some type of word analysis. Researchers usually conduct these qualitative analyses by hand or with a computer program that can assist them.

The specific processes involved in conducting both quantitative and qualitative data analysis are examined in the next two chapters. Because quantitative and qualitative data analyses are distinctly different, they are examined in separate chapters: Chapter 14 describes quantitative data analysis, and Chapter 15 describes qualitative data analysis.

Chapter Reflections

Values and Ethics, Diversity, At-Risk Groups, and Social Justice

Data analysis is not value-free or neutral. It involves numerous choices that have ethical consequences. For example, honesty, thoroughness, and accuracy are all needed in selecting and using data analysis strategies—in reporting on what is analyzed and in preventing biases from influencing what is analyzed. Avoiding reductionism with qualitative data is also a critical ethical issue.

It is also important not to overlook diversity issues in data analysis. If a variety of groups are being studied, pertinent data analysis tools are available to explore important differences and similarities among such groups. Qualitative data analysis, in particular, can help identify and clarify differences evident among a varied group of people being studied.

Qualitative data analysis strategies can also be useful for gaining more understanding about at-risk groups and in empowering the people being studied. Qualitative strategies, for example, can provide descriptive accounts of at-risk people and their circumstances that can be invaluable in revealing how we can help these individuals. Quantitative strategies can be empowering for at-risk groups as well. For example, these strategies can be used to prepare a well-documented report on the adverse impact of a social problem on thousands of people. The next two chapters on quantitative and qualitative data analysis offer additional examples of the links between data analysis and all of these issues.

Discussion Questions

1. Identify a study that primarily uses quantitative methods. You can find such a study using the Allyn and Bacon Research Navigator. Does the report explain how the data were analyzed? Describe these procedures. What specific statistical techniques were used to analyze the data? For example, were any of the following statistics

used: percentages, mean scores, standard deviation, chi-square, *t*-test, correlation, or ANOVA?

2. Identify a study that primarily uses qualitative methods. You can find such a study using the Allyn and Bacon Research Navigator. Does the report explain how the findings of this study were analyzed? Describe these procedures. Did the analysis involve any of the following approaches: preparing a case study, a theme analysis, or constructing general response categories for open-ended questions?

References

Longres, J., & Scanlon, E. (2001). Social justice and the research curriculum. *Journal of Social Work Education, 37*(3), 447–463.

Nud*ist N6. (2002). *Nud*ist* (version 6). Doncaster Victoria, Australia: QSR International. (Available through Sage Publications Software, Thousand Oaks, CA.)

NVivo. (2002). *Nvivo* (version 2). Doncaster Victoria, Australia: QSR International. (Available through Sage Publications Software, Thousand Oaks, CA.)

SPSS, *Student Version, 11 for Windows.* (2002). Upper Saddle River, NJ: Prentice-Hall.

chapter 14

Quantitative Data Analysis

Statistics are especially pertinent to this one step of the research process. After data have been collected, statistics help us condense and refine the data and discover the meaning evident in them.

This chapter is devoted to quantitative data analysis or statistics. Whenever researchers use a quantitative method of data collection and the data are available in numerical form, statistics are used to analyze the data. This is step 5a in the context of the overall research process.

This chapter covers three general topics pertaining to statistics: coding the data, descriptive statistics, and bivariate statistics. Illustrations from a variety of studies are introduced to help in explaining important concepts. These illustrations are often similar to ones that a social worker may encounter in agency research projects in the producer role.

Steps in the Research Process

1. Understanding the research topic to be studied
2. Focusing the study
3. Designing the study
   a. Selecting the participants
   b. Selecting a data collection approach and measuring concepts
      - Surveys
      - Observations
   c. Exploring causal relationships
4. Collecting the data
5. Analyzing the data
   a. **Quantitative data**
   b. Qualitative data
6. Preparing a report

Coding the Data

After the data have been collected (step 4), the data need to be prepared for analysis. **Coding** is a process used to prepare data for analysis. Quantitative data, as described earlier, are data that can be converted into numerical form. There are many advantages to having findings in numerical form when it comes time to analyze the data, as statistical techniques can be very useful.

However, a note of caution when converting data from word form into numbers: important meaning inherent in the data can be lost when reducing some types of qualitative data into numbers. This problem was discussed in Chapter 5 and is referred to as *reductionism*. If reductionism appears to be a problem, leaving the data in qualitative form and using a qualitative analysis strategy is an alternative. Qualitative analysis techniques are covered in Chapter 15.

Structured interviews, structured questionnaires, structured observations, and some existing documents and records are methods of collecting numerical findings. Let's look more closely at the types of responses that need to be coded. In Chapter 13, it was pointed out that numerical responses result from two different types of questions: questions that directly elicit a numerical response and forced-response questions.

Coding Questions That Directly Elicit a Numerical Response

One type of structured question directly elicits a numerical response. Examples of such questions are:

- How old are you?
- How many school-age children do you have that are living with you?
- What is your net weekly income?
- How many times have you been absent from school this past week?
- How many miles do you travel to get to work?

Note that the answers to each of these questions are in a particular unit of measure, such as years, dollars, and miles. Each of these questions is considered a variable at the interval/ratio level of measurement. The responses to these questions are already in a numerical form and are ready for entry into a computer file.

Coding Forced-Response Questions

The second type of question that creates a numerical response is a forced-response question. These questions are considered "forced" because they instruct respondents to select answers from an existing set of response categories. Response categories of forced-response questions need to be coded to convert them into a numerical score. The following are examples of forced-response questions:

1. What is your gender?
   ____ female
   ____ male
2. How satisfied are you with your research methods course?
   ____ very unsatisfied
   ____ unsatisfied
   ____ not sure
   ____ satisfied
   ____ very satisfied

The response categories of these and other forced-response questions can easily be converted from word form to number. For example, the first question asks for the respondent's gender. In this case, coding can occur as follows: 1 = female and 2 = male. Based on this coding, we can enter the respondents' gender into a computer file using these numbers. We need to keep in mind, however, that while we have assigned each person a numerical score for gender, this does not mean that there is an order to gender. Based on our understanding of levels of measurement, gender only meets the properties of a nominal-level variable and must be always treated as such. Nominal-level variables have categories for the values of the variable, but these categories do not have an order to them as do ordinal-level variables. One category, for example, is not higher, stronger, or preferred over any other category.

The second question described above uses a Likert scale, which can be coded numerically as follows:

1 = very unsatisfied
2 = unsatisfied
3 = not sure
4 = satisfied
5 = very satisfied

If a respondent checks "satisfied" as their response to the question, the response would be coded as a 4; if a respondent checked "very unsatisfied," the response would be coded a 1. Note that the Likert scale used in this question does have an order to it. For example, "very satisfied" is more satisfied than "satisfied," and "unsatisfied" is less satisfied than "not sure." A Likert scale question has all of the properties of an ordinal-level variable and should be treated as such throughout the data analysis process.

Coding Forced-Response Questions with Only One Response   Coding responses is different depending on whether a forced-response question permits only one response or more than one response. Some forced-response questions are crafted to instruct respondents to select one and only one response category—the one that best characterizes their views or circumstances. The response categories used with these questions should meet the requirements of either nominal- or ordinal-level variables. Nominal-level variables must have response categories that are distinct, do not overlap, and are exhaustive of all possible responses. Ordinal-level variables must have all three of these properties, and the response categories must have an order to them. You may want to review the material on levels of measurement in Chapter 6. Or you can refresh your memory below.

Levels of Measurement

Nominal—Values are in two or more categories that are distinct, mutually exclusive, and exhaustive of all possibilities (e.g., gender).

(continued)

Ordinal—Values are in two or more categories, have all of the properties of nominal variables, and have a sequential order (e.g., social class).

Interval—Values have a sequential order, and there is an equal distance between the different values. There is no true 0 value (e.g., temperature).

Ratio—Values have a sequential order, and there is an equal distance between the different values. Also, 0 is a true 0 value that represents an absence of the variable (e.g., weight).

Let's consider another illustration of a forced-response question that permits only one response:

1. What is your ethnicity? (Please check one response)

_____ African American

_____ Latino

_____ Caucasian

_____ Asian American

_____ Other (please specify _____)

TEST YOUR KNOWLEDGE **Understanding Levels of Measurement**

This test is a quick review to refresh your understanding of the levels of measurement. Assume that the response categories in question 1 are at the nominal level of measurement and that those in question 2 are ordinal. What's wrong with the response categories or their order in these two questions, based on the requirements of levels of measurement?

1. What is your religious affiliation? (Please check one response.)

_____ Catholic

_____ Protestant

_____ Baptist

2. Do you like your job?

_____ yes

_____ no

_____ somewhat (in between)

In this case, the respondent is expected to choose one and only one response to this question. Note that these response categories meet the requirements of nominal-level variables. The categories are distinct in that each one identifies widely recognized ethnic categories in the United States. Also, these categories do not usually overlap; for example, a respondent does not usually fit into more than one response category, since an African American is not a Latino or a Caucasian or an Asian American. Finally, the "other" category provides an option for respondents who do not identify with any of these four ethnic groups. For example, a Middle Eastern Arab could select "other." Also, someone who identifies with more than one of the four ethnic categories that are listed can choose "other" as well. In this latter case, the respondents' perceptions of their ethnic identity determine their responses.

Coding Forced-Response Questions with Multiple Responses   In some instances, forced-response questions are constructed to allow respondents to select more than one response category. Note that the question below is an example of a forced-response question with multiple-choice options. This question could be asked in a community needs assessment survey.

1. What services do you currently need? (Check all that apply.)
   - _____ individual counseling
   - _____ family counseling
   - _____ group therapy
   - _____ help in obtaining food stamps
   - _____ help in obtaining Medicaid
   - _____ other (explain _____)
   - _____ none

When forced-response questions with multiple-choice options are used, special consideration needs to be given to coding the responses before they are analyzed. In the question described above, a respondent could check, for example, both "individual counseling" and "help in obtaining Medicaid." In this case, the response could not be coded with only one number, as both 1 (individual counseling) and 5 (help in obtaining Medicaid) would apply. One way to address this coding dilemma would be to convert each response category into a variable. Each of these new variables would have values of 1 for yes and 0 for no. In our example, the coding would be as follows:

1   individual counseling
0   family counseling
0   group therapy
0   help in obtaining food stamps
1   help in obtaining Medicaid
0   other (explain _____)
0   none

A Code Book

Assigning numbers to response categories in word form can lead to confusion. For example, how will we remember later that female = 1 and male = 2 and not the other way around? A **code book,** also sometimes called a data dictionary, can be the answer. A code book is a compilation of all of the questions in an instrument, their response categories, and the code numbers assigned to each response category. This code book helps the researcher remember what each of the code numbers represents during the time of data analysis. SPSS (Statistical Package for Social Sciences) and other statistical programs can easily create a code book once an electronic data file is set up.

Descriptive Statistics for Data Analysis

After all of the responses have been coded, it is time to begin data analysis. Data analysis is usually conducted in two major stages. It is a good idea to calculate all of the descriptive statistics in the first stage. After reviewing the results of these statistics, a second stage is conducted involving bivariate statistics. **Descriptive statistics** are statistics that are used to summarize the responses for each variable. These statistics are also referred to as *univariate* statistics, because they analyze one variable at a time. Several types of descriptive statistics can be used, as summarized in Table 14.1. However, each of these statistics can only be used with variables at specified levels of measurement. This means that it is important to identify the level of measurement of each variable before selecting a descriptive statistic.

TABLE 14.1   Types of Descriptive Statistics

Descriptive Statistic	Purpose of Statistic	Requirements of Level of Measurement of Variables
Frequency distribution	Summarizes responses to one variable at a time	Nominal or ordinal
Measures of central tendency	Summarizes responses to one variable at a time	
a. mode		a. nominal, ordinal, interval/ratio
b. median		b. ordinal, interval/ratio
c. mean		c. interval/ratio
Measures of dispersion or variability	Summarizes responses to one variable at a time	
a. range		a. interval/ratio
b. standard deviation		b. interval/ratio

Frequency Distributions

A frequency distribution is a statistic that describes the number of times each of the values of a variable are observed in a sample. For example, in a question using a Likert scale, a frequency distribution describes how many participants selected "very satisfied," "satisfied," "dissatisfied," and so on. Frequency distributions can be presented in actual frequencies or percentages. Usually, the percentages are more easy to grasp if the sample is relatively large. Often, however, frequency distributions list both frequencies and percentages. An example of a frequency distribution for some of the demographic characteristics of the participants in a study by Debra and David Woody (2003) are presented as in Table 14.2.

Note that the frequency column of Table 14.2 is helpful because it describes the number of participants included in each category (e.g., 70 mothers completed twelfth grade) and the total number of mothers in the sample (135). Yet, the percentage column may be even more informative, as it helps to single out the categories with larger

TABLE 14.2 Demographics of a Sample of Single, Low-Income, African American Mothers

	Frequency	Percentage
Marital status		
Single, never married	98	72.6
Legally separated	18	13.3
Divorced, not remarried	16	11.9
Widowed, not remarried	3	2.2
Education		
8th grade or less	4	3.0
9th, 10th, or 11th grades	28	20.7
12th grade	70	51.9
1 year of college	12	8.9
2 years of college	15	11.1
3 years of college	5	3.7
4 years of college	1	0.7
Employed		
Yes	65	48.1
No	70	51.9
Total	135	100.0

responses. For example, 72.6 percent of the sample are single and never married, and just over half have only completed twelfth grade. Because both columns of numbers provide helpful information, both were included in this research report.

Frequency distributions are an appropriate statistic to use with categorical variables, which include both nominal and ordinal variables. A frequency distribution can also be used with an interval/ratio variable if the responses are reduced to categories.

Measures of Central Tendencies

Measures of central tendencies are another set of statistics that can be used in summarizing the responses (or scores) measuring a variable. A measure of central tendency is a statistic that summarizes an entire set of scores in a single representative number. There are three specific statistics that measure central tendencies of the responses: the mean, median, and mode. A **mean** statistic is the arithmetic average of all scores. A **median** statistic is the middle score—that is, half of the scores are above it and half are below it. A **mode** statistic is the most frequent score. Each of these statistics can only be used with variables at the appropriate level of measurement. A mean statistic can only be used with interval/ratio-level variables. A median statistic is used with either interval/ratio- or ordinal-level variables. A mode statistic is used with variables that are nominal, ordinal, or interval/ratio. A summary of the conditions required for using these statistics is provided in Table 14.1.

An example will help in illustrating how the measures of central tendency can be used. Let's assume we are interested in summarizing the ages of a group of five mothers who are participants in a study. Their individual ages are 36, 43, 35, 43, and 27. The mean age of this group is calculated as follows: the sum of all of their ages (184) divided by the number of mothers (5) equals 36.8 years. Therefore, the mean age of these mothers, calculated to the nearest tenth, is 36.8 years.

The median age of these mothers (the middle score) would be calculated as follows. First we would list their ages in chronological order. Their ages in chronological order are 27, 35, 36, 43, and 43. Next, we would count to the middle score, or age, which would be 36 years. This would be the median age. Whenever there are an even number of people in a sample, there will be two middle scores, not one. In this case, we would add these two middle scores and divide by 2 to find the median age. Let's say, for example, that there were six mothers with their ages being 27, 35, 36, 38, 43, and 43. In this example, the two middle scores are 36 and 38. We would add these two ages and then divide by 2 (36 + 38 = 74 ÷ 2 = 37). Therefore, the median age in this example would be 37 years.

The modal age of these mothers is the age that is most frequently represented. Viewing the ages in our example (27, 35, 36, 38, 43, 43), we see that two mothers are 43 and no other age is indicated more than once. Therefore, the modal age of this group is 43 years.

An important question to ask about measures of central tendency is "Which one is preferred?" A few guidelines can be helpful. First, it is important to only use a central tendency measure that is appropriate for the level of measurement of a variable. Table 14.1 describes the level of measurement requirements for each measure of central tendency. For example, it makes no sense to calculate a mean score for a nominal variable like gender or race. Try to calculate such a measure; you will find it is irrelevant, because there is no order to the categories of these variables.

Another guideline pertains to the mean score. While this score is very precise, it is also influenced by extreme values that are very large or small. For example, if one person in a sample is either extremely wealthy or very poor, this value will have an excessive influence on the mean score. Imagine a sample of participants who are mostly in the middle-income range but one has no income or is a millionaire. Such extreme scores will deflate or inflate the mean income. As another example, imagine a student with grades on several equally weighted assignments as follows: 95, 90, 89, 95, 65. Unfortunately, the "65" grade will deflate this student's overall course grade. Such extreme values should be noted along with the mean score in a report.

Sometimes the responses to a variable cluster near the two extreme scores rather than in the middle. In this case, a mean or median score may not be that helpful in summarizing the responses, because it doesn't capture the bimodal nature of the cluster. For example, let's say that the ages of a sample of students in one class are 19, 20, 20, 22, 23, 34, 35, 36, 36, and 39. Note that the students tend to cluster around 20 and 36 years. Actually, this distribution of ages has two modes, 20 and 36. In this case it may be the most helpful to report both modes as the measure of central tendency.

Measures of Variability

Finally, descriptive statistics also include measures of variability or dispersion. **Variability measures** are statistics that summarize how the responses to a question vary or disperse away from their central tendency. These statistics complement measures of central tendencies because they provide information about the variability of scores away from the clustering point. Two common statistics that measure variability of scores are range and standard deviation. Both can be used with interval/ratio-level variables only.

The **range** identifies the lowest and highest scores in the responses to a question. In viewing the ages of the mothers in the above example, we can see that the youngest mother is 27 years old and the oldest is 43. Therefore, the range in ages is 27 to 43, or a total range in age of 16 (43 − 27).

Standard deviation is a second measure of variability. A **standard deviation** statistic takes into account the extent to which each of the scores or responses to a question varies from the mean score. Standard deviation is often abbreviated in research reports as SD. The formula for calculating the standard deviation is:

$$\text{S.D.} = \sqrt{\frac{\Sigma (x_1 - \bar{x})^2}{n - 1}}$$

A standard deviation score is not as easy to interpret as a range score. A range statistic clearly reflects two scores, the lowest and highest. The standard deviation (SD), in contrast, is calculated by the above formula. Note in this formula that the distance of each score (symbolized by x_1) from the mean score (symbolized by $\bar{x}$) is taken into account.

A SD score can be most helpful when it is used to compare two or more groups. When we observe a SD score for two subgroups of people, for example, we can interpret these results by saying that the subgroup with the smaller SD has less variability in its responses than the other subgroup. If you are interested in obtaining more information about the uses and interpretations of standard deviations, you can review a basic statistics book (e.g., Montcalm & Royse, 2002; Phillips, 2000; Weinbach & Grinnell, 1998).

Bivariate Statistics for Data Analysis

Bivariate statistics are useful in investigating the relationship between two variables. **Bivariate statistics** examine two variables at a time. In other words, a hypothesis can be tested using bivariate statistics. You may want to review background material on hypotheses in Chapter 6. Once a hypothesis is formulated and data are collected measuring the two variables in the hypothesis, the next step is to explore whether or not an association is evident. This can be done by applying a bivariate statistic.

Bivariate statistics are more complicated to understand than univariate statistics, because they involve the analysis of two variables at the same time, not one. A few background concepts are introduced at this time to help in understanding bivariate statistics. These concepts are (1) significance, (2) statistical significance, and (3) statistical tests.

Significance

When we are attempting to investigate the relationship between two variables identified in a hypothesis, we are actually wanting to know how strong the relationship is. **Significance** refers to its strength. The significance of a relationship can be defined by two different standards: statistical significance or clinical significance. Definitions of both types of significance are described below. While both types can be useful in determining whether or not two variables have a strong enough relationship to each other, our focus in this chapter is only on statistical significance. Clinical significance was discussed in Chapter 11.

Two Types of Significance

1. *Statistical significance.* The significance of a relationship between two variables is determined by mathematical principles. Generally, we claim statistical significance if a statistical test indicates that there is a strong relationship based on

probability. Usually a claim of significance is made when the probability of being in error is less than 5 percent (symbolized as $p < 0.05$).

2. *Clinical significance.* The significance of a relationship between two variables is determined by the clinical judgment of professionals. In this case, we are usually exploring hypotheses that claim that a relationship exists between an intervention (IV) and a client outcome variable (DV). A claim of significance is made when the client's improvement is substantial enough to meet clinical criteria.

Statistical Significance

Let's look more closely at the concept of statistical significance. When we are claiming that a relationship between two variables is statistically significant, we are inferring that what we have found from a sample of participants is also evident in the population from which the sample was drawn. We sometimes refer to these statistics as *inferential statistics* because they provide an inference about the characteristics of the population from the characteristics of the sample.

Technically, inferential statistics should only be used if a sample is representative of the population. As was discussed in Chapter 8, a sample is representative of the population when it is selected by a probability sampling approach (e.g., random, systematic random). When we have a representative sample, we can infer with some confidence that what is evident in the sample is also evident in the entire population. Yet, some degree of sampling error needs to be expected as well. *Sampling error* is the degree of error evident when we infer from a sample to a population. We may claim that the characteristics of a sample are the same as the population, with the possibility of a small percentage of sampling error. Generally, a sampling error of 5 percent or less is an acceptable level.

In practice, inferential statistics are also often used in exploratory studies with nonprobability samples (e.g., selected from quota, criterion, or snowball sampling). In these cases, the degree to which a sample and population are similar is unknown. Inferential statistics are used in these studies to discover new hypotheses for testing in later studies. Limitations inherent in using inferential statistics in these circumstances must be recognized and reported. The conclusions drawn from such studies, at best, can only be preliminary in nature and recommended for replication in other studies.

A Fuller Explanation of Inferential Statistics

When using inferential statistics, we begin with a null hypothesis. A null hypothesis states that there is no association between the two variables. Using an earlier example of a recovery group being introduced to reduce the clients' alcohol intake, the null hypothesis would state that there is no association between attending the recovery group and a change in the clients' alcohol intake. A statistical test is administered next to determine whether the null hypothesis is rejected or not. If we

(continued)

reject the null hypothesis, we are concluding that there is a significant association between the recovery group and their drinking behavior. Conversely, if we fail to reject the null hypothesis, then we must conclude that there is no reason to suppose the recovery group has influence over the clients' drinking problem.

Statistical Tests

We are not likely to find that a population is identical in characteristics to a sample drawn from it. Instead, we investigate whether or not the findings in the sample have a high probability of being evident in the population. A statistical test is employed to determine statistical significance. The test provides an overall score and a level of significance score (symbolized as p). As a general rule, the level of significance score must be equal to or less than 5 percent (symbolized as $p \leq 0.05$) to claim with confidence that the findings in the sample are evident in the population. Put more simply, a $p \leq 0.05$ is the margin of error being accepted to claim statistical significance. If the p is higher than 5 percent ($p > 0.05$), the margin of error is too high to accept.

The ability of a bivariate test to infer statistical significance is referred to as its *statistical power*. A bivariate test's power is greater when a study's variables have higher levels of measurement. Interval/ratio variables, for example, have greater power than nominal variables. A bivariate test's power is also greater when the size of a sample increases. The larger the sample, the more confident the researcher can be that the sample is representative of a population. A random sample of 30 unemployed people, for example, is much less likely to have the statistical power of a random sample of 100 unemployed people in inferring something about a larger population of 500 unemployed people. Statistical tables are available that offer explanations for how sample size influences statistical power. For example, a sample size of 80 can only be generalized to a population of 100 with a margin of error of 5 percent, while a sample size of 278 can be generalized to a population of 1,000 with the same degree of error (Krejcie & Morgan, 1970).

The field of quantitative analysis provides us with numerous statistical tests, and the first task is to select the best test that fits each hypothesis. While the statistical tests covered in this book do not go beyond bivariate tests, there are also several multivariate tests available to investigate relationships among three or more variables at one time. A few of the most familiar multivariate tests in social work research are factor analysis, analysis of covariance, and multiple regression. It is always a good idea to consult a statistician when selecting a statistical test to make sure that you are selecting the most appropriate one.

Four bivariate statistical tests are discussed next, namely chi-square, correlation, *t*-test, and ANOVA. These tests provide a beginning social work researcher with an introduction to statistical tools for hypothesis testing. When any of these four statistical tests are used to analyze data from a study, they produce a test score and a p score that inform you about whether or not there is statistical significance.

As was mentioned earlier, if the p is equal to or less than 0.05 (symbolized as $p \leq 0.05$), then we can say that the relationship between the two variables is statistically significant. Let's consider two different types of bivariate analysis: (1) measuring the association between two variables, and (2) comparing two or more groups

Measuring the Association between Two Variables

When researchers are exploring whether or not two variables are associated with each other, they are attempting to determine if the values of one variable have a particular association with the values of the other variable. Let's use the earlier example of the hypothesis "Gender is associated with political party affiliation." If we are measuring the association between these two variables (gender and political party), what we are measuring is whether women are more often Democrats than men; conversely, we are measuring whether men are more often Republicans than women. Let's assume that we interview ten women and ten men, and we obtain the results described in Table 14.3.

According to Table 14.3, seven of the ten women, or 70 percent, are Democrats; similarly, seven of the ten men, or 70 percent, are Republicans. These high percentages suggest that there is some kind of association between the values of these two variables. In contrast, if there is absolutely no association between these two variables, the results could appear something like those in Table 14.4.

As you can see in Table 14.4, men and women are not different at all in terms of their political party affiliation. Both males and females have an equal number in each political party. In this case, there is absolutely no association at all.

 TABLE 14.3 **Political Party Affiliation by Gender**

	Women	Men
Democrat	7	3
Republican	3	7
Total	10	10

TABLE 14.4 **Political Party Affiliation by Gender**

	Women	Men
Democrat	5	5
Republican	5	5
Total	10	10

Unlike the example in Table 14.4, there is usually some kind of association between any two variables being investigated. What we need to do is to determine how much of an association exists. In this case, statistical significance is used to determine if there is a strong enough association for it to be important to us. To find out if there is a statistically significant association between two variables, we take the following steps:

1. Determine the levels of measurement of each of the variables in the hypothesis.
2. From the list of statistical tests that measure associations, select a test that is appropriate for the levels of measurement of the two variables being investigated.
3. Apply the statistical test using a statistical program on the computer.
4. Interpret the results to determine if the relationship is statistically significant (i.e., determine if $p \leq 0.05$).

As Table 14.5 points out, a chi-square test and correlation test are two of the bivariate tests that can be used to determine if there is an association between two variables.

Chi-Square Test   This is used to determine if the values of one variable are associated with the values of another variable. A **chi-square test** is also sometimes referred to as a cross-tabs, or a cross-tabulation of these variables. Tables 14.3 and 14.4 are presentations of gender and political party in cross-tabulation format. This format helps us to visualize the possibility of an association before we even administer a chi-square test.

When a chi-square test is conducted using a computer program such as SPSS (Statistical Package for the Social Sciences), the data are presented in a cross-tabulation format. Other results include a chi-square test score and a p score, among other things. Based on the p score, we can determine if the association between the two variables is statistically significant.

The chi-square test is only used when both variables are at the nominal or ordinal level of measurement. In other words, both variables must be categorical in nature. *Categorical variables* are variables with values in category form either at

TABLE 14.5	Measures of Association		
	Purpose of Statistic		**Requirements of Level of Measurement of Variables**
Chi-square	Determines whether two variables have a statistically significant association to each other		The two variables are at the nominal or ordinal levels.
Correlation	Determines whether two variables have a statistically significant association with each other		Both variables are at the interval/ratio level.

the nominal or ordinal levels of measurement. Our example of gender and political party illustrates categorical variables. The values of gender consist of two categories (female and male) and political party affiliation consists of two categories (Democrats and Republicans).

A chi-square test also requires a large enough sample size that each cell of the cross-tabulation has a value of five or more. In Table 14.3, you can see that two of the cells have values less than five (two cells have values of three). Therefore, a chi-square test should not be used with these data.

Example of a Study Using a Chi-square Test

McQuillan and Ferreeuse (1998) used a chi-square test to determine whether younger husbands in marriages are more willing to accept their wife's influence than older husbands. The first variable is "age of husbands," with values of "younger" and "older," and the second variable is "whether or not husbands accept their wife's influence," with values of "usually," "sometimes," and "never," which were determined by asking the wife. The results are as follows:

	Younger husbands	Older husbands
Usually	25%	14%
Sometimes	65%	51%
Never	10%	35%

(Note: $p < 0.01$)

A conclusion can be reached from this test. Using a chi-square test, the fact that $p < 0.01$ informs us that the association between these two variables is statistically significant with a margin of error less than 1 percent. The differences between younger and older husbands in accepting a wife's influence are also evident in a careful examination of the two columns of percentages. For example, 25 percent of the younger husbands and only 14 percent of the older husbands "usually" accept their wife's influence. Meanwhile, only 10 percent of the younger husbands and 35 percent of the older husbands "never" accept their wife's influence.

Correlation Test   The other test used to measure the association between two variables is a correlation. The term *correlation* is sometimes used in our everyday conversations. For example, we might say that there is a correlation between smoking and lung cancer, or a correlation between regular exercise and good health. A **correlation test** is used to determine if there is a statistically significant association between two variables. A correlation test can only be used when both variables are at the interval/ratio-level of measurement. Interval/ratio-level variables are not in categorical form; instead, these variables have values falling along a standard unit of measure, such as income in dollar units or age in years. Correlation tests can be used with samples of almost any size.

A correlation test has a special feature referred to as a **correlation coefficient.** The correlation coefficient is designed so that a correlation test score falls somewhere between a score of −1.0 and +1.0. With this special feature, we can interpret the results to some degree even before determining the p. The closer the score is to either a −1 or +1, the stronger the association between the variables. Conversely, the closer the score is to 0, the less likely there is a significant association. A p score is also calculated and used to determine whether or not the association is statistically significant. As with other tests, the p score must be equal to or less than 5 percent ($p \leq 0.05$) to have a statistically significant association. A correlation score is symbolized by an "r."

The relationship between two variables in a correlation is either positive or negative. A **positive relationship** between two variables is an association in which the values of both variables vary in the same direction. For example, let's assume that we have the hypothesis "Older people are likely to have more friends than younger people," and we find that the older the person, the more friends they tend to have. We refer to this as a positive relationship between age and number of friends. In this case, the correlation test score is a positive number. If the association is statistically significant, the score could be something like $r = 0.31, p < 0.05$.

In contrast, a **negative relationship** between two variables is an association in which the values of one variable go up while the values of the other variable go down. In other words, the values go in opposite directions. In our above example, let's assume that our hypothesis is "Older people have fewer friends than younger people." This is a negative relationship if we find that the older the person, the fewer friends they tend to have. In this case the correlation test score will be a negative rather than a positive number. Negative relationships are also sometimes referred to as *inverse relationships*. If the association is statistically significant, the score could be something like $r = −.46, p < 0.05$.

Table 14.6 describes an example of a set of findings from a study published in *Social Work* using a correlation test to analyze its data. This table summarizes a wealth of information that can be helpful to social workers working with people having AIDS. It also illustrates how several hypotheses were explored using a correlation test.

Let's look more closely at Table 14.6. A careful review can help you develop some skills in reading tables of data. Note that this is an exploratory study. The authors were investigating several variables to find out if any of them were correlates of "comfort level with AIDS patients" for the social workers in the sample. The extent to which a social worker has a comfort with AIDS patients was a central concept to these authors because of the potential influence on a social worker's effectiveness in providing help to patients with AIDS. Note that these potential correlates are listed in four groupings in the left column. The first grouping includes hypothesis variables such as knowledge about AIDS, evidence of homophobic attitudes, and negative moral attitudes related to AIDS. The next grouping consists of the background characteristics of these social workers. Some of their work experience characteristics are grouped next, followed by five different reactions their family and friends could have about their work with AIDS patients.

Next, note that there are two columns of data in Table 14.6, with the headings r and p. The r refers to the correlation coefficient scores, and the p represents the

TABLE 14.6 Bivariate Association with "Comfort with AIDS Patients" Index

Correlates of "comfort with AIDS patients"	r	p
Hypothesis variables		
• knowledge about AIDS	+.30	.001
• homophobia	−.41	.0001
• negative moral attitudes	−.53	.001
Background factors		
• age	+.04	ns
• marital status	+.002	ns
• gender	+.09	ns
• gay family members	+.13	.06
• gay friends	+.17	.01
Work experience		
• experience with terminally ill	+.23	.0005
• comfort with other high-risk patient populations	+.51	.0001
• years employed	−.11	ns
Reactions of family and friends		
• frightened	−.28	.0001
• concerned	−.14	.04
• angry	−.28	.0001
• supportive	−.25	.0002
• indifferent	+.13	.05

Note: ns = not significant

Source: From "Social Workers' Comfort in Providing Services to AIDS Patients," by L. Wiener and K. Siegel, 1990, *Social Work, 35*(1), pp. 18–25. Copyright 1990, National Association of Social Workers, Inc. Reprinted by permission.

level of significance for each score. It is probably most helpful to look first at the column headed by *p* to find out which of these variables have a statistically significant correlation with comfort level. As you can see, all but four of the sixteen variables are significantly correlated with comfort level (the four that are not are identified with ns, or "not significant").

Next, look at the column that is headed by an *r* to find out the correlation scores and whether they have positive or negative associations with comfort level. Note that some are positive and others are negative. This means that some of these variables have a positive or direct association with comfort level and others have a negative or inverse association with comfort level. For example, "knowledge about AIDS" (which is an overall measure of how well the social workers responded to a test of their knowledge about AIDS) has a correlation score of +0.30 and is significant at the 0.001 level. This means that the more knowledge that the social workers had about AIDS, the more likely they were to be comfortable working with people having AIDS. This makes sense, doesn't it? Keep in mind that this does not mean that the researchers can say that knowledge about AIDS causes greater comfort. All that we can say is that these two variables are positively associated with each other. A discussion question is included at the end of the chapter to offer a fuller opportunity to explore the findings in Table 14.6. I hope you can see that this table offers numerous relevant insights about the factors associated with the comfort level of the social workers who were studied.

Comparing Two or More Groups

The second type of bivariate statistical test compares the mean scores of two or more groups. In this case, the intent of this statistical test is to determine if these groups are significantly different from each other rather than associated with each other. When we are attempting to find out if two groups are different from each other, we are actually determining if the two groups are different in particular characteristics. For example, let's say we are interested in how male and female social workers employed in a public school system are different from each other based on several characteristics. One characteristic might be their longevity in their positions. We could find out if one group has been employed in the schools for a significantly longer period of time than the other. What we actually want to know is how different these two gender groups are in terms of their length of employment and if this difference is statistically significant. In this case, statistical significance tells us if the difference is large enough for us to be reasonably confident that it exists in the population.

To find out if there is a statistically significant difference in characteristics between two groups, we follow the same steps used in determining a statistically significant association, as described earlier in this chapter, namely

1. Determine the levels of measurement of the two variables.
2. Select an appropriate test.
3. Apply the statistical test using the computer.
4. Interpret the results to determine if the relationship is statistically significant (i.e., if $p \leq 0.05$).

As Table 14.7 points out, a *t*-test and ANOVA test are two bivariate tests that can be used to determine if there is a significant difference in characteristics between two or more groups.

t-Test   A *t*-test is used to determine whether two groups are significantly different based on a particular characteristic. One variable in this hypothesis would be

TABLE 14.7   Comparing Two or More Groups

Comparing the Mean Scores of Two or More Groups	Purpose of Statistic	Requirements of Level of Measurement of Variables
t-test	Determines whether two groups are statistically significantly different from each other, based on particular characteristics.	One variable is at the nominal level and has two values or categories; the other variable is at the interval/ratio level.
ANOVA	Determines whether three or more groups are statistically significantly different from each other, based on particular characteristics.	One variable is at the nominal or ordinal level and has three or more values or categories; the other variable is at the interval/ratio level.

the group variable (group 1 or group 2). The second variable would be the characteristic that is being compared. In the above example, the group variable would be gender (male group or female group), and the characteristic to be compared would be length of years employed in a public school system. The following is another example:

Example of a Study Using a *t*-Test

The National Center on Addiction and Substance Abuse (CASA) at Columbia University in New York City conducted a study on substance abuse among young people between the ages of 8 and 22. Among other things, their national survey compared the substance use of females and males. The researchers used a *t*-test to explore if there were any significant differences between the sexes. Following are some of their findings related to these comparisons:

- Puberty is a time of higher risk for substance use for girls than boys. Girls experiencing early puberty are at higher risk of using substances sooner, more often, and in greater quantities than later-maturing peers.
- Girls are more likely than boys to be depressed, have eating disorders, or be sexually or physically abused—all of which increase the risk for substance abuse.
- Substance use can sink into abuse and addiction more quickly for girls and young women than for boys and young men, even though the girl uses the same amount or less of a particular substance.
- Girls using alcohol and drugs are likelier than boys to attempt suicide.
- Girls and young women using alcohol and drugs are likelier than boys and young men to experience more adverse health consequences, such as greater smoking-related lung damage.

The *t*-test is only used when the group variable (group 1 or group 2) is at the nominal level of measurement and the characteristic to be compared is at the interval/ratio level. A *t*-test can be used with almost any sample size, including relatively small samples. When a *t*-test is calculated, it produces a number of results. The most important ones include a measure of the mean scores of the characteristic for each of the two groups, a *t*-test score (or *t*-statistic), and the *p*, which reveals level of significance.

The meaning behind these bivariate tests is that they attempt to make an inference to a larger population. "Inference" means that the two groups come from different populations, not the same one. A *t*-statistic and its *p* tell us whether there is a statistically significant difference between the two groups in the characteristic being compared. Based on the *p* score in particular, we can determine if there is statistical significance.

Two types of analysis are possible using *t*-tests. They are the dependent-samples *t*-test (also called a paired-samples *t*-test) and the independent-samples *t*-test. A *dependent-samples* t-*test,* or *paired-samples* t-*test,* is used if there is a natural way of pairing up one observation from one group with one observation from the another group. This could most easily occur when pairing up a particular characteristic of the same sample at different points in times. An example would be to compare the self-esteem scores of a group of clients before and after they have completed a special program. In this case it is natural to pair up before-program and after-program characteristics of the same client. Another example would be to pair up a subgroup of men and a subgroup of women if the data set consists of couples. In this case, it would be natural to pair up the male and female of each couple.

An *independent-samples* t-*test* is used when different groups of a sample are being compared and there is no natural way of pairing up observations from the two subgroups. For example, we could compare the test scores of a group of men and a group of women who have no natural way of being paired.

Example of a Student's Study Using an Independent-Samples *t*-Test

A social work student conducted a study of attitudes toward the death penalty based on his interest in learning more about those who supported it. He developed a questionnaire made up of ten items and administered it to the employees of his field agency. Examples of items that he included were "I believe the death penalty is well deserved by those who receive it," "I oppose the death penalty when the perpetrator has a mental illness," and "I believe that poor people are more likely to receive the death penalty." A seven-point Likert scale ranging from "strongly disagree" to "strongly agree" was used with each of these items. This scale was treated as an interval/ratio variable because of the large number of ordinal categories.

As part of this student's analysis, he wanted to find out if younger (under 30 years) and older (30 years and over) employees differed significantly on any of the items. One item compared younger and older respondents on "I believe the death penalty prevents murders." Using an independent samples t-test statistic, he found that the younger respondents were significantly more likely to agree with this statement than the older ones. The level of significance was reported to be $p < 0.04$. Because the sample was so small and limited to a specific employee group, he reported the findings as being tentative and exploratory. He recommended that the questionnaire be replicated with other groups to find out if the results would be similar.

ANOVA   An ANOVA is another test that is sometimes referred to as a "one-way analysis of variance." An **ANOVA** is a test used to determine whether three or more groups are significantly different from each other based on a particular characteristic. If there is a statistically significant difference between the groups, inference means that these groups come from different populations, not the same one. An ANOVA, for example, could be used to compare some employment characteristics of three or more groups of clients. Specifically, an ANOVA could be used to compare the salaries of three or four different ethnic groups to find out if they are significantly different. In this case, the group variable is the ethnic groups (e.g., White, African American, Latino, etc.) and the characteristic to be compared is their salaries. Note that a t-test and ANOVA are very similar. While a t-test is used in comparing two groups, an ANOVA is used in comparing three or more groups.

The ANOVA can only be used when the first of the two variables is at the nominal or ordinal level of measurement. This would be a categorical variable having at least three values or categories. The other variable, the characteristic being compared, must be at the interval/ratio-level of measurement. An ANOVA can be used when the sample size is relatively small or large. An example of a study using an ANOVA test follows:

Example of a Study Using an ANOVA

A study by Rosenheck (2003) investigated the impact of three different models of assistance to 460 homeless veterans. All of these vets were homeless, living in the streets or shelters, and had a psychiatric diagnosis. They were randomly assigned to three different groups based on different models of assistance provided to them over three years. The first group received both housing vouchers and intensive case management; the second group received only case management; the third group received standard VA treatment.

An ANOVA test was used to determine if these three groups were significantly different in the extent of their homelessness after three years. The findings

(continued)

indicate that the first group spent 25 percent more nights housed than those who received standard VA treatment and 16 percent more nights housed than those who only received case management. These differences were found to be statistically significant.

When an ANOVA is electronically calculated, a computer printout provides several helpful results. These include the mean scores of the characteristic being compared for each subgroup, the ANOVA score, and the p, which determines significance. Based on the p score, we can determine if the differences among the groups are statistically significant. If the p is significant, it indicates that there is at least one group that is different from the other groups. However, the ANOVA and p scores do not identify the particular groups that are significantly different. An additional multiple comparison test can be added to determine this.

Working with a Data Set

Several descriptive and bivariate statistics have been introduced and can be used in analyzing the data collected for a study. Let's look at how these statistics can be used in analyzing a data set. A **data set** is a computer file of data that has been collected, coded, and is ready for analysis.

A data set of an actual study is presented below as an example. This data set was reconstructed from a participant action research (PAR) study conducted by a group of adults with developmental disabilities who had not previously conducted any research. Being active with a self-advocacy group in Pennsylvania, they wanted to know if other consumers with developmental disabilities were satisfied with their jobs. With assistance from advisers who were familiar with the research process, this group participated in all of the steps of the research process, including identifying their overall research questions, constructing specific questions, obtaining informed consent, conducting the interviews, and analyzing their results. Unfortunately, a formal report was not prepared, and the results were never published. Therefore, the data set described in the chapter has been made up and is based on a general recollection of the questions these adults investigated.

These self-advocates were interested in job satisfaction, because some of the people they knew had jobs in sheltered workshops that were exclusively for people with developmental disabilities and others had newly obtained jobs in the competitive market. They wanted to know if those in sheltered workshops were less satisfied than those in competitive employment. They decided to interview a total of ten people, and they asked them five questions. They constructed simple response categories for each of their questions so that they could be easily analyzed. They developed the response categories based on the answers that they anticipated, and they added an "other" category to one of the questions to take into account unexpected responses. The questions that they asked the ten people are listed below.

Interview Schedule for PAR Study on Satisfaction with Employment

What is your age? __

What is your gender?   1. ____ female   2. ____ male

Q1. Where do you work?

    1. ____ at a sheltered workshop

    2. ____ in a competitive or "outside" job

    3. ____ don't work

Q2. Do you work part-time or full-time?

    1. ____ part-time

    2. ____ full-time

Q3. Do you like your current job responsibilities?

    1. ____ I don't like them.

    2. ____ I like them some.

    3. ____ I like them a lot.

Q4. Are you satisfied with the salary that you receive?

    1. ____ yes

    2. ____ no

Q5. How did you obtain your job?

    1. ____ I found it myself.

    2. ____ My parents found it.

    3. ____ I was referred to the job by a social agency.

    4. ____ Other (please explain) _____

The data from this study can be presented efficiently in a data set, as in Table 14.8. Note that the data have already been coded. All of the cells are in number form and represent something of importance to the study. However, to understand what each number represents, refer to the interview questions in the example.

The first column of the data set in the table is the identification number (ID) of each of the ten people who were interviewed; they were assigned a number from one to ten. The second column describes the age of each interviewee. These data are the actual ages that were given by each respondent. The third column identifies their gender. In this case, the interviewer simply recorded each respondent's gender on the interview schedule. As the schedule indicates, 1 refers to a female and 2 indicates a male. The remaining five columns describe their responses to each of the five questions, with each column representing one question.

TABLE 14.8   A Data Set

ID Number	Age	Gender	Q1 Type of Job	Q2 Part-time or Full-time	Q3 Like Job Responsibilities	Q4 Satisfied with Salary	Q5 How Obtained Job
1	54	2	1	2	1	2	2
2	46	1	1	2	2	2	3
3	31	2	2	1	3	2	1
4	45	1	1	2	1	1	4
5	54	1	3				
6	41	1	1	2	1	2	2
7	24	2	2	1	3	1	2
8	23	2	2	1	2	2	1
9	36	1	1	2	2	2	2
10	30	1	2	2	3	1	4

As indicated in the interview schedule, each of the response categories for a question was assigned a code number. For example, question 1 asks "Where do you work?" If the person indicated that they worked in a sheltered workshop, they were assigned a 1 for that question. If the person indicated a competitive job, they were assigned a 2. If they did not work, they were assigned a 3.

The first row, for example, lists the responses for interviewee number 1. According to the codes, this interviewee is fifty-four years old and is a male. He works in a sheltered workshop on a full-time basis. This interviewee reports that he does not like his job responsibilities and is not satisfied with his salary. His parents found the job he has. Can you describe the responses for interviewee 2? An exercise is provided in the Discussion Questions section for further work on analyzing this data set.

Chapter Reflections

Values and Ethics, Diversity, At-Risk Groups, and Social Justice

Values and ethics play an important role in data analysis. When analyzing quantitative data, it is most important to be as thorough, accurate, and honest as possible. As a first step, the data should be coded and entered into a computer file as meticulously as possible to minimize any possibility of error. Afterward, it is a good idea to have someone double check to make sure the data were entered accurately. Don't forget that the steps of data coding and data entry are as important as any other steps, because creating inaccurate or erroneous data at this stage could threaten the integrity of the entire study. If the data are not coded and entered correctly, any conclusions drawn from them will be misleading and potentially harmful to the users.

After a data set has been created, it can be analyzed. At this stage, other ethical concerns can emerge. It is important that the appropriate statistical tests are selected for analysis and that incorrect tests are not used. As mentioned earlier, it is wise to consult a statistician or someone who knows a lot about statistics for advice on this decision.

The data analysis process could also be biased by the researchers' deliberate manipulation of the results. Researchers are often hoping to obtain results that support their hunches or hypotheses. While this may be a natural inclination, it is important that it does not become a bias that is introduced into the analysis process. One guideline to follow is to use a range of appropriate statistical tests if possible and report the results of each test even if they are contradictory or are not consistent with the researchers' likings.

Discussion Questions

1. *An exercise in reviewing a table of findings.* Review the findings of the study by Wiener and Siegel (1990) in Table 14.6 (page 261). Then answer the following questions:
   - Was homophobia found to be significantly associated with "comfort with AIDS"? If so, was it a positive or negative correlation? Describe this association in simple words.
   - Select a background characteristic of the research participants that is associated significantly with "comfort with AIDS" and explain in simple terms the relationship between the two variables.
   - Table 14.6 lists five types of reactions that family members and friends have to AIDS. Select one of these reactions that is statistically significantly associated with "comfort with AIDS." Describe the relationship between these two variables in simple terms.

2. *An exercise in analyzing a data set.* Review the findings from the PAR study in the chapter. The interview questions are listed on page 267 and the data set is described in Table 14.8. Next, answer the following questions:
   - Describe the age and gender of interviewee number 7 and this person's responses to the five questions.
   - Determine the level of measurement for each of the seven variables.
   - Calculate the mean age (round off to the nearest whole number) and the range of ages for these ten people.
   - Calculate and present a frequency distribution for their gender.
   - Calculate and present a frequency distribution that summarizes the responses to question 1 and question 2. Include both actual frequencies and percentages.
   - Prepare a table that presents a cross-tabulation of the responses to question 1 and question 3. Use Table 14.3 (which describes a cross-tabulation) as a guide. Does

there appear to be a pattern or association between how the interviewees responded to questions 1 and 3? What is this pattern?

- Prepare one other table that presents a cross-tabulation of two other variables in the study. Does there appear to be a pattern or association between the responses to these two variables? What is it?
- What statistical test could be used to find out if there is a statistically significant difference in age between part-time and full-time employees?

3. If a computer lab is accessible, set up an electronic file of the data set described in Table 14.8. Then calculate descriptive statistics for each of the seven variables.

4. *An exercise for the entire class.* Develop a set of questions you would like to ask your classmates in a research methods course. For example, you could ask their age, marital status, number of children in their family, field of practice interest, and other background questions of interest to the class. Add two additional forced-response questions such as:

- How much are you learning in your research methods course? (Create a Likert scale to complete this question using the following three response categories: "a lot," "some," and "very little.")
- On a scale of 1 to 10, how much do you like social work research? Select a number from 1 to 10, with 1 being "not at all" and 10 being "like it the most."

Have every student in the class answer these questions. Next develop a data set. Then have the class develop a data analysis plan identifying a set of descriptive and bivariate statistics to be calculated. Carry out these calculations and present the results to each other.

R e f e r e n c e s

Krejcie, R., & Morgan, D. (1970). *Educational and psychological measurement.* Thousand Oaks, CA: Sage.

McQuillan, J., & Ferreeuse, M. (1998). Importance of variation among men and the benefits of feminism for families. A. Booth and A. Crouter (Eds.), *Men in families.* Mahwah, NJ: Erlbaum.

Montcalm, D., & Royse, D. (2002). *Data analysis for social workers.* Boston: Allyn and Bacon.

National Center on Addiction and Substance Abuse. (2003). *The formative years: Pathways to substance abuse among girls and young women ages 8–22.* New York: National Center on Addiction and Substance Abuse (CASA), Columbia University. Also available online at www.casacolumbia.

org/publications1456/publications_show.htm?doc_id=151006

Phillips, J. (2000). *How to think about statistics,* 6th ed. New York: Freeman.

Rosenheck, R. (2003). Supported housing for homeless people is more effective, but more costly. *Archives of General Psychiatry, 60,* 940–951.

Weinbach, R., & Grinnell, R. (1998). *Statistics for social workers,* 4th ed. New York: Longman.

Wiener, L., & Siegel, K. (1990). Social workers' comfort in providing services to AIDS patients. *Social Work, 35*(1), 18–25.

Woody, D., & Woody, D. (2003). Parent success among single, low-income, African American mothers: Implications for BSW education. *Journal of Baccalaureate Social Work, 9*(1), 1–17.

chapter 15

Qualitative Data Analysis

Studying quantitative research without studying qualitative research is like allowing the prosecution to present its case and not letting the defense speak. (a BSW student in Zeiger, 1995, p. 122)

The overall purpose of qualitative methods is to search for new meaning or greater understanding of a phenomenon using inductive reasoning. This purpose is in some contrast to that of quantitative methods, which is to find support for something already proposed by the researcher. Quantitative and qualitative methods have been described side by side on various topics throughout the book to help the reader understand how these approaches are both different and complementary. The previous chapter covered data analysis, with a focus on quantitative methods. This chapter focuses on step 5b, qualitative data analysis.

General qualitative methods were introduced in Chapter 2, qualitative survey methods were described in Chapter 9, and qualitative observational methods were highlighted in Chapter 10. Several data collection methods have been introduced so far that generate qualitative data, including (1) open-ended questions asked in structured and semistructured interviews and questionnaires, (2) unstructured interviews, (3) focus groups, (4) unstructured observation, (5) participant observation, and (6) examinations of existing qualitative documents (e.g., case records, logs, journals, etc.).

The data gathered through all of the above methods are in word or narrative form. In most cases, it is unlikely that the data can be reduced to numerical scores without losing important meaning inherent in the data. Note that one of the above examples of data collection methods (number 6) involves analyzing data previously gathered by someone else. Social work researchers have access to numerous types of such qualitative data gathered and stored in social agencies.

Steps in the Research Process

1. Understanding the research topic to be studied
2. Focusing the study
3. Designing the study
   a. Selecting the participants
   b. Selecting a data collection approach and measuring concepts
      - Surveys
      - Observations
   c. Exploring causal relationships
4. Collecting the data
5. Analyzing the data
   a. Quantitative data
   b. Qualitative data
6. Preparing a report

Varied Types of Qualitative Data

Qualitative data have been described as "data in word form" on numerous occasions in the book. These data can be almost any "material" that consists of single words, phrases, sentences, or longer narratives. Imagine some of the possibilities as you consider this list of examples of qualitative data:

1. responses to any open-ended questions of surveys
2. behaviors identified while observing people in a waiting room
3. suggestions for improving agency operations deposited anonymously in a suggestion box
4. client case records
5. conversations in the staff lounge
6. a process recording of an individual interview
7. summaries of group sessions
8. a journal article
9. information on a Website
10. a client's journal entries
11. observations of a family's rituals during a meal
12. exit interviews with former clients
13. an in-depth interview with a new client
14. newspapers and magazines

Only some of these examples are likely to be results of research studies (e.g., numbers 1, 2, 8, and 12). Most involve data gathered for other purposes. Virtually all of them are usually obtained by a fairly reliable source. Note that many of these examples come from client records or other material available in many social agencies.

Let's take the example of an agency suggestion box (number 3). If the administration of an agency encourages staff members to anonymously put suggestions for improving the agency's operations in a suggestion box, these data are likely to be periodically read and then discarded. If an agency frequently receives suggestions, it could conduct a qualitative analysis to uncover important patterns of concern. The point is that there are numerous sources of qualitative data that are gathered in social agencies but not systematically analyzed. Valuable information could be created from analyzing such data.

How Are Qualitative Data Analyzed?

Initially, the *unit of analysis* of the study needs to be considered in preparation for data analysis. In Chapter 8, the unit of analysis was defined as the system level (individual, family, community, city, state, etc.) that is being investigated. The unit of analysis is important because it clarifies what is being compared. Often, individuals are the unit of analysis studied, and the responses of individuals are compared to each other. However, other units of analysis could be selected as well. Let's consider them by looking at a few of the examples of qualitative data in the above list. If behaviors were observed in a waiting room (number 2), the unit of analysis would likely be behaviors, not individuals. If summaries of several group sessions (number 7) were analyzed, these summaries could be the unit of analysis. If we were attempting to identify similar patterns or themes among several journal articles (number 8), these articles are likely to be the unit of analysis.

The major question that is being asked in this chapter is "How is qualitative data analyzed?" The correct response is that there are several options, not one. We must return to the overall research questions and the methodology of a study to begin to determine which data analysis option to use. For example, let's say that the researcher wants to understand the rituals of religious Jewish families when a family member dies. The researcher could decide to conduct a participant observation study of one family. In this case, a descriptive case analysis may be the most relevant data analysis option. As another example, the researcher may want to conduct semistructured interviews with several homeless women staying at a shelter to understand their hopes for the future. In this instance, a theme analysis may be most useful, as it can uncover common patterns in their responses as well as the range of differences.

The chapter focuses on three general options for conducting qualitative data analysis. These are not the only options, but they seem most relevant for qualitative research conducted by a producer of research at an agency. These options are (1) case studies, (2) summarizing responses to open-ended questions, and (3) theme analysis.

Coding data is the first step in qualitative data analysis, just as it is with quantitative analysis. Coding qualitative data is usually an integral part of the data analysis process and can be carried out in a variety of ways. Because each of the above three data analysis options has its own unique way of coding the data, the step of coding data is described individually for each one.

Option 1: Case Studies

Purpose: to provide a detailed description of one or a few cases to promote a fuller understanding of an aspect of their lives

Number of cases: usually one to five

Unit of analysis: a case (individual, family, community, etc.)

Data collection approaches used: unstructured interviews, participant observation, focus groups, or use of archival documents

The first option in qualitative data analysis is a description of one case. You may think that there are not enough data of importance to report on one case, but case descriptions can be extremely useful. The general purpose of case descriptions is to provide a fuller understanding of someone or something of interest. A **case study** can illuminate the complexities of an individual, cultural group, family, or neighborhood that is faced with special social circumstances. These illuminations can provide insights that are relevant to large numbers of people faced with similar circumstances.

Two data collection approaches most effective in developing case studies are unstructured interviews and participant observation. Both approaches can facilitate an open search for deeper meaning or unfamiliar explanations inherent in complex social circumstances. Examples of case studies that could be helpful are a recent Mexican immigrant struggling to live as an undocumented worker in the United States, a Pakistani American family coping with conflicts arising between their Islamic faith and Western culture, or a teenager secretly trying to cope with HIV or suicidal thoughts. A case study can also be assembled using secondary data. For example, data of an archival nature can be identified and assembled into a case study. An example would be a case study of a pioneer or historical figure of importance in social work based on data from library sources. (This is a popular assignment in many social welfare history courses in social work programs.)

Case descriptions typically do not go beyond description. However, there are important issues to address. Many of these issues need to be carefully planned for when the study is being designed, such as which case or cases to select and what specific topics to explore. Other issues are important during the data analysis step. A case description must be organized to tell the story about the individual (or family, group, etc.) in the most effective way. The outline of the case study is very important in identifying the most important and relevant topics. Another issue is to determine if the topics of interest have been described throughly enough in the data or if more data need to be collected. Important information may be missing, for example, and may require additional data collection on particular topics. Another consideration in developing the case study is to discover and describe how or if the topics covered in the case are interrelated.

The professional literature provides numerous examples of case studies that have focused on individuals representing at-risk populations, a cultural group, gangs, or larger social systems (such as mental institutions and prisons, etc.). These studies have often been enormously influential in producing new insights about how to help particular groups of people and how various service delivery systems function and can be improved. Such descriptive accounts have often served as a catalyst for successful social change efforts. An example is Goffman's (1962) *Asylum.*

Example of a Case Study

In 1962, Erving Goffman conducted a two-year participant observation study of the social life of patients in a large state mental institution. In his book entitled *Asylum,* Goffman vividly depicted the stark realities of life in a mental institution and the numerous ways it depersonalized patients. For example, every patient had to follow a rigid daily routine that was set up to efficiently manage the facility with a high staff/patient ratio. Most unfortunately, these routines systematically overlooked and neglected the individual needs of each patient.

This case description was most effective in illuminating the harmful practices and processes promoted by a custodial model of institutional care. The book was timely in that it served as one of the catalysts for promoting the deinstitutionalization movement that followed soon after the book was published.

Social workers are in a strategic position to conduct important case studies because they are in daily contact with people faced with debilitating circumstances that need greater understanding from the society. An example are the growing numbers of undocumented Mexicans recently arriving in various parts of the United States. A survey of several of these families could provide useful information about their unique needs. Yet, a survey study may not be a very realistic option because of the fears that such families would have of being deported if they participated.

In contrast, a case description of one or two of these individuals could provide valuable insights. A social worker could conduct a series of unstructured interviews with one Mexican family, possibly a client, to obtain information about the difficulties they are facing while living in the United States illegally. These problems are likely to revolve around obtaining access to medical care and adequate housing, enrolling their children in day care and the public schools, having access to transportation, finding legal assistance, and getting advocacy assistance if exploited on the job. The following case description by an MSW student focused on a troubled Hispanic teenage male.

Case Study of a Hispanic Youth

A case study was conducted on a thirteen-year-old Hispanic male using unstructured interviews with the teenager, his mother, his aunt, and school officials (Oviedo-Clark, 2002). The interviewer explored the juvenile's current situation, including his home environment, his social relationships, the family's financial situation, and his legal problems. She found that the juvenile's mother was very permissive and had no power over her son. For example, in one instance, the juvenile came home at 4:00 A.M. and the mother did not punish him or even say anything to him. The juvenile's social relationships are a bad influence over him. For instance, the mother reported that he often steals magazines, knives, and movies with his friends. The juvenile is currently waiting for his court date for a larceny offense in which he stole some condoms and batteries from a local store with one of his older friends.

The juvenile's school situation is very unpleasant in that, according to school records, he is failing every class. The juvenile also has 37 unexcused absences and 18 days of suspension for a total of 55 school absences. The juvenile has many other issues, such as being aggressive toward his mother, watching pornographic movies and reading sexually explicit magazines, and showing a lot of interest in gangs. The mother reported that their financial situation was okay except that the juvenile often makes demands higher than those she can financially meet because she is a single mother.

(continued)

The juvenile was born in Mexico City and came with his family to live in the United States five years ago. However, after two years of being in the United States, his parents filed for a divorce. The mother reported that the family had experienced domestic violence for ten years prior to the divorce and that she had reported her husband to the authorities on different occasions. The teenager admitted that he was scared of his father. He also admitted to being afraid of the dark and always sleeping with the lights on. He also has problems wetting the bed. The mother also stated that her son's problems have a long history and did not begin suddenly. For instance, when the family lived in Mexico, the juvenile burned down their house.

Also, two years ago, the teenager, along with some of his friends, placed a living cat in the dryer and killed it. This teenager has many serious problems and is a high risk for dropping out of school. He also confuses reality. He said he would like to go to war so that he could meet fictional characters such as Rambo. The juvenile has also been caught smoking marijuana on school grounds. When asked what he wanted to be when he grew up, he responded "a drug dealer."

Obviously, some serious work must be done with this teenager and his family. In addition, there is a need to educate the Hispanic community with regards to the services offered in the community. For example, the mother of the teenager did not know that psychological assessment and counseling were available in the community. It is also crucial to try and find a way to educate as many parents as possible about these resources before they learn about them through a juvenile court system, as this teenager did.

Option 2: Summarizing Responses to Open-Ended Questions

Purpose: to construct a set of general categories to summarize a large number of responses to an open-ended question

Number of cases: a large number

Unit of analysis: each response to an open-ended question

Data collection approaches: open-ended questions included with interviews and questionnaires

The second option for analyzing qualitative data is to condense the responses to an open-ended question into a smaller set of general categories. The unit of analysis for this option is the individual responses to the question. By condensing these responses into a fewer number of general categories (perhaps five to ten), we summarize the results. In some ways, this option is similar to the way a frequency distribution summarizes the quantitative responses to a forced-response question. This option is useful in succinctly summarizing a large number of responses that are too numerous to absorb or include in a report in their original form. The general categories created from this option of data analysis are usually at the prenominal or nominal level of measurement and could be used as a set of response categories for a forced-response question in a follow-up study.

Open-ended questions are often asked in research studies. As described in earlier chapters, the responses to open-ended questions are in the words of the respondent. Open-ended questions are particularly useful to ask in questionnaires and interviews. Often a questionnaire will have one or two open-ended questions that encourage respondents to elaborate on concerns that cannot be adequately addressed in the forced-response questions. Interviews of all types usually have open-ended questions as well.

How to Summarize Responses for Open-Ended Questions

It is important to have two raters, working independently of each other, to create the general categories and assign the specific responses to these categories. Use of two raters ensures that there is consistency or interrater reliability between these raters. For example, if the raters disagree on which categories to use, this matter can be discussed and resolved in a rational way. In some cases, such disagreements may need to be resolved by involving a third rater. The process of condensing the responses to open-ended questions into a smaller set of general categories occurs in several stages. These stages are:

1. *Prepare the responses for analysis.* Prepare the responses for analysis by listing all of the responses to each question together on the same page so that they can be examined all together. Make sure that everyone's responses are clear.
2. *Review all of the responses.* Carefully review all of the responses so that you can become totally familiar with them.
3. *Code the data.* Code the responses that are similar or express similar themes and group these responses together. Codes can take the form of symbols, such as a letter in the left-hand margin, or highlighting with different-colored marker pens.
4. *Create a label for each category.* Create a term or label for each category of responses. Each of these labels should clearly describe the grouping of responses to which it is assigned.
5. *Count the frequencies.* Count the number of responses that fit within each category so that the results can be reported in a quantitative form.
6. *Provide a few illustrations.* General categories provide a useful summary of responses to an open-ended question, but it may also be helpful to share some of the specific responses as illustrations. You may want to select the responses that are the best reflection of a general category or you may want to select the most dramatic or unusual responses. Adding such illustrations often helps to emphasize the human side of numerical data.

An Example of Summarizing Responses for an Open-Ended Question   An open-ended question that is asked of a large number of people (ten or more) can elicit extensive data that need to be analyzed. Note below an example of the responses to an open-ended question of a structured interview. This question ("What do you like about living here?") was asked of over 1,000 clients, not just the small portion of the sample listed here. Some of these clients lived in an institution when they were interviewed, and others had recently moved from an institution to a group home in the community.

A Partial List of Responses to an Open-Ended Question

Question: What do you like about living here?

Individual responses of 22 of the more than 1,000 clients:

- Cigarettes—I can have cigarettes
- Watch TV, brush teeth, take a bath in a tub
- Go to school; take a bath, makes me feel good; like smoking, TV
- Nothing
- Some girls are mean here (Ward 37)
- Taking my bath
- Nice place—gym, vocational workshop, things to do, learned a lot
- No favorite thing but likes it
- Better than nothing, gym, basketball, baseball
- Likes to help on the ward, going out on free time
- Would rather be where he can go and others don't have to unlock the door
- Good food, watching TV, playing ball, dances
- Going on trips, going to classes
- Nothing, don't like this place
- Basketball, hug and kiss the girls
- Free time, likes to drink Mellow Yellow
- I like staying busy, my boy bear
- Eat fried chicken almost every day
- Yes, freedom
- Food, shower, bath
- TV, having a coke and peanut butter crackers
- Working in the factory, hot chocolate and graham crackers, watching TV

Note both the variability in these responses and the multiple responses of most of the clients. Imagine how difficult it would be to condense them into a small set of general categories without introducing reductionism. Nevertheless, a reader will not be able to make much sense out of a long list (well over 1,000) of such diverse responses. In addition, however, it is sometimes helpful to add some of these specific responses as illustrations in a report.

Note how the responses in this example are summarized into ten general categories in Table 15.1. Obviously, valuable meaning was lost in condensing the responses of these 22 people into ten groupings, yet this summary does provide a useful overview of their responses. The categories are presented in the order of their frequency of occurrence, beginning with the highest frequency. Even though

TABLE 15.1 A Set of General Categories for the Question "What Do You Like about Living Here?"

General Response Categories	Frequency	Percentage
Food or beverages	6	14.0
Hygiene activities (e.g., taking baths, brushing teeth)	4	9.3
Watching TV	4	9.3
School, employment, or vocational training	4	9.3
Likes nothing or mentions dislikes	4	9.3
Playing sports (e.g., gym, basketball, baseball)	4	9.3
Freedom or free time	3	7.0
Keeping busy, things to do	2	4.7
Cigarettes	2	4.7
Other	10	23.2
Total responses counted	43	100.0

the "other" category has ten responses, it is listed last because it represents a set of responses that have no similarities to each other.

It is always helpful to set up a few rules to follow in deciding on the appropriate categories and assigning each response to a category. Such a rule was established in conjunction with creating the categories in Table 15.1. It was decided that a category would not be created unless there were at least two responses that were similar. Also, another rule was that each one of the clients' responses was counted, even when a respondent had multiple responses. (For example, one client responded with "watch TV, brush teeth, take a bath in a tub," which were treated as three separate responses.) This would make the responses, not the clients, be the unit of analysis. Therefore, the percent of responses in each category was based on the total number of responses (42), not the number of clients (22). Another rule that was established permitted a client to have no more than one response for each category. For example, the responses of one client included "hot chocolate and graham crackers," but these two responses were only counted once for the "food" category.

As the general categories in the above illustration suggest, the responses of these clients are very diverse and do not cluster around a few types of things that they liked. Ten categories were identified, and the category with the highest frequency ("food") only represented 14 percent of all of the responses. In addition, the "other" category had the highest frequency, suggesting that there were many responses that were distinctly different from all others.

Option 3: Theme Analysis

> *Purpose:* to identify patterns or themes evident in several cases
>
> *Number of cases:* at least two and often several
>
> *Unit of analysis:* can be individuals, case records, behaviors, journal articles, etc.
>
> *Data collection approaches:* semi- and unstructured interviews, focus groups, participant observation, and use of archival documents

The focus of the third option of data analysis is on identifying common themes or patterns that are prevalent in several cases. Note that this option usually involves the analysis of several cases, in contrast to a case study, which focuses on one or a few cases. **Theme analysis** is useful in analyzing lengthy narrative material of a participant observation or unstructured interview study. This option is also relevant for research data that already exist from other sources, such as journal articles, case records, and other agency material. In addition, this option can be valuable in completing many of the other nonresearch tasks expected of students and professionals. The following are some nonresearch tasks for which a theme analysis can be used:

- organizing a literature search for a paper
- conducting a content analysis of your practice approach (for example, finding out the techniques you frequently use and those you use very little)
- organizing and integrating the knowledge you have collected in a particular field of practice
- a self-assessment of your strengths and weaknesses using data from instructors' and clients' feedback

The units of analysis for theme analysis can vary widely. For example, a study involving several interviews with homeless parents could use the individual as the unit of measure. Behaviors could be the unit of analysis if an unstructured observational study of a waiting room were the focus. Analysis of themes could also be collected from case records, staff meeting minutes, and other agency narratives; in these instances, the unit of analysis would likely be the records or minutes. The following example from the narrative records of a focus group describes one particular theme.

Example of a Narrative Record from a Focus Group Discussion

A social work student conducted a focus group study of volunteers of several churches involved in providing shelter to homeless people in their churches during the cold months (Leary, 2003). One theme resulting from these sessions was identified as "A perceived need of homeless people to talk to someone at the shelter." When the volunteers began discussing the needs of the homeless people they had helped, they identified the need to talk to someone who could listen and provide compassion. An abbreviated version of four of the comments found in the narrative that reflected this theme follows:

- I think one of the big needs is just to listen to them, be compassionate, and be there for them. I remember one evaluation meeting . . . when you have the homeless at the meeting with you, and I remember one of the fellows saying "just don't feed us and leave us."
- I would have loved to have one of many clergy members, deacons, priests, whatever, come and say an opening prayer with our people and it be a show of force that this whole congregation is behind this program. . . . I think that is a really important part, to have a show of force, that clergy and staff support the program 100%. I think the guests actually get a sense of being special when we are all present.
- During Lenten season, when we would have community meals on the same night as the shelter program, one of the things that was very interesting was they were much more likely to sit down with [one of the pastors]. Some of the issues that were shared actually initiated my bringing up the idea with my church about offering the possibility of some counseling services and providing that there. I see that as care, a very crucial care, to their situation, and also it's definitely a help.
- A lot of them have a lack of self-confidence; they don't believe in themselves anymore. Mainly they need someone to talk to, to reassure them they are still human beings and worth something.

Theme analysis is a process of circular stages It is often a lengthy and time-consuming process. The amount of time needed will depend on how much narrative is to be analyzed. In any case, a social worker can fairly easily develop some proficiency in completing this type of data analysis. Furthermore, this process is likely to be rewarding in uncovering new insights about a topic.

How to Conduct a Theme Analysis

Theme analysis usually takes more time, covers more data, and is more intellectually demanding than the previous two options. It has more stages as well. Similar to option 2, it is important to involve two reviewers if possible in conducting all or a portion of the theme analysis independently of each other. Use of two people ensures that there is consistency, or interrater reliability, in the results. For example, if the two people disagree on how a theme is to be described, their differences can be discussed and resolved in a rational way. In some cases, such disagreements may need to be resolved by involving a third person.

The stages involved in conducting a theme analysis are summarized here:

Stages of Theme Analysis

1. Determine the unit of analysis.
2. Prepare the narrative.
3. Thoroughly acquaint yourself with the entire narrative.

(continued)

4. Identify themes.
5. Assign a code to each theme.
6. Record your impressions separately.
7. Group the comments together by theme.
8. Clearly articulate a label for each theme.
9. Identify variations in each theme.
10. Look for other themes.
11. Generate hypotheses (optional).
12. Present the results.

A student-led theme analysis project led by Grantham (2001) is used to illustrate some of these stages. Grantham conducted a theme analysis of fifteen client charts that summarized the clients' first contact with a hospice agency. The charts were in narrative form and written immediately after the client's visit. Grantham wanted to identify the major themes evident in these narrative charts as a way of preparing herself to work with this population. (Note that while this was not intended as a research study, it could have been one).

1. *Determine the unit of analysis.* Before the narrative is prepared for analysis, it is important to identify the unit of analysis that will be used and the number of cases to be analyzed. The unit of analysis could be individuals, case records, articles, or other units you wish to compare. Once the unit of analysis is determined, identify each unit or case by a number.

Example

Grantham decided to use clients' charts for her theme analysis. She decided to compare these charts to each other. Since she planned to analyze 15 charts, she numbered them from 1 to 15.

2. *Prepare the narrative.* The data need to be organized and made available in narrative form that is easy to read. In addition, having the data in an electronic file has special advantages, as the files or portions of files can be printed, copied and pasted, and easily incorporated into various reports.

Example

Grantham used the clients' charts as the source of data for her theme analysis. These charts, being in narrative form, were ready for analysis in their current form. Since Grantham worked at the hospice agency that possessed the client charts and was conducting the theme analysis to help prepare herself for her job, she was easily able to obtain permission from the agency to analyze these forms.

3. *Thoroughly acquaint yourself with the entire narrative.* This stage consists of carefully reading all of the narrative data. It is a good idea to read the entire narrative more than once to fully acquaint yourself with it. Take plenty of time to complete this stage, as you will need to be thoroughly familiar with the data to successfully complete the stages that follow.

4. *Identify themes.* As you read the narrative, begin to identify themes that are sometimes evident. A theme is an idea, viewpoint, or conceptualization of something that is repeated over and over in qualitative materials. Some themes are identified when designing the study prior to analyzing the data. Other themes can be discovered as the narratives are being read. Themes can be expressed at various levels of abstraction. These repetitious ideas will not necessarily be stated every time, using the same words or phrases, particularly when they are at higher levels of abstraction.

Example

Grantham identified six themes from carefully reading these client charts, including

- physical health concerns identified by patients
- mental health concerns identified by patients
- social support issues facing the patient
- religious or spirituality issues (needs, beliefs, requests) identified
- legal issues related to finances, end-of-life care, and insurance
- death and dying issues

5. *Assign a code to each theme.* This stage involves setting up a coding system consisting of a code for every theme. As themes are identified, they are coded like a "bookmark" that can be easily identified later in the analysis process. Codes can be symbols, such as a letter in the left-hand margin (e.g., S = social supports evident, H = health concerns mentioned, L = legal issues mentioned, etc.), or coding can be done in different colors using marker pens. Whenever a theme seems to be evident, the appropriate code is recorded in the left-hand margin.

6. *Record your impressions separately.* Record all of your own impressions while you are proceeding through the process of data analysis. Your impressions can be your thoughts, questions, hunches, and so forth. It is important to record these impressions in a section of your notes that is separate from the narrative material. This helps keep the analysis of the narrative material untainted by your subjective reactions. These impressions can be helpful later in the process, possibly when you are trying to explain how you came up with your themes, why you selected the excerpts of narratives you did, or describing any limitations you detected in your theme development.

Example

Grantham recorded her impressions related to each theme on a separate page as she conducted the analysis. Her impressions about one of these themes, legal issues for hospice clients, are shared here. They were, in part: "This would be a very difficult area for me to address with clients. I don't think I would have any trouble with the financial concerns part, but the advanced directives part would be hard. This is because the social worker has to talk up front about the clients' impending death. Some of the clients are uncomfortable talking about their deaths and try to avoid the issues surrounding advanced directives. The social worker has to take clues from the client as to how to proceed. The worker has to phrase the questions in ways that don't cause the client undue stress, such as referring to the client as 'really sick or ill' rather than 'dying.' The words *dying* and *death* are not used by the agency unless the client uses them first."

7. *Group the comments together by theme.* After the entire narrative has been thoroughly reviewed and all of the important themes have been identified and coded, group the specific comments pertaining to each theme together, possibly on a separate page, so that they can be easily analyzed. If the narrative is on an electronic file, it can be easily organized by themes, using the "copy" and "paste" commands of a word processing program. If the narrative is on paper, an extra copy can be made. Then this extra copy can be cut up and pasted using scissors and Scotch tape. Note an example of the comments of a theme grouped together.

Example

One of the themes identified by Grantham was "legal issues related to finances, end-of-life care, and insurance." Some of the specific comments coded in the client records that illustrated this theme were

End-of-life planning is completed, including advanced directives.

DNR (do not resuscitate) in home.

Patient unwilling to discuss advanced directives.

Patient may want to have a legal will prepared.

Patient has a legal will and DNR.

Patient desires DNR.

Patient has no apparent financial concerns.

Insurance recently changed—insurance company will only pay 30 percent of bill.

8. *Clearly articulate a label for each theme.* By this point in the analysis, each grouping of comments reflecting a theme is listed separately. You may have a few

or several such groupings. Now you will need to articulate a label for each theme that captures the content of the comments. Keep in mind that your labels are to be a clear and accurate depiction of each theme. Feel free to use a single word, several words, or even a phrase for your labels. Once you come up with a label for each grouping, you may find that one or more of the comments in that grouping does not belong. In this case, remove them.

9. *Identify variations in each theme.* This stage is important to complete if the narratives of a particular theme are expressed in different or contrasting ways. Identifying variations is helpful in further delineating what the theme actually means. For example, you may find that a theme is presented both positively and negatively. Sometimes variations in a theme can even be used in a later study as a measure of a nominal or prenominal variable.

Example

In Grantham's project, the comments that documented the legal theme identified in stage 7 had variations in the ways they were stated. Variations in the comments about legal issues seemed to be about one of three things: finances, a legal will, or advanced directives. Comments could also be grouped by whether these clients had problems in these areas or seemed to have them resolved.

10. *Look for other themes.* To be thorough, you may want to review the narrative again to make sure that all of the supporting evidence for each theme has been located. Also, this review may lead you to find evidence of other themes or a few interesting comments that are not frequent enough to constitute another theme. Any new themes that are found can be added to the results, and perhaps some of the isolated comments in one or two cases may have enough merit to be included in a report as well.

11. *Generate hypotheses (optional).* This stage is optional. After identifying each of the themes in the narrative, you may want to explore the possibility that some themes are related to one another. In other words, comments about one theme may be associated with comments of another theme. In this instance, it may be possible to generate a tentative hypothesis that could add more meaning to the analysis. This hypothesis could then be explored in a follow-up study.

Example

Grantham identified several themes and discovered that some of them were associated with one another. For example, the clients that had strong religious beliefs and spiritual supports (religion and spirituality theme) tended to have an easier time discussing their pending death and dealing with related legal issues (legal theme).

12. *Present the results.* By this point in the process, you will have identified several themes, with each having numerous examples or comments from the narrative. A presentation of your themes is largely done at this point. You could, for example, have each theme stated as a heading in a table under which is a list of all or some of the comments reflecting that theme. You could also review your impressions and attempt to see if they are consistent or contrary to the results. After reviewing the results, your impressions, and the pertinent literature, you could craft a set of helpful recommendations supported by the results. Of course, the recommendations should be tailored to the needs of the users of your report or presentation.

Data Collection Approaches and the Three Options

Several methods of qualitative data collection were identified initially in the chapter. The data analysis options that are most suited for each of these approaches are summarized as follows:

Data Analysis Options Used with Different Methods

Data Collection Methods	Data Analysis Option
1. Open-ended questions of a survey	Option 2
2. Unstructured interviews	Options 1 or 3
3. Focus groups	Option 3
4. Unstructured observation	Options 1 or 3
5. Participant observation	Options 1 or 3
6. Examinations of existing qualitative documents	Options 1 or 3

As this summary indicates, open-ended questions of surveys are usually analyzed by summarizing the responses into general categories. Focus groups are most likely to be analyzed using theme analysis. The remaining qualitative data collection approaches can be most effectively analyzed using either a case study approach or a theme analysis.

Other Types of Qualitative Data Analysis

The chapter has focused on three distinct types of qualitative data analysis—case studies, theme analysis, and summarizing responses to open-ended questions. These three options are highlighted because they are most relevant for producers of research in an agency. They are also basic approaches that can be easily modified to fit the needs of a particular research project. For example, a case study of one can be increased to two or three cases for comparative purposes.

Other strategies are also available for conducting qualitative data analysis. Some are more advanced strategies that may be of interest to readers who want to develop these skills. Many of the more advanced strategies are similar to the three options that have been covered in this chapter, except that they use more complex tools. Some of these strategies are:

- *Content analysis:* Content analysis is a strategy similar to option 3. **Content analysis,** however, focuses specifically on the repetition of different types of recorded communication, such as words and phrases. It helps to answer questions central to communication research, such as "Who says what, to whom, why, how, and with what effect" (Babbie, 2001, p. 305). This strategy also tends to use quantitative methodology and analysis more often than qualitative. Allen-Meares (1984) points out the relevance of content analysis to social work research.
- *Qualitative data analysis with observations:* Most of the material that has been covered in this chapter focuses on qualitative data obtained from surveys. Lofland and Loftland (1995) offer helpful guidelines for analyzing qualitative data resulting from unstructured observations.
- *Constant Comparative Method of analysis:* The stages that are used in option 3 in this chapter are a simplified version of an approach described by Glaser and Strauss (1967, pp. 101–115). This approach, the Constant Comparative Method, is designed to aid a researcher in generating a theory that is integrated, consistent, plausible, and grounded in the data.
- *Validating data:* Taylor and Bogdan (1984, pp. 140–142) suggest that researchers should view their qualitative data with skepticism. They suggest that one of the final stages in qualitative data analysis is to challenge the validity of the data by considering such questions as "Was the data solicited or volunteered?" "Are the findings direct or indirect data?" "In what ways did the researchers influence the settings being studied?" "Who, if anyone, was present and may have influenced the views that the participants shared?" "Are the views of a few participants being used too often, resulting in the data being overgeneralized?" and "What influence has the researchers' assumptions and presumptions had on the findings?"
- *Proposing hypotheses:* Proposing hypotheses is another strategy in qualitative data analysis. This strategy focuses on discovering relationships among concepts that are in qualitative form (Marlow, 2001). Such a strategy is similar to hypothesis testing with quantitative data, as described in Chapter 14. However, this type of analysis is generating new hypotheses, while the quantitative version is testing existing hypotheses.
- *Constructing causal flowcharts:* Another type of analysis investigates the relationships among several concepts in qualitative data (Marlow, 2001). In this case, the findings are presented in the form of a flowchart that shows the possible relationship among several concepts, all in word form, not numbers.

Chapter Reflections

Values and Ethics, Diversity, At-Risk Groups, and Social Justice

Values and ethics play an important role in qualitative data analysis. The problem of reductionism is one such issue. Reductionism occurs whenever an effort to create a numerical measure of a concept results in losing some of the properties of the concept. This ethical problem can occur with numerous concepts important to social work such as stress, clinical depression, family functioning, racism, happiness, communication skills, and being suicidal. In these and other instances, measuring a concept in qualitative form is preferred to reducing it to a numerical measure in which much of its meaning is lost.

Concerns about reductionism are also relevant for diversity issues. All of the characteristics of importance to each group should be considered in data analysis. If a study is investigating people of various nationalities in Central and South America, for example, each of the nationalities should be considered in the analysis of factors related to nationality rather than lumping them all together.

Populations at risk have similar issues. Qualitative methods and data analysis are often the best fit for many populations at risk, because less is known about these groups and it is often paramount to fully hear what they have to say. Analyzing the views of vulnerable groups by keeping the data in their own words avoids reductionism. Further, doing so is empowering and can go a long way in furthering social justice. This chapter offers several examples of data analysis involving populations at risk, including Mexican teenagers, patients with terminal illnesses, people in psychiatric hospitals, and those who are homeless.

Discussion Questions

1. Construct your own set of general categories for the responses to the open-ended question, "What do you like about living here?" on page 278. Do this without looking at the general categories that were created for the responses in Table 15.1. After you have completed this task, compare your results with those in Table 15.1. Discuss any differences between how you completed this task and how it was completed there. This is an exercise in interrater reliability.

2. Conduct a theme analysis of a collection of narratives using the following stages:
   - Go on the Internet and access the Child Trends Website (www.childtrends.org).
   - Once you are at the Website for Child Trends, go to Publications. Then select one of the following topics: Welfare and Poverty or Adolescent Sexual Behavior. Next, select two or three of the articles on that topic that are online.
   - Attempt to obtain electronic copies of the articles you select, if possible, so that you can use the cut, copy, and paste commands of your word processing program.
   - Complete the stages involved in theme analysis summarized on pages 281–282 and described in the chapter. This assignment could take many hours to do if it

were to be completed thoroughly. However, spend only one to two hours completing stages 1 through 6 and identify only one theme. Then take one to two hours to complete stages 7 through 12.

- Prepare your theme analysis work to be turned in, as follows:
    a. Cite the material sources you analyzed (use full citations for articles).
    b. Identify the theme you discovered and all of the specific comments reflecting it.
    c. Explain variations within the theme.
    d. Record your impressions separately.
    e. Share what you have learned from doing this assignment.

3. Assume that your university is investigating the need for a new MSW program. Conduct a case study by interviewing one undergraduate social work major. Some topics to cover with the student are (1) why they are interested (or lack interest) in an MSW program, (2) their expectations of an MSW program if they were to enroll, and (3) what knowledge and skills they hope to develop by the time that they graduate. Next, craft the specific questions you will ask to cover these three topics, conduct the interview, and organize the information obtained. Be prepared to describe the process of crafting the questions, completing the interview, and organizing the data into a presentation. What did you learn from doing this assignment?

4. Assume that you are conducting a qualitative study investigating the weekend entertainment wishes of college-aged students (This is an exercise for two students.) Craft the questions you will ask and the method that you will use in collecting data. Next, collect the data from three students. Condense the individual responses into themes, using frequency counts. Determine interrater reliability. Be prepared to describe the process of crafting the questions, collecting the data, and organizing the data into themes. What did you learn from doing this assignment?

5. You are conducting a qualitative study investigating the types of information that are displayed on three university bulletin boards (This is an exercise for two students.) Decide on the general types of information you will consider by looking at one bulletin board. Next, collect the data from the three bulletin boards. Then collapse the individual observations into themes, using frequency counts. Determine interrater reliability. Be prepared to describe the process of determining the types of information, collecting the data, and showing how you organized it into the themes and how you determined interrater reliability. What did you learn from doing this assignment?

6. You are conducting a qualitative study investigating the type of clothing worn by college-aged students. (This is an exercise for two students.) Decide on the general types of clothing you are going to observe. Collect the data through observation. Then organize them into categories. Collapse the individual clothing items observed into the categories, using frequency counts. Determine interrater reliability. Be prepared to describe the process of deciding what to observe, collecting the data, organizing the data into the themes, and determining interrater reliability. What did you learn from doing this assignment?

7. Divide the class into smaller focus groups of eight to ten students. Select a facilitator who will lead the discussion and a recorder who will record the responses of the

group members. Select one of the following two topics: (1) the impact of the students' parents and (2) learning from field experiences.

A. The facilitator asks the following questions:

Topic: impact of parents

- How was your father (or mother) important to you during your childhood?
- What was missing or problematic in your relationship with your father (or mother)?
- If your father (mother) was absent, what do you think you missed by not having a father present?

Topic: learning from field experiences (e.g., the field practicum, monitoring legislative activities for a policy course, volunteer work, etc.)

- What have you learned about practice that can be applied in your job after graduation?
- What were you exposed to that seemed irrelevant or not useful?
- What was relevant but not covered very well?

B. List all of the responses on the board so that all can be viewed at once.

C. Identify themes having at least three responses that illustrate them.

References

Allen-Meares, P. (1984). Content analysis: It does have a place in social work research. *Journal of Social Science Research, 7,* 51–68.

Babbie, E. (2001). *The practice of social research,* 9th ed. Belmont, CA: Wadsworth/Thomson Learning.

Glaser, B., & Strauss, A. (1967). *The discovery of grounded theory: Strategies for qualitative research.* Chicago: Aldine.

Goffman, E. (1962). *Asylum: Essays on the social situation of mental patients and other inmates.* Chicago: Aldine.

Grantham, V. (2001). Theme analysis of client records. Student assignment, University of North Carolina, Charlotte.

Leary, A. (2003). Room in the inn: Exploring church involvement in serving the homeless. Student research project, University of North Carolina, Charlotte.

Lofland, J., & Loftland, L. (1995). *Analyzing social settings: A guide to qualitative observation and analysis,* 3rd ed. Belmont, CA: Wadsworth/ Thomson Learning.

Marlow, C. (2001). *Research methods for generalist social work,* 3rd ed. Stamford, CT: Thomson Learning.

Oviedo-Clark, M. (2002). A case study of a Hispanic youth. Student research project, University of North Carolina, Charlotte.

Taylor, S., & Bogdan, R. (1984). *Introduction to qualitative research methods: The search for meanings,* 2nd ed. New York: Wiley.

Zeiger, S. (1995). A case for the inclusion of qualitative methodology into research course content. *Journal of Baccalaureate Social Work, 1*(1), 11–124.

chapter 16

Preparing the Report

How well this step is completed can "make or break" an entire study! A poorly written research report can easily negate all of the hard work that has been completed on a study up to this point.

After the data have been collected and analyzed, it's time to prepare a report for the stakeholders. The stakeholders are the people who are expected to read the research report. Stakeholders should also include the clients. Even though they may not read the report or even be aware of it, they could be affected more than anyone by its consequences. Preparation of a report is the sixth and final step of the research process.

Several tasks are involved in preparing a report and are the focus of this chapter. These tasks are presented for both the consumer and producer roles of research. The chapter provides producers with several strategies for preparing their reports, and consumers with insights about how to critique a report for clarity, relevance, and completeness. Attention is given to preparing reports of both qualitative and quantitative studies.

Tasks Involved in Preparing a Report

Preparing a report involves five general tasks. First, background material about the study needs to be summarized. The reader will want to know about such things as the research problem or topic, the research questions that were investigated, and the research design. Next, considerable forethought and planning need to go into organizing and focusing the findings into a readable presentation. Next, recommendations need to be developed that help the reader consider the practice and policy implications of the

Steps in the Research Process

1. Understanding the research topic to be studied
2. Focusing the study
3. Designing the study
   a. Selecting the participants
   b. Selecting a data collection approach and measuring concepts
      - Surveys
      - Observations
   c. Exploring causal relationships
4. Collecting the data
5. Analyzing the data
   a. Quantitative data
   b. Qualitative data
6. **Preparing a report**

findings. A report of all of the steps is prepared and written (or presented). Finally, efforts must go into disseminating and utilizing the results.

> ### Tasks Involved in Preparing a Report
> 1. Highlighting background material on the study
> 2. Organizing the findings
> 3. Developing recommendations
> 4. Writing or presenting the report
> 5. Disseminating and utilizing the results

Task 1. Highlighting Background Material on the Study

The research report follows the order of the steps of the research process. In a traditional research report, the following background information is provided to help the reader understand the larger context for the findings:

1. *Statement of the problem.* The research problem or topic is usually summarized in a few paragraphs. Varying views of the problem can be mentioned, along with the viewpoint of the researcher. The relevance and importance of the research topic are emphasized here, and a summary of pertinent literature is also included.

2. *Research questions or hypotheses.* The research questions or hypotheses describe the purpose of the study and are central to understanding the study. They should be easy for the reader to find and in a central place.

3. *Design of the study.* Specific information about the design of the study is also important to highlight. Material to be covered can include:

- important demographic characteristics that describe the research participants
- the sampling approach used in selecting the research participants and an explanation of whether or not the findings can be generalized to a larger population
- the data collection approach and specific measurement instruments used and a brief explanation of why they were selected
- a brief description about the data collectors and whether they received any training
- a summary of how the data were analyzed

Task 2. Organizing the Findings

Organizing the findings is a very important task. The effort that goes into completing this task may well determine the extent to which the findings of the study will be read, taken seriously, and utilized. Too often, findings are put together without giving enough forethought to such things as (1) how to focus the findings, (2) ensuring their accuracy and clarity, and (3) creatively using graphics for visual effect.

Focusing the Findings

The initial concern is to determine a focus for the presentation of findings. Sometimes, all of the data collected are included in a single report, but more often only some of the data are included. A report that has too much data, particularly when the data are not well organized and focused, is difficult to understand, and this diminishes the report's impact. When there are extensive data, it is important to ask:

- Which findings should be emphasized?
- Which findings should be left out?
- Which findings can be included in an appendix?

The best way to begin to answer these questions is to review the general research questions of the study (step 2). These research questions can provide a focus and possibly an organizing framework for the presentation of findings, since the findings are supposed to answer these questions. The research questions may even become the overall outline for the findings.

In completing step 6, you may discover that the original research questions are too vague to be used in organizing the presentation. In this case, it's possible that the research questions were not crafted with enough specificity. This could pose difficulties in the preparation of the report. Another possibility for inconsistencies between the initial research questions and the findings is that the initial focus changed since data have been collected. This is permissible, particularly in unstructured or qualitative studies that do not use a standardized set of instruments. In these studies, the inductive research process is flexible enough to shift the study's emphasis to optimize what can be learned from the people being studied. In these instances, the focus for the findings can be addressed by considering both the initial research questions and the actual findings in preparing an outline for the report.

Example of Focusing a Report for a Qualitative Study

A focus group study was conducted of several volunteers of Room in the Inn, an ecumenical program that offers overnight shelter to small groups of eight to ten homeless people during the winter months (Leary, 2003). Initially, the researcher identified three overall research questions that focused the study as follows: (1) What are the needs of their homeless guests? (2) What efforts have the churches tried to meet these needs? and (3) What efforts might churches try in the future?

While all of these questions were asked by the researcher in focus groups, the third question was given much more attention by the participants and was

(continued)

perceived by both the sponsoring organization and the participants to be the central set of findings. Therefore, it was decided that the major focus of the report would be on question 3. The researcher ended up presenting the findings from the first two questions in an appendix.

Another factor to consider in the organization of the findings is the stakeholders or those who will read the research report and how these findings can be helpful to them, whether they are agency colleagues, agency administrators, policy makers, clients, or the general public. The above example of a qualitative study reflects an effort to be responsive to the stakeholders, in this case an ecumenical agency, the local churches, and individual volunteers.

Accuracy and Clarity

It is also important to present the findings in an accurate manner. Accuracy also presumes that the findings are being presented with clarity. Some of the questions to ask at this stage include:

- *Are the correct tests used in presenting the descriptive statistics?* For example, frequency distributions are appropriate for variables at the nominal and ordinal levels of measurement, while measures of central tendency and variability are used with interval/ratio-level variables.
- *If hypotheses are tested, are the correct bivariate and multivariate tests used? Also, are the results of these tests reported correctly and in enough detail?* Usually, the results of a statistical test include the test score (e.g., χ^2(chi-square) = 7.68, or r = 0.13), and the level of significance (e.g., $p < .05$). At times, the degrees of freedom are also included (e.g., $df = 45$).
- *Do the tables and graphs focus on the most important findings?*
- *Are the tables and graphs prepared accurately and easy to understand?*
- *Do the text summaries describing the contents in each table or graph accurately reflect the table or graph? Also, are these summaries limited to highlighting the most important contents in each table rather than providing a total review and repetition of what is in the table?*

Use of Graphics

A report composed solely of uninterrupted written material can be boring and tedious to read, and it may discourage some from reading it at all. Therefore, in preparing a report, serious consideration should be given to using tables, graphs, and other visual aids to creatively highlight and summarize important findings. SPSS (Statistical Package for the Social Sciences), Microsoft Excel (2002), and other computer programs can be used in preparing these graphics. Let's look at some tables, bar charts, and pie charts in particular.

Tables   Tables are quite useful in consolidating data into one visual presentation that highlights an important set of findings. For example, a table can highlight the characteristics of the research participants or their responses to a question. It can compare two different subgroups or compare measures of an outcome variable at two or more points in time. Examples of two such tables are presented in Tables 16.1 and 16.2. Table 16.1 describes the responses of students to a study on social work students' career plans conducted by Rome (1997). The forced-response question reported in Table 16.1 asked what they perceived to be the most attractive features of child welfare practice. They could choose more than one response.

Table 16.2 presents a summary of the demographic characteristics of a sample and is more complicated than Table 16.1. Two subgroups of teenage female participants, those who were maltreated in childhood and those who were not, were described so that their differences could be highlighted. Note that this table reveals that these two subgroups were significantly different, based on whether or not they were welfare recipients, their family structure, and their race/ethnicity.

Bar Charts   Pie and bar charts are other visual ways to highlight some of the findings. **Bar charts** use bars as a graphic to summarize the frequency distribution of a particular variable. Bar charts provide a visual way of comparing two or more groups of people based on a particular measure. Figure 16.1 provides an example. In this case, mothers and fathers were compared on their responses to whether or

TABLE 16.1   Positive Features of the Child Welfare System

Positive Features	Percentage
Serving children	89.3
Strengthening families	86.2
Using many social work skills	68.2
Contributing to society	59.1
Seeing positive outcomes	56.0
Learning community resources	51.3
Diverse practice settings	48.5
Being a role model to clients	42.7
Good training for other social work jobs	36.2
Working with other professionals	30.6
Salary	12.0

Note: Total valid responses = 784.

Source: "The Child Welfare Choice: An Analysis of Social Work Students' Career Plans," by S. Rome, 1997, *Journal of Baccalaureate Social Work*, 3(1), 31–48. Reprinted by permission.

TABLE 16.2 **Prevalence of Maltreatment in Female Teenagers, by Demographic Characteristics**

| Characteristics | Whether Maltreated | | |
	Yes	No	*n*
Total sample	14%	86%	249
Welfare recipient[a]			
Yes	19	81	134
No	6	94	96
Parent education			
Not high school graduate	13	87	137
High school graduate	14	86	111
Family structure[a]			
Other	17	83	180
Both biological parents present	4	96	64
Race and ethnicity[a]			
White	33	67	16
Hispanic	5	95	33
African American	13	87	200

[a]$p < 0.05$, one-tailed.

Source: From "The Link between Childhood Maltreatment and Teenage Pregnancy," by C. Smith, 1996, *Social Work Research*, 20(3), pp. 131–141. Reprinted by permission.

not they know whom their adolescent children ages 12 through 14 are with when they are not at home (Moore et al., 2002). The bar chart reveals that a higher percentage of mothers than fathers report that they know whom their adolescent is with, yet 27 percent of the mothers do not know this information.

Pie Charts   Pie charts are a special type of bar chart displayed in circular form. **Pie charts** are useful when a circular display communicates more effectively than a linear bar chart. Note an example of a pie chart in Figure 16.2. As you can see in this figure, members of the National Association of Social Workers responded to a survey about their access to the Internet (O'Neill, 2003). As the pie chart indicates, all but 3 percent have access to the Internet. Of those who do have access, over half have access both at work and home.

Task 3. Developing Recommendations

As the findings are being organized and assembled, the researcher should be thinking about their implications: "What do these findings suggest?" "How can they be helpful to the reader?" The section following the findings of a research report is

FIGURE 16.1   **Example of a Bar Chart**

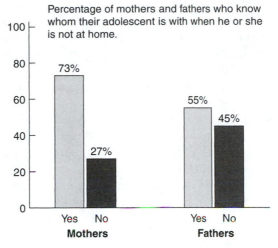

Source: From "Family Strengths," by K. Moore et al., 2002, *Child Trends Research Brief.* Reprinted by permission.

FIGURE 16.2   **Example of a Pie Chart**

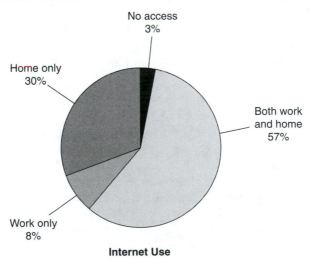

Source: From "Nearly All Members Linked to Internet," by J. O'Neill, 2003, *NASW News,* 48 (2), p. 9. Reprinted by permission.

typically referred to as the Discussion Section, Recommendations, or Practice Implications. While we will focus mostly on the recommendations, several types of information are often shared in this section of a research report, including:

- *general conclusions,* including possibly a summary of the findings
- *interpretations* that may glean meaning from some of the findings without offering recommendations
- *recommendations* that offer suggestions about how the findings can be used by the reader
- *limitations of the study* that need to be taken into account before considering whether the findings can be generalized to the clients in the reader's work setting (Examples of the types of limitations to cite in the report are listed below.)
- *consistencies/inconsistencies between the findings of this study and other studies* that are relevant to the research topic (Many of these studies have been reviewed in the introductory section of the report as part of the literature review.)
- *new research questions* that could be investigated in future studies, based on what was found or not found in this study (This is a special type of recommendation suggesting the need for further research.)

Types of Limitations in a Study

Examples of the types of limitations in a study that could be reported are:

- Questions were poorly formulated.
- Particular questions were not asked.
- The sample was too small.
- There was a low response rate.
- The sample could not be generalized because a nonprobability sampling approach was used.
- No baseline data were available.
- Important extraneous variables were not controlled.

The recommendations are usually the most important topic to consider in the discussion section of a research report, so let's focus on them. How do you develop useful recommendations that are based on the findings being reported? Morris, Fitz-Gibbon, and Freeman (1987) suggest that the recommendations may be the most important part of the report, because the stakeholders tend to turn to this section for guidance on what to do. Since recommendations are so important, these authors suggest preparing this section extra carefully.

Several guidelines that can be helpful when preparing recommendations for a research report include:

1. *Attempt to draw some general conclusions from the findings.* Overall, what do the findings seem to say?

2. *List some initial recommendations.* Recommendations should be stated in such a way that they are relevant and useful to readers, whoever they are.

3. *Recommendations must be supported by the findings.* Recommendations should not be a wish list or an excuse to promote a particular viewpoint if it is unsupported by the findings. A helpful exercise to conduct to fulfill this principle is to identify each recommendation in a report and then identify the specific findings of the study, if any, that support each of these recommendations. When there are no findings to support a recommendation, it should be omitted. An exercise used in assessing the recommendations of one study is described here:

Exercise to Assess the Recommendations of One Study

Several recommendations were provided by Wiener and Siegel (1990) in their research report on the factors that influence the comfort level of social workers in providing services to AIDS patients. (Some of their findings are presented in Table 14.6 on page 261, illustrating the use of a correlation test in analyzing findings.) Two of their recommendations are identified here to illustrate an exercise in critiquing how well recommendations are supported by findings.

Almost all of the recommendations were strongly supported by specific findings, including one recommendation that stated that social work education needs to do more to dispel myths and stereotypes about gay people. This recommendation was strongly supported by the finding that research participants who were more likely to be homophobic were also less likely to be comfortable with AIDS patients.

A second recommendation, however, was only partially supported by qualitative comments of a few participants. This recommendation stated that work with AIDS patients entails an emotional investment that not all social workers may be willing to make.

---

4. *The discussion of the recommendations of a study should mention any limitations that need to be considered in implementing them.* For example, a study about the school adjustment of children born and raised in the United States may not have direct applicability for children who are recent immigrants.

5. *Be tentative about recommendations.* It is good to be cautious unless your recommendations are strongly supported by the findings of your and other studies

6. *Don't hesitate to present selected naturalistic data as illustrations.* While qualitative findings are interpreted tentatively because they represent only a few people, these findings can be rich with meaning in their natural form. The insights and experiences of a few research participants can be very useful in illustrating a point that could possibly be relevant to larger numbers of people known to the readers.

7. *Recommendations should be directly connected and relevant to the overall research questions* (step 2). In other words, remember why this study was conducted in the first place when developing recommendations.

8. *Offer alternative recommendations on an important issue when one recommendation may not seem sufficient.* Sometimes, the more ideas that are offered, the more helpful the recommendations can be to readers. An example of alternative recommendations follows:

Example of Recommendations for a Staff Morale Study

A student conducted a study that found that staff morale generally was low, based on surveys of a sample of staff members. Instead of focusing on one overall recommendation for addressing morale, the findings suggested several ways that morale could possibly be improved, such as raising salaries, improving supervision, having more in-service training workshops, and reducing caseloads. All of these suggestions were mentioned by various staff in the survey.

A useful report will suggest all of these alternative recommendations and leave it up to the readers to select the ones that are most relevant to them.

---

9. *In suggestions for further research on the topic, be specific.* Indicate what could be done in a follow-up study and base your suggestions on what has been learned from your study.

10. *Make reference to the findings of other studies that either support or refute the recommendations of this study.* The more studies that can be considered on the same topic, the more that can be learned about it.

Task 4. Writing or Presenting the Report

Writing a research report is the next step in the research process. Like the other steps, it is very important to spend an adequate amount of time thinking about and planning this step. A poorly written research report can easily negate all of the hard work that has been completed on a study so far. A research report can take many different forms and formats, including any of the following (Morris et al., 1987): a traditional research report, an executive summary of a report, a special report for consumer use, a professional journal article, a brochure, or a poster presentation. Reports can be presented orally as well, for example, as a press conference, a community forum, or a staff meeting or workshop. Other forms are possible as well.

Considering Potential Readers of the Report

Let's concentrate here on research reports relevant to you in the producer role within a social agency. An initial question to consider in preparing the report is who the potential users or readers of will be. These may include funding agencies, board members, advisory committees, administrators, program service providers, legislators and other policy makers, current or potential clients, community groups, professional advocacy groups, professionals, and the public. Each of these groups is likely to have different needs related to a report. It is most important that the targeted readers find the report easy to read and relevant and useful to them. Since there are often different types of readers, different types of reports may need to be prepared for the same study.

It is a good idea to consult any stakeholders who have a special investment in the study and its results before the report is written. If the research report is developed by a social agency, the stakeholders could be agency administrators, funding agencies, clients, and so on. Morris and others (1987) suggest asking stakeholders several questions, such as:

- What do stakeholders want to know and why? What expectations do they have for the report?
- Will the stakeholders be answering any important questions or making any decisions about policies, programs, or practice, based on the findings of the report? If so, what are these questions or decisions?
- Are there any ethical or political considerations that need to be carefully thought out before preparing the report? For example, are there controversial issues that need to be addressed very cautiously and in a delicately balanced way? Is there any potential resistance to some of the findings that could come from particular groups?
- Should the results of the study be made available to clients? If so, in what form?
- How can the clients benefit from the findings? What can be done to maximize client benefits? (The participant action research approach gives special emphasis to the step of writing and disseminating the report.)

Contents of a Traditional Research Report

Now let's discuss the contents of a traditional research report, which is usually the most comprehensive and complete type of research report. This type of report is mostly relevant to you in the consumer role. Other shorter reports, such as an executive summary or press release, can be developed fairly easily from "cutting and pasting" and editing sections of a traditional report.

A traditional report contains a succinct description of all of the steps in the research process. An outline of a traditional report is as follows:

- A *title* that is brief and succinct and describes the focus of the study
- An *abstract* that summarizes the purpose of the study, methods and sampling approach used, findings, and recommendations
- *Background* information on the research problem or topic, including relevant viewpoints and theories that help to explain the topic and a literature review
- The *purposes of the study,* which include the overall research questions and/or the hypotheses
- A description of the *characteristics of the sample*
- The *sampling approach* used in selecting the sample
- A description of the *informed consent protocol* used

- A description of the *data collection approach* and the *specific measurements* that were used
- A *data analysis plan*
- The *findings*, including an overall summary, highlights of the most important findings in tables and graphs, and statistical results (The findings section is usually the longest and offers greater detail than the other sections of the report.)
- *Recommendations*
- *Limitations* of the study
- *Other important conclusions*
- A *bibliography* or reference list

Each of the above sections of a research report can be critiqued for quality. Several criteria are used to evaluate a research report. These criteria and the procedures for critiquing a research report have been covered throughout the book and are summarized in Appendix A.

Reporting on Qualitative Studies

Qualitative studies are likely to be reported differently than quantitative studies. Qualitative studies tend to be more difficult to publish in journals, partially because the findings are more exploratory, samples are smaller, and the word form findings usually require more space than quantitative studies. Also, many professional journals do not consider qualitative studies to be as rigorous in methodology as quantitative ones. Often, qualitative studies are published in books because the findings are so extensive.

Opportunities for publishing qualitative studies have diversified in recent years (Tutty, Rothery, & Grinnell, 1996). Besides books and Websites, these studies are often available through nonprint outlets such as videotapes and audiotapes, and their findings are increasingly used in staff training and conference presentations.

Tutty and colleagues (1996) suggest three criteria for determining whether qualitative studies should be disseminated. They include:

- Do the findings extend current theory pertinent to social work?
- To what extent are the findings useful in informing social work practice issues?
- Do the findings have strong validity and reliability?

Generally, the traditional format used in reporting qualitative findings is similar to the format used in quantitative studies. A report has four basic sections: (1) the introduction, (2) a description of the research design of the study, (3) findings, and (4) recommendations. The findings section of a qualitative study is the one that is most dissimilar to the findings section of a quantitative study. Instead of having findings presented in statistical form, a findings section is often organized by subheadings reflecting the major themes that were identified. Several illustrations of these themes are often described under each of these themes.

For example, a Canadian study by Antle and colleagues (2001) investigated parenting themes among families living with HIV/AIDS. Their findings section was organized by the following themes, which were the subheadings: Family Life as "Precious Time"; Preparing Children through Focused Parenting; HIV Makes Parenting Difficult; Future Care Planning, Guardianship, and Preparing Affected Fathers; and Parenting Children Who Are Infected and Affected: Differing Needs. Note that these themes are phrases that are already somewhat self-explanatory.

Task 5. Disseminating and Utilizing the Results

Too often, research reports are forgotten soon after they are written. They simply sit on a shelf and collect dust. Yet, arguably, disseminating the results of a study should be a prerequisite for claiming that a study has been successfully completed. Let's look at a variety of ways that research results can be disseminated and utilized.

Some research reports are presented in a form that automatically leads to dissemination. Having a study published in a professional journal is an example. In this case, the results can be disseminated widely to hundreds or even thousands of readers of the journal across the country and world. A press release published in a local newspaper can be another example of successful dissemination. Thousands of people are likely to read such an article as a news story. Also, a study that becomes a legislative report for a congressional hearing is intended to be disseminated to key policy makers. More often, however, a research report is not likely to be disseminated without persistent effort on the part of the researcher. In most cases, a study does not become a journal article, a news story, or a legislative report. Let's look at some of the ways we can disseminate and utilize the results of studies in various circumstances.

Utilization by Staff Members

The producer role has been described throughout the text as occurring primarily in a social agency where a social worker is employed. Agencies are likely to be conducting studies in a variety of areas, including community needs assessments, client satisfaction studies, evaluations of programs and practice, quality assurance, staff satisfaction initiatives, and so on. In all of these instances, the stakeholders include the staff members of the agency. For example, staff members can greatly benefit from the findings of a practice evaluation or a staff satisfaction study. They can also give helpful feedback to the agency on hearing about these findings.

Dissemination of the results of a study can occur in numerous ways. Staff satisfaction findings, for example, offer an excellent opportunity for a discussion of varying perceptions of the agency and its programs between the administrators and staff members. Staff can offer suggestions for improving their work conditions, supervision, and benefits as well. These discussions can help staff feel more committed to their agency's mission and appreciative of their work environment. In a sense, these studies can be used to boost satisfaction and morale. Dissemination of such results could occur in a staff meeting, a personnel committee, or a staff retreat. Those who present these findings must be prepared to effectively handle any staff anger or resentment that may emerge related to areas of staff dissatisfaction.

Staff members also have much at stake in hearing the results of a practice or program evaluation. Evaluation findings can be quite useful in helping staff examine their practice, consider alternative approaches, and strengthen their professional performance in the agency. Dissemination of evaluation findings can occur in numerous ways, including staff retreats and workshops, in-service training sessions, quality assurance deliberations, and supervisory sessions.

Administrative staff of these agencies will also be very likely to utilize the findings of such studies. They can use them for documenting program effectiveness in reports to funding agencies. They can incorporate such findings into agency brochures and annual reports that promote the agency's identity and also can pass them on in presentations to board members. These findings can be useful in supporting agency accreditation efforts, government licensing of programs, auditing, program monitoring, and quality assurance.

Informing and Empowering Clients

Another group of stakeholders central to the agency are the clients. Hopefully, every agency-sponsored study has as its ultimate purpose benefiting the clients. Why? Because this is the primary reason why an agency is in business. All kinds of agency studies can be relevant to share with clients, even though confidentiality and other privacy matters must be arranged. The results of a community needs assessment, for example, can inform clients of the reported needs of a larger group of clients and potential clients, and they can respond by validating, challenging, or adding to these findings. Clients are in a unique position to offer insights into the needs of clients generally.

As another example, evaluation studies inform clients how well the agency is performing and the extent to which clients are achieving their goals. Client satisfaction findings inform them of the satisfaction levels of other clients and remind them of the ways that their agency is beneficial to them. Findings reflecting client dissatisfaction can also open up fruitful discussions about program areas needing improvement. These discussions also provide the agency with a special opportunity to remind clients of the importance of their voices. By responding favorably to some of their concerns, the agency sends a message to clients that they are important to consider.

Prior to disseminating research findings to clients, an agency must give careful attention to confidentiality issues and other privacy protection requirements. Clients need to know that they are not being exposed arbitrarily to outsiders and that their lives are being considered with the highest regard and respect. Keeping this in mind, disseminating research results to clients can occur in numerous creative ways. Individual and group counseling sessions can be a place for reporting on pertinent evaluation findings. Client brochures and information sheets can be developed to highlight findings of particular relevance to new clients. Community forums and other public meetings should be considered for reporting on and dialoguing about findings of relevance to the public. Client advisory boards can be involved in both discussing findings and helping disseminate them to other clients. And all of these and other types of dissemination can be an enormous benefit to clients and the larger community. Disseminating research results should be seen as an effective strategy for building closer partnerships between the agency and its clients.

Reporting on the Research and the Consumer Role

The consumer of research reports should have an overall understanding of what a good report looks like and when a report may have inherent weaknesses. Some specific questions should be asked that relate to the topics covered in the chapter.

1. Can you give a summary statement of the major findings?
2. Were the findings presented clearly?
3. Were the tables easy to understand? If not, can you describe what was unclear or missing? Also, can you identify the variables that are presented in each table?
4. Are the findings useful to social workers? In what ways can a social worker like you use these findings in your practice?
5. Can you identify the recommendations in the Discussion Section? For each recommendation, can you identify a specific finding, if any, that supports this recommendation. In your opinion, is each recommendation adequately supported by a specific finding?
6. Are limitations of the study discussed? What are these limitations? Are any obvious limitations not reported or mentioned?
7. What recommendations were useful to social workers? How can these recommendations be implemented by a social worker like you?

Chapter Reflections

Values and Ethics, Diversity, At-Risk Groups, and Social Justice

Ethical issues are important to consider in preparing a research report, whether written or oral. Several questions can be asked. Is the description of the research design represented accurately and completely in the final report? Are the specific procedures that were used in selecting a sample and collecting data accurately described? Also, are the findings represented accurately? Findings that refute a hypothesis, for example, may be as important as supporting evidence. Finally, are the recommendations based on the findings, or are they distorted in favor of the researcher's biases?

Diversity and social justice issues are also extremely relevant in preparing a final report. For example, have the various stakeholders been consulted for their ideas on what they would like to have included in a report? Will the report be readable to all stakeholders? Is a report being prepared for clients and others who can directly benefit from it? Is such a report delivered to them in a manner that is most useful to them rather than as an afterthought?

Discussion Questions

1. Select a research article from a social work journal. Critique its Findings Section by answering the following questions:
   - Provide a summary statement of the major findings in your own words.
   - Were the findings presented clearly? If not, what was unclear? How could they be presented more clearly?
   - Were the tables easy to understand? If not, explain how they were unclear. Can you identify the variables that are presented in each table?
   - How are the findings useful to you as a social worker?
2. Using the same research article used to answer question 1, critique the Discussion or Recommendations Section by answering the following questions:
   A. Identify the recommendations in the Discussion Section, as follows:
      - Identify each recommendation.
      - Identify the specific finding, if any, that supports each recommendation.
      - In your opinion, decide if each recommendation is adequately supported by a specific finding. If it is not, explain why not.
   B. Are the limitations of the study discussed? What are these limitations?
   C. What recommendations were useful to you as a social worker?

References

Antle, B., Wells, L., Goldie, R., DeMatteo, D., & King, S. (2001). Challenges of parenting for families living with HIV/AIDS. *Social Work, 46*(2), 159–169.

Leary, A. (2003). *Room in the Inn: Exploring church involvement in serving the homeless.* Student research project, University of North Carolina, Charlotte.

Microsoft Excel. (2002). Microsoft Corporation, 1985–2001.

Moore, K., Chalk, R., Scarpa, J., & Vandivere, S. (2002). Family strengths: Often overlooked, but real. *Child Trends Research Brief.* Washington, D.C.: Child Trends. Also available online at www.childtrends.org.

Morris, L. L., Fitz-Gibbon, C. T., & Freeman M. (1987). *How to communicate evaluation findings.* Newbury Park, CA: Sage.

O'Neill, J. (2003). Nearly all members linked to internet. *NASW News, 48*(2), 9.

Rome, S. (1997). The child welfare choice: An analysis of social work students' career plans. *Journal of Baccalaureate Social Work, 3*(1), 31–48.

Smith, C. (1996). The link between childhood maltreatment and teenage pregnancy. *Social Work Research, 20*(3), 131–141.

Tutty, L., Rothery, M., & Grinnell, R. (1996). *Qualitative research for social workers.* Boston: Allyn and Bacon.

Wiener, L., & Siegel, K. (1990). Social workers' comfort in providing services to AIDS patients. *Social Work, 35*(1), 18–25.

The Consumer Role
Questions to Ask When
Critiquing a Research Report

Step 1: Understanding the Research Topic (Chapter 4)

1. Is this research topic or problem relevant to social workers? How is it relevant? Is it relevant to your interests? How can this study help you?
2. Do you understand what the research topic or problem is? Can you explain it to others in an understandable way?
3. Do you think that the research topic or problem is clearly and concisely stated? If not, what is not clear? Is important information missing? Or is the terminology or subject matter largely foreign to you? Or possibly the article was written poorly?
4. Do you detect any biases in how the research topic or problem is described? Possibly you may think that it favors one view and leaves out another. If so, can you identify the viewpoints that are left out? Or possibly important groups of people that are left out or omitted from the problem description? This could be an important diversity issue to consider.
5. Can you detect any theories, whether they were identified as theories or not? An important component of the research problem is a description of any explanations, or theories, that are given for the causes.
6. Do you think that the review of the literature is adequate? The literature review is presented to help describe the research problem. Some of the articles in a literature review are studies conducted on the topic, while others may be conceptual or theoretical contributions. It is almost impossible to fully know whether the literature is adequate without being familiar with the literature on a particular topic. Four simple criteria follow that offer a starting point for evaluating a literature review when you are not at all familiar with the topic:
   - Are there a reasonable *number of references* cited? Usually, about eight to ten references is reasonable, even though the number will vary with the topic.
   - Are these references *fairly recent*, such as within ten years of when the study was conducted? Count back ten years from the date the study was likely conducted, not ten years from today. Keep in mind that the study was likely conducted as long as two years before the publication date of the study.
   - Does the literature *focus on the research topic* and not on some peripheral or unrelated topics?
   - Does the researcher attempt to describe *differing viewpoints* that are cited in the literature? Any views that are different from the researcher's may be easy to identify, because they are not usually presented as persuasively as the researcher's.

Step 2: Focusing the Research Study (Chapter 6)

1. What are the research questions or the hypotheses that are explored in the study? Usually, a study focuses on either research questions or hypotheses and occasionally on both.
2. If research questions are identified, what seem to be the most important concepts and variables in the study? These are often identified in the research questions.
3. If hypotheses are being explored, what are the independent and dependent variables of each hypothesis? Also, are any extraneous variables identified, and if so, does the researcher attempt to control them? In addition, can you detect any important extraneous variables that are not identified?
4. Are the research questions or hypotheses stated clearly? Anticipate the possibility that they are unclear or confusing. For example, often researchers do not describe the general research questions in a question format. Instead, they write them as a purpose statement of the study. While this can be confusing, it can be fairly easy to convert a purpose statement into a question format.
5. Do you detect any biases in how the research questions or hypotheses are described? Possibly the researcher left out an important group or an important concern of some groups. If so, can you identify the groups or issues that are left out? Diversity issues are most important to consider during this step of the study, since concerns important to some groups can be overlooked. It is important to realize that these omissions could be biases, intentional or inadvertent, of the researcher.
6. Is this research focus relevant to social workers? How is it relevant? Is it relevant to your interests? Most important, how can these research questions or hypotheses help you as a social worker? If the focus does not have much relevance to your work, you may want to discontinue reading this study and move on to one that is more relevant and useful to you.

Step 3: Designing the Study (Chapters 7–11)

1. What sampling approach did the researcher use? Is it a probability or nonprobability type of sampling approach? Can you describe the specific procedures followed in selecting the sample?
2. Is the population of interest to the researcher clearly identified? If not, what do you think the population is? Can the findings about the sample be generalized with any degree of confidence to this population?
3. Is the sample made up of a diversity of people? What relevant groups may be left out, if any?
4. What data collection approach is used (e.g., participant observation, interview, experiment, etc.)? Can you describe the specific procedures or steps that were followed in collecting the data? What are the advantages and limitations of the data collection approach for the topic being researched?
5. Does the data collection approach seem appropriate for the group studied? If not, what seems problematic?

6. Is there an adequate description of how each of the important variables is defined and measured? Can you explain what each of these definitions and measures are?

Step 4: Collecting the Data (Chapter 12)

1. If either interviews or observations are used as data collection approaches, is there any evidence in the research report that the data collectors were trained to collect data for this study? If so, what was the nature and extent of their training, if reported?
2. Was anything noted in the report about selecting research interviewers with particular demographic characteristics (e.g., race, gender, age, etc.) that match the characteristics of the research participants? If so, do you think that this was a good idea? Why or why not?
3. Does the report indicate that the data collectors have any special qualifications, such as research skills, work experience, or knowledge about the topic, that could facilitate data collection? If so, do you think this was helpful? Why or why not?

Step 5: Analyzing the Data (Chapters 13–15)

1. If *quantitative* data analysis was used, what specific statistical techniques were utilized to analyze the data? For example, were any of the following statistics mentioned: percentages, mean scores, standard deviation, chi-square, *t*-test, correlation, or ANOVA?
2. If *qualitative* data analysis was used, what specific data analysis strategies were employed? For example, did the researcher prepare a case study, conduct a theme analysis, or construct general response categories to summarize responses to open-ended questions?

Step 6: Preparing a Report (Chapter 16)

1. Can you give a summary statement of the *major* findings?
2. Were the findings presented clearly?
3. Were the tables easy to understand? If not, can you describe what was unclear or missing? Can you identify the variables that are presented in each table?
4. Are the findings useful to social workers? In what ways can a social worker like you use these findings in your practice?
5. Can you identify the recommendations in the Discussion Section? For each recommendation, can you identify a specific finding, if any, that supports this recommendation? In your opinion, is each recommendation adequately supported by a specific finding in the study?
6. What recommendations are useful to social workers? How can these recommendations be implemented by a social worker like you?
7. Are the limitations of the study discussed? What are these limitations? Are any obvious limitations not reported or mentioned?

Ethical Standards of the National Association of Social Workers

Approved by the 1996 NASW Delegate Assembly and revised by the 1999 NASW Delegate Assembly

Ethical Standards

The following ethical standards are relevant to the professional activities of all so-cial workers. These standards concern (1) social workers' ethical responsibilities to clients, (2) social workers' ethical responsibilities to colleagues, (3) social workers' ethical responsibilities in practice settings, (4) social workers' ethical responsibilities as professionals, (5) social workers' ethical responsibilities to the social work profession, and (6) social workers' ethical responsibilities to the broader society.

Some of the standards that follow are enforceable guidelines for professional conduct, and some are aspirational. The extent to which each standard is enforce-able is a matter of professional judgment to be exercised by those responsible for reviewing alleged violations of ethical standards.

1. Social Workers' Ethical Responsibilities to Clients

1.01 Commitment to Clients

Social workers' primary responsibility is to promote the well-being of clients. In general, clients' interests are primary. However, social workers' responsibility to the larger society or specific legal obligations may on limited occasions supersede the loyalty owed clients, and clients should be so advised. (Examples include when a social worker is required by law to report that a client has abused a child or has threatened to harm self or others.)

1.02 Self-Determination

Social workers respect and promote the right of clients to self-determination and assist clients in their efforts to identify and clarify their goals. Social workers may limit clients' right to self-determination when, in the social workers' professional judgment, clients' actions or potential actions pose a serious, foreseeable, and im-minent risk to themselves or others.

1.03 Informed Consent

(a) Social workers should provide services to clients only in the context of a pro-fessional relationship based, when appropriate, on valid informed consent.

Social workers should use clear and understandable language to inform clients of the purpose of the services, risks related to the services, limits to services because of the requirements of a third-party payer, relevant costs, reasonable alternatives, clients' right to refuse or withdraw consent, and the time frame covered by the consent. Social workers should provide clients with an opportunity to ask questions.

(b) In instances when clients are not literate or have difficulty understanding the primary language used in the practice setting, social workers should take steps to ensure clients' comprehension. This may include providing clients with a detailed verbal explanation or arranging for a qualified interpreter or translator whenever possible.

(c) In instances when clients lack the capacity to provide informed consent, social workers should protect clients' interests by seeking permission from an appropriate third party, informing clients consistent with the clients' level of understanding. In such instances social workers should seek to ensure that the third party acts in a manner consistent with clients' wishes and interests. Social workers should take reasonable steps to enhance such clients' ability to give informed consent.

(d) In instances when clients are receiving services involuntarily, social workers should provide information about the nature and extent of services and about the extent of clients' right to refuse service.

(e) Social workers who provide services via electronic media (such as computer, telephone, radio, and television) should inform recipients of the limitations and risks associated with such services.

(f) Social workers should obtain clients' informed consent before audiotaping or videotaping clients or permitting observation of services to clients by a third party.

1.04 Competence

(a) Social workers should provide services and represent themselves as competent only within the boundaries of their education, training, license, certification, consultation received, supervised experience, or other relevant professional experience.

(b) Social workers should provide services in substantive areas or use intervention techniques or approaches that are new to them only after engaging in appropriate study, training, consultation, and supervision from people who are competent in those interventions or techniques.

(c) When generally recognized standards do not exist with respect to an emerging area of practice, social workers should exercise careful judgment and take responsible steps (including appropriate education, research, training, consultation, and supervision) to ensure the competence of their work and to protect clients from harm.

1.05 Cultural Competence and Social Diversity

(a) Social workers should understand culture and its function in human behavior and society, recognizing the strengths that exist in all cultures.

(b) Social workers should have a knowledge base of their clients' cultures and be able to demonstrate competence in the provision of services that are sensitive to clients' cultures and to differences among people and cultural groups.

(c) Social workers should obtain education about and seek to understand the nature of social diversity and oppression with respect to race, ethnicity, national origin, color, sex, sexual orientation, age, marital status, political belief, religion, and mental or physical disability.

1.06 Conflicts of Interest

(a) Social workers should be alert to and avoid conflicts of interest that interfere with the exercise of professional discretion and impartial judgment. Social workers should inform clients when a real or potential conflict of interest arises and take reasonable steps to resolve the issue in a manner that makes the clients' interests primary and protects clients' interests to the greatest extent possible. In some cases, protecting clients' interests may require termination of the professional relationship with proper referral of the client.

(b) Social workers should not take unfair advantage of any professional relationship or exploit others to further their personal, religious, political, or business interests.

(c) Social workers should not engage in dual or multiple relationships with clients or former clients in which there is a risk of exploitation or potential harm to the client. In instances when dual or multiple relationships are unavoidable, social workers should take steps to protect clients and are responsible for setting clear, appropriate, and culturally sensitive boundaries. (Dual or multiple relationships occur when social workers relate to clients in more than one relationship, whether professional, social, or business. Dual or multiple relationships can occur simultaneously or consecutively.)

(d) When social workers provide services to two or more people who have a relationship with each other (for example, couples, family members), social workers should clarify with all parties which individuals will be considered clients and the nature of social workers' professional obligations to the various individuals who are receiving services. Social workers who anticipate a conflict of interest among the individuals receiving services or who anticipate having to perform in potentially conflicting roles (for example, when a social worker is asked to testify in a child custody dispute or divorce proceedings involving clients) should clarify their role with the parties involved and take appropriate action to minimize any conflict of interest.

1.07 Privacy and Confidentiality

(a) Social workers should respect clients' right to privacy. Social workers should not solicit private information from clients unless it is essential to providing services or conducting social work evaluation or research. Once private information is shared, standards of confidentiality apply.

(b) Social workers may disclose confidential information when appropriate with valid consent from a client or a person legally authorized to consent on behalf of a client.

(c) Social workers should protect the confidentiality of all information obtained in the course of professional service, except for compelling professional reasons. The general expectation that social workers will keep information confidential does not apply when disclosure is necessary to prevent serious, foreseeable, and imminent harm to a client or other identifiable person. In all instances, social workers should disclose the least amount of confidential information necessary to achieve the desired purpose; only information that is directly relevant to the purpose for which the disclosure is made should be revealed.

(d) Social workers should inform clients, to the extent possible, about the disclosure of confidential information and the potential consequences, when feasible before the disclosure is made. This applies whether social workers disclose confidential information on the basis of a legal requirement or client consent.

(e) Social workers should discuss with clients and other interested parties the nature of confidentiality and limitations of clients' right to confidentiality. Social workers should review with clients circumstances where confidential information may be requested and where disclosure of confidential information may be legally required. This discussion should occur as soon as possible in the social worker-client relationship and as needed throughout the course of the relationship.

(f) When social workers provide counseling services to families, couples, or groups, social workers should seek agreement among the parties involved concerning each individual's right to confidentiality and obligation to preserve the confidentiality of information shared by others. Social workers should inform participants in family, couples, or group counseling that social workers cannot guarantee that all participants will honor such agreements.

(g) Social workers should inform clients involved in family, couples, marital, or group counseling of the social worker's, employer's, and agency's policy concerning the social worker's disclosure of confidential information among the parties involved in the counseling.

(h) Social workers should not disclose confidential information to third-party payers unless clients have authorized such disclosure.

(i) Social workers should not discuss confidential information in any setting unless privacy can be ensured. Social workers should not discuss confidential information in public or semipublic areas such as hallways, waiting rooms, elevators, and restaurants.

(j) Social workers should protect the confidentiality of clients during legal proceedings to the extent permitted by law. When a court of law or other legally authorized body orders social workers to disclose confidential or privileged information without a client's consent and such disclosure could cause harm to the client, social workers should request that the court withdraw the order or limit the order as narrowly as possible or maintain the records under seal, unavailable for public inspection.

(k) Social workers should protect the confidentiality of clients when responding to requests from members of the media.

(l) Social workers should protect the confidentiality of clients' written and electronic records and other sensitive information. Social workers should take reasonable steps to ensure that clients' records are stored in a secure location and that clients' records are not available to others who are not authorized to have access.

(m) Social workers should take precautions to ensure and maintain the confidentiality of information transmitted to other parties through the use of computers, electronic mail, facsimile machines, telephones and telephone answering machines, and other electronic or computer technology. Disclosure of identifying information should be avoided whenever possible.

(n) Social workers should transfer or dispose of clients' records in a manner that protects clients' confidentiality and is consistent with state statutes governing records and social work licensure.

(o) Social workers should take reasonable precautions to protect client confidentiality in the event of the social worker's termination of practice, incapacitation, or death.

(p) Social workers should not disclose identifying information when discussing clients for teaching or training purposes unless the client has consented to disclosure of confidential information.

(q) Social workers should not disclose identifying information when discussing clients with consultants unless the client has consented to disclosure of confidential information or there is a compelling need for such disclosure.

(r) Social workers should protect the confidentiality of deceased clients consistent with the preceding standards.

1.08 Access to Records

(a) Social workers should provide clients with reasonable access to records concerning the clients. Social workers who are concerned that clients' access to their records could cause serious misunderstanding or harm to the client should provide assistance in interpreting the records and consultation with the client regarding the records. Social workers should limit clients' access to their records, or portions of their records, only in exceptional circumstances when there is compelling evidence that such access would cause serious harm to the client. Both clients' requests and the rationale for withholding some or all of the record should be documented in clients' files.

(b) When providing clients with access to their records, social workers should take steps to protect the confidentiality of other individuals identified or discussed in such records.

1.09 Sexual Relationships

(a) Social workers should under no circumstances engage in sexual activities or sexual contact with current clients, whether such contact is consensual or forced.

(b) Social workers should not engage in sexual activities or sexual contact with clients' relatives or other individuals with whom clients maintain a close personal relationship when there is a risk of exploitation or potential harm to the client. Sexual activity or sexual contact with clients' relatives or other individuals with whom clients maintain a personal relationship has the potential to be harmful to the client and may make it difficult for the social worker and client to maintain appropriate professional boundaries. Social workers—not their clients, their clients' relatives, or other individuals with whom the client maintains a personal relationship—assume the full burden for setting clear, appropriate, and culturally sensitive boundaries.

(c) Social workers should not engage in sexual activities or sexual contact with former clients because of the potential for harm to the client. If social workers engage in conduct contrary to this prohibition or claim that an exception to this prohibition is warranted because of extraordinary circumstances, it is social workers—not their clients—who assume the full burden of demonstrating that the former client has not been exploited, coerced, or manipulated, intentionally or unintentionally.

(d) Social workers should not provide clinical services to individuals with whom they have had a prior sexual relationship. Providing clinical services to a former sexual partner has the potential to be harmful to the individual and is likely to make it difficult for the social worker and individual to maintain appropriate professional boundaries.

1.10 Physical Contact
Social workers should not engage in physical contact with clients when there is a possibility of psychological harm to the client as a result of the contact (such as cradling or caressing clients). Social workers who engage in appropriate physical contact with clients are responsible for setting clear, appropriate, and culturally sensitive boundaries that govern such physical contact.

1.11 Sexual Harassment
Social workers should not sexually harass clients. Sexual harassment includes sexual advances, sexual solicitation, requests for sexual favors, and other verbal or physical conduct of a sexual nature.

1.12 Derogatory Language
Social workers should not use derogatory language in their written or verbal communications to or about clients. Social workers should use accurate and respectful language in all communications to and about clients.

1.13 Payment for Services
(a) When setting fees, social workers should ensure that the fees are fair, reasonable, and commensurate with the services performed. Consideration should be given to clients' ability to pay.

(b) Social workers should avoid accepting goods or services from clients as payment for professional services. Bartering arrangements, particularly involving services, create the potential for conflicts of interest, exploitation, and inappropriate boundaries in social workers' relationships with clients. Social workers should explore and may participate in bartering only in very limited circumstances when it can be demonstrated that such arrangements are an accepted practice among professionals in the local community, considered to be essential for the provision of services, negotiated without coercion, and entered into at the client's initiative and with the client's informed consent. Social workers who accept goods or services from clients as payment for professional services assume the full burden of demonstrating that this arrangement will not be detrimental to the client or the professional relationship.

(c) Social workers should not solicit a private fee or other remuneration for providing services to clients who are entitled to such available services through the social workers' employer or agency.

1.14 Clients Who Lack Decision-Making Capacity

When social workers act on behalf of clients who lack the capacity to make informed decisions, social workers should take reasonable steps to safeguard the interests and rights of those clients.

1.15 Interruption of Services

Social workers should make reasonable efforts to ensure continuity of services in the event that services are interrupted by factors such as unavailability, relocation, illness, disability, or death.

1.16 Termination of Services

(a) Social workers should terminate services to clients and professional relationships with them when such services and relationships are no longer required or no longer serve the clients' needs or interests.

(b) Social workers should take reasonable steps to avoid abandoning clients who are still in need of services. Social workers should withdraw services precipitously only under unusual circumstances, giving careful consideration to all factors in the situation and taking care to minimize possible adverse effects. Social workers should assist in making appropriate arrangements for continuation of services when necessary.

(c) Social workers in fee-for-service settings may terminate services to clients who are not paying an overdue balance if the financial contractual arrangements have been made clear to the client, if the client does not pose an imminent danger to self or others, and if the clinical and other consequences of the current nonpayment have been addressed and discussed with the client.

(d) Social workers should not terminate services to pursue a social, financial, or sexual relationship with a client.

(e) Social workers who anticipate the termination or interruption of services to clients should notify clients promptly and seek the transfer, referral, or continuation of services in relation to the clients' needs and preferences.

(f) Social workers who are leaving an employment setting should inform clients of appropriate options for the continuation of services and of the benefits and risks of the options.

2. Social Workers' Ethical Responsibilities to Colleagues

2.01 Respect

(a) Social workers should treat colleagues with respect and should represent accurately and fairly the qualifications, views, and obligations of colleagues.

(b) Social workers should avoid unwarranted negative criticism of colleagues in communications with clients or with other professionals. Unwarranted negative criticism may include demeaning comments that refer to colleagues' level of competence or to individuals' attributes such as race, ethnicity, national origin, color, sex, sexual orientation, age, marital status, political belief, religion, and mental or physical disability.

(c) Social workers should cooperate with social work colleagues and with colleagues of other professions when such cooperation serves the well-being of clients.

2.02 Confidentiality

Social workers should respect confidential information shared by colleagues in the course of their professional relationships and transactions. Social workers should ensure that such colleagues understand social workers' obligation to respect confidentiality and any exceptions related to it.

2.03 Interdisciplinary Collaboration

(a) Social workers who are members of an interdisciplinary team should participate in and contribute to decisions that affect the well-being of clients by drawing on the perspectives, values, and experiences of the social work profession. Professional and ethical obligations of the interdisciplinary team as a whole and of its individual members should be clearly established.

(b) Social workers for whom a team decision raises ethical concerns should attempt to resolve the disagreement through appropriate channels. If the disagreement cannot be resolved, social workers should pursue other avenues to address their concerns consistent with client well-being.

2.04 Disputes Involving Colleagues

(a) Social workers should not take advantage of a dispute between a colleague and an employer to obtain a position or otherwise advance the social worker's own interests.

(b) Social workers should not exploit clients in disputes with colleagues or engage clients in any inappropriate discussion of conflicts between social workers and their colleagues.

2.05 Consultation

(a) Social workers should seek the advice and counsel of colleagues whenever such consultation is in the best interests of clients.

(b) Social workers should keep themselves informed about colleagues' areas of expertise and competencies. Social workers should seek consultation only from colleagues who have demonstrated knowledge, expertise, and competence related to the subject of the consultation.

(c) When consulting with colleagues about clients, social workers should disclose the least amount of information necessary to achieve the purposes of the consultation.

2.06 Referral for Services

(a) Social workers should refer clients to other professionals when the other professionals' specialized knowledge or expertise is needed to serve clients fully or when social workers believe that they are not being effective or making reasonable progress with clients and that additional service is required.

(b) Social workers who refer clients to other professionals should take appropriate steps to facilitate an orderly transfer of responsibility. Social workers who refer clients to other professionals should disclose, with clients' consent, all pertinent information to the new service providers.

(c) Social workers are prohibited from giving or receiving payment for a referral when no professional service is provided by the referring social worker.

2.07 Sexual Relationships

(a) Social workers who function as supervisors or educators should not engage in sexual activities or contact with supervisees, students, trainees, or other colleagues over whom they exercise professional authority.

(b) Social workers should avoid engaging in sexual relationships with colleagues when there is potential for a conflict of interest. Social workers who become involved in, or anticipate becoming involved in, a sexual relationship with a colleague have a duty to transfer professional responsibilities, when necessary, to avoid a conflict of interest.

2.08 Sexual Harassment

Social workers should not sexually harass supervisees, students, trainees, or colleagues. Sexual harassment includes sexual advances, sexual solicitation, requests for sexual favors, and other verbal or physical conduct of a sexual nature.

2.09 Impairment of Colleagues

(a) Social workers who have direct knowledge of a social work colleague's impairment that is due to personal problems, psychosocial distress, substance abuse, or mental health difficulties and that interferes with practice effectiveness should consult with that colleague when feasible and assist the colleague in taking remedial action.

(b) Social workers who believe that a social work colleague's impairment interferes with practice effectiveness and that the colleague has not taken adequate steps to address the impairment should take action through appropriate channels established by employers, agencies, NASW, licensing and regulatory bodies, and other professional organizations.

2.10 Incompetence of Colleagues

(a) Social workers who have direct knowledge of a social work colleague's incompetence should consult with that colleague when feasible and assist the colleague in taking remedial action.

(b) Social workers who believe that a social work colleague is incompetent and has not taken adequate steps to address the incompetence should take action through appropriate channels established by employers, agencies, NASW, licensing and regulatory bodies, and other professional organizations.

2.11 Unethical Conduct of Colleagues

(a) Social workers should take adequate measures to discourage, prevent, expose, and correct the unethical conduct of colleagues.

(b) Social workers should be knowledgeable about established policies and procedures for handling concerns about colleagues' unethical behavior. Social workers should be familiar with national, state, and local procedures for handling ethics complaints. These include policies and procedures created by NASW, licensing and regulatory bodies, employers, agencies, and other professional organizations.

(c) Social workers who believe that a colleague has acted unethically should seek resolution by discussing their concerns with the colleague when feasible and when such discussion is likely to be productive.

(d) When necessary, social workers who believe that a colleague has acted unethically should take action through appropriate formal channels (such as contacting a state licensing board or regulatory body, an NASW committee on inquiry, or other professional ethics committees).

(e) Social workers should defend and assist colleagues who are unjustly charged with unethical conduct.

3. Social Workers' Ethical Responsibilities in Practice Settings

3.01 Supervision and Consultation

(a) Social workers who provide supervision or consultation should have the necessary knowledge and skill to supervise or consult appropriately and should do so only within their areas of knowledge and competence.

(b) Social workers who provide supervision or consultation are responsible for setting clear, appropriate, and culturally sensitive boundaries.

(c) Social workers should not engage in any dual or multiple relationships with supervisees in which there is a risk of exploitation of or potential harm to the supervisee.

(d) Social workers who provide supervision should evaluate supervisees' performance in a manner that is fair and respectful.

3.02 Education and Training

(a) Social workers who function as educators, field instructors for students, or trainers should provide instruction only within their areas of knowledge and competence and should provide instruction based on the most current information and knowledge available in the profession.

(b) Social workers who function as educators or field instructors for students should evaluate students' performance in a manner that is fair and respectful.

(c) Social workers who function as educators or field instructors for students should take reasonable steps to ensure that clients are routinely informed when services are being provided by students.

(d) Social workers who function as educators or field instructors for students should not engage in any dual or multiple relationships with students in which there is a risk of exploitation or potential harm to the student. Social work educators and field instructors are responsible for setting clear, appropriate, and culturally sensitive boundaries.

3.03 Performance Evaluation

Social workers who have responsibility for evaluating the performance of others should fulfill such responsibility in a fair and considerate manner and on the basis of clearly stated criteria.

3.04 Client Records

(a) Social workers should take reasonable steps to ensure that documentation in records is accurate and reflects the services provided.

(b) Social workers should include sufficient and timely documentation in records to facilitate the delivery of services and to ensure continuity of services provided to clients in the future.

(c) Social workers' documentation should protect clients' privacy to the extent that is possible and appropriate and should include only information that is directly relevant to the delivery of services.

(d) Social workers should store records following the termination of services to ensure reasonable future access. Records should be maintained for the number of years required by state statutes or relevant contracts.

3.05 Billing

Social workers should establish and maintain billing practices that accurately reflect the nature and extent of services provided and that identify who provided the service in the practice setting.

3.06 Client Transfer

(a) When an individual who is receiving services from another agency or colleague contacts a social worker for services, the social worker should carefully consider the client's needs before agreeing to provide services. To minimize possible confusion and conflict, social workers should discuss with potential clients the nature of the clients' current relationship with other service providers and the implications, including possible benefits or risks, of entering into a relationship with a new service provider.

(b) If a new client has been served by another agency or colleague, social workers should discuss with the client whether consultation with the previous service provider is in the client's best interest.

3.07 Administration

(a) Social work administrators should advocate within and outside their agencies for adequate resources to meet clients' needs.

(b) Social workers should advocate for resource allocation procedures that are open and fair. When not all clients' needs can be met, an allocation procedure should be developed that is nondiscriminatory and based on appropriate and consistently applied principles.

(c) Social workers who are administrators should take reasonable steps to ensure that adequate agency or organizational resources are available to provide appropriate staff supervision.

(d) Social work administrators should take reasonable steps to ensure that the working environment for which they are responsible is consistent with and encourages compliance with the NASW Code of Ethics. Social work administrators should take reasonable steps to eliminate any conditions in their organizations that violate, interfere with, or discourage compliance with the Code.

3.08 Continuing Education and Staff Development

Social work administrators and supervisors should take reasonable steps to provide or arrange for continuing education and staff development for all staff for whom they are responsible. Continuing education and staff development should address current knowledge and emerging developments related to social work practice and ethics.

3.09 Commitments to Employers

(a) Social workers generally should adhere to commitments made to employers and employing organizations.

(b) Social workers should work to improve employing agencies' policies and procedures and the efficiency and effectiveness of their services.

(c) Social workers should take reasonable steps to ensure that employers are aware of social workers' ethical obligations as set forth in the NASW Code of Ethics and of the implications of those obligations for social work practice.

(d) Social workers should not allow an employing organization's policies, procedures, regulations, or administrative orders to interfere with their ethical practice of social work. Social workers should take reasonable steps to ensure that their employing organizations' practices are consistent with the NASW Code of Ethics.

(e) Social workers should act to prevent and eliminate discrimination in the employing organization's work assignments and in its employment policies and practices.

(f) Social workers should accept employment or arrange student field placements only in organizations that exercise fair personnel practices.

(g) Social workers should be diligent stewards of the resources of their employing organizations, wisely conserving funds where appropriate and never misappropriating funds or using them for unintended purposes.

3.10 Labor-Management Disputes

(a) Social workers may engage in organized action, including the formation of and participation in labor unions, to improve services to clients and working conditions.

(b) The actions of social workers who are involved in labor-management disputes, job actions, or labor strikes should be guided by the profession's values, ethical principles, and ethical standards. Reasonable differences of opinion exist among social workers concerning their primary obligation as professionals during an actual or threatened labor strike or job action. Social workers should carefully examine relevant issues and their possible impact on clients before deciding on a course of action.

4. Social Workers' Ethical Responsibilities as Professionals

4.01 Competence

(a) Social workers should accept responsibility or employment only on the basis of existing competence or the intention to acquire the necessary competence.

(b) Social workers should strive to become and remain proficient in professional practice and the performance of professional functions. Social workers should critically examine and keep current with emerging knowledge relevant to social work. Social workers should routinely review the professional literature and participate in continuing education relevant to social work practice and social work ethics.

(c) Social workers should base practice on recognized knowledge, including empirically based knowledge, relevant to social work and social work ethics.

4.02 Discrimination

Social workers should not practice, condone, facilitate, or collaborate with any form of discrimination on the basis of race, ethnicity, national origin, color, sex, sexual orientation, age, marital status, political belief, religion, or mental or physical disability.

4.03 Private Conduct

Social workers should not permit their private conduct to interfere with their ability to fulfill their professional responsibilities.

4.04 Dishonesty, Fraud, and Deception

Social workers should not participate in, condone, or be associated with dishonesty, fraud, or deception.

4.05 Impairment

(a) Social workers should not allow their own personal problems, psychosocial distress, legal problems, substance abuse, or mental health difficulties to interfere with their professional judgment and performance or to jeopardize the best interests of people for whom they have a professional responsibility.

(b) Social workers whose personal problems, psychosocial distress, legal problems, substance abuse, or mental health difficulties interfere with their professional judgment and performance should immediately seek consultation and take appropriate remedial action by seeking professional help, making adjustments in workload, terminating practice, or taking any other steps necessary to protect clients and others.

4.06 Misrepresentation

(a) Social workers should make clear distinctions between statements made and actions engaged in as a private individual and as a representative of the social work profession, a professional social work organization, or the social worker's employing agency.

(b) Social workers who speak on behalf of professional social work organizations should accurately represent the official and authorized positions of the organizations.

(c) Social workers should ensure that their representations to clients, agencies, and the public of professional qualifications, credentials, education, competence, affiliations, services provided, or results to be achieved are accurate. Social workers should claim only those relevant professional credentials they actually possess and take steps to correct any inaccuracies or misrepresentations of their credentials by others.

4.07 Solicitations

(a) Social workers should not engage in uninvited solicitation of potential clients who, because of their circumstances, are vulnerable to undue influence, manipulation, or coercion.

(b) Social workers should not engage in solicitation of testimonial endorsements (including solicitation of consent to use a client's prior statement as a testimonial endorsement) from current clients or from other people who, because of their particular circumstances, are vulnerable to undue influence.

4.08 Acknowledging Credit

(a) Social workers should take responsibility and credit, including authorship credit, only for work they have actually performed and to which they have contributed.
(b) Social workers should honestly acknowledge the work of and the contributions made by others.

5. Social Workers' Ethical Responsibilities to the Social Work Profession

5.01 Integrity of the Profession

(a) Social workers should work toward the maintenance and promotion of high standards of practice.
(b) Social workers should uphold and advance the values, ethics, knowledge, and mission of the profession. Social workers should protect, enhance, and improve the integrity of the profession through appropriate study and research, active discussion, and responsible criticism of the profession.
(c) Social workers should contribute time and professional expertise to activities that promote respect for the value, integrity, and competence of the social work profession. These activities may include teaching, research, consultation, service, legislative testimony, presentations in the community, and participation in their professional organizations.
(d) Social workers should contribute to the knowledge base of social work and share with colleagues their knowledge related to practice, research, and ethics. Social workers should seek to contribute to the profession's literature and to share their knowledge at professional meetings and conferences.
(e) Social workers should act to prevent the unauthorized and unqualified practice of social work.

5.02 Evaluation and Research

(a) Social workers should monitor and evaluate policies, the implementation of programs, and practice interventions.
(b) Social workers should promote and facilitate evaluation and research to contribute to the development of knowledge.
(c) Social workers should critically examine and keep current with emerging knowledge relevant to social work and fully use evaluation and research evidence in their professional practice.
(d) Social workers engaged in evaluation or research should carefully consider possible consequences and should follow guidelines developed for the protection of evaluation and research participants. Appropriate institutional review boards should be consulted.

(e) Social workers engaged in evaluation or research should obtain voluntary and written informed consent from participants, when appropriate, without any implied or actual deprivation or penalty for refusal to participate; without undue inducement to participate; and with due regard for participants' well-being, privacy, and dignity. Informed consent should include information about the nature, extent, and duration of the participation requested and disclosure of the risks and benefits of participation in the research.

(f) When evaluation or research participants are incapable of giving informed consent, social workers should provide an appropriate explanation to the participants, obtain the participants' assent to the extent they are able, and obtain written consent from an appropriate proxy.

(g) Social workers should never design or conduct evaluation or research that does not use consent procedures, such as certain forms of naturalistic observation and archival research, unless rigorous and responsible review of the research has found it to be justified because of its prospective scientific, educational, or applied value and unless equally effective alternative procedures that do not involve waiver of consent are not feasible.

(h) Social workers should inform participants of their right to withdraw from evaluation and research at any time without penalty.

(i) Social workers should take appropriate steps to ensure that participants in evaluation and research have access to appropriate supportive services.

(j) Social workers engaged in evaluation or research should protect participants from unwarranted physical or mental distress, harm, danger, or deprivation.

(k) Social workers engaged in the evaluation of services should discuss collected information only for professional purposes and only with people professionally concerned with this information.

(l) Social workers engaged in evaluation or research should ensure the anonymity or confidentiality of participants and of the data obtained from them. Social workers should inform participants of any limits of confidentiality, the measures that will be taken to ensure confidentiality, and when any records containing research data will be destroyed.

(m) Social workers who report evaluation and research results should protect participants' confidentiality by omitting identifying information unless proper consent has been obtained authorizing disclosure.

(n) Social workers should report evaluation and research findings accurately. They should not fabricate or falsify results and should take steps to correct any errors later found in published data using standard publication methods.

(o) Social workers engaged in evaluation or research should be alert to and avoid conflicts of interest and dual relationships with participants, should inform participants when a real or potential conflict of interest arises, and should take steps to resolve the issue in a manner that makes participants' interests primary.

(p) Social workers should educate themselves, their students, and their colleagues about responsible research practices.

6. Social Workers' Ethical Responsibilities to the Broader Society

6.01 Social Welfare

Social workers should promote the general welfare of society, from local to global levels, and the development of people, their communities, and their environments. Social workers should advocate for living conditions conducive to the fulfillment of basic human needs and should promote social, economic, political, and cultural values and institutions that are compatible with the realization of social justice.

6.02 Public Participation

Social workers should facilitate informed participation by the public in shaping social policies and institutions.

6.03 Public Emergencies

Social workers should provide appropriate professional services in public emergencies to the greatest extent possible.

6.04 Social and Political Action

(a) Social workers should engage in social and political action that seeks to ensure that all people have equal access to the resources, employment, services, and opportunities they require to meet their basic human needs and to develop fully. Social workers should be aware of the impact of the political arena on practice and should advocate for changes in policy and legislation to improve social conditions in order to meet basic human needs and promote social justice.

(b) Social workers should act to expand choice and opportunity for all people, with special regard for vulnerable, disadvantaged, oppressed, and exploited people and groups.

(c) Social workers should promote conditions that encourage respect for cultural and social diversity within the United States and globally. Social workers should promote policies and practices that demonstrate respect for difference, support the expansion of cultural knowledge and resources, advocate for programs and institutions that demonstrate cultural competence, and promote policies that safeguard the rights of and confirm equity and social justice for all people.

(d) Social workers should act to prevent and eliminate domination of, exploitation of, and discrimination against any person, group, or class on the basis of race, ethnicity, national origin, color, sex, sexual orientation, age, marital status, political belief, religion, or mental or physical disability.

Source: National Association of Social Workers. (1999). Section on Ethical Standards, Code of Ethics of the National Association of Social Workers. Approved by the 1996 NASW Delegate Assembly and revised by the 1999 NASW Delegate Assembly. Washington, D.C. Reprinted by permission.

Afrocentric research a theoretical perspective based on an African American perspective, strongly identified with African American heritage

alternate form method a test of reliability in which two different forms of an instrument that are very similar are administered to determine if the responses to one instrument are strongly associated with the responses to the other instrument

anonymity the circumstance in which the researcher does not know the names of those who have participated in the study, which in itself ensures that the participants' names will not be known to others

ANOVA a bivariate statistical test used to determine whether three or more groups are significantly different from each other based on a particular characteristic (also called "one-way analysis of variance")

bar chart a special type of table that summarizes the frequency distribution of a particular variable using bars

baseline a measure of the client's goal prior to introducing an intervention

bivariate statistics used to investigate the relationship between two variables

case study a detailed description of one or a few cases to promote a fuller understanding of one or more aspects of the lives of these cases

central tendency measure a statistic that summarizes an entire set of scores in a single representative number; three specific statistics measuring the central tendencies of the responses: the mean, median, and mode

chi-square test a bivariate statistic used to determine if the values of one variable are associated with the values of another variable; also referred to as a cross-tab, or cross-tabulation of these variables

clinical significance a way to determine if enough improvement occurred in the client's outcome variable after implementing the intervention, based on clinical criteria established by a professional group

cluster sampling a multistage sampling approach used to obtain a representative sample when the people in a population of interest cannot be initially identified in any direct way

code book a compilation of all of the questions in an instrument, their response categories, and the code numbers assigned to each response category; also called a data dictionary

coding a process used to prepare data for analysis

community forums sessions in which several people in a community come together to discuss a topic of interest to all of them

comparison group a group of clients that is similar but not identical to the group receiving the intervention in a group design

concepts ideas or thoughts about which we have a mental image

confidentiality the circumstance in which the researcher knows the names of each participant but promises not to disclose these names to anyone outside the research team

constant unlike a variable, a concept that doesn't change

construct validity a measure used to consider how a variable to be measured is logically associated to other variables

consumer role a research role taken on by a social worker when reading and critiquing research reports; involves understanding a study, evaluating how well it was conducted and presented, and applying the findings to social work practice

content analysis a type of data analysis that records the repetition of different types of recorded communication, such as words and phrases

content validity the degree to which a measure covers the range of meanings included within the concept; used to determine if the questions you selected reflect all of the dimensions of the variable

control group a group of clients in a group design that is considered identical to the group receiving the intervention, based on either random assignment or matching

convenience sampling a sampling approach in which the people who are the easiest to find are selected as a sample; also referred to as availability sampling

correlation coefficient a special feature of a correlation test score designed to help in interpreting the results

correlation test a bivariate statistical test used to determine if there is a statistically significant association between two variables; can only be used when both variables are at the interval/ratio-level of measurement

Council on Social Work Education (CSWE)   a social work education's agency that accredits BSW and MSW programs and promulgates standards for BSW and MSW programs, including the mandates described in this book

criterion-related validity   a measure that is valid if its scores correlate with the scores of another measure of the same construct

criterion sampling   a sampling approach that selects research participants based on a set of criteria related to the purpose of the study; also referred to as purposive sampling

critical thinking   a careful examination of beliefs and actions, with attention to the process of reasoning; considers alternative points of view; uses standards of fair-mindedness, clarity, accuracy, relevance, and comprehensiveness

cross-sectional studies   studies using a research design in which data are collected at only one point in time from research participants

data analysis   a process of transforming data into useful information

data set   a computer file of data that have been collected, coded, and are ready for analysis

deductive research   a research philosophy that involves crafting a theoretical statement to explain why something is happening in the real world and collecting data to find support or a lack of support for this theoretical explanation

dependent variable   the effect variable, or the variable that is changed by the independent variable

descriptive statistics   statistics used to summarize the responses for each variable; also referred to as univariate statistics, because they analyze one variable at a time

ethical principles   attempts to operationalize general values into action statements, which point to some behaviors that are important to follow and other behaviors to avoid

ethnic-based research   a theoretical perspective based on a specific ethnic perspective and strongly identified with a particular ethnic group and heritage, its history, unique values, and concern for the current needs of its people and their culture

exemplar case   one type of criterion sampling; a case that exemplifies or illustrates what is desired or preferred

explanatory studies   studies conducted to find support for theoretical explanations that have already been crafted by the researcher; usually have hypotheses to confirm or refute

exploratory studies   studies conducted to learn more about a phenomenon when not much is currently known; have general research questions to answer

external validity   addresses the issue of generalizing the results of a group design to other people not in the group

extraneous variables   variables that have not been identified in the hypothesis; sometimes referred to as control variables

face validity   when a measure of something appears to be valid "on its face" (i.e., based on what you know about the concept or based on what your mental image of it is)

feminist research   a theoretical perspective informed by feminist theories and defined both by the research methods that feminists prefer and the research topics that they choose to study

focus groups   a method used to find out the views of several people on a particular topic; conducted as a group interview in which the participants are invited to discuss a particular topic

forced-response questions   questions that restrict the respondent's answer to a predetermined list of response categories; sometimes referred to as closed-ended questions

frequency distributions   a statistic that describes the number and percent of times that each of the values of a variable are observed in a sample

generalizing   inferring that the findings from a study of a sample of research participants apply to a larger population

goal attainment scale (GAS)   a scale with widespread use in social work practice that is useful when measuring clients' progress in reaching their goals

group design   designs that measure the impact of an intervention on a group of clients, not one client, and explore a causal relationship between an independent and dependent variable

Guttman scale   a scale that recognizes that statements used in the scale can vary in degree of importance and takes into account the fact that some statements of a scale may be more extreme indicators of a concept than others

hypothesis   a hypothetical explanation describing the relationship between two variables

independent variable   the causal variable; presumed to cause a change to occur in the dependent variable

inductive research   a research philosophy that involves gathering data about a phenomenon before an explanation is hypothesized or suggested; the explanation emerges from the observation of the phenomenon

informed consent   the practice of informing research participants fully about the study before they are expected to consent to participate

institutional review boards (IRBs)   a group of people at an institution who have been designated to promulgate ethical standards and approve and monitor the ethical provisions of all studies sponsored by the institution

internal validity   addresses the question of whether the intervention, rather than some other factors, is responsible for improvement in the client outcome variable in group designs

interrater reliability   a test of reliability in which two or more people, referred to as raters, measure the same episode independent of each other to determine how consistently they observe and record the same behaviors

interval variables   variables at a level of measurement that does not have response categories; values of these variables are individual numerical scores based on a standard unit of measure

interview   a type of survey in which a researcher asks questions of a research participant and records the responses on a form called an interview schedule

key informants   people who have special knowledge and/or experience on a topic

levels of measurement   the degree to which the values of a variable can be quantified

Likert scale   a set of response categories that proceeds in order from one extreme to the opposite extreme, such as strongly agree, agree, not sure, disagree, strongly disagree

longitudinal studies   studies that have research designs in which data are collected from research participants at two or more points in time

mean   the arithmetic average of a set of scores

measurement   the process of determining the values of a variable for the people being studied

median   the middle score of a distribution of scores (i.e., half of the scores are above it and half are below it)

mode   the most frequent score in a distribution of scores

National Association of Social Workers (NASW)   a national association representing all professional social workers that acts, among other functions, as the organizational sponsor of the Code of Ethics for Social Workers

negative relationship   an association between two variables in which the values of one variable go up while the values of the other variable go down (i.e., the values go in the opposite direction)

nominal variables   variables at a level of measurement that have categories as values and meet three properties: being distinct, mutually exclusive, and exhaustive

nonprobability sampling   sampling in which we do not know if every person in the population has an equal chance of being selected

observational research   the process of using all of the senses, particularly sight and hearing, to collect data about something, particularly on the behaviors of people

open-ended questions   questions that permit respondents to answer questions in their own words and do not provide a restricted set of response categories from which respondents must choose their answers

ordinal variables   variables at a level of measurement that have categories as values, all three of the properties required of nominal variables, and a sequential order

participant observation   an observational data collection approach in which the researcher participates to some extent with the people being studied; used to help the researcher observe people and their social context from the inside out

participatory action research (PAR)   a specific approach that focuses on topics relevant to the research participants and actively involves them in all or some of the steps of the research process; considered an empowering approach to research

philosophy   the underlying intentions or reasons for conducting the research process, including the basic values and beliefs about research

pie chart   a special type of bar chart displayed in circular form

population   all of the people of interest to the researcher conducting a study

positive relationship   an association between two variables in which the values of both variables vary in the same direction

prenominal variables   variables in qualitative studies that have not yet fulfilled the requirements of nominal-level variables

probability sampling   sampling in which every person in the population has an equal chance of being selected

probability theory a theory that predicts the chance or likelihood that a given event will occur

producer role a research role taken on by social workers who conduct their own studies or assist others in conducting research; requires learning several applied research skills

qualitative methods an approach to data collection that attempts to discover the quality of something—its peculiar and essential character—and uses inductive methods to attempt to discover new explanations

quantitative methods an approach to data collection that measures the quantity of something and attempts to find support in the real world for a theoretical explanation developed by the researcher

questionnaire a type of survey in which questions are recorded on paper or on an electronic computer file and given to the research participants to answer

quota sampling a sampling approach used when either an equal or proportional number of people are selected from each subgroup of the population so that they can be compared

random sampling a sampling approach in which each person in the population has an equal probability of being selected by chance

range identifies the lowest and highest scores in the responses to a question

ratio variables variables at a level of measurement that is similar to interval variables except that zero is a true 0 value

reactivity a problem that occurs whenever the researcher's presence interferes with how people respond to a survey or how they behave when they are observed

reductionism a problem that occurs whenever an effort to create a numerical measure of a concept results in losing some of the properties of the concept

reliability a standard used to determine whether an instrument measures something consistently from one time to another and among different people

representative sample a sample in which the characteristics of the sample accurately reflect the characteristics of the population

research design a plan that describes how the study will be conducted

research participants the people being studied in social work research

response rate the proportion of people who complete and return a survey

sample a subgroup of the population that a researcher selects to study

sampling error the degree of error to be expected when generalizing from sample to population

sampling frame a list of all of the units (usually individuals) in the population

secondary research research that analyzes data already collected in a prior study

semistructured interviews interviews in which most of the questions are already formulated but can be asked in a different order

significance the strength of a relationship; can be defined by two different standards: statistical significance or clinical significance

single system design (SSD) a practice evaluation tool that measures whether or not there is a causal relationship between the practitioner's intervention and an outcome variable for a client system; typically used with only one client system at a time

snowball sampling a sampling approach used when the population of interest is "hidden" or difficult to identify

split-half method a test of reliability that involves splitting the items of an instrument into two random groupings and finding out if there is a strong association between the responses to the two sets of items

standard deviation a measure of variability that takes into account the extent to which each of the scores or responses to a question varies from the mean score; often abbreviated SD

standardized scales structured data collection instruments composed of a set of questions or statements that measure important concepts otherwise difficult to measure and have strong evidence of validity and reliability

statistical significance a way to determine if enough improvement has occurred in the client's outcome variable after implementing the intervention; calculated by applying a statistical test that determines if the probability of an association between two variable is high

stratified random sampling a sampling approach that stratifies the population into subgroups and then randomly selects a sample from each subgroup

structured interviews interviews that use questions formulated before the data are collected, questions asked in predetermined order, and little variation in how the interview is conducted

structured questionnaires questionnaires with forced-response questions that are easy to answer without any assistance from the researcher

survey a data collection approach that involves asking questions of research participants and has two types: interviews and questionnaires

systematic random sampling a sampling approach in which each person has an equal chance of being selected by systematic choice, not by random chance

t-test a bivariate statistical test used to determine whether two groups are significantly different based on a particular characteristic

test-retest method a means of determining reliability through evaluating whether a question is answered consistently by administering it to the same person at two different points in time and comparing to see if the participant's responses are the same or similar

theme analysis a type of qualitative data analysis that involves identifying common themes or patterns prevalent in several cases

theory several interrelated explanatory statements or propositions about a phenomenon; useful in explaining the nature and causes of important phenomena

Thurstone scale a scale created by consulting a group of outside experts in which statements consistently rated most strongly by most of the judges are included in the questionnaire while the weaker statements are discarded

time series design a type of quasi-experimental group design that involves obtaining several measures of the client outcome variable prior to the introduction of an intervention and several additional measures of the client outcome variable after the intervention has been implemented

triangulation a process of using multiple methods to measure one concept

typical case one type of criterion sampling; a case (individual, family, agency, neighborhood, etc.) that has many of the characteristics evident in other cases of a larger group

unit of analysis the level of the system being compared in the study

unobtrusive measures measures of nonhuman entities such as social artifacts, deterioration or improvements in physical materials, and physical settings (i.e., an office or home)

unstructured interviews an interview method most similar to a conversation, with a very flexible format; also referred to as in-depth interviews

validity a standard used to determine whether an instrument measures what it is supposed to measure and whether it measures it accurately

value one specific measure of a variable (not to be confused with social work values)

variability measures statistics that summarize how the responses to a question vary or disperse away from their central tendency

variable a concept that has two additional properties: (1) it varies or changes, (2) it is measurable; a variable provides a means of measuring a concept